D1524924

Deliverance at Hand!

The Redemption of a Devout Jehovah's Witness

James Zimmerman

Minneapolis–St. Paul

Library of Congress Control Number: 2013947107

Cover design by David Orr
Interior design & production by Robaire Ream

ISBN: 9780988493803

Printed in the United States of America
10   9   8   7   6   5   4   3   2   1

To Jennifer, Owen, and Isla.
And the Future.

You can let others tell you what you are allowed to think and believe.
Or you may wish to investigate some of the evidence yourself and
reach your own conclusion.

—*Awake!* (September. 2006)

My Special Place

My special place is at the Kingdom Hall.
You listen and learn and have lots of friends.
I like giving talks and taking written reviews and singing the songs.
It is the best place you can go to.
The books we study are very educational.
They talk all about Jehovah and his son Jesus.
Not only do you learn, but you get good association with your friends.
I wish I was there right now.
Someday I want to work at Bethel and then I can be there all the time.

—James Zimmerman
February 5, 1987 (11 years old)

Contents

Note on Sources

When confronted with incriminating statements in their own literature, Jehovah's Witnesses resort to two arguments:

The first is that the literature being cited does not reflect current teaching; it is "dimmer light."[1] For that reason, I have used only contemporary citations (literature currently published in print or electronic form) when addressing Witness beliefs.

The second argument is an attempt to bog down incriminating statements with semantics regarding the source. Witnesses insist that there are fundamental differences between the Governing Body, the Little Flock, the Watch Tower Society, the Watchtower Society, the Christian Congregation of Jehovah's Witnesses, and the Faithful and Discreet Slave. This is merely a ruse; the differences only serve to confuse. Witnesses never make such an argument unless their religion is being challenged. For simplicity's sake, I have avoided using most of these esoteric terms.

Verbal conversations are close approximations, though their contents have been verified to the extent possible. All email, blog, and letter excerpts appear as originally written, aside from minor grammar and spelling edits. Some names have been changed.

All Bible citations are from the *New World Translation of the Holy Scriptures, with References*. Published by the Watch Tower Bible and Tract Society of New York. © 1984.

Unless otherwise indicated, all books, brochures, magazines, and videos referenced are published by the Watch Tower Bible and Tract Society of New York.

Prelude

Millions of Jehovah's Witnesses have come before me; millions will come after. Each has his or her own story. Claims of mistreatment abound among many who have left the religion. Some claim they never believed it—only participating because their family members were Witnesses. Some claim they left because fellow Witnesses were uncaring, rude, hypocritical, or even stupid.

I claim none of those things.

I claim to be merely one who lived and breathed the Jehovah's Witnesses and the Watch Tower Society. My story, lasting nearly a third of a century, is really just the story of a single prayer. That prayer, however, only makes sense in the context of my life, my story. And so I will start at the beginning.

BALSAM IN GILEAD

Diane and I eavesdropped on the revelries from the hallway window, peering obliquely to avoid detection, and shaking our heads at the sins. There were ten or twelve kids, running around a yard festooned with crepe paper and balloons, celebrating the neighbor boy's birthday. Aaron was six. He invited us, of course, but my Dad had put an end to our neighbors' naivety when he marched across the small patch of grass that separated our mobile homes and Witnessed to Aaron's father. Bible in hand, my Dad logically showed the sincere but mistaken Lutheran why birthday celebrations were a sin against God.

"They're having fun now, but they're gonna die at Armageddon," I said.

My sister, being five years younger than me and only three years old, didn't have much to add. But she scrunched up her face in an attempt to wink at me, and we continued watching. A few minutes later, it was time to get ready for the meeting.

My parents brought me to the meetings before I could even walk. The meetings were held at the local Kingdom Hall, which was the fancy term we gave our houses of worship. In the earliest days, I didn't understand a single word spoken there, but nonetheless I sat in awe of the intelligences standing on stage before me. These men knew everything! They confounded me with their complex explanations of deep—often obscure—Bible references. I sat stoically, masking the uncomfortable combination of admiration and confusion that bubbled in my belly. If I listened closely, I thought, maybe one day I, too, could instill those same feelings in my fellow Witnesses.

We often heard about the promise of everlasting life on a Paradise Earth. To bring this hope alive to their audiences, speakers regularly turned to Isaiah: "Jehovah of armies will certainly make for all the peoples, in this mountain, a banquet of well-oiled dishes, a banquet of [wine kept on] the dregs, of well-oiled dishes filled with marrow, of [wine kept on] the dregs, filtered."[2] *What?* I thought. I understood the appeal of a banquet, but *well-oiled dishes?* Who cared how much oil was on the dishes—and why? And who cared about wine kept on the dregs? What did this mean?

Oil was a recurring theme. Speakers sometimes likened our meetings to oil that runs down beards and under collars. I understood our command to congregate, but I didn't see how oil poured on my head was a good metaphor. It sounded unappealing, uncomfortable, and unnecessary.

For me though, the most bothersome scriptural reference to oil was Jeremiah 8:22: *Balsam in Gilead.* What the heck was balsam? Where—or what—is Gilead, anyway? And why should I care?

We often sang *Balsam in Gilead* during the meetings:

> *There's balsam in fair Gilead;*
> *This from God's Word we hear.*
> *It comfort brings to troubled hearts*
> *And helps grief disappear.*
> *It soothes us when we're sorely tried*
> *Or deeply are distressed,*
> *Or we have lost some loved dear one,*
> *Who in death's sleep does rest*[3]

The song rattled me. Its melancholy tune, its calm, almost morose melody, its lack of a beat, and its utterly boring chorus—these things tortured me, sure. Almost as much as the prose itself: What was this balsam? Unlike many of our songs, which seemed to increase our collective courage as outcasts from the world, this one highlighted our frailness and mortality. Singing this song brought me nearly to tears, and I wasn't even sure why. It made me think I couldn't even pull myself out of bed in the morning without Jehovah lifting my tired body. The song concludes by exhorting us to seek out depressed, tired people and to comfort them, that they, too, might know of the balsam in Gilead. Perplexed, I concluded that if I ever had some of that balsam, I would never be sad again.

My clearest explanation of balsam in Gilead came from a speaker who pointed out that the prophet Jeremiah was depressed over the lack of love among his people, and the imminent destruction of Jerusalem. The speaker explained that Jeremiah became "shattered," finally crying out: "Is there no balsam in Gilead? Or is there no healer there?"[4] The prophet was crying out for answers. He wanted—*needed*—to know if someone could ease his mind and restore his wretched condition.

I desperately wanted to know more, so I asked my Dad about the importance of all that oil—specifically the balsam—in the Bible.

He didn't know. But he suggested I research the subject. Research, I knew well, was a key way to verify our faith as the one true religion, and I had no desire to be found wanting in this area.

GENESIS

I was born into a family with a rich history as Jehovah's Witnesses. My parents were Witnesses, as were their siblings, and their parents. But this did not mark us as extraordinary. As Jehovah's Witnesses, we were all family. We were each other's brothers and sisters.

Though Jehovah's Witnesses only trace their organizational history to the 1870s, we considered ourselves descendants of faithful followers from millennia past. We were not so much a new religion as a renaissance; a return to the way God intended Christianity to be.

But it wasn't simply a rich past that kept Witnesses faithful and zealous. There was also the future—the glorious hope of living forever in a Paradise Earth. Jehovah soon intended to execute judgment on this wicked world and usher in a new order—a "New Earth"[5] where only the meek live. The Earth would finally become as it was meant to be: no war, no poverty, no pollution, no sickness, no death. This Paradise would be a panacea for humanity's problems. Absolutely every tribulation facing mankind would be exterminated. Even more thrilling, I had a good chance of never dying. Provided my faith stayed intact, I would live through the last days, through Armageddon, and be among the faithful Witnesses granted life eternal; full, satisfying life in a Paradise where centuries pass as weeks do now.

Life in this world, then, was temporary and fleeting. It was an inconsequential stroke of the clock compared with all that had come before and all that would come after. I was powerfully thankful to God that He allowed me to be born, and that He afforded me the chance to enjoy an incalculably beautiful, endless life. I loved Jehovah. I owed my life to Jehovah.

In the meantime, though, life was busy.

Sunday started the week with a two-hour meeting. After the meeting, we joined our brothers and sisters out in service, which was our term for going door-to-door witnessing to our neighbors about God's kingdom.

On Monday, my Dad read the daily text during dinner. And, since there was a meeting on Tuesday, we set aside time to study for that meeting.

On Tuesday we attended a one-hour bookstudy.

Wednesday night was ostensibly for our family study. Every family head was encouraged to conduct a study with their family. My Dad maintained no consistency in this regard, but he tried.

Thursday night we attended another two-hour meeting. Sometimes, my dad or mom had a talk, so sometime in the days before, they had to set aside time to prepare. Later, I began giving talks and my mom spent hours helping me prepare and rehearse.

On Friday my Dad and I sat on my bedroom floor and studied the Bible.

Saturday was Service Day. We *always* went out in service on Saturday. There was no question. It was our pattern, and we patterned ourselves after the directive in *The Watchtower*, the flagship periodical of the Witnesses governing organization, The Watchtower, Bible, and Tract Society in Brooklyn, New York. Saturday was heavily promoted as a day to go out in service; the Watchtower Society's calendars had "share in field ministry" printed on every single Saturday. In the afternoon and evening, my sister Diane and I often reenacted biblical dramas for one another or played Service by knocking on each other's bedroom doors. At night, my dad turned on the cassette player and Diane and I fell asleep listening to a recording of the Watchtower Society's children's book.

The meetings were extraordinarily important. I felt terrible if illness forced any of us to stay home. One evening, while dressing for the meeting, my four-year-old sister burned her hand on a curling iron. Faithfully, we still attended the meeting, and she sat on the floor with her hand in a cup of cold water. When my school held open house, inevitably on a meeting night, we dressed in our meeting clothes, ventured briefly to the open house, then quickly drove to the meeting. The next day, my classmates laughed, joking at how stupid I looked dressed in a suit, and asking if my parents made me dress that way all the time.

For many years, my dad was assigned the privilege of manning the literature counter. This necessitated arriving about a half hour before each meeting began and staying just as late to be available to the other Witnesses who needed to order or collect literature for their personal study and the door-to-door work. When my sister complained of leaving the Kingdom Hall so late and being tired for school the next morning, my mom told us to be thankful: "When I was a little girl, Grandpa sometimes had to meet with the other elders after the meeting, and we all had to wait in the car for him for hours."

"Couldn't Grandma just drive you guys home and let him get a ride with one of the other elders?"

"Oh no," my mom insisted. "Grandpa said we needed to set a good example by leaving together as a family." She laughed at the silliness. "Of course, no one could see us setting a good example, because everyone else was already home in bed by one a.m."

The four of us were dedicated members of the congregation. All of my grandparents, uncles, aunts, and cousins were Witnesses. So was every person I called a friend. Being one of Jehovah's Witnesses then was not merely *a part* of my life, or even *my way* of life. It *was* my life.

And I mean that literally. My parents were born and raised on Long Island, and met when their fathers were assigned to move to a neighboring congregation. It was easy to move around elders in New York; the high concentration of Witnesses meant there was no shortage of willing brothers for any duty. Indeed, the Witnesses were practically tripping over each other, knocking on the same doors several times a year. This, coupled with the degrading morals of the Big City, caused several elders to offer to move someplace where there was more need for Witnesses. A few old men at the Watchtower Society pooled their opinions, looked at a map of the country, and pointed to a hinterland between the oceans - a place more civil due to its being less civilized. Beginning in the 1970s, a few elders and their families made their way west of the Burned-over District to the Land of 10,000 Protestant Denominations. My Dad's family was among them. My Mom's family follow suit soon after. My parents, young and recently married, were left stranded in New York, until they, too, decided to strike for Minnesota; a great place to wait until the Paradise arrived.

THE LAST GREAT DECADE

Let's see what we need to do to make sure that God will give us everlasting life in his new paradise.

—*My Book of Bible Stories*, p. 253

1975: I was born at the right time. The Watchtower Society's ideology avowed that we were living in the last days, which began in 1914, and that the generation of that year would not die before Armageddon began. The old world couldn't last much longer. According to Psalms, a generation is seventy or eighty years[6]—so God would *have* to act shortly. I knew I would live to see it. Even if God delayed the Paradise until the year 2000, I would still be a young man. Barring disease or accident, I would live through the momentous events set to commence any day. Deliverance was at hand!

The Watchtower Society, which is the Jehovah's Witnesses' governing organization and the source of its ideology, instructs Witnesses to "make the truth their own."[7] This meant we couldn't ride on the faith of our spouse or parents. Jehovah intended to judge each human individually.

This thought scared me. I worried that I didn't know enough about God. I worried that I sinned too often. I worried that my parents would be granted eternal life but that God would kill me at Armageddon because I hated wearing neckties, or because I wasted an hour reading about astronomy instead of studying the Bible. Though only six years old, I needed to decide what I was going to do with my life.

In making such a decision, it became apparent that there were two questions I needed to ask.

The first was this: *Do I want it to be true?*

By "it," I meant not just the modern-day Jehovah's Witnesses. I meant the whole world-view: God, the Bible, and the history of the Israelites and the Jews. Did I want the twentieth century to be "the Last Days"? Did I want Armageddon to arrive? Did I want God to bring Paradise? Did I want to be there?

The answer was yes.

How could I have answered otherwise? Yes, it was a lot of work. We sustained an intense routine of meetings and service, talking to cold, often

9

rude, strangers. I had to avoid bad movies and bad music. I couldn't celebrate holidays or my birthday. But it was worth it. I mean, who wouldn't want to live forever in perfect health on a clean Earth? Who wouldn't want to have their dead loved ones resurrected? Who wouldn't want to meet all the millions of faithful worshippers of Jehovah that had fallen asleep in death? Who wouldn't want to witness a world where disease is extinct . . . where children are not abused . . . where animals are not mistreated . . . where we have time to study anything we desired . . . where we are with our friends and family for all eternity without pain or sorrow? Yes, without any doubt, I *wanted* it to be true. That was my answer then. That is my answer now.

The second question was this: *Is it true?*

This really was the larger question. It was the tougher question, too, for it meant looking not within, but externally. And though I hated to admit it, the answer was not dependent upon the answer to the first question. Just as I wished my Dad didn't have to work long hours and I wished my grandparents didn't grow old, I had to admit: wishing didn't make it so. Whether or not I wanted the Watchtower Society to be true did not affect its inherent trueness in any way. I was just a little boy. I had no influence over these truths.

So, the answer to this question was . . . I don't know. Yet.

And how could I know? The Bible was an epic book. I hadn't even read it. It was a complex tome that necessitated five weekly meetings just to keep up with studying it. The Watchtower Society published dozens of new books and magazines each year in an effort to explain the Bible's history, prophecies, and promises. People far older and smarter than I were still learning about the Bible. In a way, this was consoling; I believed that my parents and grandparents had already conducted the research and arrived at the answer that, yes, the Watchtower Society was true. When elders gave talks at our meetings, they sounded so smart. *How could I ever be that smart?* Maybe I couldn't, but at least I knew that there were smart people, and they *knew* that our religion was the truth. So much so, in fact, that they called it the Truth.

Someday I would be smarter. Then I would figure everything out. In the meantime, Armageddon was imminent. I may not have been old enough or smart enough to fully grasp the Bible and the Watchtower Society's teachings, but I couldn't wait. For if I decided to not do anything in God's service until I knew fully that it was true, I risked running out of time. The best move was to wager on the safe side. If I was right, I would win the world. If I was wrong, well . . . at least I wasn't hurting anyone.

I worried about more than just my own plight, though. I was concerned about my sister. Knowing Jehovah's plan to judge each person individually,

I wondered where a child like her would stand. God was loving and merciful, so I hoped that when He brought Armageddon, He would let my sister live. Yet I also knew from biblical stories that God had murdered millions of children and babies—even when they had not sinned. I was bothered by this apparent contradiction.

Any time I tried to convince myself that a loving God wouldn't destroy children, something else disaffirmed my uneasy peace. Nothing depicted this more forcefully than the Watchtower's book for children, *My Book of Bible Stories*. The gilded cover was embossed with the deep red words of the title in large, gothic calligraphy. Filled with illustrations and fascinating stories, it was my favorite book. I loved the way it showed the progression of God's people. Although I was enthralled with the story of Noah and the Ark, the picture on that page was the most troubling in the whole book.[8] In the background, the ark drifted on the water, with its passengers securely inside. Heavy rains flooded the image. Lightning split the scene. The foreground portrayed people scurrying to safety, vainly scaling above the morass of death to one of the only remaining outcrops. One man was trying to swim to a tiny purchase of land that rose above the rising tide, while another shook a fist at the ark in one last act of rebellion. Still another man stood on the shrinking mountaintop and held his hands to his head, cursing his lot. A woman gripped the rocky precipice in futile agony, climbing out of the deluge and buying herself a few more minutes of her wicked life. Rodents, great reptiles, and wooly mammoths shared the foothold, and appeared to cry out to the heavens for amnesty.

But there was another woman on the peak, too. Having clambered above the din and the deluge, she was serenely seated in a crevasse and faced out toward her coming fate. She was enraptured in a crimson tunic and her long auburn hair fell around her. In her arms, she held her infant child, who clung tightly, seeking solace. Now, I understood why the woman was condemned. God instructed Noah to tell everyone about the impending deluge. Noah and his family preached that the only means of survival was to board the ark. But this woman did not listen to Noah. She stayed outside the ark. She probably even laughed at Noah.[9]

The child was a different matter. *Why did God feel the world would be a better place if He executed that child? Did the child get a chance to make a decision? Did he say: "No thanks, I'd prefer to die"?*

Perhaps the child would receive another chance to serve God. *Yes, that was it. God will resurrect this child in the Paradise where he'll be raised amongst other worshippers of God in a perfect world. Surely, then, as he grew into adulthood he would decide to please God.*

But then I wondered why God bothered murdering the child in the first place, only to have to resurrect him later.

And so, I worried about my sister. Armageddon was imminent, yet I hoped it held off long enough so that my sister could reach an age to declare her love for God and to serve Him. When I prayed in private, I always beseeched God to watch over my sister.

At the start of each school year, my parents met with my teacher. They made it clear that I was one of Jehovah's Witnesses, and would therefore not engage in any holiday activities; including Halloween, Christmas, Valentine's Day, and Easter, or even nonreligious holidays like Thanksgiving and Mother's Day. Also, I would not join the children in singing the National Anthem or celebrating birthdays. On some school days, particularly Halloween and Valentine's Day, the day became a big party for the students. My parents kept me home on those days. Sometimes, a classmate stopped by after school, assuming I was home due to illness, and dropped off party favors, candy, or Valentine's cards. We did not answer the door; we pretended we weren't home and allowed the classmate to simply leave the package on the doorstep. Later, my mom retrieved the package and threw it in the trash.

On Halloween, we stayed home, quiet, with the lights off, and shushed each other when costumed trick-or-treaters knocked. "Why do they have to bother us," my mom lamented, "Can't they tell we don't want them coming to our door?" For my part, I preferred when Halloween landed on a Tuesday or Thursday, because then we left for the meeting, and didn't have to sit in the dark all evening.

Thanksgiving was somewhat easier to tolerate. My parents shook their head at the stupidity of worldly people, who needed a special holiday set aside to force them to get together with one another. My Dad often received a complimentary turkey from his employer, and my mom cooked it up on Thanksgiving Day, apologetically remarking that we were not, in fact, celebrating the holiday, "It's just that it takes so long to cook a turkey, and so this is a perfect day for me to do it."

Diane and I laughed. "Why don't you make it tomorrow?" we chided. But my mom explained there was no room for the turkey in our mobile home's small freezer. Then we left for the Thursday night meeting.

Indeed, I enjoyed driving to and from the meetings the best during those final months of each calendar year. The sun set before we left home, and we often drove through neighborhoods looking at the dazzling holiday lights of the increasingly populated suburb as Christmas drew nearer.

Every December, my classmates excitedly asked each other what they wanted for Christmas. When they asked me, I told them that I wasn't allowed to celebrate Christmas. Soon, though, my parents told me that it is better to say that I didn't believe in Christmas, or that Christmas was displeasing to God. This phraseology, they insisted, made it clear that my stance wasn't due to being *prohibited* from celebrating Christmas, but due to my *desire* to please God. When my peers asked if I felt bad that I didn't get any presents, I told them that I didn't feel bad because my parents and grandparents gave me gifts all year long.[10] One classmate said: "I suppose you just get more presents on your birthday." When I told her that Witnesses don't celebrate birthdays, she said: "God, I'm glad I'm not you." When asked if I was sad that Santa Claus didn't stop at my house, I confidently told them that Santa is not real and that their parents were lying to them. This was not the most tactful retort, and at parent-teacher conferences, the teacher told my mom that maybe I shouldn't push my religion on others. That evening at home, my mom said to my Dad: "Don't they realize how much they're pushing their religion on us, with their songs, and decorations, and all that?" She was right, and I was more convinced than ever that we had the right religion. Nevertheless, my parents said that in the interest of giving a good witness, I shouldn't taunt other kids with the knowledge that Santa is bogus. "The kids will like you better," my Dad added.

I was little concerned with my schoolmates' friendship. To the contrary, I needed to avoid getting too close. My classmates occasionally invited me to their birthday parties, and I said no, or they invited me to a sleepover, and I made up excuses why I couldn't attend. I was more comfortable at the meetings. There, I could really befriend my peers. We could do activities together. I visited their homes, and they came to mine. They didn't seem to mind that I was a small, scrawny nerd. They didn't make fun of me. Partly, I'm sure, this was because we were instructed to love one another. But I also felt that they were decent people. They were, after all, the ones who would be living forever with me in Paradise.

Sometimes, though, I wondered why other kids in the congregation didn't take the religion seriously. Some children had the audacity to spend their time at the meetings playing with coloring books.[11] While I took notes at the meetings, most of my peers did not. They didn't look up the scriptures or follow along in their own copy of the publications. I figured maybe they weren't sure if the Truth was the truth or not; but they'd better decide soon—the End was nigh.

My exemplary behavior at the meetings was also due to my fear of being spanked. Any time I couldn't force myself to sit still—any time I got a bit antsy, as my mom called it—my dad hauled me downstairs to receive corporal discipline. This was always embarrassing, particularly as I got older. I tried to get my dad to linger in the basement—lying that I had to pee, or that I needed a drink of water—anything to remain downstairs as long as possible in the hopes my bloodshot eyes would dry before returning upstairs where everyone would look at me. "Jimmy got spanked," I imagined them whispering, "I thought he was a good boy, I wonder what happened?" My Dad said spankings were commissioned by Jehovah, and that, though it "hurt him more than it hurt me," he would be shirking his God-given duties if he did not spank. My Dad frequently delivered a talk entitled "Parents— Are You Building with Fire-Resistant Materials?" In it, he noted "Isn't it amazing Jehovah created parents' hands the same size as their children's behinds?" This solicited chuckles from parents as they nodded in approval.

Despite my occasional lapses into childish misbehavior, the religion was my singular motivating aspect; everything else in my life fit around it. I looked for opportunities to preach to schoolmates and teachers. Many were decent people and I knew that if they only gave me a chance, with open-mindedness, they would realize the Witnesses had the one true religion. When I was assigned a book report in second grade, I chose to write about *My Book of Bible Stories*. I brought *The Watchtower* on the bus with me to have something to read, and when we had free time in class, I pulled out the latest *Watchtower* and proudly read this life-giving literature.

Essentially, I liked being different. During birthday parties at school, I reveled the opportunity to diverge from the norm. During the holidays, when I overheard people talking about how busy they were, and saw the frantic behavior of parents at the toy stores and heard how people forced themselves to get together with family they didn't like, I recalled how glad I was to be free from those false religious traditions. Being different gave me purpose. It gave me drive. It made me feel like I stood for something.

In fact, this made me the perfect Witness. Or, at least, it made me perfectly suited to being a Witness. Many struggled with having to make a stand for their faith, but I sought out such opportunities. Many children in the congregation were too nervous to raise their hand and comment. One little boy, in particular, was so nervous he cried during his comments. I had no such fear. More than speaking, I loved reading and studying. Many Witnesses had a tough time keeping up with everything the Society published. I often overheard comments of people forcing themselves to read. Not me. I didn't care for sports, and I was indifferent to television, but I loved reading. I read nonfiction almost exclusively. I made lists of books I read, took notes, and kept track of remarkable bits of trivia.

Books were my best friends. They accompanied me everywhere. Once, while at my grandparents' house, I was reading my dinosaur book. One of my aunts passed by and saw what I was reading. "You know what you have to remember when reading books about dinosaurs, don't you?"

I had a suspicion that I knew, but I wasn't entirely sure, so I asked: "What's that?"

"A lot of those books teach that the dinosaurs were around for millions of years and died out long before Jehovah created people, but you know that's not true, don't you?"[12]

"Yeah, I know that." I smiled.

At age six, I attained the privilege of publisher, meaning I was now expected to turn in a monthly report of the time I spent in Service. The very first month, I placed a *Watchtower* magazine with two householders. Dutifully, I returned to those householders a few weeks later to see if they wanted the latest magazine. They didn't, but my Dad assured me that the important thing was that they received the message and had been given a chance to accept the Truth. I shouldn't lose heart if not everyone accepts, my Dad insisted. "Remember Noah? Noah preached for forty years and no one listened to him."

I wasn't fond of service, but I knew it was an important work. Jehovah wanted me to give my all, so I did. Sometimes at the meetings, when brothers and sisters gave comments, they said that the more we engage in Service, the more we enjoy it. I accepted this at the time, though I would have to wait for a future day before I could go out in service more.

While Service was difficult, there was an aspect of Jehovah's service that I enjoyed: talks. I greatly wanted to give talks. My parents were happy to oblige my desire. My mom, being a woman, could only give a certain kind of talk: Instead of standing at the speaker's stand, she sat at a table and faced another sister, who played the role of householder. The two of them role-played as if one woman was teaching the other.

The good thing about these role-playing talks was that it gave me a place to start. I accompanied my mom on stage and sat next to her while she and the other sister role-played. Soon, though, I graduated to being my mom's householder. We practiced the talk many times, so much so that we memorized our lines.

The first time I was her householder, I knew my lines so well that I decided to change the script. During the talk, my mom asked: What are some things that Jehovah provides? "Service and meetings," I said, following the script. Then she prompted me by asking what else he provides, and I was supposed to say food and water and shelter, but instead, I said: "sister." My sister was still new, and I was thankful that Jehovah had provided me with a friend. My mom laughed at my extemporaneous answer, looked out at the audience and said: "I never know what he's going to say!"

At the seasoned age of eight, I received my first talk assignment. No longer being a lowly householder for my mom, I would now give talks straight from the lectern, directly to the audience, like the other boys and men in the congregation. My mom wrote the talk for me.

I read and reread the manuscript until I committed it to memory. My mom called my grandpa to see if it was acceptable for me to go on stage without my Bible and, while he agreed it was not improper, he advised me to bring it up on stage anyways, so as not to appear to be a show-off.

When the big day arrived, I was more nervous than I had ever been. My mom selected my best suit, and purchased a new clip-on tie for the occasion. She combed my hair just right, using the curling iron to get it perfect. I put on my suit jacket and buttoned it. I was ready before anyone else. As we left the house that evening, my mom checked and double-checked that I had my notes with me. "Don't cry," she said. I replied: "I'm not gonna cry."

When the meeting began, my nervousness increased. My hands were sweaty and cold. My mouth was dry, but I was too nervous to use the water fountain. My breathing was shallow and my heart was bent on cracking my ribs. My mom leaned over and whispered in my ear. "Don't forget to pray."

"I did pray."

"Pray again," she said. So I bowed my head and prayed.

"We have a new student this evening," the Theocratic Ministry School Overseer announced. "Brother James Zimmerman, junior. Out of the book of Exodus. He's using as his theme: "Do you have faith and love in your worship to Jehovah?"

I rose from my seat, walked past my mom (who patted me on the back), my sister, and my dad. I counted the steps as I walked on stage and, being too short for the lectern, approached the table. A brother adjusted the microphone; fiddling with the stand and cord for a few seconds. Then . . . it was just me. I looked out at the audience and the sprawling aisles converging on me and sensed the overwhelming fear of being an eight-year-old about to talk to two hundred people for five straight minutes. Unlike most Halls, ours was wide instead of deep, so a good speaker had to crane his neck left and right to see everyone sitting in the arching rows.

I opened my mouth. "Do you have—" I was supposed to start by asking a question, but it was quite some time before I finished that question. Instead, I started crying. I had in my mind the suggestion of crying, from the story my dad told me about his first talk. I thought I could catch myself quickly and regain composure, but the microphone, unblinking and intrusive, pointed directly at my mouth and the stuttering whimpers of my cries were amplified beyond any hope of calling back the tears.

The audience stared, and their silence surged up the wide aisles. After what felt like a half hour, but was scarcely half a minute, I saw through the blur of light my dad rising from his seat. He walked down the aisle and came on stage. For a transient second I imagined him taking my hand and leading me off the stage. Instead, he stood behind me, and put his massive hands on my shoulders. He bent down and whispered into my ear so quietly that even the invasive microphone could not eavesdrop. "It's okay, buddy, you can do it."

I craned my face up to see his and whispered: "I can't do it."

"Yes," he said calmly, patting my shoulders. "You can do it."

I took two halting, stuttering breaths and wiped the tears off my eyelashes. I sniffed a couple more times. Then, at a time when the talk should have been nearly a quarter over, I began again.

"Do you have faith and love for Jehovah?" My voice wavered and the sound of it through the speakers scared me. But I had said the first sentence. Others followed. In the audience, I saw my mom, my sister, my grandmother Nana, and even some non-relatives crying along with me. As I neared the end of the introduction, my dad began to take his hands off of my shoulders. When I felt his hands leaving my shoulders, I started to break down again. My voice became higher and the words came out faster. I tried to get my thoughts out before my throat became gripped by emotion. The microphone picked up my precarious voice and amplified my nerves. I was going to cry, but just as the floodgates were about to release again, my dad returned his hands to my shoulders.

By the end of the introduction, I could breathe normally. I asked everyone to please open their Bibles with me as I read the assigned scriptures. I maintained full eye contact with the audience the entire time. I altered my voice to show emotion during some of the scriptures, making sure to gesture where my mom had instructed me to do so. I slowed my speech and tried to connote a feeling of tenderness when I read:

> And Jehovah went passing by before his face and declaring: "Jehovah, Jehovah, a God merciful and gracious, slow to anger and abundant in loving-kindness and truth, preserving loving-kindness for thousands, pardoning error and transgression and sin."[14]

Finally, with my dad still holding my shoulders, I reached the conclusion: "Happy are you, my brothers and sisters, and I, Jimmy, because our God is Jehovah and only Jehovah." I added: "Thank you."

The applause boomed, and continued while my dad and I walked to our seats. A few minutes later, my grandpa leaned over my chair. He placed his giant, powerful hand on my shoulder and handed me a note. In the note, he compared me to Moses, who once told God that he was not a fluent speaker; that he was slow of mouth and tongue.[15] But God told Moses that it was He who appointed a mouth to men. God reminded Moses that He had assigned him the task of going to Pharaoh, and who was Moses to question that assignment? My grandpa wrote that I was faithful for having fulfilled my assignment from God and that, just like Moses, I too would one day be used for great things.

After the meeting, many brothers and sisters shook my hand and congratulated me on my first talk. An older woman handed me a note saying she was encouraged by my example. Several people told my dad that he had done a great thing. A couple of sisters assumed he had planned to come on stage, but my dad assured them it was spontaneous. Nana hugged me tightly. She gave my dad a hug, too, and asked him what made him think of going up on stage, and he told her that when he was a little boy and began crying during his talk, no one came to stand by him, and he would have given the world if his dad would have done so.

Instead of going home that night, Nana and Papa invited us over for snacks. This was quite a treat, because it was already late. My dad's sister Janet, and his brother Cal rode in the car with us. I sat quietly. After the high of a barrage of compliments, I finally had a few minutes to reflect on the evening.

When we pulled into the driveway, everyone got out, but I stayed in the car. "Everything okay, buddy?" my dad asked.

"I feel bad because I didn't do a good job."

My dad shook his head in disbelief: "What are you talking about, Jimmy? You did excellent. Everyone was so proud of you."

I argued that the brothers and sisters only said they were proud of me because they wanted me to feel better. My dad insisted it *was* a good talk. He pointed out that I actually finished it—which was more than some people do for their first talks. He reminded me that I had eye-contact. I gestured. I had good inflection in my voice. I never mispronounced a single word.

So I sat for a moment and thought. Perhaps I *had* done a good job. At the very least, I *did* finish it, and that counted for something. Surely, any talk I ever gave in the future could only be an improvement, so that was good. "But I was nervous," I said.

"That's okay," my dad said, his voice a calming force. "Everyone who gives talks gets nervous. I still get nervous when I give talks. It shows that you care about what you're doing."

"I prayed to Jehovah to not be so nervous."

"Well, Jehovah probably wants you to be a little nervous; it shows that you care about what you're doing."

"But I wasn't a little nervous, I was a *lot* nervous."

My dad laughed. "That's good! I'm sure Jehovah was with you up on stage."

I felt humbled that night. The thought of how far I would have to progress to become as capable and smart as the adults was overwhelming. But that night was a beginning, and it precipitated a decade-long streak of progress and privileges as one of Jehovah's Witnesses. It was also the most humble I would be for a long time.

In the months that followed, various members of the congregation asked my parents for me to spend time with their sons. I was considered a good influence, and these parents hoped my love of studying Watchtower literature and staging Bible dramas for my sister would influence their kids. My mom was not keen on this, arguing that if someone needed me as a good influence, then they were, by default, a bad influence. In time she relented. "Just try your best to be a good influence," she offered.

I did try, but I didn't feel like the shining example most people assumed I was. I began spending time with Ryan, a wiry and dark-haired kid who was more interested in music and computers than the Bible. He loved reading, and we talked often about our books.

"I keep a list of every book I read," I told him.

He looked at me funny, then shrugged as if it made sense. "What if you don't read the book all the way through?"

"Then I don't count it."

"But what if you read, like, the whole book, but skip one chapter because it's boring."

"I'd never do that," I asserted. "If I read almost a whole book, I'd be sure to read the tiny part I didn't like, too. That way I could add it to my list."

Ryan contemplated this for a moment, mulling over the eccentricity. He asked if I knew how to play guitar.

"No, but I like music," I said, and then I listed off my three favorite non-Watchtower songs, and reminded him that a lot of worldly music is bad. Ryan knew I felt that way, as his mom repeatedly encourage him and his brother to model themselves after me, including the style in which my hair was combed. His mom, it seemed viewed me as a benchmark for her sons. Others, I soon found out, viewed me similarly.

During my penultimate week of third grade, the teachers herded the students into the gymnasium to sit on the floor and watch a talent show. The lights dimmed. The curtain parted. And there, before my eyes, was Tia Starling—a girl I knew from the Kingdom Hall. She was frozen in profile, with one hand on her hip and one on the brim of a black hat. One of her feet was flat on the stage and one leg bent at the knee, toe on point. She wore a black jacket. She wore one glove. The music began. Tia looked up at the audience and with a quick flick of her wrist, spun the hat off of her head. I was immediately mesmerized. For the next four minutes, Tia lip-synced to Michael Jackson's song "Beat It". It was obvious she had practiced her routine. She moved with soul and style. I loved every second.

After school, I ran home and bolted in the front door; I had to tell my mom about the talent show. She was sitting on the floor cutting coupons out of the newspaper and she looked up—a bit surprised that I was so excited about a day at school.

When I told her about Tia's performance, my mom tilted her head slightly. "Michael Jackson? She shouldn't have done that."

"Why?" I asked, "She was just dancing."

"Yeah, but Michael Jackson? Jimmy—she should know better than that."

"Oh. Well, anyway, I liked it."

I went into my room and changed my clothes to go play.

At dinner that evening, I toned down my excitement about the show. I didn't mention Tia's performance to my Dad. Witnesses shied away from Jackson and I felt guilty for enjoying the performance.[13]

No one mentioned the matter for the rest of that day. That weekend, I awoke and hobbled into the kitchen. My mom was preparing breakfast. I noticed my Dad wearing jeans. "Aren't we going out in service?" I asked.

"We're not going out in service this morning." He set down his tea mug. "The Starlings are coming over; Tia wants to apologize to you."

"What?" I didn't understand. "Why's she doing that? I'm not mad at her."

My Dad explained that it was good I wasn't mad, but that she wanted to apologize anyway. I furrowed my brow in continued confusion.

I dressed and sat on the couch just as the Starlings knocked on our door. My heart raced. My Dad opened the door and said hello. Tia flew past my parents and ran to me. She knelt on the ground and put her hands on my knees. She began sobbing. "Oh Jimmy, I'm so sorry. I'm so sorry." She sniffed and wiped her nose on her sleeve. "I didn't mean to do anything wrong. I'm so sorry." She repeated her apology over and over again. Her copper hair draped over my legs; she was too disgraced to look me in the eyes.

I stared at the back of her head, simultaneously fascinated and frozen by her display. I carefully patted her head, absolving her of sin. "It's okay." I looked at the adults, who kept their distance and smiled, and then over at my sister, whose face indicated that I wasn't the only one who wanted this to be over.

Tia gained her composure and sat on the floor by my feet. The adults sat around the living room as Tia's parents told us they were so glad we called and told them about what had happened. My dad asked if I understood what Tia did wrong. I nodded. "Okay, you kids can go play in the other room now," he said.

Tia followed me into my room and, once there, grabbed my arm, bowed her head, and again started crying. She repeated her apology. "I'm so sorry. . . . I'll never do something like that again, Jimmy." Her tears soaked into my sleeve. I shook my head at the ridiculousness of the event but adopted a sympathetic tone: "It's alright, Tia. I don't even care."

I couldn't determine why Tia was so remorseful. Witnesses, it's true, are instructed not to offend their brothers and sisters, but even at a young age, I saw becoming offended as merely a means to gain the advantage. Ecclesiastes 7:9 states that "the taking of offense is what rests in the bosom of the stupid ones," and that was all I needed to make up my mind never to be offended. And why would I? Granted, there may be some music or movies or behaviors that I felt were not Christian, but I just refrained from participating in them. Why should I care what Tia did? That's her relationship with God. That's her conscience. Moreover, if something is a matter of conscience, then it was okay by me. Who was I to be stricter than God?

Every so often, while out in service, the householder asked questions that left me speechless. I didn't like not knowing what to say, because I wanted to give a good Witness. Usually, there was an adult with me at the door who could step in and defend our faith, or at the very least, tell the householder that we will research the topic and return. But I wanted to be able to defend my faith without any help. I accelerated my study of Watchtower literature and I felt it was incumbent upon me to read the Bible all the way through. I began by reading the Bible aloud to my sister, but the circumlocution of Leviticus and Numbers left her bored, so I continued alone. I soon had an entire folder set aside for Bible research: lists of the Israelite kings, the fourteen apostles, the miracles in the Bible, the number of times Jehovah's name appeared in each Bible book, and the longevity of the patriarchs (for which I also made a wall chart).

I enjoyed knowing the answers to so many mysteries. When people argued about the afterlife, I handily showed from the Bible that life in heaven was not what God promised. God created Adam and Eve to inhabit Earth. If they had not sinned, they would not have died and they would still be on Earth. But they *did* sin, and the punishment was death. Since death is a punishment, Adam and Eve would not be rewarded with heavenly resurrection.

A schoolmate claimed that the Bible was fictitious because Adam and Eve only had two sons—so how did we all come to be? With aplomb, I quoted the scripture showing that Adam and Eve became parents to sons *and* daughters. I loved that I could logically explain my faith.

One householder said she didn't believe the Bible because the Earth is obviously more than six thousand years old. I happily told her that we, as Jehovah's Witnesses, agreed with her. Genesis gives no indication as to the time of creation of the heavens and earth, so there is no conflict in accepting both the Bible and the scientific proofs that the universe is billions of years old.

Thirty-seven days after my first talk, my family was out in service with the Brewer family. There were four of us, and five of them, but somehow all nine of us fit into the Brewers' enormous car. Their son Eddie was two years my senior. He and I frequently went to the doors together, and on this day, a man opened the door and Eddie began his presentation. As soon as the man learned we were Witnesses, he cut off Eddie's sermon: "You know what I don't like about you Witnesses? You guys don't believe in the Trinity." Eddie was taken aback by this sudden attack, but he bounced back swiftly and explained that the word 'trinity' is not found in the Bible. The usual back-and-forth retorts transpired. I stayed out of it. I didn't know what to say. I had only researched *my* faith; I hadn't researched concepts like the Trinity that were not Biblical anyway.

As the conversation waned, I figured I should contribute. "You know what the Son's name is—Jesus—but do you know the name of the Father?"

The man said: "God."

I said: "But 'God' is just a title. There are many gods, but what is the name of the god of the Bible? You should look up Psalms 83:18."

The man said he would, and we said our good-byes.

Eddie and I walked back to the car, where our families were waiting. They asked what took so long, and we told them the story.

A few weeks later, while talking with Eddie after a meeting, two elders approached. I was a little nervous about this, because elders never just walked up and started talking to young kids, at least not the well-behaved kids. The older one asked if he could talk to me for a second, and I meekly agreed. The other one put his hand out, pushing Eddie away, and said: "Eddie, leave us alone, we need to talk to Jimmy privately." Eddie walked away, head hanging down. My nerves accelerated.

The older elder put his hand on my shoulder. "Would you like to be on the Circuit Assembly?"

They explained how the Circuit Overseer heard about what I had said to that householder and how I turned the conversation from something I didn't know about into something I did. "It took great courage for an eight-year-old to speak up like that, Jimmy."

"Well, I need to ask my parents."

"We already did."

Of course it was okay with my parents; having your child interviewed at a Circuit Assembly is every Witness parents' dream. So I agreed.

This was a great privilege. The two-day Circuit Assemblies only occurred semiyearly. All the speakers were elders. A few of the talks called for demonstrations or interviews. Maybe a dozen people in the entire Circuit of twenty congregations were invited to participate in the demonstrations or interviews. Everyone used in this capacity was an exemplary Witness; impeccable in their dress, conduct, and attitude. Being interviewed required several rehearsals in front of the Circuit Overseer and other elders. It involved showing up at the assembly early to participate in a dry run on the stage.

And so, mere months after crying during my first performance on stage at the Kingdom Hall, I found myself on a much larger stage, being interviewed in front of nearly two thousand people. I was the youngest person on the stage that weekend, and my family assured me that it was a great privilege I should treasure always.

Twenty months later, I was interviewed again. This time, I was invited to share with everyone my tenacious reading and personal studying habits. The elder began the interview by saying that I was reading the Bible . . . for the second time. Audience members gasped, unable to believe that a ten-year-old had already read the Bible.

At age eleven, I was on the assembly again. This time I delivered a five-minute talk. "You know buddy," my grandpa said, "this is a special privilege. It's your own talk. You're not being used in someone else's talk." I nodded, feigning humility. He also said my assignment was special because Circuit Overseers choose only the finest speakers in the Circuit, and I had been chosen from amongst hundreds of candidates. He would know. My mom's father had a powerful, commanding voice. He was a tall man with broad shoulders, large muscles, complete with a tattoo from his worldly days as a drill sergeant in the Navy, before my mom was born. When he gripped the lectern and spoke about Jehovah, it was impossible to not listen. He sternly charged of the upcoming day of God's judgment, yet balanced his exhortations with parables and illustrations he had collected over his decades of working up talks from the Watchtower's outlines. He imbibed the Watchtower's literature, reading it even during breakfast. His smile showed off his hound's teeth, and his eyes sparkled one evening when I sat on his lap and he shared with me the profoundness of Ecclesiastes. He had a scripture scribed in wood affixed above his doorpost and had handpainted an image of Samson felling the pillars on his two-story living room wall. His love for Jehovah's one true organization was so embracing, so enthralling, that he—a man who had lost his own mother when he was a boy—referred to the Watchtower Society as "Momma." To me, he was the tip of the Watchtower's sword; the ideal Witness who let nothing intervene in his devotion.

The next year, I was interviewed at the assembly again, this time concerning a Bible study I conducted on the bus ride to and from school.

The year after that, I was interviewed again—only this time I was interviewed at a District Convention. Instead of standing before two thousand people, I stood before twenty thousand.

The next year, I was interviewed at the District Convention again. Ryan and other kids in the congregation referred to me as "Assembly Boy." The sobriquet was partially a tease; a joke for exuding a religious fervor normally seen only in older Witnesses, such as my grandfather, and new recruits, who were still in the infatuated throes of a romance with the religion. But I reveled in the nickname. It indicated to me that I was on the path to surviving Armageddon. And Armageddon was close.

Having dinner at Nana and Papa's home one evening, I complained that I wished the Paradise would be here by now. Papa gently assured me it was coming. "Look how long I've had to wait," he said with his head tilted back to see through his trifocals.

"Jimmy," Nana said, clutching her chest, "The End is so close, it'll be here before you know it." Deigning to provide me instant evidence, she leaned forward and lifted the remote, turning the television louder. "Do you see what's on the news, Jimmy? You can open your Bible to Matthew 24 and follow along. It's all being fulfilled! Wars, and famine . . . but we know the good news, right? We know that this is good, because Jehovah said all these things have to happen and then the End will come."

She was right, of course, and as I thought about the recent world events, I recalled how they served to bolster my faith. Alone among my classmates and teacher, I did not cry on the morning of the Challenger disaster, for I knew those astronauts were in God's memory and would now have their sins forgiven. I did not fret about the meltdown in Chernobyl, knowing in my heart that God would clean up the earth and resurrect the people who had died.

About a month before each convention, the elders announced that any who wished to be baptized should contact them. I asked my parents for years, and they consistently said no. Just after turning twelve, I leaned over during the meeting and asked my dad again. He just shook his head. "Why?" I asked. He said we'd talk about it later. A week passed, and one evening my dad came into my bedroom. He sat on my bed.

"Do you still want to get baptized at the convention next month?"

I looked up from the book I was reading.

"Because if you want to, then we shouldn't hold you back."

I later discovered that the Circuit Overseer, during his visit to our congregation, took my dad aside and asked why I was not baptized. The Overseer said I certainly seemed ready. My dad felt I wasn't ready. He and my mom thought I was too young and didn't fully know what I was getting into. Nevertheless, at the Overseer's insistence, my dad agreed that it wasn't his place to stand in the way of my spiritual progress.

The next month at the District Convention, I sat in the front row. All baptismal candidates sat in the front rows. The talk discussing the importance of baptism was, essentially, a restating of the baptism talk from previous conventions, so I had the majority of the talk memorized. The talk culminated in the baptismal candidates being asked to stand. The audience applauded. The elder asked two questions, and requested that we respond in a loud, clear voice:

> On the basis of the sacrifice of Jesus Christ, have you repented of your sins and dedicated yourself to Jehovah to do his will?

> Do you understand that your dedication and baptism identify you as one of Jehovah's Witnesses in association with God's spirit-directed organization?[16]

Maybe it was because I was only twelve, or maybe it was because the organizational aspect of the religion was uninteresting, but I didn't understand the questions. Fortunately, I knew from dozens of previous assemblies and conventions that the answer to both questions was Yes!

An elder dunked me underwater at 12:17 that afternoon. I was the twelfth person baptized that day. My family congratulated me with open arms. While my mom hugged me, I noticed Aunt Janet hugging my sister.

She said, to no one in particular: "Poor Diane, everyone pays attention to her big brother. She keeps thinking, 'Hey, when am I gonna get some of this attention?'" I looked at my sister and winked. She winked back.

There are two bizarre consequences to getting baptized, and both of them frightened me. First, it was now possible to get disfellowshipped—evicted from the congregation and shunned by my brothers and sisters. I had no intention of ever doing anything bad. But I knew that, as a human, I was imperfect. Temptation, or the Devil, could lead me down the wrong path, and I would have to pay for my actions. Disfellowshipped people scared me; I had no idea how to act around them—how to nonchalantly ignore them while simultaneously acting out judgment on God's behalf.

One afternoon, I accompanied my dad to an automotive store. While he was busy talking to an employee, I wandered off to look at the car fresheners. And then . . . I saw *him*. His name was Thom. He was recently disfellowshipped. My heart raced. I turned to look down, feigning interest in the selection of fuzzy dice. But I could sense him. He was right there—at the other end of the aisle—and he was walking in my direction. It was a peculiar feeling: He was not a Witness anymore. He had willfully turned his back on his family and the opportunity to live forever in God's love. He was dead; he was a spiritual zombie. Or, at least, he was supposed to be dead. But there he was, scanning the merchandise on the shelves, walking my way. I looked out of the corner of my eyes, then turned my head to see him. He looked up, noticing me for the first time. He nodded, politely, but did not speak. I nodded in reply—a gut reaction—and instantly felt remorse.

Later, at my grandparents' house, I confessed that I saw Thom. My dad, sitting next to me on the couch, jumped back as if my experience was contagious. "You didn't tell me that, buddy."

I shrugged. "Well, you were busy, and I didn't want you to get mad at me."

"Why would I get mad?"

"Because I nodded at him," I said, sheepishly.

Nana jumped into the conversation. "Well, did he talk to you?"

"No." I turned to face her. "But he looked at me, and I just kind of nodded without thinking about it."

Aunt Janet shook her head in disgust, and her thick, black hair swayed in response. "It just goes to show how much they've fallen. Disfellowshipped people sometimes come into the bank where I work, and I just help them politely, but I don't act like they're my friends anymore." She added: "Because they're not."

"I just felt bad if I would've ignored him." I looked down at the coffee table.

Nana sat forward in her rocking chair. She was a short, plump woman with striking silver hair who wore a muumuu whenever she was home. But despite appearances, she wielded a fiery personality and loved God with an unyielding zeal. With sternness in her voice, she asked: "Now why would you feel bad for Thom, Jimmy?"

"I don't know." Sensing that everyone wanted to hear more, I added: "Well, you know, no one talks to him anymore."

"Jimmy!" Nana yelled, exasperated that she had to spell things out so clearly. "No one forced him into that position. Is that what you think? Do you think the elders didn't know what they were doing? He got what he deserved—"

"No one pushed him to do that," my dad interjected. "What he did was what he wanted to do."

Nana nodded, reminding me that the elders had formed a judicial meeting, met with Thom in the basement and found him unrepentant. "It's a good lesson, don't you think? We just need to make sure we never stop loving Jehovah like that."

"We just need to make sure we never end up in the basement with the elders," Aunt Janet added, half in jest.

The second consequence of being baptized was that I was now the head of every female in the Organization. It didn't matter if the woman was twice or seven times my age. It didn't matter if she worked at the World Headquarters of Jehovah's Witnesses, or if she was the wife of an elder. It didn't even matter if the woman was my mother or my grandmother. In matters of spirituality, I was superior. This immediately became apparent when my dad was out of town; it fell to me to say prayers before mealtime. And when I accompanied Nana to the home of a woman with whom she studied the Bible, she donned a head covering to demonstrate submission.

During summer break, my mom took my sister and me out in service every Wednesday. I didn't mind the additional day of service. What I minded was the lack of men during midweek service. Before my baptism, I often watched as one of the sisters wore a head covering to conduct the meeting. But after my baptism, I was nervous to show up for service. I tried to make us late with the hope that another baptized male would arrive first and begin conducting the meeting for service. Just weeks after my baptism, we showed up at a meeting for Service, and of the twenty-one people there, I was the only one who was both baptized and male. I breathed a heavy sigh of relief when Eddie showed up and offered to conduct the meeting. Another time, I wasn't so lucky. We arrived four minutes late, and a sister was conducting. She awkwardly demurred to my authority and slinked back to her seat. Organizing two dozen women into car groups was an uncomfortable task. I didn't even have a driver's license. The women were my aunts and baby-sitters and seniors. I felt silly. I nervously read from the lectionary, then arbitrarily divided the women into car groups. Once out in service, the situation was no better. The sisters knew that when a male is present, he takes the lead. So, I sat in the back seat and laughed with my sister until some woman, many years my senior, looked at me in the rearview mirror and asked: "Okay, Jimmy, who should go where?"

As popular as I was in the congregation, things were exactly the opposite at school. The accolades my fellow Witnesses afforded me were more than balanced by the lack of respect from schoolmates and teachers. My family was poor, I was scrawny, and those are two cogent reasons to be picked on at school. But I was also the kid who sat off on the side during flag salutes and stayed home on Halloween. As a Witness, I needed to minimize association with worldly people, so I didn't make friends with my classmates. They were "bad association," and I knew that soon they would all die in Armageddon.

In fifth grade, our class held a celebration for Native American Day. A local television news station filmed our class dancing Native dances and eating Native food. My mom ordered me to not participate, fearing that such activities were tantamount to worshipping false gods. That evening, I watched my class, on TV, dancing in a circle. I was marginally visible, sitting off on the side. The next day my peers riled me for looking like a reject on television.

In sixth grade, on the day before winter break, my math teacher distributed worksheets to the class. The worksheets were Christmas-themed, so I raised my hand.

"Mrs. Lark?"

"Not now, Jimmy, I'll answer all questions at the end."

When finished, she turned to me. "Now," she asked, exhaling loudly, "does anyone have any questions?"

I raised my hand.

"Yes, Jimmy?"

"I don't think I can do these worksheets."

"Why not?"

"Because they have Christmas stuff on them."

She stomped to her desk and opened a drawer. Walking to my desk with scissors in hand, she cut off the Christmas aspects of each worksheet. Some had pictures of Santa, others depicted reindeer, and some featured

Christmas stories in the instructions. She cut off all of this. I sat sweating and shaking as I felt two dozen sets of eyes glaring at me. I stared at the floor and watched the hacked up paper fall to the carpet.

Finally, she asked: "Is that better?"

As a Witness, I knew better. The situation reminded me of the morning flag salute ritual. It was unthinkable that I stand up like the rest of the class, or that I place my hand near my heart, keeping it a couple of inches from my body, and merely lip-sync the pledge. Technically, I would *not* be saluting the flag, so I could argue that I did not sin. But how would it look? I would not be giving a good Witness, as anyone watching me would assume that I *did* salute the flag. It would be a lame attempt to blend in while avoiding sin on a technicality.

I told Mrs. Lark her hurried edits did not alter the situation. "It's still Christmas stuff."

She grabbed the remnants of the worksheets, crumpled them and ordered me to sit outside the classroom. I sat in the commons area and six classrooms full of students stared at me.

When my classmates made fun of me the next day, pushing me in the hall and laughing at my ability to get in trouble for the dumbest reason imaginable, I stiffened my upper lip. But then one of them grabbed my pencil and tore off the eraser top my sister had given to me. He threw it across the room and spat at me. I took the hall pass and went into the bathroom to cry for a while.

I hated school. I liked learning, but my classmates were rude and irreverent. The pedantic teachers didn't really care if the students learned, and they reveled in the power they held over the students. And since, as Witnesses, we knew the end of the world was imminent, my parents said higher education was pointless.[17] Compulsory school was viewed as having some value, as the reading and writing skills would assist in the study of God's Word, but college was off-limits. A bevy of jobs were available to non-college graduates and, besides, college life was rife with immorality, drunkenness, and exposure to satanic ideas like philosophy and evolution. No one in my family held a college degree, and there were no plans for me to obtain one. Once, when I expressed some concern about what I would do for a job upon graduation, Aunt Janet flicked her wrist as if tossing my worry in the trash: "Don't worry, Jimmy, the new system will be here before you even get to high school."

School, then, was little more than a distraction from Jehovah's service. The knowledge that I was wasting my life in school gave way to depression.

I often cried while sitting in class. I sat alone at lunchtime and on the bus. I was sullen and withdrawn. "You don't seem like a happy boy anymore," my dad remarked. He told me that if I didn't show more enthusiasm, I might not get to give any more talks. "No one wants to listen to a monotone speaker."

In eighth grade, I imagined methods of suicide. At first, the idea frightened me. But then its allure became a source of comfort, as if, at any time, I could hit the reset button. I figured suicide was a fast way to the Paradise: I would die, my sins would be forgiven, and I would wake up in Paradise. But the caveat was this: maybe taking my own life showed such disregard for life, that God would not forgive me. I thought about killing myself with the fumes from glue and correction fluid; even going to the point of brushing the stuff on my nose and breathing it. But this just made my face swell up.

Soon I did not see any point in going to school, despite repeated arguments with my parents. My dad claimed it was my duty before Jehovah to do what the secular authorities require. When I countered with the idea of being home-schooled, he dismissed this as impossible. One morning, with my coat and backpack on, I collapsed on the couch and cried; begging my mom to let me stay home. I pleaded, begging her to let me home-school myself. With my sister looking on, my mom grabbed my arms and shook me. "Jimmy, you have to go to school. I don't want any more of this." Locking eyes with my sister, I dragged my depressed weight off the couch and left for school. Diane offered me a tissue from her coat pocket as we walked to the bus stop. I was spineless; afraid to stand up for myself.

My sister was given all the genes for gumption. Once, on the walk to the bus stop, Diane looked up and said: "I don't want to go to school today." She turned around and walked back home. I was supposed to watch over her, so I decided to follow her back home. When we got home, my sister just walked in the door, threw down her backpack and told my mom she wasn't going to school. My mom laughed at the audacity of her little daughter. She drove us both to school.

Meanwhile, my love of learning caused irritation. Without exception, every zoology book was written by a proponent of evolution. Most books mentioned it in passing, saying things like "birds have evolved into masters of the air," but some devoted entire chapters to the godless theory. I didn't like reading those words. Jehovah created everything; I couldn't understand how such smart people had studied creation and then arrived at the wrong conclusion. Shouldn't a close look at the physical world have revealed creation to be the best, if not the only, explanation for life on earth?

I was ecstatic, then, when the Watchtower Society published *Life—How Did it Get Here? By Evolution or by Creation?* I expected the book to thouroughly, logically prove that life was not the product of blind chance, but of a purposeful Creator. We received the new book at a District Convention and I read it within the week.

But I was disappointed. The book claimed to weigh fairly the evidence on both sides of the issue, but was clearly biased towards creation from the start. I was mad at my secular books for being predisposed to evolution, and this book suffered from the same kind of slant—only towards creation.

If anything, *Life—How Did it Get Here?* made me realize that the proponents of evolution possessed valid arguments, such as when it showed pictures of the reptile-bird *Archaeopteryx*.[18] I was confused; had this creature really existed? From the wording in the captions I was unsure, so I asked my dad. He looked at the pictures with furrowed eyebrows. He handed the book back briskly. "Yep, it was real. Why?"

"Just wondering," I said, dejectedly.

I couldn't believe it. I had no idea that a creature like that—a creature with hands *and* wings and with a beak *and* teeth—actually existed and, further, that the Watchtower Society did not dispute its authenticity. Staring at the picture, I was flooded with the disturbing notion that evolution deserved more credence than I had given it.

The most disheartening paragraph in the entire book began on page 55:

> If evolution were founded in fact, the fossil record would be expected to reveal beginnings of new structures in living things. . . . There should be reptiles with front limbs changing into bird wings, back limbs changing into legs with claws, scales changing into feathers, and *mouths changing into horny beaks.*[19]

Did the Society somehow miss the *Archaeopteryx*—the very creature they depicted on two separate pages? If that wasn't a beast with a mouth changing into a beak, I didn't know what was. I didn't have to look far at all to knock down their line of logic; I simply had to turn the page.

But there was no benefit in getting tripped up by little problems. The important thing was to endure to the End. Once the Paradise was here, God would restore humans to perfect mind and body. Then, new scrolls would be opened and our superior intellects would be able to handle even the most perplexing concepts.

And that End was excruciatingly soon. In early 1989, Aunt Janet even opined that the pregnant sisters in our congregation were "putting Jehovah to the test." I couldn't speak for my aunt, but I secretly believed 1989 would be the final year of the wicked world. It marked the 75th year since 1914. The generation of that era was old. World events confirmed my theory: The Soviet Union granted independence to the Baltic States. The nations of Eastern Europe were democratizing. Demonstrations in China hinted at a relaxing of their government's grip on the people. Reagan and Bush were shaking hands with Gorbachev. The Berlin Wall fell. The Cold War ended.

This was all good news. Every Witness memorized Matthew 24:14. The verse is part of Jesus' answer to his apostles regarding the 'sign' of the end times: "This good news of the Kingdom will be preached in all the inhabited earth for a witness to all the nations and then the end will come." It doesn't take a biblical scholar to see the application: Before God brings the End a witness must be given *everywhere*. For decades, many nations were not receiving this witness. But now they would. Additionally, 1 Thessalonians 5:3, another scripture Witnesses identify as a 'sign' of the Last Days, states: "Whenever they are declaring peace and security, then sudden destruction is to be instantly upon them." For this scripture to be fulfilled there could be no wars—not even cold wars. The world of 1989 was headed towards complete fulfillment of these scriptures.

Since the first president of the Watchtower Society, Charles Russell, identified October 1, 1914 as the exact start to the Last Days, I reasoned that God would begin Armageddon on the anniversary. October 1, 1989 was a Sunday. At the meeting that afternoon, I paid close attention. I took notes. I commented during the *Watchtower* study. I was nervous that evening, I kept looking at the sky to see if the clouds portended anything unusual. After dusk, while my parents and sister watched television, I went into my room and opened the curtains. I grabbed my desk chair and sat, staring. I shut off the light and watched the birds flying south. I looked at the street, the neighbors' trailer homes, and the sky. I prayed and breathed slowly and tried to stay calm.

Nothing seemed to be happening, so I only sat there for seventeen more minutes. I went to bed that night hoping Armageddon would commence in the middle of the night. I fell asleep thinking about it.

October came and went. So did November and December. Soon, a new decade was under way.

SCHOOL AND JEHOVAH'S WITNESSES

> Any "future" this world offers is no future! Wisely, then, let God's Word influence you in selecting a course that will result in your protection and blessing. Make pioneer service, the full-time ministry, with the possibility of Bethel or missionary service your goal. This is a life that offers an everlasting future!
>
> —*The Watchtower*, March 15, 1969, p. 171

The calendars were not the only change in January 1990. Our congregation, and two neighboring congregations, had swelled in size so much that a new congregation needed to be formed. The elders split the three large congregations and divided them along new geographic lines to make a fourth congregation in the city of Apple Valley. Coincidentally, we moved to a new house only two months after the formation of the new congregation. This new house was within the borders of Apple Valley congregation's territory.

I was eager to attend a new congregation. It brought with it excitement and anticipation. About a third of the members had been in my previous congregation, so I knew many of them. And since Witnesses are such a tight community, I had heard of most of the people I did not already know. In time, I came to view Apple Valley as the perfect congregation—the one where I expected to stay through the Last Days and into Armageddon.

I wasn't sure anymore when Armageddon would arrive. *The Watchtower* stated the preaching work "would be completed in our *20th century*."[20] While the Bible clearly states that no one knows the day or the hour,[21] the magazine's guess seemed plausible. But I had to face the facts: Through my youth, the Society consistently indicated that the End was extremely close. And yet, it had not come. The Last Days had already lasted longer than anyone suspected. With all my heart I hoped Paradise would arrive in the next couple years, but I had to acknowledge that there was a minuscule possibility that the Last Days would last several more years.

So I devised a plan. First, I would begin regular pioneering as soon as possible. This entailed devoting one thousand hours a year to going out in service—knocking on doors, standing on the street corners passing out literature, and conducting bible studies. As long as I pioneered, I would have God's approval. After graduating high school, I would apply to work at the Watchtower Headquarters, called "Bethel." Once accepted, I would be required to stay a year, but could stay as long as I wanted. This was a good position to be in. If I held to my plan, I could look forward to finishing out the twentieth century—and thus this wicked world—busy in full-time service to Jehovah. In the rare chance that I didn't get accepted to Bethel, I would stay home and continue pioneering.

Most Witnesses are well intentioned when they begin pioneering. They are zealous and sincerely desire to please Jehovah. But most don't last more than a year. They would, in a fit of zeal, reduce their hours at their job, then be unable to succeed financially. Or, they would concoct some special arrangement, such as staying with their parents, then end up falling in love, getting married, moving out, and increasing their expenditures.

I wasn't going to fall for such vicissitudes. When I began high school, I met with a guidance counselor. I told her I wanted to be on the school's work program, wherein students are allowed to leave early to go to work. If I could get on the work program, I could start pioneering as soon as I completed eleventh grade.

I was also interested in graduating early. I had long since written off school as a waste, so I determined to conclude it post-haste.

The counselor was not pleased. She suggested I use my senior year to take classes that interested me without worrying about credits, or to get a head start on college. But I had no desire to waste my time in worldly pursuits; to the contrary: I was going to participate in a volunteer work that required no secular schooling.

With my parents' marriage becoming increasingly strained and my sister becoming more difficult to control, my parents were clueless about my high school career. I coasted through tenth grade. When the guidance counselor informed me that my grades were too high to be on the work program, I argued that as a good student I should be allowed the freedom to do what I want. When she replied that there was no way a student with my grades would be accepted for the work program, I started to purposely neglect assignments, and intentionally answer incorrectly on tests.

The Watchtower Society encouraged pioneers not to burden others.[22] So if I was going to pioneer, I needed transportation. My parents offered me their old car. It was in good condition, it had four doors, and they were willing to sell it cheap. To get money, I needed a job, and so I obtained employment at the public library. I worked three evenings a week for minimum wage. By March of my sophomore year, I had enough money to buy the car.

During these final years of high school, I became good friends with my peers in Apple Valley congregation. The person whose companionship I enjoyed most was Ryan Sutter. Ryan was a polymath, and we often spoke for hours on arcane subjects. He was equal to my height, but had sharper features and thin, black hair and bony, double-jointed fingers.

At first, my parents were hesitant to let me associate with Ryan and his older brother Rhett. The Sutters were musicians, an identity second only to their religiosity. They were heavily into music, even recording their own albums. Their tastes were eclectic; they listened to artists I had never even heard of. They talked about music incessantly. This wasn't balanced, and my parents felt a Witness must be balanced in all things. But as I became a teenager, they relented and agreed that the Sutters were acceptable friends. Eccentric, but acceptable.

I managed to wrangle my talentless self in amongst them. We went to movies together; we went out to eat after the meetings together. I slept over at their house as often as I was allowed, as my parents had a rule of "be home and lights out by ten" and so, if I wanted to go have a fun evening without worrying about the clock, I slept at the Sutters' home. Ryan always had strange ideas; like his thought that no two physical objects ever touched, no matter how close they were. He claimed that one day we would only use computers to write things down, and he thought his life was a balancing act of ensuring the good outweighed the bad.

During the summer of 1991, Ryan and I auxiliary pioneered. Auxiliary pioneering is a temporary version of regular pioneering; instead of working toward a thousand hours in a year, an auxiliary pioneer pledged to devote sixty hours in a single month. Ryan and I pledged all three summer months, so were together nearly every day. Ryan also secured a job at the library. He helped me come to terms with being a nerd, and not to care what others thought about me. I soon came to view Ryan as my best friend, although I never said as much, because I knew he had so many friends that there was no way he felt the same about me. Ryan introduced me to new ideas and new ways of looking at the world. I had much respect for him and his logic, and I decided that he was the most intelligent peer I had. He was a self-trained philosopher, a non-drugged Ginsberg who demanded an explicit rationale for the world. Indeed, the fact that he was logical and intelligent *and also a Witness* strengthened my faith, because it indicated that anyone with sufficient intelligence, who looked at the evidence, couldn't help but be a Witness. It was the correct way to be; it was the Truth.

Returning from Florida after a vacation with my grandparents, I learned that Ryan had been publicly reproved, that is, the elders announced that Ryan had sinned and been disciplined. I was conflicted and betrayed about this turn of events. Was it okay to still associate with Ryan? Was he now "bad association?"[23] How would I, Assembly Boy, look if I was in his company?

It wasn't difficult to determine Ryan's sin. Naomi, a girl from a neighboring congregation, had also been reproved. I knew Ryan liked her; I just didn't know he liked her *that* much. I couldn't believe a friend of mine had committed such a grievous sin.

After not being with Ryan for two weeks, my dad asked if I was avoiding him. I lied: "No."

"You know," he said, "You should make sure you show Ryan that you're his friend now more than ever. Ryan made a mistake, but he was repentant, so he could probably use some encouragement. It'd be a big help to him."

I called Ryan that night and invited myself to his house. But I didn't ask about his sin, and I didn't ask about his future intentions with Naomi. I almost didn't want to know.

SAVING MY OWN LIFE

Therefore, if you, although being wicked, know how to give good gifts to your children, how much more so will your Father who is in the heavens give good things to those asking him?

—Matthew 7:11

onathan Kamber and I first met at a wedding reception, and whenever we crossed paths, we talked for hours. His dark eyes and dark hair stood out against his pale skin. He was overweight and he stood with his feet splayed out. He was self-conscious, to the point of distraction, and his ego was easily bruised. We fought often. "How do you manage to get a beer belly when you're too young to drink beer?" I asked him the day we met. He laughed affably, sucking in his gut and stretching out his neck to assure me I was no match should we come to blows.

He fit a perfect role in my life. Johnny *wanted* to be with me and soon called me his best friend. He had a variety of interests, but wasn't a reader. He had good know-how when it came to the utilitarian tasks in life and reveled in asking bizarre questions about the world around him.

Johnny came from a large family; he had three younger siblings and so many older half-siblings that I never learned all their names or exactly how many there were. Johnny was impressed with his dad for having provided for them all. He told me that his dad, as a truck driver, had unfortunately been forced to miss meetings while out on the road providing for his family. Jehovah understood, Johnny reasoned, because first and foremost a man must provide for his family.

But while Johnny felt that he and his dad had reasons for justifiably circumventing *Watchtower* suggestions, I was dogmatic about the issue. "That's just wrong," I argued one afternoon at a restaurant.

"What do you mean?" he asked, springing back and gesturing grandly.

"I mean that Jehovah says we're supposed to seek *first* the kingdom and then all the other things will be added to us, so if your dad would have gone to all the meetings, Jehovah would have seen to it that you all were provided for."[24]

"Jim, you don't understand," Johnny said, "My dad was a truck driver, and there were ten kids at home, so he had to do what he could to make money." He leaned forward and grabbed a handful of fries.

"The Bible doesn't say 'seek first the kingdom, unless you have lots of kids, then it's okay to miss meetings'! It just says to seek first the kingdom. Period," I said, as if there was nothing left to discuss.

"Jim, what else could my dad have done if he wasn't a truck driver?"

"I don't know; that's not what I'm saying. All I'm saying is Jehovah would have seen to it that all of you were provided for. Are you saying that Jehovah couldn't have done that?"

Johnny was defensive. "All I'm saying is that my dad did what was best for the family."

"Right, and now all of your older brothers and sisters are not in the Truth, so maybe your dad was able to feed and clothe them, but obviously their spiritual needs were never met."

"Okay, that's crossing the line," he said sharply. "My brothers and sisters have to answer to Jehovah for themselves; they can't tell Jehovah that they didn't want to do his will because dad wasn't with them at the meetings."

"Fine. Whatever," I snapped, folding my arms.

In May of 1992, my high school counselor granted my request to be on the work program for the following school year. I saw no reason why I shouldn't start regular pioneering on June first. Though my junior year didn't finish until two weeks into June, I knew that I had the drive and determination to get in the required hours by August 31st. So, in late May, at the meeting, the elders announced that I was joining the ranks of regular pioneers beginning in June. Everyone clapped, and a few people looked over and nodded approvingly. Some were even surprised; it was unusual for someone to begin pioneering while still in school.

After the meeting, Ryan walked over to me: "Way to go, man."

Rhett gave me a hug. "I'm proud of you, buddy," he pointed heavenward, "but more importantly, so is He."

The first of June was like any other day. It was a Monday, and I dragged myself to school. It wasn't until later that morning, when I wrote the date on a worksheet, that I realized it was June first. *This is it. This day marks a divider in my life between all that came before and all that will follow.* I was only a sixteen-year-old eleventh-grader, but I knew I was in a perfect position to spend the rest of the Last Days serving Jehovah full-time. Nothing—not even school—could stop me now. I had a good job and a good car. I had a growing bank account and no bills.

For the first two weeks, I didn't feel like a pioneer. I couldn't go out in service, as school was still in session. I went out on Saturday, but hardly got in any time. The problem with Saturdays was that everyone in the congregation went out in service. We met at nine o'clock to divide into car groups. Then everyone started talking with everyone else, because they haven't seen each other since the last meeting, two days ago. By nine thirty, if I was lucky, I could finally start counting time. At eleven, the group took a break. This meant patronizing a donut shop or fast food dive. Witnesses from several car groups often planned to meet at the same place; they descended upon an innocent establishment like a swarm of locusts.[25] The break often exceeded forty-five minutes, then we'd cram back in the car for one or two return visits, or just to drive back to the Kingdom Hall. All told, from arriving at the meeting for service at nine, until getting back in my car at twelve thirty, I was fortunate if I could count two hours. This never bothered me before, because Jehovah knew we were doing a difficult work, and I felt that leisurely knocking on doors and wasting the better part of the morning was okay. But now, my mentality changed. Now I needed to accumulate hours.

The day after the school year ended, I woke up and went out in service. I stood at the first house—a house far nicer than any I had ever lived in—and rang the bell. And waited. Just waited. Just waited there with my clean-shaven face, my Montgomery Wards suit, my ten dollar neck tie and my bag containing a Bible, copies of the latest *Watchtower*, and assorted other Witness literature. I looked out across the street at the other Witness working on the other side of the road. No one was home midweek. Everyone was at work or school. The few people home were sleeping or too busy to say hello.

For every minute I was at a door, I was sitting in a car for five minutes. Sometimes I was in the car because we were driving. Other times I was in the car because I finished working the houses, and I was waiting for the others to return. Sometimes I was in the car because two other people in the group were making a return visit.

There wasn't much variety in the people in the car. Rhett was there, thankfully, always the moral compass and ready with a quirky conversation about music. He looked much like his brother Ryan, his junior by just over a year. In fact, he looked so much like Ryan, people in the congregation often confused the two. But Rhett was a tad taller and had a heftier build.

Eddie Brewer was also pioneering, and even though we had little in common, we had a kindred nature, as our parents were friends. Then there was Scott Pallas, a tall, lanky teen with a shock of chestnut hair. Despite his haggard appearance of tousled hair and untucked shirts, he was allowed to begin pioneering that fall with the stipulation that he remove the skull-and-crossbones decals from the side of his car.

Service soon became more challenging. After complaining about this to Johnny one evening, he suggested I quit pioneering before I developed a negative attitude, but I would have been too humiliated to quit. After spending years of my life preparing for the task, I couldn't give up only months after starting. I conceded that Johnny might be right, but that I wanted to give it a fair chance. "Maybe I'll quit after going to Pioneer School," I said.

I had an unexpectedly tough time accumulating the required number of hours. If the problem of getting in enough hours was due to my own negligence, it wouldn't have been so bad. But by and large the problem was my fellow Witnesses.

One morning, no one else showed up for service. There were seven other regular pioneers in the congregation, plus auxiliary pioneers, not to mention the assorted publishers, but not a single person showed up. I was baffled. I didn't know that sort of thing ever happened. Not a single person in the entire congregation could find the time to do this most important work? So I just sat there. As if holding my own private meeting, I thumbed through the *Watchtower*. I said a prayer. Then I went home. I had nothing to do. I was discouraged. This occurred eleven times that year.

On another occasion, after we stopped for lunch, one of the sisters in our group was nowhere to be found. At first, we assumed she was using the ladies' room, but then five minutes turned into fifteen. Finally, after thirty-three minutes, she trotted out of the adjacent grocery store with a cart of groceries. That evening, I told my parents how ridiculous that was. "Stuff like that happens from time to time," my mom said. "I don't like it either." My dad said that if that happens again, I should offer magazines to the people in the parking lot to keep my time going.

That was the thing about pioneering: you had to keep your time going. One pioneer joked that he had a time juggernaut; that is, once he started counting his time for the day, it was tough to stop. Scott claimed that he started counting his time as soon as he tied his tie every morning. Rhett laughed, assuming it was a joke, but I looked at Scott with a questioning look, causing him to add: "Maybe it's one of those don't ask/don't tell things."

I was split. Part of me wanted to accrue the required hours as easily as possible. I wanted to lazily drop off *Watchtowers* at bus stops and laundromats, or sit in the car while two people spent a half hour at a door arguing with someone, or tag along with Rhett while he studied the Bible with Jamin, a young boy in our congregation. But part of me wanted to do what was right. The important thing wasn't clocking in a thousand hours; the important thing was bringing the good news to people.

Still, the goal itself suggested what the Society felt was important: A regular pioneer was not someone who studied with twenty people, or placed two hundred magazines a month or made five hundred return visits a year. No, a regular pioneer was someone who spent one thousand *hours* out in service every year.

I argued about this with Nana. Not only was counting and reporting time a direct violation of Galatians 6:4, I felt it was wrong to classify Witnesses by the quantity of service they performed; it should go by quality. Nana reasoned that, by increasing quantity, quality rose, too. "Not necessarily," I said. I wasn't placing more magazines or making more return visits as a thousand-hour-a-year pioneer than I was as a twenty-hour-a-month publisher. But she said the important thing is that Jehovah saw I was trying that much harder. I argued that instead of reporting my time each month, I should just report how hard I tried. Obviously, trudging through the snow in freezing temperatures going door-to-door is a lot harder than sitting on Jamin's floor. Nana claimed, though, that as a pioneer, I was doing much more for Jehovah than I had before—the easy and the hard stuff.

She was right, of course. That was the whole gist of our culture. People who have never been Witnesses wonder what keeps them going. Why do Witnesses keep going to people's doors when so many are not home, and when the people who are home are rude or apathetic? The reason is this: Witnesses go door-to-door to *save themselves*. It's a Bible-based truth. Remember Noah. He preached for forty years, and no one listened to him. But Noah was not a failure. God told Noah to preach; He didn't say anyone had to listen. I was like Noah. God commanded me to preach. There was no reason to get discouraged if no one listened, or even if no one came to the door. The important thing was doing my duty. In doing so, I was saving my own life.

The new service year began in September. I had 365 days to accrue one thousand hours. One thousand hours of knocking on doors, sitting in cars, leaving magazines at laundromats, and knocking on more doors.

My final year of compulsory school commenced mere days after the service year began, so I had little chance to get a head start. My routine made for tiringly full days. On Mondays, I attended school from 7:30 to 11:08 each morning. As soon as my fourth and last class finished, I drove home, ate a lunch my mom prepared, and dressed in a suit. A car group picked me up at noon. I began counting time immediately. I stayed out in service for three hours, after which I quickly ate a snack and, time permitting, changed back into more casual clothes. I showed up for work at the library at three thirty and worked there until closing time at eight thirty. I then spent an hour studying the Bible with a young boy named Ben. Around ten, I drove home.

A few weeks after the service year began, Johnny and I attended a going-away party for a brother who had been accepted to the Watchtower Headquarters. The fall day was cool, but not cold. The sun shone low in the sky and a slight breeze made me shiver. I watched some of the Witnesses playing volleyball.

Johnny went to get some food, and I stood alone for a few minutes until Rhett's girlfriend, the ever-chipper Moriah, came towards me with someone in tow. She was pulling a boy with thick, swept-up hair, olive skin and deep-set eyes by his jacket, stretching out the sleeve. He flipped his long hair to one side, reached out his hand and said: "You must be Jim Zimmerman."

I smiled large, knowing this man was destined to be my friend. "Yes," I laughed, "Are you Jeremy Davis?"

"Yes I am," he said, proud of his own name. He was a couple inches taller than I. He wore cowboy boots and fitted jeans. He smelled like cologne. "Moriah kept telling me 'You've got to meet this guy! And I said, 'You mean the guy that's always on stage at the assemblies?' and she said, 'he's pretty nice once you get to know him.'" He laughed, and I nodded in agreement; Moriah had repeatedly said much the same to me.

During our conversation, which lasted fifty-eight minutes, there were two thoughts that kept going through my mind.

The first thought was this: This guy is gay.

He wasn't just effeminate. I had seen effeminate. There were brothers in the local congregations known for their excessive flair, the lilt in their step, the way they giggled instead of guffawed. But there was something different about Jeremy. There was no one trait I could point to as evidence, but when he told me he was enrolled in nursing classes at the local community college, and when he said he loved 1980s pop music and enjoyed figure skating, well, I combined all that with his loud gestures, the overeager way he ran his fingers through his hair and the fact that his wardrobe showed that he actually cared about fashion . . . and I concluded that this young man was absolutely, unequivocally gay.

The second thought was this: There's no way this guy is gay.

I mean, how could he be? He was one of Jehovah's Witnesses, and there was no such thing as a homosexual Witness. The Bible clearly states: "Neither fornicators, nor idolaters, nor adulterers, nor men kept for unnatural purposes, *nor men who lie with men* . . . will inherit God's kingdom."[26] To be sure, Jeremy fit the profile, but he must have simply been unmasculine. I resolved the issue in my mind by assuming he was just fully comfortable in his manhood; he didn't need to hide behind standard manly mannerisms or professions.

On the drive home, Johnny asked what I thought about Jeremy. "Didn't you think . . . you know . . . ?" Johnny's question trailed off.

"That he was gay?"

Johnny laughed. "Well, I wasn't going to say it, but now that you mention it."

"No. No way. He seems like a good Witness; he even said he admired me for pioneering. If he was gay he wouldn't bother being a Witness."

"Yeah, I suppose."

Ryan married Naomi that fall. They were young, but what else could they do? They had feelings for each other, and when you have feelings for someone you want to hold their hand . . . and then you want to kiss them . . . and then . . . well, then you have violated God's law. Ryan and Naomi had already made a serious error at least once before; doing so again would show an unrepentant attitude and surely lead to being disfellowshipped. They wanted to live forever in Paradise, but they also want to have sex. The only way to resolve this is to get married. Even the Apostle Paul argued: "It is better to marry than to be inflamed with passion."[27] Even if you are still a teenager. Even if you have no clear way to support yourself and your new mate.

Ryan asked me to be a groomsman, and I was honored. Some of the older persons in the congregation grumbled that the wedding would just be a bunch of kids playing dress up, but I figured that was an easy judgment to make when your hormones are withered.

I loved the fact that school was almost finished. I could taste it. I felt liberated. Never again would I attend any sort of schooling (except the Theocratic Ministry School). My days of compulsory time-wasting were completed. A few of my schoolmates knew that I would not be back after the end of the trimester. Most assumed I was getting a jumpstart on college or that I was joining the military. Nope, I told them, I'm not doing either one. If they persisted, I made up a phony answer. I didn't feel like explaining that Armageddon was coming, so career planning was moot, and my job was decent enough so that I could continue in it for the final years that remained.

Commencing the very next Monday, I began going out in service all day, every day.

Within a month, however, my new lifestyle dragged my spirits. I confessed to Rhett that I was feeling down. He launched into a big discussion about depression, and how he had the blues sometimes. He said it was important to rely on Jehovah and throw our burden on Him in prayer.

Rhett was right, but no one could pray like Rhett. When I prayed, I felt like I was talking to myself. When Rhett prayed, it was like he was talking to his best friend. I nodded in agreement during Rhett's prayers, as if I was saying: "Yes Jehovah—what Rhett's saying, that's what I mean!" He said, in two sentences, what most elders couldn't say in two hours. Rhett was absolutely right: Certainly Jehovah took care of Rhett. Could Rhett actually feel the Holy Spirit? Could he detect God influencing his life? I wanted to ask. But I didn't.

Pioneers were supposed to be especially blessed due to their decision to give so much of themselves in God's work. In those rare moments when I allowed myself the indulgence of intellectual honesty, I had to admit that I did not feel blessed. I had to keep pioneering, at least until Pioneer School. Everyone, without exception, said they enjoyed Pioneer School. Rhett claimed that Pioneer School helped him to make the Truth his own;[28] it made the Truth sink into his heart.

So I prayed to like pioneering. I didn't want to dislike it, but in my discreet solitude, I hated it.

One blustery afternoon as autumn waned, Rhett and I talked with a householder who sternly told us: "Even if you guys have the right religion, I won't join because I am mad at God for the way he does things." Rhett reasoned that God has a purpose for everything, and that soon He will make everything right. But the man was mad that, despite his prayers, God let his wife die of cancer. Rhett explained that our deliverance from this wicked world was at hand, and God would resurrect his wife soon.

Though I said nothing to Rhett, I felt the man made a good point. God could have cured that woman's cancer. In doing so, the man's faith would have been strengthened, and he and his wife would have surely become Witnesses. But that's not what happened. She died, and her widowed husband became a man without faith. I was sullen for the rest of the week.

In the spring, there was another Circuit Assembly. A pioneer shared in an interview how during the previous winter, on a freezing, snowy morning with ice on the roads, she was driving to the Kingdom Hall. Her car hit an ice patch. Her car spun in a circle and plowed into a large snow bank on the side of the road. The faithful pioneer was unharmed, but she had no way to signal for help and, even if she did, there were no other cars on the road. She couldn't leave her car, because she was miles from town. So she prayed.

She did not relate the exact wording of her prayer, but whatever she said, it worked. As soon as she finished praying, her car slid down the embankment and back onto the road. She put her car in gear, and drove to the Hall. When she arrived, the other Witnesses helped her get her car to a mechanic and then went out in service.

The Watchtower taught that God does not perform miracles today.[29] Hadn't that sister described a miracle? Granted, it wasn't the parting of the Red Sea, but it fit the definition of a miracle. God deliberately and directly altered the laws of physics for His servant.

I wished I could pray like that sister. What had she said to catch God's ear? What had she done that I had not done? I prayed fervently many times that week, asking Jehovah to please let me know if I was doing what he wanted me to do.

Only months earlier, I had lambasted Johnny's father for not trusting in Jehovah; for not believing that Jehovah would provide for his family. Yet, here I was unable to see how Jehovah could have stepped in to help that sister. I reasoned that every time any Witness prays, they are asking for a miracle. If we pray before a meal, requesting that God bless the food, then what are we really asking? And what are we asking him for at night when we pray that he "help us have a good night's sleep"? If no change happens when we pray before meals or bedtime, then why bother? Was it just to give thanks? Then why not thank God for every minute detail of one's life? Why the tired routine of thanking Him for a meal, but not for a safe car ride, or a relaxing bowel movement?

I tried to feel His Holy Spirit. I tried to convince myself that He had answered my prayers by bringing a calm over me. In a dark corner of my mind, a corner I feared ever shining a light into, I had to concede that I felt nothing.

I wondered if Jehovah would answer a prayer in which I asked for proof of His existence. I was hesitant to pray in such a manner; primarily because it forced me to face the fact that I had been serving Him all these years without any proof. I pondered on scriptures and concluded that God would answer such prayers.[30] He wanted to answer them. So I prayed before going to sleep. And this is the prayer that I said:

> Dear Jehovah God my heavenly father
> I know that you do not perform big miracles anymore,
> but I know that you perform little miracles
> so I am humbly asking you to please give me some sign
> and I hope it is not wrong to ask for this.
> Please give me some sign, some indication,
> that I'm doing what is right so that I may know for sure,
> without a doubt, that you really do exist and that you really are God.

I promise that if I really know that you really exist then
I will be the best Witness I can possibly be.

Before closing my eyes to pray, I looked up at one of my bookshelves. There sat four porcelain bird figurines. I scrutinized their positions and for one blasphemous moment, I fancied that Jehovah could perform a tiny little miracle and ever so slightly move one of the birds.

The birds were the first things I looked at when I woke up the next morning. None of them had moved.

Maybe it was silly to want Jehovah to move a porcelain bird. I was embarrassed to think about it. If I asked any other Witnesses about this, I knew what their answer would be. They would say that Jehovah doesn't perform miracles today. Then I would remind them about the pioneer who got her car stuck. Then they would respond by admitting that Jehovah would, perhaps, perform a miracle if it was in line with His will.

The next night, I laid one of the birds on its side. Since Witnesses are told to be specific in their prayers, I spelled out my request very plainly. I asked Jehovah to make it so that when I woke up the next morning, the bird would be upright.

The bird was still on its side the next morning. I was discouraged. Jehovah didn't seem to care enough to give me the tiniest bit of evidence of his existence. Worse, I had possibly angered Him by daring to request a miracle in the first place.

A few weeks passed. One Thursday, before the meeting, two elders asked if we could talk for a minute. I walked with them into a back room, all the way wondering what I had done wrong. After closing the door, one elder said: "James, the body of elders feels that you would make a good ministerial servant. Would you like that?"

Stunned, I took a loud breath of relief. "Yeah, definitely." Being appointed ministerial servant was a grand privilege. After obtaining consensus from both the Circuit Overseer and the Watchtower Society headquarters, congregation elders were permitted to appoint men to this position. Ministerial servants were charged with assisting the elders; they were doled out sundry tasks not given to other men. Ministerial servants were able to give more talks, and they were put in charge of various duties, such as the literature and sound department.

"Well I have to ask, is there any reason why we shouldn't appoint you a ministerial servant?"

I felt it would be cocky to say no, so I asked if maybe I was too young. The position of ministerial servant, generally perceived as a precursor to becoming an elder, was normally reserved for men twenty years old and up. I couldn't determine, in that moment, if this privilege was being granted to me, a mere seventeen year old, because I was some sort of wunderkind, or due to my pedigree in the Witness aristocracy, but I assumed both were substantial contributors.

The elder chuckled. "Well, you *are* young; the Circuit Overseer said you're the youngest person he's ever recommended for appointment. But you're an outstanding brother, so we felt your age shouldn't hold you back."

Thus, at the next Service Meeting, the Presiding Overseer, a mousy individual named Eugene, was called up to the platform to read a special announcement. He briefly mentioned some of the qualifications for a ministerial servant, then said he was happy to announce that Apple Valley congregation now had two new ministerial servants: Rhett Sutter and James Zimmerman. The congregation clapped. My mother looked over at me in surprise, as I had not told her of my appointment. My Aunt Valerie, sitting in front of me, turned around and nodded. Her hand was on her chest as if the announcement had taken her breath away. I looked at Rhett, across the auditorium. He was already looking in my direction. He stiffened his lower lip and nodded as if to say *good job*.

After the meeting, some asked how old I was; it was unheard of that someone less than eighteen be appointed as a Servant. One elder, while congratulating me, told me that I was now the youngest ministerial servant in the entire Circuit. My Aunt Valerie was so overwhelmed with happiness that I thought she was going to cry. She hugged me. "How in the world did you manage that? I can't believe I'm your aunt."

A few weeks later, Rhett and I went out in service in a neighboring congregation with his girlfriend Moriah. She told us that she was taking a bus trip to the Watchtower Headquarters in the coming summer, and asked if we wanted to join her. I asked if she was going to go on the trip with anyone that I knew, hoping with all my heart that she'd say Lizzie. Lizzie Browne attended the same congregation as Moriah, and I had an intense crush on her. Instead, she said Pauline, a sister I hardly knew. Still, I liked the prospect of a vacation, and I figured I should visit the Watchtower Headquarters, especially since I planned on working there in the near future.

I looked over at Rhett: "Rhett, we have *got* to go on this trip! Wouldn't it be great?"

Rhett shrugged his shoulders. "The thing is, I just don't have the money. I lost that one cleaning job, remember, and I'm not sure what I'm gonna do for cash."

I told Rhett Jehovah would provide. He bobbed his head back and forth, unsure what to say. I decided not to push the issue, but I made plans to join Moriah on the bus trip.

I didn't need to ask Rhett again. Not only was unemployment taking a toll on his finances, he was diagnosed with a hernia. Rhett was the unhealthiest friend I had; he slept in a musty basement; his four food groups were candy, chocolate, fast food, and cheap Chinese restaurants. He was gaining about a pound every month and didn't seem to notice his shirts were crying for mercy at each button.

Johnny, by contrast, said yes before I could even provide him with all the details. Despite his job at a fast food establishment, Johnny never saved any of his money. But due to his impending graduation party, he knew his financial status would improve, if only for that week.

I also asked Jeremy. Like Johnny, he would be done with school just a week before the trip. Like Johnny, he'd be having a graduation party, wherein he would easily garner enough cash to pay for his seat on the bus. When I chaperoned Rhett and Moriah, Moriah and I excitedly talked about our upcoming trip to Bethel. She promised "non-stop fun." I worried that Rhett felt left out. But in early June, about a week before the bus trip, Jeremy called. Something was wrong. He did not sound as if he was calling merely to socialize. He informed me that Moriah had decided not to be a Witness anymore.

I spent the rest of the evening alone in my room. I sat at my desk and stared at nothing. *How could Moriah, only the most compassionate girl I had ever known, decide that she just didn't love Jehovah anymore? And what of Rhett? Did he know his girlfriend had left the Truth? What kind of girl could date such a spiritual, talented, kindhearted man for a year only to dump him without warning?* I felt simultaneously sad for Rhett and mad at Moriah. I was thoroughly perplexed. Certainly, I had known people to leave the religion before. Typically, they were the bimbos who just wanted to sleep around, or guys who were just into girls and cars and drugs. *But Moriah?* Her leaving the religion was an anomaly, an aberration that I could not explain. I cried.

A few days passed, and I asked Rhett if he would still be willing to go out in service with Inver Grove congregation with me. For over a year, Rhett had been visiting Inver Grove to be with his girlfriend, and I followed along like a sidekick with ulterior motives of being in Lizzie's presence. There was nothing stopping me from visiting Inver Grove without Rhett, of course, but having him with me added an air of legitimacy.

Rhett answered: "Yeah, why wouldn't I?"

"Well, I didn't think you'd want to go anymore, you know, because Moriah's family and people who knew her well are all there, and I thought it might be kind of weird for you."

"Moriah's the one who left Jehovah," he said. "I still love all of our friends in Inver Grove, that hasn't changed." He sat forward and ran his hands through his thinning black hair. "My relationship with Moriah was just something of this earth, you know, man? Just an earthly thing, and nothing more. It's not what really matters in the whole scheme."

On the first evening, the buses stopped in Mackinaw City, Michigan. Johnny, Jeremy, and I visited the local state park. Later, we met up with Pauline. Pauline had spent the past week hurriedly looking for a substitute for Moriah. She ultimately found a friend of a friend in a neighboring congregation, a girl named Jenni who none of us—Pauline included—had known prior to the trip.

We joked and laughed together during dinner. We were filled with the excitement of a vacation that had only just begun. Johnny and Jeremy turned out to be the perfect pair to have with me. Jeremy, of superior intellect, picked on Johnny regarding anything intellectual while Johnny, of superior heterosexuality, picked on Jeremy for his mannerisms. It all seemed to be in good humor, though, and I was glad to have assembled such an ideal group of friends. Jenni sat across from me and we both noticed the same old man acting strange at a table across the room. We laughed. She was shy, which I initially attributed to the fact that she knew no one else on the bus. She was pretty: slightly taller than Moriah, a fairer, clearer complexion, and brownish hair that brushed her shoulders. But not even a God-fearing Witness boy looks at only a woman's head.

A rule among Witnesses is that women must wear skirts or dresses to all the meetings and while out in service. All the sisters I knew were always in dresses. It was almost strange to see Witnesses in casual clothes and, with the exception of my closest family and friends, I rarely saw them in such attire. But there was one problem with dresses and skirts. It was quite impossible to precisely estimate the size and shape of the butt.

As the five of us left the restaurant, I lingered back at the table to polish off my iced tea. I then hurried to catch up, and it was as I approached that I first got a good look at Jenni. In jeans. I nearly fumbled over my feet as I allowed my eyes to drink in the way the denim hugged her body; curving in and out to show the shape of her female form.

Later that night, Johnny and Jeremy and I played cards in the hotel lobby. Jeremy paused while shuffling. "Well I thought Jenni was a very nice young lady."

Johnny and I nodded. Then Jeremy continued: "I mean, I was kind of sad that Moriah wasn't gonna be on the trip, but after tonight I realized that Jenni seems pretty cool in her own way."

I nodded again. "And she does have a sweet ass."

Johnny's face flushed with embarrassment and he scanned the lobby to make sure none of the hundred other Witnesses in the building overheard my crass language.

Jeremy held up his hand, soliciting a high-five, and said: "All right, James!"

On the last day, I sat next to Jenni. In the final hours of the drive, she drew me a picture, and we exchanged phone numbers and addresses. When the bus pulled back in town, Jenni's parents and two sisters were waiting. While Jenni was talking with her parents, I ran over and said goodbye and reminded her to call me. I promised to write a letter within the week. I asked if the people with her were her family, and she said yes. I then went down the line, shaking hands with her dad, her mom, her sixteen-year-old sister Sarah, and her little sister Roberta. "Thanks for letting Jenni come on the bus trip. I had a great time getting to know her; she's a marvelous young woman." I spoke with the New York bravado that my family embodied so well. It was a little overwhelming for Jenni's quiet family and they couldn't do much in return besides laugh at me.

At the next yearly District Convention, an elder was assigned the task of interviewing our family, which had been exemplary in the Truth for many years. We all walked on stage: Papa and Nana, my dad, mom, me and my sister; then my dad's brother Peter and his wife, then Aunt Janet, then my dad's youngest brother Cal and his wife. The elder extended his hand in a grand gesture. He proceeded to tell the audience of five thousand that the Zimmerman family had served Jehovah a combined total of 213 years. To thunderous applause, he regaled everyone with our credentials: My grandfather was an elder, as was my dad and his brother Peter. My dad's older brother, who lived in Florida, was also an elder. My dad's brother Cal and I were both ministerial servants, as was my Floridian cousin. And three of us standing on stage—Uncle Cal, his wife, and I—were all regular pioneers.

Again, there was applause.

This was the Zimmerman family: A striking example of three generations of Jehovah's Witnesses. Speaking of her children, Nana said, "From infancy, we tried to make the Truth the center of their lives, because it was the focal point of our lives." She added: "I used to tell them I couldn't see everything they did, but Jehovah could see them no matter where they were." When asked if she had any fond memories of watching her children continue on as Witnesses, she said: "An especially precious memory that I have relates to our teaching our children that they should never turn down an assignment," and then she told all in attendance how I cried during my first talk.

Then my dad took the microphone. "We've tried to help our children appreciate that the Truth is not just a part of their life, but their whole life. We've always helped our children to appreciate that they should never let a day go by without doing something for Jehovah."

When my uncle handed me the microphone, I related how thankful I was to have such a spiritual family and what a grand privilege it was to serve Jehovah alongside my parents, aunts, uncles, and grandparents. I looked out past the bright lights and raised my head to see people high in the bleachers. The people who liked to sleep and be inattentive sat up in the top row. I was glad not to be among them. It felt good to hold my head up.

Perhaps this was the answer to my prayer. At scarcely eighteen years old, I was a ministerial servant with over a year of pioneering behind me. This was my ninth interview at an assembly, and I would have another one the very next day. I was scheduled to attend Pioneer School next month. If all of that wasn't blessing enough, I had an outstanding family: shining examples of how a Witness family should be; spiritual pillars in the congregation. And I was one of them.

All we had to do was endure to the End.

MY INAMORATA

B ut my family, as one cohesive unit, did not endure.

The fact that my dad didn't want to be married to my mom anymore was not shocking news, but the fact that he didn't come home from work one evening was unexpected. My mom, hysterical with emotion, claimed he had given no indication that morning that anything was different. He just didn't come home. My grandpa delivered the news. As soon as he showed up at our door, I knew something was wrong. My dad was already an hour late, and my mom had not heard from him all day. My grandpa wouldn't drive forty-five minutes out of his way on a meeting night just to be social.

As it turned out, one of my dad's co-workers called my grandpa to explain that my dad had had a nervous breakdown at work. He was so distraught he couldn't even get his welding gloves off without help. Another co-worker drove him to a doctor's office, and no one was sure where he went from there.

My mom was a pile of tears. She was the same woman who panicked if I was ten minutes late getting home from service, so this development was beyond her ability to cope. My sister fell on the couch and cried.

Through her sniffling, my mom reminded me that my dad was assigned to give a talk at the meeting that night. So I called Carl Brewer, the Ministry School Overseer. Within a half hour, he, too, showed up at our door to console us. My mom was worried that he was missing his duty of conducting the meeting that night, but Carl reassured her that he had handed the duty off to another elder.

I was worried about my dad. No one was sure where he was, and I didn't trust his co-workers. They were worldly people, and I knew there were some among them who harassed my dad for being a Witness. I was worried they had taken him away somewhere, and we'd never hear from him again.

After my grandfather and Carl left, the three of us sat trying to make sense of the situation. My mom asked if I could say a prayer aloud for us, so I did. I didn't really know what to say; what I should ask for or what I should be thankful for. I never liked praying aloud. A family prayer was my dad's responsibility, and I was mad at him for thrusting it upon me without warning.

My dad's brother Cal called two days later telling us something about a nervous breakdown and that my dad was okay and would be staying at his place for a little while. I was relieved, but only for about a quarter of a second, because then my relief turned to anger. I was mad at my dad. Questions arose, and I was unable to satisfactorily answer them. *Why would he just leave without even letting us know? Was he afraid we wouldn't understand? Why would he do this on a meeting night? Didn't he know that he had a talk? His actions caused three of us—my mom, sister and me—to miss the meeting that night; didn't he know that would happen? What about his marriage vows? Didn't he know that "Jehovah hates a divorcing"?*[31] *How could he expect to remain in God's favor if he abandoned his family?*

All week, my mom and I talked extensively about the near future. She was worried that my dad would not continue to provide for us. She was extreme in thinking this; suggesting that she may have to begin working more hours and I, having recently quit my job at the library, may have to get a steady job to help with our expenses.

Pioneer School was imminent, and the thought of not being in attendance due to the actions of my very own father was too much to bear. I didn't want to quit pioneering and work in some futile worldly dead-end job, underpaid and overtaxed and unable to serve Jehovah full-time. The thought made me sick.

A week later, my dad stopped over to give my mom some paperwork regarding their health insurance. They stood in the entryway diverting their glances and speaking in clipped sentences. I could hardly breathe from the tension, so I went downstairs into my room and closed the door. After he left, my mom spent the night crying. I hated living at home. I thought of killing myself, but I had no idea how to go about doing the deed. Besides, Pioneer School was just a week away, and I didn't want to miss it.

Pioneer School lasts ten days. The students consist of Witnesses in the Circuit who had been pioneering since at least September first of the previous year. The Circuit Overseer is the primary instructor. He passed out our textbook, *Shining as Illuminators in the World*, on the first day of class. The highlight was lunch, where students had the opportunity to tell their experience, generally a brief story telling how they had come into the Truth, or, more commonly, the obstacles they needed to overcome in order to pioneer. Giving one's experience was not compulsory, but most did it. In an effort to apply the things we were learning, there were also four mornings set aside for us to go out in service.

I had looked forward to Pioneer School since Rhett attended it the year before, returning with glowing reviews. He had been so moved by the School, that he threw away all of his Frank Zappa albums.

I was disappointed that first day, flipping through my very own copy of *Shining*. There wasn't much to the book—it was mostly margins; nothing about Frank Zappa. The pages consisted of simple sentences like this priceless counsel:

> Whom can you assist in the field service?
> Why may the elders take the initiative in arranging for this type of assistance?
> Why may it be necessary at times for you to take the initiative in offering assistance?
> Why might such assistance be mutually encouraging?
> What have you found to be helpful to those with whom you share in the field ministry?[32]

That's it. During class, we expounded upon these questions, but the Circuit Overseer, far from being a teacher, was merely a conductor. He asked the questions, and then called on pioneers in the audience to offer Watchtower-guided thoughts on the matter. I was frequently bored.

During the second week, our class went out in service three times. Sister Becard, a shapely woman of nineteen who would have attracted my gaze more often if it wasn't for the blinding glare of her engagement ring, asked everyone in the car group if we felt it was appropriate to count the time while we were out in service for Pioneer School.

Sister Willet, the eldest Witness in the vehicle, pursed her lips. "I don't think so. They are already giving us fifty hours towards our goal, so I think it would be cheating to count this time extra."

"They *only* credit us with fify hours, and we're in class for eighty hours," I chimed in. "I think we're more than justified if we want to count this time."

Sister Becard smiled. "I'm sticking with you James, I like the way you think."

Sister Willet objected: "Well, you two do what you want, just don't tell me about it."

On day eight, we again went out in service. The Circuit Overseer was in my car group, and he asked if any of us had any return visits. The other two pioneers began flipping through their books and talking over each other like they were trading on the stock market floor. I offered to go back to one elderly gentleman I spoke with a week ago. He had been the only person home that day: a bearded, well-mannered geriatric with Buddhist leanings. Being completely at a loss as to how to bring a Buddhist into the Truth, I told the Circuit Overseer that I would appreciate his expertise.

We knocked on the man's door. He graciously invited us in. "Thanks for letting us come in, Victor. I wanted to come back today and see what your thoughts were on the brochure I left you last week."

Shuffling into his den, and groaning as he sat, he said, "Oh, it was fine. I liked it." He coughed. "A good read. Real good read." He smacked his dentures.

I didn't know what to say. Victor wasn't forthcoming. He was neither opposed to the message, nor overly interested. Besides, he was Buddhist. I didn't know what sort of common ground—if any—we shared. If I had been alone, or with a peer, I would have just left him with more literature, but I was in the presence of the Circuit Overseer. Besides, I had just completed seven days at Pioneer School where we were repeatedly instructed to start Bible studies. I glanced at the Circuit Overseer, and he took over the conversation.

For the next half hour, I sat on the couch and didn't say a word. The two of them went back and forth; not arguing, just discussing religion in general. I was roundly impressed with their knowledge. Victor had researched every major religion and concluded that the teachings of Buddha were his cup of Darjeeling. The Circuit Overseer, meanwhile, had examined several branches of Protestantism in his youth, before he was contacted by the Witnesses. I kept trying to find something to say, some way to contribute, to no avail.

Getting back into the car, I asked the Circuit Overseer if he felt I should call back on Victor. The Overseer rubbed his chin. "I'll leave that up to you, James, but I don't think you'll get anywhere with him. He's very well grounded. He's made up his mind."

So that was it. Twenty years as a Witness, a week and a half in Pioneer School, and the Circuit Overseer by my side . . . and there was no way to bring a knowledgeable, sincere, humble man into the Truth? Surely someone who had researched all the world's religions should have discovered Jehovah's Witnesses as the one true religion. I wished intently that the Circuit Overseer would have given me something tangible that I could take back and share with Victor so that he would accept the Truth before it was too late.

Two days later, Pioneer School was over.

Most Witnesses never have the circumstances to pioneer, and many who do sign up don't survive a full year. I was in the minority, and I'd succeeded. This pleased me, yet I had to admit that it hadn't fulfilled my hopes. I still was uncomfortable showing personal interest in the householders, and none of the lessons caused me to make radical adjustments, like throwing out Frank Zappa recordings. Mostly, I had wished that some proof of belief, some "evident demonstration of realities" had been forthcoming.[33] I wished the School would have usurped my doubts and caused the Truth to sink into my mind.

I sat with my mom that evening and talked about Pioneer School. She was distant, distracted by the uncertainty of her marriage. I looked out the window at the sun, setting earlier and earlier each day. "Man, this time of year used to be so depressing to me. The summer is almost over and all those poor kids have to go back to school next week."

"Be glad you're a Witness, then," she said. "If we weren't Witnesses, your dad and I would have made you go to college. You'd be starting school this fall."

Arriving home from service one day that autumn, my mom told me that she was going to meet with my dad yet again. These meetings only served to get in the way of the day-to-day routine that we were trying to rebuild. I wished my parents would either reunite and act like a married couple, or divorce. Their teeter-tottering relationship was taxing all four of us, and I was sick of it. Leaving home for the Watchtower Headquarters couldn't come fast enough.

My mom came home with the news that my dad was going to move home on Saturday. It was tough to believe that all the wounds of the last three months had been sufficiently healed, but Diane and I simply accepted it.

Our family had been invited to a wedding reception that Saturday. I arrived late, but when I walked into the reception, I spotted my mom sitting at a table right next to my dad. They looked like newlyweds: my dad had his arm around my mom, and their hands were folded together, gently resting on the table.

"Look who's home!" my mom said with atypical glee.

"So that's it?" I asked. "You guys are back together now?"

My dad concurred that they were a couple once more.

Somehow, that didn't seem to fit within the parameters of possibility, but I said I was glad. Then I got up and looked for my friends.

Rhett slept at my house often, as his own bedroom was located in a musty basement that caused trouble for his respiratory system. This was usually a spur-of-the-moment decision. He never came over to my house prepared with a change of clothes and toothbrush in tow. He would just show up in his suit, and he slept in his suit. He never loosened his tie or bothered to unbutton his suit coat. I would wake up the next morning early enough to shower, have breakfast, and brush my teeth. Exactly five minutes before it was time to leave for service, I'd wake up Rhett.

Rhett had a dilapidated compact car in such horrid shape that the road was visible through the floor in the back seat. During those endless hours in the car, he was always doing something with his hands. If he wasn't playing air drums (the result of his constantly composing music in his head) or scratching a rash that developed along his wrists and didn't abate for years, or flipping through his notebook of return visits, he was putting clear polish on his hacked nails, his way of battling against nail biting. It was a losing battle.

Despite his flaws, I wanted to be like Rhett. For months I pondered the question of Rhett: how was he able to get along with everyone in our congregation? How was it that nothing dampened his spirit? How did he maintain a good attitude about everything? He was honest without being rude, sincere without being cloy, humorous without being sarcastic, and confident without being arrogant.

My attempts at emulating his attitude failed horrendously.

In the teeth of winter, as we drove to the local university to pass out magazines to pedestrians, I argued with Rhett about our hourly requirement. Rhett had failed to meet the requirement by a mere five hours, and I lashed out at him for not trying harder to get in those final few hours. He meekly noted that it was more important that his service be meaningful, but when we arrived on campus, Rhett could sense I was still seething. He let me out at one end of a long footbridge, then drove around and stood at the other end. For nearly an hour, I stood shivering and angry, and shaking my head in dismay at the college students—my peers—who were wasting their time shuffling from one class to another. In a flash, a bicyclist sped toward me, and held out his hand to grab the Watchtower. He snatching the magazine, and then kept pedaling towards his next class. I reached into my bag for another *Watchtower* and buried my face in my scarf.

At last, Rhett covered the quarter mile between us. His ears were bright red, and there was frost on his thinning black hair. "Let's go get something to drink, buddy." When I hesitated, he smirked. "You can keep your time going, if you want."

A few weeks later, I realized something. In fact, I had always known it—but on this particular day, it rose from my subconscious to my conscious.

Trudging up a snow-filled driveway, we approached a door, and Rhett knocked. A young man answered the door. Rhett began by asking the man about the violence and crime we see in our world. The young man began smiling at us, and he didn't stop. His smile was insincere. It was a smirk. When Rhett asked if he would like to live in a world where violence was a thing of the past, he answered: "Why yes, yes I would. Please, tell me more." All the while he was nodding his head and grinning widely. He smiled at Rhett, and Rhett smiled back. Looking over Rhett's shoulder, he smiled at me, and I stared an icy stare back at him.

Rhett asked if he was a Bible reader and he answered: "Oh, yes, absolutely. The Bible's a great book. I wouldn't go without it, no sir." Rhett set his bag down on the chilly stoop and pulled out his Bible. Rhett offered the man a small tract that talked about the importance of Bible reading. The man agreed to take it, saying: "Why, yes, I will put it in my pocket right here and I will read it just as soon as I have the time."

On the way back to the car, Rhett looked up at the sky and inhaled deeply. "It's so refreshing to meet a friendly person at the door."

I yelled at him through my chattering teeth: "Rhett! Are you crazy! That guy was mocking us the whole time!"

"Really? How do you know?"

"What do you mean 'how do I know?' He had a smirk on his face a mile wide the whole time and he kept looking at me like what we were saying was just a big joke."

"Wow, I guess I didn't notice that. That's the good thing about having two people at the door; one can be observant while the other gives the presentation."

Rhett pulled out his decade-at-a-glance and wrote down the man's name and address. I couldn't believe it.

"Rhett! Are you seriously planning on going back to that guy?"

"We're supposed to call back on anyone who takes any literature."

I closed my eyes and shook my head. "Well, I ain't going back with you."

Rhett had not noticed the man's mocking behavior. Rhett had not noticed his condescending demeanor, his sarcastic tone. No wonder Rhett was always so kind to other people—he didn't have to constantly strive to ignore the bad side of people because he didn't even notice their bad side. His inability to see the dark side of human nature had made him a better person.

I would never be like Rhett.

Soon after, I received an invitation to a wedding reception. The invitation was addressed in a way I had never seen before: "James and guest." *James and guest? Who am I supposed to bring?* I didn't understand. I showed the invitation to my mom, and she explained that it is customary to allow unmarried adults to bring a guest with them to weddings and receptions so they don't have to show up alone.

I liked the idea of getting to pick from among friends and bring them along with me to a fancy party. The problem was everyone was already invited. My sister was already invited. Johnny was invited. Rhett was invited. Jeremy was invited, and he planned to bring his friend Gabriel Tomanek.

Gabe was the antithesis to Jeremy: brooding and introverted. While Jeremy loved 80s pop music, Gabe was lost in a world of Pink Floyd and Pearl Jam. I couldn't figure out what they had in common, besides a long history together. Countering Jeremy's fashion, Gabe wore loose-fitting, ragged jeans, threadbare t-shirts and the same forest green boots whether he was hanging out with friends or sitting at a meeting. His orange hair was curled in front of his face, and covered the tops of his ears. He was, like Johnny, somewhat overweight, and preferred to hide his belly behind his guitar.

For a few days, I considered attending the reception solo. But then I decided upon Jenni, who accepted.

We arrived at the reception hall at the same time as my parents. Jenni and I went to the coatroom to hang up our coats. My dad was there and gave Jenni a hug, since it was the first time he had seen her since the bus trip. I turned to hang up my coat, and when I turned back, I watched Jenni take her coat off. She wore a red dress that buttoned down the front. The neck line came down in a V-shape in the center of her chest. The opening was wide enough to just barely allow the up-curve of her breasts to be exposed on both sides of the V. The dress cinched slightly at her waist and ended midway down her thigh, leaving plenty of nylon-laden leg exposed for me to steal quick glances.

The moment my gaze alighted upon Jenni's dress, my anxiety heightened. I feared my dad, or one of the elders present, would see Jenni and castigate me for being in the company of an immodest girl.

I compelled myself to stop fretting long enough to enjoy the evening. During dinner, Jenni got reacquainted with Johnny and Jeremy. Gabe, forcing himself to not be so shy for once, tried out his social chops. Near midnight, I drove Jenni home and watched as she got out of the car and went up the steps to her house. The bottom of her coat swung back and forth in rhythm as she walked. It gave me a chance to check out her legs.

"You're such a good guy James," Rhett said, bringing me back to reality.

"Oh yeah? Why's that?"

"'Cause, man, you made sure she got in to her house nice and safe. Like a true gentleman."

Gabe continued spending time with me. He was making a concerted effort to improve his life in every way imaginable. He desired to be a rising star in the congregation. He didn't qualify as outgoing, but he was noticeably more comfortable in social situations. He had this ability to target the best qualities in each of his friends and then emulate the quality within himself. Socially, and with public speaking ability, Gabe looked to me. "How do I get on the assembly like you, James?" he asked in all earnestness one afternoon while we were out in service together. Laughing, I explained he needed to be born into my family, but Gabe shrugged aside the suggestion of nepotism in the Watchtower's back rooms and repeated his question.

"Just keep doing what you're doing, I guess." Gabe scowled at my limp answer, and so I added: "Don't sit up in the back bleachers at the assemblies. Make yourself more visible and extroverted. Let the elders see you're trying to be well-rounded."

Really, the only issue keeping Gabe from becoming the most well-rounded Witness possible was his brooding manner. He endured episodes of depression, and on occasion he broke down and cried at his inability to get life to proceed smoothly. His music of choice was alternative and grunge rock, and simply being in his car long enough to hear Pearl Jam belt out of the speakers was enough to make me suicidal, too. Perhaps, though, Gabe had good reason for feeling down. His mother had cancer. One week, Gabe called me, exuberant with the news that the disease was in remission. The next week, he asked me to tag along as he brought his mother in for treatment. His mom alternated between bouts of health and sickness, but the trend was undeniably terminal.

Rhett and I, meanwhile, met early each weekday morning and drove to the local laundromats to leave *Watchtowers*. It was easy time: most of the morning was taken up simply by driving from one laundromat to another. One cold spring morning, I sat in my car waiting for Rhett to arrive. He showed up fifteen minutes late. He fell into my car. He looked disheveled, even by his own standards. He propped his bag up on his lap and began thumping out a song with his hands. He apologized for being late.

I was about to drive to a laundromat, but I noticed Rhett's thoughts were distant. "Are you okay, Rhett?" I asked.

"Well, I got a lot on my mind."

I hated playing psychiatrist. "What's the matter?"

"Just more trouble at home," he said, implying his parents' recent separation. "Oh man, my dad was real bummed this morning." Rhett had let his dad cry on his shoulder, literally, helping to give him the strength he needed to start the day. Rhett again apologized for being late, "I rushed here so fast I even skipped breakfast."

"Well, how about we go have breakfast, together, at the Country Diner?"

"No, no, that's okay. Just go through a drive-through."

"Rhett," I said, patronizing. "What would Scott say if he heard you talk like that?"

He laughed. "He'd say I should treat my body like a temple."

"Exactly! So let's bring your temple to a place where you can get something besides grease and lard."

Rhett laughed again. He told me he had no money. "I sold some of my CDs yesterday for gas money, but I only have a dollar left." Begrudgingly, I told him I would pay. The restaurant smelled like bacon and eggs. Our waitress donned a starched dress under her apron. She wore white running shoes and nylons. In between his plate of fruit and pancakes, Rhett continued talking.

We left the restaurant just in time to make the meeting for service. When the meeting was over, a sister asked if we had a good time going laundromat-to-laundromat. I bemoaned the fact that we didn't go visiting laundromats, and now I was two hours behind on my schedule for the day.

"Oh James," Rhett pinched my cheek like I was a little kid. Then he put his arm around me, "He's just being modest. I was feeling down and this guy here bought me breakfast."

Scott, sitting with his chin tucked into his coat and his gangly legs stretched out under the seat in front of him, turned to look at us. "Get out of town," he said. "James paid for you?"

"Yes he did," Rhett answered. "And I love him for it."

Scott shook his head in amazement. "I didn't think it was possible to squeeze a quarter out of that wallet."

Spring came, and I took advantage of the warmer days to get ahead on my hourly requirement. Johnny was flagging on his hours, but I encouraged him to keep at it, reminding him that he made a commitment to Jehovah.

Then one evening, he called to tell me he was accepted to Bethel.

"Wow, congrats," I told him. "When are you leaving?"

"June tenth—so I got a month and a half here to get everything squared away."

"Oh, man, I'm gonna miss you." Johnny annoyed me, the way he was always morphing our lives into an ongoing competition, and the way he called every day wanting to know what I was doing. But, truthfully, I liked him. He often said I was his best friend, and he tried extracting the same comment from me. I would weasel out of it by telling him that I had no one *best friend*, but rather a few *good friends*. That always irritated him.

"Hey, you'll be joining me soon enough," Johnny said. "I'll save a spot for you, maybe we can be roommates."

"Yeah, maybe."

On June tenth, Johnny boarded an airplane for New York. I stood in the terminal and watched as his plane ascended. I was proud of my friend. At his going-away party, an elder from Johnny's congregation extolled him for being the only one in his family that "amounted to anything," since he was the only one of his siblings to stay in the Truth upon reaching adulthood. Though Johnny's parents balked at the insinuation, I was in complete agreement. Still, as I watched the plane vanish, I wondered how long Johnny would last at Bethel. Especially if I wasn't with him.

I languished in boredom without Johnny. I had not expected to miss him. I spent the next few weeks in a fog. I stayed home from service a couple of days. The days I went out in service, I was poor company. I had been a dutiful pioneer, but otherwise, the past year had been a waste. I just drifted along through life. I wasn't making my life better and I wasn't accomplishing anything.

At the convention that summer—as at every convention—a speaker used the phrase: "Jehovah's people are the happiest people on Earth." But I had trouble reconciling that statement with the facts I knew. Gabe certainly was not one of the happiest people on Earth. His mom was dying, and he spent every day sitting by her side at the hospital or rocking back and forth to grunge music, trying to wriggle free from his depression. Rhett was no better. His carefree nature of a year ago had been replaced with an uncertainty regarding his family and a looming worry of his own mental state. My parents, meanwhile, had fallen out of love years ago, and their pieced-together marriage was simply an exercise in the limits of tolerance. And though I was trying to do all I could in Jehovah's service, I had to admit that I felt no holy spirit. I would not qualify myself as among "the happiest people on Earth."

Later, when Nana asked if I was happy pioneering, I told her I wasn't. She groped for encouragement. "Are you sure it's what you want to be doing, then?"

"Yeah," I said, defensively.

"Why is that?"

"Well, how could I not do it? We're supposed to do all we can do to serve Jehovah, and if I don't do all I can, then I'm not really pleasing Him, am I?"

My aunt brought up her hand defensively. "But I am not pioneering. Do you think Jehovah isn't pleased with me?"

"I can't answer for you," I told her. "If you could be pioneering, but aren't, then no, I don't think Jehovah is pleased with you. But we all have different circumstances and abilities. I have the circumstances and ability to pioneer, so I *have* to do it."

Nana reminded me that we have to *want* to do it.

"I *do* want to do it."

"Then you should be enjoying it." She added that if our service is not done with joy, then we are not pleasing Jehovah.

I threw up my hands. "I'm not enjoying it. I don't know why. I pray to Jehovah that he make me enjoy it."

My aunt then noted that we need to let Jehovah know we are willing and ready to do whatever he asks of us.

I *was* willing. I *was* ready. The fact that I didn't like pioneering was a distant secondary concern. My primary motivation for pioneering was that I knew I had to do what God asked of me. Indeed, I told them that I felt my service to God was acceptable to Him because I do it even though it does not come easy to me and even though I do not like doing it.

Aunt Janet patted me on the knee: "Well, just pray about. And, you know, the more you do it, the more you'll like it."

By August, I only needed thirty more hours to make the thousand-hour goal. Jeremy had helped me get a job at the eyeglass store where he worked, and I spent most of my time working there, trying to rebuild my floundering savings account. After three weeks of work, I received my first paycheck.

I announced my new wealthy status to Rhett and Scott the next day while out in service. We celebrated by heading into the city to eat at Rhett's favorite restaurant. I picked up the tab.

But my days of hanging onto Rhett and Scott's coattails were coming to a close, not because of anything I was planning on doing; rather, it was they who were changing their lives. Rhett couldn't escape his depressed funk. He was continually saddened by his parents' divorce. His chances of achieving the thousand-hour goal were looking dim. He was incessantly tired, although I couldn't quite determine if it was due to poor health or eating habits. He was always battling some virus. To that end, he was going to try a new path. There was a small congregation an hour southeast of the cities, and they needed more ministerial servants. After consorting with the Circuit Overseer, Rhett made it his goal to move to a cheap apartment in that congregation's territory as soon as his finances were in order. He prayed about it, and felt Jehovah's hand guiding him into this new avenue of service.

A new life, where Rhett could breathe country air would, he believed, do him much good.

Scott, meanwhile, was going to move farther than Rhett. Over a year since turning in his application, he was finally accepted to Bethel. He would ship out before summer's end.

Listening to them talk about their life-changing plans, I felt like such a child. I had no plans to move out, and I secretly wished I would not be accepted to Bethel. I joked to Rhett and Scott that they would forget about me now that they were going to see the world. Rhett put his arm around me. "Oh, you! We could never forget about our buddy! We wouldn't be where we are today without Assembly Boy!"

Scott agreed, "My mom and dad used to talk about that fine young example up on stage at all the assemblies. I hated you for years before I finally got a chance to meet you."

That night, I telephoned Jenni and complained about my lot in life. I told her how I missed Johnny, and that soon I would also be losing Scott and Rhett. She reminded me that I still had a large group of friends. I slept better that night.

Such calls, in fact, turned out to be a common occurrence. So much so, that I realized Jenni was the perfect girl for me—she had been there all along as my friend, and that, ultimately, is the definition of a good relationship. A week later, Gabe and I spent the day with Jenni and her sister Sarah. We ended up at a scenic overlook, high on a ridge over the confluence of two rivers, with the airport in the distance and the downtown skylines tracing a path along the horizon. I told them it was such a beautiful evening that I felt like going for a walk. Gabe, as planned, said he wanted to stay in the car. Sarah predictably stayed in the car to be with Gabe, giving the two of them time to toy with their marginally platonic relationship. Jenni and I went for a walk, then sat on a brick ledge and watched the sun set.

As I had done too often, I talked too much. Eventually, I came around to asking her to be my girlfriend.

"Why do you want to date me?" she asked, surprised.

In the immediacy of the moment, I was taken aback by her inquiry. "I like you," I said. "You're a sincere, good person. That's the kind of girl I want to marry. The things that attracted me to other girls weren't the important things. I was just attracted to the idea of those girls. You're a way better girl. You're honest. You're a good person." To conclude my case, I added: "And you're pretty."

Her answer was so meek, and so calm—"Okay"—but it held the prospect of influencing our lives immensely. By agreeing to date each other, we were, by Watchtower standards, beginning down a path towards marriage.[34] Jenni was, in effect, saying that one day she would be willing to move away from her parents and live with me for the rest of her life. For eternity. She was saying that she would become my best friend now and for millions and billions and trillions of years. Forever.

To ensure that Jenni understood the gravity of our decision, I said: "I want you to know that I only want to date someone with a view to marriage—not just for the fun of it like some people do."

"Me, too," she agreed.

I told Jenni I wanted to keep our dating a secret for the time being, at least until we had time to process our newly revealed feelings for each other. Jenni agreed.

I asked Jenni if she wanted to wear my ring for the rest of the evening.

"Don't you think Sarah will see it?" she asked. "'Cause Sarah's got a big mouth and she'll tell everyone."

"She's too concerned with Gabe to notice us. Just keep it hidden, if you can."

Jenni put my ring on her finger.

With much apprehension, I asked: "Do you want to hold my hand?"

I offered my right hand and we fumbled our fingers for an awkward few seconds, laughing at our own innocence. We were nineteen years old, yet neither of us knew how to hold hands.

Adjusting her seat on the wall, Jenni set our hands on her lap. She was wearing shorts, and the side of my hand landed on her soft, feminine leg.

I felt nervous. I felt excited. I felt guilty.

QUESTIONS YOUNG PEOPLE ASK

> What justification could there be for two people of the opposite sex to begin spending a lot of time together other than to investigate the possibility of marrying each other? In the long run, dating for any other reason is likely to result in anything but "fun."
>
> — *Questions Young People Ask – Answers that Work!*, p. 226

Dating Jenni created a whole new set of worries for me. Would we, in fact, get married one day? What about getting engaged—how did dating someone "with a view to marriage" differ from being engaged? What would my family think when they found out I was dating? What about chaperones? Would I have to ensure that there was someone with us at all times? And what if Jenni and I "went too far"?[35] What exactly was "going too far"?

I investigated the matter to the fullest extent, reading everything the Society published regarding courtship. The important thing, it seemed, was to make sure I kept Jehovah's service in the forefront, putting His interests first in my life. Still, I felt more comfortable keeping our budding relationship out of the public eye for a time.

When not with Jenni, I spent most of my time with Gabe. He had a profound desire to not be alone. His mom was not faring well. We often stayed up late talking, mostly about his inability to come to terms with his mom's looming death. He called late one night, hours after I had gone to bed. He was on the verge of tears. I asked him, as nicely as I could, if he could maybe go talk to his dad or his sister. But they weren't Witnesses and, therefore, were miles away in spirit despite their close physical proximity.

He kept asking: "Why does she have to die, James? Why does she have to die?" I could hear his tears threatening to break. I tried to comfort him by speaking of the Paradise. Gabe sobbed that the Paradise was a nice future, but he was heartbroken that his mom had to suffer now, lying in the hospital wasting away.

After two hours of listening to Gabe cry, I said good-bye for the evening. I sat on the floor of my room and stared at the phone. The Watchtower Society taught that, due to Adam and Eve, we were all condemned to lead imperfect, sinful lives ultimately resulting in our deaths. This I could accept. What bothered me, though, was why some people seemed destined to have lives of greater suffering than others. The Society passed this off as random chance, but it hardly seemed fair. All humans were expected to remain faithful to God and to stay by his organization, yet some people, simply by chance, were forced to have a much harder time than others.

Gabe's mom died twenty-two hours later.

I attended the funeral, but then refrained from contacting Gabe. Four days later, he called me and asked me to come over. I didn't want to go, because I knew Gabe would still be depressed from his loss, but I had no real reason to decline.

We sat out on his deck that night, as we had done many times before. The stars filled the expanse, and I marveled at their beauty, wondering how any idiot could fail to see God had created them all. Gabe stared off, straight ahead, and told me he didn't know what to do with his life. He didn't like his congregation, he felt he had no chance with Sarah, and his mom had just died.

"Why did she have to die, James?" He said casually, as if he was asking me why the sky was black.

"Gabe, it wasn't up to . . ."

He cut me off. "Why did she have to die? Why did she have to die! Why did she have to die!"

I swallowed my words, not sure if there was an answer to satisfy him.

"Gabe," I finally broke in, "You have to remember that you will see her very soon. Do you know that we are now eighty years into the last days? The End is coming soon, and you'll see your mom in the New World."

Gabe took comfort in this reminder. Or, at least, it appeared to calm him down.

Jenni and I continued dating in secret, but she was sick of the secrecy. I initially asked her to keep our relationship a secret so that we might have time to get used to the idea of dating. But it had been nearly two months, she argued, and continued secrecy just made it seem like I was embarrassed. "No, not embarrassed," I said, "worried." I thought my parents and grandparents would be disappointed, but the time for a clandestine courtship was over. We agreed to both tell our parents the news on the same evening.

"What would you guys say if I told you I wanted to start dating girls?" I asked.

My mom and dad looked at each other and then darted their eyes around the room. I was unsure if they didn't know what to say, or if they were reeling from the idea that they suddenly had a child old enough to begin dating.

My dad was intuitive enough to know I wouldn't just pull this topic out of nowhere. "Is there someone in particular that you are interested in?"

"Jenni."

"Jenni Meissner? She's nice," he admitted. "Is she pioneering?"

In smug defensiveness, I asked: "Why, does that make her a bad person if she's not?"

"No, it's just that . . . well, it's nice to find someone that's compatible, someone who has the same goals."

"I think Jenni would like to pioneer. She thinks it's a good thing to do; she's just really shy."

We talked for an hour, mostly about the importance of a chaperone. My mom sternly reminded me that as a pioneer *and* a ministerial servant, people looked up to me, and a lot was expected of me. I nodded dutifully as they doled out their rules.

I called Jenni that night. She had told her parents the big news, too. They guessed right away who she was dating, with her sister Sarah even claiming "I knew it!"

Rhett didn't go out in service the next day. I called him in the evening. He answered the phone with a cough. "I've been sick all day," he sputtered. He had spent the day lounging on the couch, nursing a chest cold. "I think I can probably make it out in service tomorrow. Can you give me a ride? My car isn't running and I can't afford to bring it into the shop right now."

I picked him up and gave him a ride to the Hall. He spent most of the day with the seat lowered so he could lie down during the ride.

He told me he had secured a low-rent apartment in the small Wisconsin town of Nelson, and he arranged his cleaning jobs so that they all were scheduled during three consecutive days. His plan was to live in Nelson and pioneer and go to the meetings there. Then, on Thursday night, after the meeting, he would drive an hour back to the cities, and work at his cleaning jobs. He would spend the night at his dad's house, and then spend all day Friday and early Saturday morning working at his other cleaning jobs. He would drive back to Nelson Saturday morning, just in time for service.

On the last day Rhett and I went out in service together as pioneer partners, we came upon a householder who allowed Rhett to go through his presentation and pull the latest *Watchtower* out of his bag. Rhett drew the man's attention to an article about creation. Finally, the man stopped the conversation. He asked: "So, you guys don't believe in evolution?"

"No," Rhett answered proudly, "We know from our studies of the Bible that God created everything. It didn't happen by chance."

"Uh-huh. I see. So then what does your religion teach about fossils?"

"What do you mean exactly," Rhett asked. He started coughing, so I jumped in: "Well, we know that there are fossils, and we do believe that animals have been around for millions of years, so that doesn't change our beliefs."

"Really?" he asked, jumping on my confidence, "And what about humans, you believe they have been around since . . ."

"Since Adam and Eve," Rhett answered.

"Huh. But what about the fossils?"

"Not sure I follow—" Rhett said.

"If your religion does allow you to accept fossil evidence, then surely you believe the massive amounts of fossil evidence proving that humans have existed for hundreds of thousands of years."

Rhett did an admirable job of explaining that science can sometimes be wrong, and that just because a fossil is estimated to be a certain age doesn't mean it really *is* that age.

I jumped in. "From what we've learned of Carbon-14 dating, we believe it's not a reliable way to estimate the ages of fossils."

"Is that so?" he quickly responded. "From what I've learned—and I studied radiocarbon dating for eight years while attending the University to become a paleontologist—Carbon-14 dating, coupled with other methods, is a reliable method of assigning ages to fossils."

I looked away from him, embarrassed that I tried to go head-to-head with a doctor of paleontology on the subject of carbon dating. Rhett picked up the slack and concluded: "We don't wish to argue with people. Maybe I could just leave you this tract and we'll be on our way." Rhett held out a tract titled *Will This World Survive?* The householder declined the offer.

Our experience at that door left me melancholy. If only there was something I could have said that would have convinced him that we had the Truth. Yet I knew that, ultimately, Rhett did the right thing by excusing us from the door. Some Witnesses claimed that meeting people like that was Satan's way of wasting our time and preventing us from finding people who were sincerely hungering for the truth. I supposed they were right.

Ten days later, Rhett stuffed his earthly possessions into his car and moved away from home. I asked him if we would ever go out in service together again. He smiled. "Sure, man, we'll visit each other all the time."

One evening, after going out to dinner with Jenni and her sister Sarah, I came home to find a letter from the Watchtower Society. I immediately tensed up, and opened the envelope with shaking hands. I knew what was in the envelope, because there was nothing else it could be. I was accepted to Bethel.

As I opened the letter and began reading it, I silently asked Jehovah how he could allow me to be accepted to Bethel when he knew I didn't want to go. I took a deep breath and exhaled with relief, therefore, when I realized the letter was an invitation to work at Bethel *temporarily*. I had almost forgotten that I had applied for temporary work as well as a permanent position. *Yes, I can handle temporary work. Three weeks in New York at the Watchtower Headquarters will be an awesome experience.*

A month later, I flew east of the Burned-over District to Watchtower Ground Zero: the Witnesses' Mecca was in Brooklyn, New York. My apartment had a bedroom, a living room, a dining area, a kitchen and a living room. It also had five roommates. One young man lived on Long Island, another was from California. The lone roommate over twenty-one was an elder from Georgia named Amos. Another roommate was an Iowan with a French accent. I held out my hand to shake, and he held out his hand with the fingers pointing down, as if he was royalty and I was supposed to kiss his ring. His name was LaRoy Volière, and he was, as another roommate would later describe him, "so flaming gay it's a wonder he doesn't set the building on fire."

I hardly had enough time to learn everyone's names when there came a knock at the door. Amos opened it. "Good afternoon brother, can I help you?"

I came around the corner and saw Johnny. He pointed at me. "I'm here for that guy." We shook hands and gave each other a hearty hug. After being with Johnny every day for years, it was hard to believe I hadn't seen him in five months. We left for pizza. I returned late that night to several snoring roommates.

I awoke the next day to a chaotic morning of guys running around the room in various stages of dress. "Come on Brother Zimmerman, get up!" I sat up and looked at the clock, it was eight minutes to seven, and morning worship began promptly at seven. LaRoy overslept. His alarm, he claimed, was defective. Since he wasn't awake to get anyone else up, we all overslept. There was no time to shower, so I just stood up, shoved my cot under a bed, and put on a suit. I used water from the kitchen sink to mat down my greasy hair.

Within five minutes, I was down in the dining hall where a man with a clipboard escorted me to my assigned seat.

This is life as a Bethelite:

On Monday through Friday we were in our assigned seats for breakfast by 7:00. Morning worship consisted of a scripture and comments by members of the governing body. Breakfast commenced thereafter, to be finished by 7:30. All were expected to begin their assigned work by 8:00. I vaulted from the breakfast table into a nine-block jaunt to a building where I could change from my suit into work clothes, then took another one-block run to the worksite.

At 11:45, I had a half hour to shower and change back into a suit. Lunch began punctually at 12:15. Then it was back to the lockers to get ready for work again by 1:00. The work day was over at 5:00, but for those in dirty work clothes, going straight back to rooms was not an option. They first had to shower and don suits before walking back to their rooms.

Tuesdays and Thursdays were meeting nights, and since too many Witnesses lived in too small an area, many of them were assigned to congregations miles away. Most Bethelites were unable to afford a vehicle, so carpooling is the order of the day, with riders expected to give the driver a dollar for each trip to the Kingdom Hall and back again.

Wednesday evenings were family study night. Through the televised links, the governing body conducted the *Watchtower* Study for the family in preparation for the actual *Watchtower* Study on Sunday.

Saturday was essentially a repeat of the previous five days, except the workday ended at noon.

Sunday was the *Watchtower* Study and Public Talk. Since most Bethelites had no other time to go out in service, they typically went out on Sunday.

For those who were permanent members of the Bethel family, the work load was even heavier. The young brothers were on a dish-washing rotation. They were also on night watchman rotation. Johnny had performed this task twice already, and both times he got less than four hours of sleep, yet still was expected to show up for his normal duties in the shipping department. Additionally, new Bethelites attended an orientation class on Monday nights teaching them how to properly care for themselves and their rooms. Scott called this class the "Wipe Your Butt" class.

Bethel is a tireless, efficient Rube Goldberg edifice that belches Witness apologetics. It is a moving fluid wherein the location and trajectory of each drop is accounted for. And, for three weeks, I became a cog in the machine; a number stamped on the inside of my underwear. I became part of the grease to keep the machine running cool.

As an unskilled laborer, I was placed in the tiling department. I had never laid or cut a tile in my life, but I was assigned to man the diamond-edged saw. Renovators continually brought me tiles with markings identifying how the piece needed to be cut in order to fit around this pipe, or that outlet. In between cuts, I passed the time by pressing my thumb against the blade, letting it polish my fingerprints away.

I was a slow learner. I frequently wandered around asking to help. One sister asked me to help her pull out the spacers between the dried tiles. Another day, my duty was to place duct tape over every exposed spot on a wet-dry vacuum. Johnny called me at work every day to see what I was doing that evening. I lingered on the phone, preferring the fun of chatting with a friend over the uncomfortable uncertainty of my assignment.

On Tuesday and Thursday evenings, I joined Johnny at his meetings. Johnny and I carpooled to the meetings with another Bethelite who owned his own car. Johnny never had money to give the driver, and judging from the driver's reaction to Johnny's lack of funds, this was what he had come to expect. I dutifully gave two dollars for each ride, and even offered to give four dollars to cover Johnny one night, but the driver refused the extra two bucks. Leaving the car, Johnny said not to worry about giving the money, but I told him that was what we were instructed to do. When I asked Johnny if I was mistaken, he hung his head in shame. "I guess it just makes me look bad."

I didn't understand what he was doing with the monthly stipend he received. My time at Bethel straddled two months, and even on the first day of the new month, when all the Bethelites received their stipends,[36] Johnny still didn't have a dollar to give his carpooler. Though his room and board, food and laundry were all paid for, Johnny was in debt to his roommate Cory, accruing and repaying debt each month. Primarily, Johnny was spending his money on phone calls. Johnny should have refrained himself from calling his friends back home so often, but he thrived on friends. He needed the friendships just to maintain his sanity.

All the food I could ever eat was supplied by the Society; fresh, healthy, and grown locally at Watchtower Farms. The problem, though, was the difficulty in obtaining it. In only three short weeks, I grew tired of the forty-five minutes alloted for lunch, during which time I was expected to shower and suit up just to run into a dining hall and rigidly follow the Watchtower rulebook of eating. I began leaving Bethel for lunch, briskly walking to local fast food restaurants where I was free to walk in the door in dirty jeans. I put my feet up on the benches. If I needed a napkin, I just grabbed one; I didn't have to politely ask someone. This food cut into my funds, and it was not as tasty or healthy, but the time afforded me an opportunity to center myself; to unwind momentarily before the afternoon shift. Johnny joined me for those lunch excursions as he often did with Cory. With a monthly income of eighty dollars, Johnny spent a third of his income on lunch alone.

The tiling task was put on hold while a new cement floor was poured for the kitchen. I didn't know what to do, so I sat to one side on an upturned bucket. Every few minutes, I asked if I could be of any help. "Yeah, can you hand me that screwdriver?" I'd fetch the requested tool, and then sit back down and wait until someone else looked like they needed help.

On our way to the lockers before lunch time, one of the brothers in charge grabbed me. "I noticed you weren't really helping out as much as you could have."

I felt dejected, especially since my reason for volunteering was to help out where Jehovah needed me. I told him that I often wasn't sure what to do. I told him I didn't want to mess anything up, and I didn't want to break anything. He said: "Well, some of us were talking, and we think it'd be nice if you helped out a little more." Cryptically, he added: "Let's just say that if you were here as a permanent member of the Bethel family, you would have already been talked to."

After my co-worker's comment, I felt like I was being looked at suspiciously; that no one could count on me to do any work. When I got back to my apartment, the phone was ringing. I ignored it, assuming it was Johnny telling me I had exactly thirteen seconds to myself before it was time to leave for the meeting. When it rang again, I picked up. "I'm sorry, Johnny, but I just can't go to the meeting tonight."

He sounded like I had just told him I had cancer. "Is everything alright?"

"I just need some time to myself."

Johnny answered calmly, "I understand."

"I just walked in the door. I still have my shoes on, for goodness' sake."

"James, I said I understand. It's okay. We all need some time to decompress now and then."

I felt guilty for ever missing a meeting unless I was sick. It was comforting to know that my friend understood.

With an empty wallet and an empty stomach, I spent the lunch break on my final day sitting on a park bench. I was starving, but I couldn't afford food from a vendor, nor could I stomach any food that was served with a litany of rules.

After work, I didn't bother to shower. I walked right into the apartment building in grubby, tattered, work clothes. The front desk attendant raised an eyebrow, but said nothing. I rode the elevator with an elder who commented that I "must've been working hard." I went in to the bathroom and with no roommates rushing me for once, took a proper shower. I washed away three weeks' worth of grime and rules.

Two notices were waiting on my dresser. The first was a letter thanking me for volunteering my time and energy to assist in God's work. It reminded me that I should feel free to leave a contribution to help pay for any long-distance calls I may have made during my stay. The second notice stated that I neglected to ensure my clothes were fully tucked into one dresser drawer.

As the airplane began its decent, I waited in anticipation. I missed my girl-friend. I missed my friends and family. And I was excited for the simple reason that I was back in the great state of Minnesota. Never before had I been away so long. In my absence, I had come to appreciate the beautiful home I had. Contrary to what the bumper stickers in Brooklyn suggested, I *hated* New York. I hated the rudeness and the fastness; the bravado and the accent. I hated the unending gridlines of building after building cordoned off by constant traffic. I even hated the way they drank out of cans using straws. Clearing the clouds, I saw my hometown: there was no bubble of smog enveloping the Twin Cities as in Manhattan. I smiled at the sights I saw through the little oblong window, and it was a joy to identify the landmarks. There was no need to live elsewhere. I was useless outside of my familiar surroundings.

I called Jenni, and we talked for hours. I loved hearing her voice. For the first time in three weeks, I was able to talk without roommates in earshot, and without feeling guilty for charging up a long-distance bill.

There was no doubt in my mind that I did not want to be a Bethelite, yet I was unable to bring myself to withdraw my application. I kept telling my-self, and Jenni, that Jehovah knew I didn't want to go, and so he wouldn't allow me to be accepted. One cold December day, we spent the day leisurely touring a history museum. Reflecting on the past caused me to consider my future. I felt as though my future was being written without my consent, with the opposing prospects of marriage and Bethel closing in on me. *Is Jehovah mad at me for not liking Bethel? Does he want me to go regardless? If he wanted me to go, why didn't he help me to enjoy Bethel? Why did he allow me to meet Jenni? Didn't he know I would fall in love with her?* Surely Jehovah could have fixed things so that they turned out differently, if he so desired.

Any hope I had of delaying my decisions vanished that night. I returned home to find a letter telling me I had been accepted to work at Bethel on a permanent basis. More specifically, I had been accepted to the Watchtower farm in upstate New York, hours away from the Headquarters in Brooklyn. My legs numb, I fell into my desk chair. *The Watchtower Farm?* Once again, my prayers, if they were answered, were answered in the most baffling manner possible. *Why did Jehovah allow me to get accepted to Bethel? And why the farm? I won't be able to support Johnny if I am hours away from him.*

I called Jenni and told her the news. She could tell I was upset. Being more supportive than I would have liked, she offered: "Well, why don't you just go for a year. We're not gonna be married within a year from now, anyways."

"I don't know if I'm even going. I don't know what to do."

While on the phone, my dad came into my room. He must have known that the letter was regarding my application to Bethel.

Frustrated, I said: "I guess I need a plane ticket." I threw the letter in his general direction and told Jenni I would call her back.

My dad asked if I wanted to go to Bethel, and I confessed I didn't. I reminded him how much I hadn't liked Bethel, how I had even called him one evening upset that it was not what I thought it would be. On that night, he suggested that maybe Jehovah was testing me. *Perhaps He was testing me then, but is He testing me now? Why does everything have to be a test?*

Over the next several days, I prayed dozens of times, asking Jehovah why he insisted on being so cryptic, so ambiguous. I did not enjoy my time at Bethel, and I knew that Jehovah was aware of my feelings. Did He really want someone to work at Bethel who didn't enjoy it? I was growing tired of serving God in ways that didn't make me happy. Was there no good way to both serve Jehovah with all of my strength and enjoy life? Was I not a member of the 'happiest people on Earth?

By week's end, I still had no idea of what God wanted. My parents continually asked what I planned to do. An elder helpfully offered, "Any boy doesn't want to go to Bethel, I think there's something wrong with him"—a baffling proclamation, considering his own son was not a Bethelite. With no answer from God forthcoming, on Friday night, with rain streaking down the window pane and tears in my eyes, I did what *I wanted* to do: I wrote to Bethel thanking them for accepting me, but declining their offer. I closed up the envelope and, in my pajamas, marched to the mailbox. I ripped up the acceptance letter and threw it in the trash.

Worried about my future, I exhausted the midnight hour begging Jehovah to bring the Paradise.

THE HEART IS TREACHEROUS

> The heart is more treacherous than anything
> else and is desperate.
>
> —Jeremiah 17:9

With Bethel becoming more and more a lost path each passing day, I turned my attention fully, for the first time, to a future with Jenni. We would need to start arranging our lives inexorably towards marriage. To that end, it was important to me that I still be able to serve Jehovah as much as possible.

As it stood, I was employed part-time, with no medical benefits. I was spending hours every day serving Jehovah and the congregation. Jenni had a full-time job. She was not a pioneer.

When I told Jenni of my desire to ensure at least one of us be able to continue pioneering after marriage, she suggested what seemed logical: She would continue working full-time, thereby providing us with much needed health insurance, while I would continue to work part-time and pioneer. I had, after all, the more gregarious personality, making me better suited to dealing with the varied Witnesses and householders. Furthermore, Jenni was well established at her job, having worked there over three years.

This was the logical, reasonable answer to my worried conscience.

But primarily, the idea of the woman providing for the family bothered me. Both the Bible and the Society made it clear that the responsibility of providing for a family's necessities fell squarely upon the man. I therefore deemed Jenni's plan for our future unsuitable.

Instead, I wanted Jenni to be my pioneer partner. The two of us had never been out in service together, a situation I immediately wanted to change. When the calendars changed over, Jenni was granted a new supply of vacation time and promptly took off the first Friday of the new year. The two of us went out in service together for the first time.

A day out in service with my girlfriend was a great day indeed, but I felt we needed to do more as a dating couple. I insisted she look for another job, one that would allow us to go out in service together weekly. Actually, it wasn't so much that I *insisted* as *forced* her to get a new job. Ostensibly, I bemoaned the early start time her current job required, which resulted in Jenni being too tired to stay out late most nights. I also lamented her decision to work at a full-time job in the first place—a young Witness fresh out of high school and still living at home with mom and dad is in a perfect position to pioneer. *What if the Paradise came next week; would she be happy that she'd devoted the last couple of years in this wicked system to working for an insurance agency instead of taking part in the most important work in human history?* When Jenni claimed she was too shy to pioneer, I told her I too struggled with all aspects of pioneering, "but with God, all things are possible."[37] I actively participated in finding a part-time job for Jenni, one that would offer at least one day a week off for us to go out in service together.

There was another, more insidious reason for wanting Jenni to quit her job: I was jealous of it. Not jealous in the sense that it took up too much of her life—time that should have been spent with me—but that it was one of several ways in which Jenni was, at least in my obsessive brain, better than me. As the male in our relationship, I felt that I should be better than Jenni in every way. I was jealous of anything and everything that could, in some semblance, be viewed as a way in which Jenni was better than me. I tried, at times, to rid myself of such unhealthy thoughts. My dad suggested speaking with a therapist, but doing so bothered my conscience. I read more Watchtower literature regarding women, and I couldn't help come to the conclusion that women were inferior and, as such, any way in which Jenni appeared superior, must be altered.[38]

So, I made her quit her job. I was waiting for her at her house when she came home from work for the last time. I smiled a big smile for her, but she only upturned the corner of her mouth, as if she was trying to put a positive spin on her career change, but couldn't quite convince herself. She lay on her stomach on the couch and stared at the floor. I watched her from across the room. Her eyes looked sad and nervous; I could tell she was unsettled by what I had made her do. Jenni had quit a good job. She was comfortable there. A bit of remorse opened up in my heart. I wanted to tell her that I made a mistake and that she should go back to doing what she wanted to do with her life, but I couldn't bring myself to say anything.

I tried reminding her how exciting her new job would be. Her new job would be working as a teacher's aide at a day care. It meant less pay, with no benefits; but she would be able to sleep in later and, best of all, she would not be working on Fridays, so we would go out in service together. I told her these things, and she nodded, making the best of it.

Her dad was no help. He kept repeating the same phrase: "You gave up a good job," over and over again. In a way, he was right; Jenni had been promoted and received good reviews. But I told Jenni that her father was looking at things the wrong way. This was the perfect time for us to curb our income and devote our time to Jehovah. Besides, it seemed to me that her dad was just upset that Jenni's decrease in income would mean a decrease in the rent she paid him.

Still, seeing her lying there on the couch, and hearing her mom try to console her about the anxiety of leaving one job and beginning a new one, nearly broke whatever heart I had. I resolved to curtail the manner in which my rampant jealousy was manifesting itself.

Fridays became our days. I looked forward to it all week. We were together the whole day; arriving at the meeting for service at nine o'clock and staying out in service until three, then off to one of our homes for dinner. We alternated going out in service with each other's congregations.

I preferred the Fridays when she came out in service with my congregation. Rhett was gone now, so having Jenni there helped me look forward to at least one day out in service each week.

Her congregation was quite different. The only other Witnesses to show up for service on Fridays were an elder named Howie, his wife and kids, and his Bible student. He stared at Jenni and me when we walked in to the Kingdom Hall, neither nodding nor smiling, just dryly giving us a "Good morning." His struggle to arrange the car groups (he wanted to work out in service with his family, but couldn't send an unmarried couple off by themselves), coupled with the incessant eye-rolling, led me to conclude that we simultaneously bored and inconvenienced him. I decided it was best to bring other people out in service with us.

Service on the other days of the week became increasingly difficult. Retail hours made it challenging to get in service time. Because of the meetings, I couldn't work Tuesday or Thursday evenings, and I had requested not to work on Fridays to be with Jenni. This left me with frustratingly small chunks of time to work and go out in service. I began working every Saturday, as it was a good day to make commission.

But someone who is both a pioneer and a ministerial servant can only go so long without supporting Saturday service. As it was the only day most Witnesses went out in service, it was incumbent on those taking the lead to be there to support the rank and file. It was only a matter of time until an elder took notice of my absence on Saturdays. That elder was my dad's brother Peter.

Uncle Peter approached me one evening after the meeting was over. "Got a second?" he asked, pointing his pen in my direction. We walked to a corner of the Hall.

He began: "So tell me, how's pioneering going?" He excelled at pumping people for information.

"It's fine. No problems."

"Your time . . . are you getting in your time?"

"It's a little tougher this year, with my job—but I'm managing."

"No trouble with the other brothers and sisters?"

"Eh, no, they're not so bad." I knew he was building to something. There was a formulaic and predictable way elders delivered compliments and feigned interest only to then hit a person with counsel.

"What about Saturdays? You able to get out on Saturday?"

"That kind of goes back to my job. Since I work in retail, Saturday's a great day to make commission. Besides, Saturday isn't a good day to get in any time."

"Do you think you'd be able to get out maybe one or two Saturdays a month, at least?"

I shrugged. "Maybe, I don't know. Like I said, my boss likes if I work on Saturdays, and I make good money that day to support myself in the pioneer work."

He blinked slowly, ignoring my response. He tapped his pen in his hand. "Here's the deal, the elders would really like having your support out in service on Saturdays."

I found this ridiculous. Saturdays received the best support of any day. I already went out in service almost every other day of the week. Supporting the congregation was not something I needed to improve upon. "Well I'd really like having your support out in service on Mondays, Tuesdays, Wednesdays, Thursdays, and Fridays."

He nodded and raised his eyebrows. "We all do what we can."

Wishing to avoid my uncle, I skipped the meeting the following Sunday. Jenni invited me to a family picnic, and I figured that was a good excuse. Her family was the antithesis of mine: mostly laid-back Scandinavians. Their relatively quiet nature and Minnesotan heritage both paled next to the one thing that made her family vastly different from mine: Not a single one of them was in the Truth. They were heathens, pagans, worldlings—every last one of them. Jenni's parents had only accepted the Truth as married adults and thus had no relatives who shared their faith, apart from their own children.

Even that's not entirely correct. Jenni, her parents, and her two sisters were in the Truth, but Jenni had one more sibling: a brother five years her senior. Though raised as a Witness, he had turned his back on the Truth in his teens. Lester was a long-haired, overweight, tattooed, pot-smoking rebel who loved television and his non-Witness girlfriend, with whom he lived in sin. He was the stereotypical fallen sheep: he knew the Witnesses had the Truth, but nixed it all in favor of living a life of hedonistic debauchery. I could easily imagine Lester's face depicted in Watchtower literature showing what not to do with one's life. Jenni revealed to me that Lester had caused much trouble for his parents; his disregard for the religion spilled over into a disregard for the rules of his parents. There was fighting and screaming, and Lester was kicked out of the house.

I didn't meet Lester until many months after I began dating his sister. But the very idea of Lester fascinated me. He would, one day, be my brother-in-law . . . my *worldly* brother-in-law.

Les was a little shorter than I. His partial mullet and jean jacket announced to everyone that in an era of Radiohead and No Doubt, he was living in a world of Iron Maiden and Metallica. I wanted to ask him why he decided to not be a Witness. I wanted to hear, from his own lips, what was so appealing about the world that he threw away the promise of perfect life in a Paradise earth? But I didn't ask. I just smiled like a goon when I met him. He put his arm around me. "So you're dating my sister, huh?" He laughed a deep belly laugh and asked: "How's that goin' for ya?"

He winked when he said it, and I knew he was referring to the physical delights. I just nodded. "It's fine."

As for Jenni's extended family, I had no qualms with them. I trekked with them to her Grandma's house every few months for a "family day." Family days were non-holiday occasions concocted with the implied purpose of ensuring that Jenni and her immediate family would be able to attend without having to compromise their Witness-trained consciences. I tried getting to know the people in Jenni's family, knowing that at some unspecified date in the future, they would also be my relatives. I couldn't find much wrong with them, except, of course, the fact that each and every one of them was going to die at Jehovah's hand very soon.

Soon after, while out in service one afternoon, a sister in the car group asked how long everyone thought it would be until God brought the Paradise. Three of the people in the car agreed that two years was an outside maximum; with one young woman even expressing her doubts that this wicked world would outlast the calendar year. I very much wanted to agree, but I also reveled in playing devil's advocate, a role left noticeably vacant since Scott's departure. I told the group I thought we still had five years until Armageddon commenced.

The other brother in the car shook his head at my words. "How can you say that, James?"

A sister said, "Oh, James, I don't know about that. That's a bad way to think."

Jenni and I also talked about Armageddon's imminence. Though we agreed it could come any day, we knew it could be years off. Besides, there was still the immediate future to worry about, and so we felt it would help me grow up if I moved out from under my parents' roof and experienced life as a real adult. We talked about which congregation we would join upon getting married. I felt that, as the man, I should take the lead and bear the brunt of switching congregations. I had a far easier time warming up to people than she did, so I decided I would move to Jenni's congregation.

Any reservations I entertained regarding moving out of my congregation were soon put to rest, due to another confrontation with my Uncle Peter. Once again, I couldn't determine if he was counseling me on behalf of the elders, or if he was trying to offer avuncular advice. He was concerned that I was spending time out in service with other congregations on occasion instead of with my own. When I asked him to clarify, he mentioned my routine of going out in service with Jenni.

"Let me guess," I cut in, "is this because Aunt Nancy is mad that she went out in service last Friday and there were no brothers there?"

Uncle Peter smirked nervously. "Sure, that's part of it. The sisters need someone to take the lead. If none of us are there, . . . well, they expect a brother to be there to conduct the meeting."

He suggested I refrain from going out in service with Jenni's hall, at least on a regular basis, but I explained how the two of us had rearranged our schedules to be together. As always, he provided no scriptural or *Watchtower* support to back up his suggestion, but I had documentation to support my case. I told him the *Young People Ask* book said that carrying on a successful courtship included going out in service together.[39] Uncle Peter shrugged. "I see we're not gonna resolve this."

I found it particularly disturbing that the events that proved most discouraging were the ones that occurred out of a sincere desire to do the right thing. There were times when I was trying my hardest to be the best Witness I could. Every so often, I would see an opportunity for spiritual growth, or a way in which I could help my fellow Witnesses in their faith, and it would result in extreme discouragement.

Valerie was my absolute favorite aunt. She was the definition of a good person: unlike most of my relatives, she was quiet and soft-spoken, a good listener, and she held a deep love for Jehovah and the religion. She also had her share of difficulties in the faith. Her husband, my mom's older brother Tommy, was not an active Witness. Like his wife, he was an agreeable person, and I often prayed on his behalf that his one flaw (his complete inactivity in Jehovah's service) would be corrected before it was too late.

Aunt Val put forth extensive effort to see to it that her two sons did not fall into the same pattern as her husband. She brought them to all the meetings and requested that a couple of young brothers study the Bible with them. As their older cousin, I figured I should do my part to encourage them, too. So I asked if I could bring her twelve-year-old son Matthew out in service on Friday. She was so pleased to hear my request that she put her hand over her mouth and grabbed my forearm, squeezing it gently. "That would be wonderful," she whispered. "But you better check with Sal and see if it's alright."

According to Sal, an elder in our Hall, Matthew was only to go out in service with his mom, or with people who were assigned to instruct him in the proper way to go door-to-door.[40] My aunt was genuinely concerned that I follow the policy. I complied, assuring her that Sal would be happy to hear I was trying to encourage my cousin.

So I informed Sal of my plan. Before I could finish speaking, Sal shook his head. "Are you serious?" I asked. I thought he was joking. It wasn't like the aging Sal to be sarcastic, but I couldn't comprehend why he would have a problem with my plan.

"Oh yeah, I'm serious," he deadpanned, nodding with sufficient force to jiggle his jowls.

I asked why, and he explained exactly what Aunt Val had told me: Matthew was not a publisher and, thus, was not authorized to go out in service with just anyone. Certainly Matthew could join his mother out in service, and naturally it was acceptable for Sal, being an elder, to take Matthew door-to-door.

Since this sounded woefully illogical to me, I asked Sal if he could explain this to my aunt. Sal agreed. A few minutes later, I saw Aunt Val gathering up her books and her coat. I approached her and saw she was crying.

"Did Sal tell you I can't take Matthew out in service?" I asked.

She swallowed hard, unable to speak.

"Sorry about that," I said.

She wiped a tear from her cheek. "That's okay, Jimmy," she whispered, patting the side of my face. "It's not your fault." She turned and left the Hall.

In the car on the way home, I told my parents the story. My dad suggested that maybe the Watchtower Society had written to the elders explaining this, but I argued that if such a letter existed, why hadn't Sal shown it to me as supporting evidence? My mom said that if I was so sure the elders were wrong, maybe I should check with elders from another congregation. And what better elder to check with than her father? He was my grandpa, and my cousin Matthew's grandpa. As such, he gave priority to ensuring that his family continued in their worship to Jehovah. Many of my grandpa's children and grandchildren were floundering in the religion; he was intimately troubled by this and would certainly not allow anything to discourage any of them.

I called my grandpa the next morning. He fully agreed with me. He even reminded me of the scripture that says look after orphans and widows.[41] Matthew was not a literal orphan, but since his father was completely inactive in the religion, Matthew could be thought of as a spiritual orphan. Late Friday afternoon, after Jenni and I had completed our day out in service, we returned to my house. As I took off my necktie, the phone rang. It was an elder, Uncle Peter.

He began by asking how my day had been, and I told him I'd spent six hours out in service that day with my girlfriend. He then turned to the matter at hand, asking how I felt about what happened at the meeting.

"I feel that I was right," I said with conviction.

He stifled a laugh. "Why's that?"

"Like you've said, I should be visible to the congregation and I should be an example. I was trying to set a good example for my cousin. Besides, Matthew is pretty much a spiritual orphan, so I should help take responsibility for him in learning about Jehovah—especially since I'm his relative."

Uncle Peter hesitated, then admitted that, essentially, I was correct. He confessed that the elders had erred. I roundly agreed, citing Aunt Val leaving in tears as the most blatant evidence that they had done something wrong. He apologized on behalf of the elders, and I accepted his apology. When I asked if he was going to call Aunt Val, he responded: "You don't have to worry about that, just go ahead, take him out in service with you next week if you want." I explained that spring break was this week. "He'll be back in school next week, so he can't go out with me then."

I let the matter rest for the time being, but I was continually vexed that the elders had been wrong. In being wrong, they brought harm to a good person. Good Witnesses skirt the issues to the best of their abilities before they'd say something as blasphemous as "the elders are wrong" or "the Society is wrong." Yet, out of the other side of their mouth, they will reason that the Society and the elders it appoints are not perfect. Witnesses are told not to let this discourage them, as the men in the Bible were also imperfect. By creating a needless rule, the elders discouraged my aunt and me. They behaved as the Pharisees of Jesus' day, which he blatantly denounced.[42] What if the issue had been bigger? What if the elders had been wrong about something that could've cost me my health, or my life, or the life of a friend?

I aired these questions to my friends eight days later. Johnny managed to amass a few vacation days, and his parents footed the bill for him to visit. Johnny only had five days to be in town, but he spent every waking moment—and many sleeping moments—in the company of his friends. One evening, he, Jeremy, and I sat in Gabe's basement and consumed two large pizzas. Everyone's life was getting busier. We were moving apart. Johnny lived in New York. Jeremy had a girlfriend named Bridgette and was now living in a duplex in the city. Gabe, meanwhile, was still figuring out what to do with life since the death of his mother. He finished high school, and set the goal of pioneering; but he was reluctant to pioneer in his own congregation, claiming the elders there were too stifling.

Gabe sat back and tuned his guitar. I took the opportunity to question my friends: how did they feel about the recent events concerning my aunt and cousin?

Before I could explain precisely what irked me about the whole situation, Jeremy cut me off: "Do you mean to tell me that Matthew has never gone out in service with anyone besides his mom and the elders?"

Johnny swallowed his bite of pizza. "Couldn't they just let you take your own cousin out in service? What does it hurt?"

I didn't know how to answer such a logical question. "I guess even though I'm Matthew's cousin and a pioneer and a ministerial servant, I'm just not good enough."

"Gosh," Jeremy said, using the Lord's name quasi–in vain, "If that's true, then who *is* good enough?"

This I had an answer for. I sat up and blurted: "Norman Penna—he's good enough!"

"Norm?" Jeremy could hardly believe what he had heard. "They let Norm take Matthew out in service? Why?"

"Because he's Sal's son, I suppose," I sputtered with disgust. "You know elders' kids get more privileges."

Putting his hands on his hips, Jeremy asked, "Well is Norm a ministerial servant or an elder?"

"Nope," I said, "He's just an elder's son."

"I don't care whose son he is, he's a dork," Jeremy said.

"Not only that," I agreed, "He's also a freakin' pedophile."

Johnny squeezed his lips together nervously, and gave me a look that told me I shouldn't say that. "Just because he has a pink feather boa in his house doesn't make him a pedophile," Johnny argued. Then he laughed. "It just means he's *probably* a pedophile."

I responded that Norm never was with anyone his own age. He was always going to restaurants and inviting over boys who were several years younger than him. At every meeting, he sat with boys half his age—sometimes with my cousins, sometimes with other preteens. I told Johnny of rumors that Norm had a housewarming party for himself in which the only people invited were boys between the ages of eight and fifteen.

Johnny shook his head. "Weird."

"Yeah, I know."

Later that night, I talked to Johnny about his future plans. He was approaching his one-year anniversary at Bethel. He was still having a difficult time, to the point that he had, more than once, came back to his room after a day of work and wept in front of his roommate Cory, crying that the elders were too hard on him. "I just don't think you're cut out to be a Bethelite," I said.

Johnny sighed deeply. "You're right. I've been out there almost a year now, so it's not like I'm a failure."

"I didn't mean to insinuate that you are. I'm just saying, they say to give Bethel a year, and you did that. Now you're done."

Johnny admitted he didn't know what to do with his life after Bethel. He folded his arms like he always did when deep in thought, with his fingers tucked into his armpits. I told him my plan to join Jenni's congregation, and that I would spend the next few months searching for an inexpensive duplex where he and I could live. We'd share the price of rent, and together we would be pioneer partners, helping out a congregation.

Johnny agreed this was a fabulous idea. It was so fabulous, in fact, that he even said he couldn't think of anything negative about the whole scenario.

Johnny flew back to Brooklyn for the last time, and over the next three months I searched for a rental house, found a third roommate, and packed up my belongings. During one of my last meetings at Apple Valley, Rhett visited. I told him I had the house free that evening, if he wanted to come over and visit.

"Hey man, have you ever had a beer?" he asked. I confessed that, apart from a few sips of my dad's drinks many years back, I had never consumed alcohol.

Rhett arrived that evening with two cans of beer in tow—one for each of us. It didn't taste especially good, and I felt mildly sinful. Yet I loved every sip. It was my birthday, and though birthday celebrations were sinful, I couldn't help but hold the can over my head and toast: "Here's to my teens!"

My mind felt lifted from its pedestals, submitting to the alcohol, and an agreeable calm came over me. Rhett aired his concerns about finances, worried that he wouldn't be able to last much longer in a town with no employment opportunities. I, meanwhile, told Rhett about my plans to move into the city.

So there we were: two old friends, ministerial servants and regular pioneers alike, getting buzzed on cheap beer and a laughably low tolerance. Rhett slouched back in the sofa. I laid my head back and thought about the future. I'd live with Johnny for a year, than marry Jenni and live with her as trillions of millenniums unfolded. The future was nigh, despite any misgivings Rhett and I entertained. As the sun set on my twentieth birthday, I told Rhett it would be funny to see what we'd be like in exactly ten years. Rhett reminded me we'd be in the Paradise by then. I wholeheartedly agreed. Then I poured the rest of the alcohol down my throat.

FIRST WHEELOCK

Many years after that conversation with Rhett, during the hot, sticky days of late summer, Jenni and I were vacationing at a bed and breakfast to celebrate our eighth wedding anniversary when she handed me a book with a "Form for Reacquaintance."[43] This "form" asked all manner of questions: *What are your biggest fears? What is your favorite meal at restaurants?* The idea is, both spouses fills out the form and then discuss their answers. Maybe they learn something new; maybe they talk about things that they've had trouble discussing before. While sitting in a hot tub with my wife, I filled out the form, including:

My greatest regret in my life _____.

Hardly a second passed before I decided upon an answer.

My greatest regret in my life <u>was going to Wheelock Parkway Congregation</u>.

In retrospect, I should have seen the warning signs. Shortly before joining Wheelock congregation, Jenni and I met up with Ryan and Naomi for dinner. Over chicken salads and French fries, Ryan told us that he and his wife happened to be at a gathering with Dick and Gina Jacobs. Dick, a distractingly insecure man who hid behind a large moustache, was an elder in Jenni's congregation. His wife, Gina, was an overbearing, dominant woman with a mouth larger than her thighs. Jeremy once commented that it was his firm belief that Gina kept Dick's testicles in her purse. Whereupon Johnny asked: "Where does she keep her own?"

Ryan explained that during the course of that evening, Jenni and I came up in conversation. Ryan told them of our long friendship, and Dick and

Gina told him that they had known Jenni for many years. As Dick and Gina did not know much about me, they asked Ryan for details. He spoke of my accomplishments in the religion. The Jacobs were impressed, but then noted that Jenni seemed like a poor match. They shook their heads in dismay. They said they weren't sure how theocratic Jenni was. They explained that Jenni did not come from a family with a rich spiritual heritage. They even divulged the shocking horror that Jenni was not a member of the Theocratic Ministry School. Ryan and Naomi merely took in the information and assured the gossiping elder[44] and his wife that they were "sure James knows what he's doing."

Visiting Jenni's meeting the following month, I introduced myself to the congregation's Presiding Overseer, Oskar. Oskar was a far cry from Eugene, the Presiding Overseer from my congregation. He was several inches taller than me. His large frame was topped with an authoritarian dome of graying hair.

We shook hands, and I cringed at his powerful clamp; he could have crushed my fingers if he wanted. I told him my name, and where I was from. "I've already heard of you, James," he said. His German accent, very much alive despite having lived in America for decades, didn't make him any less imposing. We exchanged the names of people we mutually knew. I quickly realized that Oskar's harsh exterior did not go down to the core. He was genuinely enjoying our conversation.

As if to perpetuate German stereotypes, Oskar leaned towards the blunt side. He folded his arms. "So tell me, what are your intentions with Jenni Meissner?"

I swallowed hard. "My intentions?"

"Ja, I think it's a fair question, don't you? You come around here often and you are always sitting with Jennifer. So I only think it's fair I ask."

I shifted my weight like someone on a witness stand being interrogated, and told him my plan. I said I wanted to join Wheelock to help out as a pioneer, that I wanted to marry Jenni and pioneer with her here in Wheelock.

"Do you really think that will happen, James?" For having known me exactly four minutes, Oskar wasted no time with pleasantries.

"Yeah, I think it will. Do you think there's something wrong with my goals?"

"It's just that, you see, Jennifer is not a spiritual person." He said it off-handedly, as if I had doubted the color of grass and he was simply stating a basic fact in saying it was green. I wondered why an elder would make such a claim about a member of his congregation. *Is it really true that Jenni is not a spiritual person? Did Jenni call Oskar and tell him she was going to leave the religion and join an atheist movement? Why does Oskar feel qualified to make such a claim?*

While it was obvious that Jenni had not done as much in the organization as I had, there were good reasons for this. Most significantly, she was female. Try as she may, Jenni would never qualify to handle the microphones or be a ministerial servant for the simple reason that she lacked sufficient testosterone. The things she could do were all, at the present, insurmountably difficult given her shyness. After thinking the matter over, the best response I could come up with was: "Huh?"

"She's not." He repeated. "Jenni is not a spiritual person."

"So, are you saying I shouldn't date her?"

"I'm not telling you to do anything, I'm just making you aware, you see?"

"Okay."

"You seem to have all these goals, and I am just preparing you for the possibility that they might not come to pass."

Jenni walked up to us and said that her family was leaving. I shook Oskar's hand goodbye, careful to tighten my grip this time.

I asked Gabe to be roommates with Johnny and me, and though he didn't think he was ready to move out from his dad's house, he liked my idea of switching to a new congregation. He joined Wheelock that week, and at his very first meeting, he approached Luther Lawson, Wheelock's Theocratic Ministry School Overseer. Luther was a sharply dressed man in his midforties. His suits alternated between light green and mustard; his ties were impeccably knotted, his shoes polished to a blinding shine. He topped all this off with a meticulously trimmed thin moustache and a neatly cropped Afro subtly turning a distinguished gray.

Flanked by Jenni and Sarah, Gabe introduced himself and said that he wanted to join the Ministry School. Luther was glad to have a new member for the School and heartily welcomed Gabe. Ever the salesmen, Luther leaned in to Gabe and said: "I'll tell you what, you should get your shy friend here to join up, too."

Jenni had never been on the School, feeling that the sisters' role-playing talks were silly and demeaning to women. But standing there, with the pressure of the School Overseer, her sister, and Gabe, Jenni said, "I don't know."

Luther asked if there was anything he could do to convince her to join. Jenni was nervous to use the microphones, so she asked if it would be possible to only give talks in the second school.[45]

"You bet," Luther said, as if they were old pals.

Two weeks later, I moved into a duplex in the city. The night before my first meeting as a member of the Wheelock congregation, I sat alone in my new bedroom. I spent my last few waking minutes that night beseeching Jehovah, asking him to help me succeed in my new congregation and get along with the elders and other pioneers.

SECOND WHEELOCK

Within weeks, I noticed that service in Wheelock wasn't going to fulfill my dreams. The Bradleys, a young married couple joined Wheelock at the same time as I did. The husband, Melvin, was a Witness dynamo who reveled in doling out encouragement, and his smarmy, faux-sincerity was grating. Melvin wanted to swaddle the world and nurse it to Paradise. His wife, Lisa, meanwhile, had all the symptoms of a woman pregnant with Holy Spirit. One day, when I got back in the car after being yelled at by a householder for "not believing in Jesus," I sarcastically said: "Well, that was pleasant."

Melvin, who evidently had lived his entire life without coming across sarcasm, stared at me as if I had said the most blasphemous comment ever. Fancying himself to be the voice of wisdom, Melvin counseled: "You know, James, that man might be one of our brothers one day, so we need to watch what we say about him."

And when householders in quick succession lambasted me for "bothering people at their homes" and then for "not accepting the Trinity as holy truth," Melvin tried to offer consolation. "Brother Zimmerman, the longer you pioneer, the better it will get, and eventually you'll view the householders as potential brothers and sisters."

I asked: "So how long do you think I need to pioneer? One year? Two years?" Melvin quickly said no, and assured me that I would enjoy pioneering much sooner than that. I then told him I had already been pioneering for over three years. His jaw dropped and he stared at me with such intensity that I feared his eyeballs would spring out of their cavities. Melvin assumed that I had only begun pioneering that autumn, like Sarah and Gabe. Three years of pioneering meant that I had been pioneering longer than he had even been baptized.

Johnny planned initially to come home in late August, but he was forced to delay his plans as he had no funds for a plane ticket. This worried me, as

93

I assumed anyone unable to pay for a plane ticket would subsequently be unable to pay rent, but when I asked if he'd be able to pay first month's rent, Johnny said: "Don't worry, Jim, I'm good for it."

But Johnny didn't pay the first month's rent, because he was still in New York. Logan, our other roommate, and I each paid half the rent as opposed to our budgeted third. Logan used up what little savings he had in doing so, but even that left him twenty dollars short. He offered to sell me his *Star Trek* trading card set to make up the remainder. I accepted.

The solution to Johnny's airline ticket dilemma was a childhood friend who was getting married in late September. He wished Johnny to be one of his groomsmen. Knowing that Bethelites seldom have cash to pay for plane tickets and tuxedo rentals, he offered to buy Johnny a roundtrip ticket. Johnny told him to make it a one-way ticket. On September 22nd, Johnny arrived with little more than the clothes on his body. I could see in his face he was happy to be home. It wasn't Bethel, but Johnny and I would finally be roommates, working shoulder to shoulder in God's full-time ministry.

Johnny had no money for the last two weeks of September, a problem I rectified by telling him his first two weeks were rent-free—my gift to him for returning home. But as kind as I was about September, I was equally harsh about October. Johnny lacked employment. He made a few paltry attempts to find jobs, predominantly by contacting other Witnesses who worked in the trades.

Several days into October, Johnny still insisted he was "good for it." I yelled that he was not good for it, because his portion of the rent was already past due. I vented in fury at Johnny—he was not making money, nor was he using his time as an unemployed pioneer to get in his service time. If he couldn't pay rent, I felt he shouldn't have agreed to live with me. If he wasn't going to get a job, the least he could do was go out in service and accrue time. But he was timid in the new congregation and didn't know many people. He was reluctant to go out in service unless I was with him.

Socially, Johnny always insisted on being with me; he even sat by me at the meetings. At one point, I joked to Johnny that he should find a girlfriend to sit by instead, citing the fact that there were several comely young ladies in our new congregation. When Johnny asked if I had any suggestions, I jokingly pointed out Tonya. Johnny looked over at her and, nodding, readily admitted she had a great body. Bursting his bubble, I said: "Yeah, there's two things you should know about Tonya first. One, she's pregnant. And two, she's disfellowshipped." Then I patted him on the back. "Otherwise, go get 'er, cowboy!" Johnny looked at me half in anger, half in embarrassment. I was having a difficult time respecting Johnny.

A third of the way into the month, Johnny flabbergasted me by walking into my bedroom and slamming the rent money down on my dresser. From where he acquired the cash, I didn't care. I took it, thanked him, and reminded him that the next month's rent was due in twenty days.

When the talk schedule for the next month was posted at the Kingdom Hall, Jenni and I went up together and checked it out. I was pleased to see that I had three talks in the upcoming month. Jenni pointed to her name, the first time she had ever seen it in such a place, and I smiled. "You're first talk, that's great."

"No it's not. See where it is?" She pointed again.

Her talk was to be given in the main school.

"I thought you told Luther you only wanted to give talks in the second school."

"I did."

I stroked my chin in confusion. "Well then why did he put you down for the main school?"

"I don't know." I could hear the anger in her voice. I told Jenni I would talk to Luther and rectify the problem and, though she felt that would be embarrassing, I insisted.

In my old congregation, I knew the elders well and I would have felt comfortable broaching this subject with any of them. I hardly knew Luther. Elders are instructed to "use good judgment in making assignments,"[46] and I had no reason to believe that Luther willfully went against this counsel. Yet I could not think of an effective way to tell him he made a mistake and to request he fix it. I resolved to approach Luther humbly, but confidently, telling him he was in error and needed to adjust my girlfriend's scheduled talk.

After the next meeting, I walked up to Luther and held out my hand in a gesture of goodwill.

"Hello, Luther."

"Hey, Brother Zimmerman, how's my brother doing? What can I do for you?"

"Well," I cleared my throat, "you know how Jenni asked to be on the School recently?"

"Jenni Meissner? Sure."

"I don't know if you recall, but she asked to only have talks in the second school, and . . . you assigned her to give a talk in the main school in a few weeks."

Luther's face lit up with a big smile. "Oh man, is that the problem?" He was half laughing, and so I laughed too. For a brief moment I felt all was right. I had brought the matter to Luther's attention, and he now planned to remedy the matter.

That was a very brief moment. Luther followed up his lighthearted question by adding: "You just have Jenni come talk to me and I'll ease her mind."

Luther moved to walk on, but I persisted. "That's the thing, you see? Jenni's really shy, so she's too shy to approach you about it. That's why I'm telling you."

Luther's smile faded. "If she's not gonna talk to me, Brother Zimmerman, there's not much I can do to help her, is there?"

His comment was utter bullshit, primarily so because elders are supposed to seek out those that need assistance and encouragement, not the other way around. "She *did* talk to you, when she first agreed to join the school. That was a big moment for her, and she was nervous about doing it. All she asked was that you not give her talks on the main school."

"Brother Zimmerman, I can't be letting people join the school with all sorts of stipulations." He paused to see if I was going to respond. When I didn't, he added: "My job would be impossible if that were the case."

I shrugged. "This isn't everyone asking for all sorts of stipulations. This is one person asking for one favor. Half the talks are given in the second school anyways, so it shouldn't be so hard to assign Jenni second school talks exclusively."

He squeezed my arm as a substitute for shaking hands, and again prepared to walk away. "I'll see what I can do."

"What you can *do*," I said with all due sternness, "is let Jenni give her talk in the second school."

Luther upturned the corner of his mouth, as if he wasn't sure if he should yell at me or run for safety. Our eyes locked in a stare-down, until a smile again washed over Luther's face. "Alright Brother Zimmerman, I'll see what I can do." Not wanting to totally ruin my chances of friendship with Luther, I nodded in agreement. He walked on.

I continually rehashed the dialogue, wondering how it escalated from a simple request to a borderline-argument fraught with gumption. I kept wishing that Luther had been more understanding, as if willing would make it so. I could not reconcile the qualifications for eldership with his actions. Elders are often compared to loving shepherds who treat their flock tenderly, but justifying his actions proved paradoxical.

Weeks later, days before Jenni's talk, Luther approached me and asked if he and Dick "could have a word" with me.

Before they spoke one word, I felt certain they were going to counsel me on my aggressiveness. Surely, I figured, they would tell me that I spoke out of line, or that I acted disrespectful or inappropriate.

I was quite taken aback, therefore, when Dick said the nature of their concern was the way my friends sat together at the meetings.

"Our seating arrangement?" I asked, fully believing I was missing a key issue.

"Yes, James," Dick offered, helpfully, the glare of the fluorescent lights glinting off his receding hairline. "We've noticed that for the last some-odd weeks you and Jenni always sit by Sarah and Johnny."

I stared at Dick, and then looked at Luther, in the vain hope that one of them would explain themselves more fully. I had no clue how to tactfully tell them that I understood nothing they were telling me. "You guys know I'm dating Jenni . . ." I let my words hang, hoping one of them would jump in and tell me that everything had been a big misunderstanding. They just stared, waiting for me to finish. "And, so I like to sit by her . . . and I'm probably going to sit next to her at every meeting . . . from here on out."

Luther mercifully broke in: "Brother Zimmerman, what Dick and I are trying to say is, we're concerned with Johnny and Sarah."

I let out a small laugh. "I'm sorry, guys, I just don't get what the problem is here."

Dick put his hands in his pocket. "It looks bad."

"It looks *bad* that I sit with Johnny and Sarah?"

"It looks bad that Johnny and Sarah are sitting together."

Luther picked up where Dick left off: "We got ourselves a lot of young kids in this congregation. They're good kids. We love 'em. We want what's best for 'em. But, you know, a lot of them are at the age where they wanna be around the opposite sex, right?" He slapped me on the shoulder. "You been there, right? It's the same with these young ones. They look up to people like you and Gabe and Johnny, and so when they see people like Johnny and Sarah pairing off like that, they think it's cool if they pair off, too."

"Johnny and Sarah aren't paired off," I corrected. "They're not dating."

"That's what makes it look bad, you see? Other young brothers look at them and they think it's okay to just have fun with the opposite sex like that. They look at the people a little older than them, like Johnny, and they think to themselves, 'He's a strong brother and he's been to Bethel and he's pioneering and whatnot,' and then they think it's okay for them to sit with girls instead of their parents."

I nodded. I assured them that I would relay the information to Johnny and Sarah. They shook my hand and reminded me that I was a valuable member of the congregation.

Over lunch with Jenni, Sarah, and Johnny, I relayed the entire conversation. Their first response was wonder at how I was able to remain so calm and polite to Dick and Luther. I told them that I wanted to come across as obedient and humble. While Jenni and Sarah said it was ridiculous that Johnny couldn't sit by whomever he chose, Johnny was outright angry. He asserted that if any elder had anything to say about his behavior, then they should come to him.

"I'm a grown man," Johnny shouted, "Do they know that I'm twenty-one? I don't live with my parents anymore—heck, I was a Bethelite for fifteen months. I'm older than you, anyways," he said, pointing in my direction.

The more we talked, the more we agreed that the elders had acted immature, even rash. They had placed me in the unenviable position of having to instruct my friends as to how they should behave. Instead of enjoying lunch, I was an unsuspecting messenger speaking in defense of an arbitrary rule for which Dick and Luther provided no scriptural support. It was humiliating, Johnny said, to be told, secondhand, where and with whom he could sit at the meetings.

"I agree it's all petty crap," I said. "But what are you gonna do? The elders are imperfect, just like us. Sometimes they make us suffer for no good reason."

"I'm not suffering," Johnny replied, pointing to himself. "And I ain't gonna sit somewhere else."

"Come on Johnny," I moaned, "Just do it."

"Just do what? The elders never told *me* anything."

"Come on, man, can't you just sit somewhere else?" I pleaded. "Why make an issue of it?"

"Who should I sit with?"

"I don't know. Go sit with Gabe. Or just sit by yourself, for goodness' sake. You keep saying that you're an adult and that they should treat you like an adult. So, be a big boy and sit by yourself."

Johnny looked away. Appealing to his ego ended the argument. He agreed to sit elsewhere.

A few days later, I came home from work to discover Johnny and Sarah were now dating. My mouth gaped at the news; I had never pictured the two of them together. I kept hoping that Sarah and Gabe would get together. I couldn't really picture Johnny with any girl at the moment; his life was in such disarray. Johnny got the most important issue out of the way right away by telling me that he would now definitely be sitting by Sarah at the next meeting.

The best part of that meeting, though, was Jenni's very first talk. She was extremely nervous before the meeting and very serious. I was nervous for her—and as she got up to give her talk, I felt more nervous than I had for any of my own talks in years. She performed flawlessly. She never stumbled on her words and never lost her place in her manuscript. Most importantly, Jenni gave her talk in the second school. Just before the meeting, I noticed two arrows drawn in pencil on the master schedule: one arrow pointed to Jenni and the other pointed to the sister originally assigned to give the talk in the second school. The pencil marks were subtle, but their message was loud: Jenni and the other woman were to switch locations. When I saw that, I couldn't help but smile. It was one small victory.

Though Logan was able to pay rent each month, he seemed to have little money for other necessities. When it was Logan's turn to buy toilet paper, he stole a roll from his Kingdom Hall. It bothered my conscience to use purloined paper, so I bought my own and kept the rolls hidden in my closet. When his car broke down beyond repair, he came to me and requested a loan. He claimed he needed a car to get to work. If he couldn't get to work, he couldn't make any money, and then he couldn't pay rent.

My relationship with Johnny also grew increasingly strained. He seemed to concoct an excuse for everything: he couldn't get out in service enough because he had to make money. He couldn't make enough money because he had to go out in service. What little money he did have was snatched away into an unknown vortex of consumables. He tried negotiating his way out of paying a third of the rent, claiming that I should pay more because I had the nicest room.

One Friday Jenni went to work instead of joining me out in service. She didn't really want to go to work, but her boss had coerced her, telling her that they were short-staffed. I was mad at Jenni for foregoing our day out in service together just to go to work; I pointed out to her that by going to work on Friday, she was negating her entire reason for switching jobs in the first place, not to mention the rearrangement of my schedule to ensure I was free every Friday. Jenni profusely apologized, promising not to let it happen again.

With the notable absence of Jenni, the service group that morning was typical: Howie and his wife and four children, Sarah, Melvin and his wife Lisa, a woman named Lory, and Luther's wife Jackie. Howie organized us into car groups. He naturally desired to stay with his family, who filled up his van. With no vehicle among us that could comfortably fit six people, Howie split us into two groups of three each. The Bradleys would stay together and take one of the women, Lory, with them, while Sarah and I would stay together and take Jackie with us.

Jackie was visibly agitated, as if Howie had dumped fire ants down her blouse. She kept looking over at Lory – the only other married, middle-aged pioneer in the congregation – trying to get her attention. Lory paid no heed. So, huffing, Jackie raised her hand. "I was really hoping to work with Lory this morning," she said. Jackie didn't actually say that she had made arrangements with Lory, only that she wished to be with her. Sarah and I looked at each other with expressionless faces, knowing each what the other was thinking.

Howie reassigned Jackie to work with Lory with the Bradleys, leaving Sarah and me as a group of two. Sarah and I again exchanged glances, and Howie offered up prayer.

After the prayer, I walked up to Howie. "Hey," I asked him, "What are Sarah and I supposed to do?"

"Well, do you have some return visits or territory?" he said in his distinctive melancholy fashion.

"Yeah, but I mean, it's just us two—is that okay?"

Howie looked over my shoulder at Sarah, as if to ensure that she was the only other person in my group. "Aren't you picking up Jenni?"

"Jenni's not coming out in service today. She had to work."

"Oh, well usually you bring her with you on Fridays."

"She had to work today."

"Is there anyone else you can get to work with you?"

My gut reaction was to say, "How about you just rearrange the groups into a sensible fashion?" but the truth was, I didn't want to work with any of them. Judging from his resistance to shuffle around the car groups, I guessed he felt the same about me. "Kyle said he might want to come out with us today."

"Yeah, why don't you call Kyle and see what he says?"

"I'll do that."

I broke away from Howie. Sarah walked over and asked what was going on. I told her I'd tell her in a minute, but first I had to use the bathroom. As I pushed open the bathroom door, I heard Jackie behind me. She was wishing Sarah a good day out in service.

I went in to the bathroom stall and leaned against the wall. I stared at the fixtures and thought about the toilet paper Logan had stolen. I was trying to do the right thing by pioneering and encouraging others, like Sarah, to pioneer with me. I wished I could better understand God's grand purpose.

When all was quiet, I emerged from the bathroom. Sarah was sitting down, thumbing through a *Watchtower*. She turned to face me. "I can call my friend Raven and see if she wants to go out," she offered.

"Nah, I don't feel like it," I said, sounding spent. "I guess I'll take you home."

Sarah gathered up her coat and her books. For a few minutes, we were the only two people at the Kingdom Hall. A Witness man is not to be alone with a woman to whom he is not married. Yet here we were: alone, abandoned at the Hall by an elder.

That winter, Jeremy asked me to be a groomsman at his upcoming wedding. He selected four of his friends to serve as his groomsmen: Gabe, Logan, Johnny, and me.

Most Witnesses seemed happy for Jeremy, as if he was proceeding down the correct path. Bridgette was an abrasive woman, and Jenni and I disliked the way she bossed Jeremy around as if he was incapable of buttoning his shirt without her assistance. She wasn't a *bad* person; we generally enjoyed her company. Johnny and I agreed that her harsher, tomboyish demeanor complemented Jeremy's effeminate leanings. At one point, Johnny, half-joking, asked: "So what do you think would happen if I just walked up to Bridgette and told her Jeremy was gay?"

I laughed. "Johnny, that would only make her upset; obviously she knows Jeremy isn't going to win the testosterone-of-the-year award, but Jeremy certainly isn't gay. Why else," I reasoned, "would he be marrying a woman?"

"I guess if there was one thing that would keep Jeremy on the straight and narrow," Johnny said, laughing at his own words, "it would be having a woman alongside him in bed every night."

"That'd keep me hetero," I chuckled.

Jenni and Sarah constantly hounded me to say something to Bridgette. "You're his best friend," Jenni said, "You should tell him not to get married. Or at least tell Bridgette that he's gay."

"He's not gay!" I yelled.

"Jimmy, he *is* gay. Bridgette just doesn't know it. She must not have a gay-dar."

"If Jeremy is gay, maybe he's trying his best to fit in," I said. "Maybe this is his way of staying straight, you know, to please Jehovah. Maybe he figures that this is the best thing he can do. Besides, I'm not his best friend. Gabe is."

"Gabe thinks Jeremy is gay . . ."

"Yeah, and he's the best man. So if he doesn't feel the need to say anything, than I'm not going to, either. Maybe he should just be a confirmed bachelor, I don't know. But if I say something to Bridgette, like, 'Hey, Bridgette, your fiancé is gay,' then she'd just get mad at me. She'll yell at me and tell Jeremy, and then he'll get mad at me."

So, on the third Saturday of the new year, at three o'clock in the afternoon, I was standing in the back of a Kingdom Hall wearing a tuxedo. The chairs were full, and the audience was quiet. Gabe leaned forward and whispered in my ear: "This is your last chance to tell Bridgette he's gay."

"No deal," I whispered back.

A half hour later, as the officiating elder asked if anyone had just cause why Jeremy and Bridgette shouldn't wed, Gabe turned his head in my direction. He didn't alter his expression, he didn't clear his throat; he merely turned his head slowly, slightly, for my eyes' only. We had just cause—but we said nothing, preferring to let the marriage commence rather than admit the truth.

Jeremy's wedding day was a fleeting respite from the world of Wheelock. Every day brought new trials. If I wasn't arguing with my girlfriend about our impending wedding while straining my strength to remain chaste, I was arguing with my roommates about their deplorable lack of funds while trying to remain as their friend. Both situations might have been manageable if serving the congregation brought some solace, some comfort. I repeatedly prayed to God that he would help me to find joy in the ministry.

For a time, I turned to Gabe. Though young, Gabe was maturing quickly and he was able to carry his own weight. With Gabe, I didn't have to worry about anyone but myself. I didn't have to talk at all the householders' doors, I didn't need to be the one who always drove, and I didn't need to set the example for everyone; I could just be me.

Gabe came to my house early the following Monday. We planned to drive around, leaving magazines at the nearby laundromats but the mercury was huddled in the bottom of my outdoor thermometer and the wind was roaring through the cracks in the house. So we sat at the dining room table and began writing letters to people in security apartments. As nine o'clock approached, Gabe asked if we were just going to go out on our own, as we had done several times in the past month, but I was worried that Melvin or some other pioneer might catch us and realize that we didn't want to be out in service with him. Worse, they might report to the elders that we were not supporting the group. So we met up with the group like proper pioneers.

I called my dad that night and told him pioneering was making me depressed. He suggested I stop pioneering. Laying there, on my bed, half drunk, I couldn't contain my emotions. I started crying, saddened that the only way to stay happy was, it seemed, to discontinue pioneering.

"You don't even like doing it, buddy," he said empathetically. "Jehovah wants us to be happy serving Him, and listen to yourself—you don't sound happy at all."

I rolled over and sat up, as if to call upon a newfound resolve. "We're supposed to serve Him with all our soul and strength, and if I'm not pioneering, then I'm not doing that."

My dad reminded me that I needed to stay happy in my service to Jehovah. "Maybe this is a test, and Jehovah is trying to see how you'll react, and what do you think He's seeing right now?"

I didn't know the answer. The idea of abdicating my responsibilities as a pioneer had a certain appeal. But I had made a goal of pioneering for as long as I could. I was trying to encourage my shy girlfriend, and it was my hope that we would be able to, someday, pioneer as a married couple. In the meantime, I had agreed to help Sarah, Johnny, and Gabe. Quitting pioneering would let them all down. I couldn't picture my life without pioneering. I did not enjoy being with most of the pioneers; I disliked going door-to-door, hoping each time that the householder was not home, but I knew Jehovah would not judge me on how much enjoyment I derived, but on the effort I put forth. I was saving my own life. Surely, I could hack pioneering for a little while longer.

I asked my dad: "Do you think I should see a therapist?"

"A therapist?" he sounded shocked. "What for?"

"I was talking to Jenni about it. I guess I have trouble calming down about things, and I'm always anxious and depressed."

"Well, I'll tell you what. A lot of Witnesses don't like the idea of going to see a psychologist or whatever, but I say you should do whatever you need to do to get through these last days."

On Tuesday I malingered home and wrote letters. I went out in service on Wednesday and got stuck in a car group with Melvin Bradley. Melvin was in rare form, even for him. In an effort to generate some kind of interesting conversation, I asked if he'd seen any good movies lately. "Oh, there are no good movies," he informed me, "They're all just part of Satan's world."

That evening, during the meeting, an announcement was made saying that Gabe, along with Oskar and his wife, would be transferring to the Como congregation to assist there.

Instantly, I was crushed. Over the past year, Gabe had become my best friend. Gabe was my support, my confidant while out in service. He was an invaluable leader in the door-to-door work. I felt as if my legs were kicked out from under me. I also felt mad, for many reasons; among them: *why wasn't I asked to go to Como?* I didn't like Wheelock congregation, and a Circuit Overseer-sanctioned move to a new congregation would have afforded me a respectable way to get out.

When I griped to Gabe that I wished I had been asked to go, Gabe admitted that he wondered the same thing. He even asked the Circuit Overseer why he had been chosen to switch congregations instead of me, and was told that, as someone who was dating a girl from Wheelock, I was unlikely to move out of her congregation. "Wow, he really missed the mark on that one, Gabe; I would have left in a heartbeat."

I became more depressed. At the meetings, I had trouble feeling like I fit in, especially with Gabe gone. I enjoyed being with Jenni's family, but they themselves were treated like outsiders despite having been members of the Wheelock congregation for over twenty years.

As winter turned to spring, nothing seemed to be going right. Dating Jenni grew increasingly stressful. We argued constantly. One week I would be angry at her for needing to quit service early, the next week we argued about wedding plans, then we argued about where we were going to live once we got married. Above all, I felt frustrated at being unable to be with Jenni. I was mad that I was stuck trying to squeeze money out of Logan and Johnny's wallets in search of rent money, when my girlfriend lived just down the road. Jenni, living in her small house with her parents and two sisters, was eager to move out. It only made sense that we should pool our finances together and live together.

Neither Jenni nor I had insurance to pay for therapy visits, but Jenni discovered that, as very-low-income adults, we were eligible for a medical assistance program in our neighborhood. By signing up for this program, at the low price of twenty-five dollars a month, I was eligible to drone on about my life to a therapist once a week.

Sitting there in her office felt inappropriate, as if I was knowingly sinning. She was some years older than me, a short, sturdy woman with curly blonde hair. Wrinkled lines drew towards her eyes, pointing at what once had been pretty. A writing utensil was never far from her hand. She didn't sit behind a desk, but positioned her office chair facing mine with nothing in between. Her skirts were too short for my conscience.

I didn't know what to say. I spoke about my roommates and how they were barely able to cough up rent money. I told her of Logan's plan to get married before our lease was up. I told her about Johnny, and how he had to borrow money from me to pay for the current month's rent, and that I was nervous he wouldn't be able to pay for the upcoming month.

The therapist nodded and acted as if she cared, but the more I spoke, the more I got the feeling that my problems were nothing special—certainly nothing to see a therapist about. *So my roommate isn't paying rent? People have money troubles; they get into car accidents; they get fired from their jobs; they break their legs. These things happen. What is the point of telling her?*

During another session, she tried prying more deeply: "There's more bothering you than just that, though, isn't there?" I began to divulge how difficult a time I was having pioneering. Only the day before, I had gone out in service with Gabe in his new congregation. There were six of us in the car. Gabe sent the two sisters to a door. He sent two young brothers to another door, and then he and I got out of the car to work the other side of the street. As we began walking, though, Sister Triller came waving her arms and yelling to Gabe, her purse falling off her shoulder and her glasses sliding down her nose. "Brother Tomanek! It is *not* appropriate to send those two young boys together! Neither of them is baptized."[47] This was a completely ludicrous statement, substantiated by neither scripture nor Watchtower doctrine. I began laughing as she came towards us, surprised that a woman acting so inane could think she was being a good Witness. I stopped laughing, though, when I saw she was most serious and, further, that her actions caused Gabe embarrassment.

I did not know how to even begin explaining this to the therapist. How could I explain that Sister Triller, though the wife of an elder and half a century older than us, was actually supposed to be in subjection to Gabe? How could I explain why her ranting served to only turn off any householders that may have been watching from their windows, and how could I explain why that was important? How could I explain why such an amalgam of individuals was out knocking on people's doors in the first place?

Later, I tried telling her how frustrated I felt having a girlfriend and being unable to have sex with her. I told her that I felt like a mere conduit for hormones, a catalyst that turned thoughts about women into sperm. I felt guilty. Admission was like a sin in itself. She asked why my girlfriend and I did not have sex, and I told her it was a mutual decision in an effort to please God. She broached the option of masturbation, and I mentally exited the conversation, sickened that a professional such as herself suggested self-mutilation, as the Witnesses saw it. I nodded in agreement, pretending to listen, but inside I told myself I would just need to pray for more strength.

Such strength wasn't forthcoming that evening. Jenni and I stopped back at my place after going out for dinner, and we found ourselves in an empty home. I brought her in my room and, on cue, we embraced and kissed. The fight between doing more and not doing more was an intricate battle, and I took the liberty of sliding my hand down the back of her pants and gently squeezing her bottom. I threw her onto my bed, and she let out an *oomph* as she absorbed the impact of my weight against the mattress. I continued kissing her neck.

She stretched out from under me. "We're gonna get in trouble."

I dropped my head on the pillow. "Ugh. You're right. I can't stand it."

"Me either," she agreed, reaching up to put her hand on my face.

"I don't want to get in trouble."

We stayed motionless for ten minutes. We did not talk and we did not kiss. Laying on top of Jenni, listening to her breathing, I cursed the fabrics that separated our bodies, and I cursed my conscience for preventing me from doing anything about it. At the same time, I condemned my heart for leading me so close to sin, worried that God would not forgive me. Above, I heard moans and squeaks and a bedpost rubbing on the hardwood floor. The renter upstairs had brought home another woman.

During my next session, the therapist asked if I had taken her suggestion. "What do you mean?" I asked, hoping she'd say something—anything—other than the M-word. But say it she did. "No," I curtly answered, in a tone that let her know that discussing prurient practices was an affront to my morality. "I don't want to talk about it." She clicked her pen and wrote. I left early.

The next week, I came home to find a message waiting on my phone's answering machine from the landlord asking when Logan and I planned to send the rest of the month's rent. "You guys are ten days overdue," he said coldly, "and I don't know what this 'I owe you' notice is for. I need a check, not a note."

I ran to my room, opened my file cabinet and pulled out the lease agreement. According to contract, rent was due by the fifth. There was a fee for paying late, increasing each day. We were already in debt an extra fifty dollars on top of the rent that was past due.

I spent the evening at Jenni's house, and we talked the matter over. The more we thought about the situation, the more we realized there was no good way out. I could evict Johnny, but that would result in Logan and I having to pay more for rent. "Even if Logan agrees to that, though," Jenni said, "that still only solves the problem temporarily—Logan's getting married in June, remember, and he told you he's not paying for rent after that."

What irked me more was Johnny's covert behavior. "He must have been too ashamed to admit he didn't have the money." I told Jenni that I wished

Johnny would come home that evening and apologize for his debts, confess what he had done, and pay the money he owed. Jenni pointed out I was being delusional.

When we drove back to my place after dinner, Johnny's car was parked out front. "Come in with me," I said, "I want you here as a witness in case something goes bad."

We walked inside, I with the full bravado of a man ready for a fight. I swung the door open, allowing it to hit the wall. Johnny sat at the kitchen table, about to take the first bite of a peanut butter sandwich on white bread.

"Oh, hey Jim!" he said, nonchalantly.

"Hi Johnny." I said the words, but I didn't like the way his friendliness was so disarming. This was a time for serious discussion, not pleasantries. I crossed my arms and inflated my chest. Jenni walked in behind me and before Johnny could start in with the niceness to her, I spoke. "So when were you gonna tell me about this month's rent?"

Johnny looked up from his sandwich, his eyes moving from me to Jenni and then back to me. "What do you mean? It's taken care of."

"Oh, you mean you've paid for this month's rent?"

"Well no, but I plan on it."

"And you discussed this with the landlord, and he said it was just fine and dandy that you not pay him?"

"No," Johnny said, drawing out the word, "I'm not on the lease. I don't deal with the landlord; you and Logan do."

"So you talked the matter over with me and Logan, and we agreed to just paying part of the rent this month, is that what happened? Because I don't remember that."

"Okay, Jim, first of all, calm down. I gave Logan the I-owe-you notice, and he didn't care. He just took it and put it in the envelope with the check."

"Johnny—why didn't you have the money? Why don't you ever have money? I don't get it." I brought my hands to my head as if to pull out my hair. "Maybe you can enlighten me a little bit here. You make more money per hour than I do, you work more hours than I do, you have no bills apart from rent and electric, and you still don't have money. What's the deal?"

The next day, I called the landlord to cancel our lease. Though he took every opportunity to charge us various fees, he relented. Logan, Johnny, and I would have to be out of the duplex by noon on April thirtieth.

My roommates were more than eager to leave. By week's end, Logan had packed and moved in with his parents. Johnny, too, began sleeping alternately at the duplex and at his parents' home, depending on which was more convenient each night.

He stopped by the following week to pick up the last of his belongings. Tonya, no longer disfellowshipped, was with him. Her son had been born a month earlier and Johnny had spent the intervening weeks helping her with the baby at the meetings. Tonya helped carry Johnny's bags to his car. She set down her sleeping baby and scanned the duplex. "Looks like you guys had a cool place here."

"Yeah, we did," I answered. I wanted to add, "Too bad your boyfriend Johnny screwed us all over," but I didn't.

Three days later, I sat in silence on the one remaining dining room chair in the duplex. The electricity had already been disconnected, and the room darkened as the sun descended. I sat, looking out the window, and watched the geese flying overhead. I was still a member of Wheelock congregation, but now I would feel more alienated than ever. I would be living further from the Kingdom Hall than anyone else in the congregation. I finished the remaining beers in the fridge.

The next morning, I packed my car until it was so full I couldn't see out the back window. At 11:55, I removed the key from my key chain, dropped it on the floor, and locked myself out of the house. I set my camera on the car roof and took a picture of myself standing in the threshold. Then I got in my car, and drove back home.

JUST MARRIED

Jenni repeatedly recommended our wedding be a small affair. Her quiet, unassuming nature steered her towards the idea of a wedding with as few people as possible in attendance. She considered an outdoors wedding or a party room wherein the reception could commence on-site immediately thereafter. I summarily nixed these ideas. Family members alone would account for nearly one hundred in attendance, then there were our close friends, and all the people in Wheelock and Apple Valley congregations. Maybe a small wedding worked for her worldly relatives, but we were Witnesses and had a large circle of friends. A small wedding was out of the question, as was the option of a non-Kingdom Hall wedding. The blasphemous thought of turning down the privilege of being married in Jehovah's house served to convince me there was no other place to say our vows than in the Kingdom Hall.

I approached Dick one afternoon after the meeting to request usage of the Kingdom Hall for the wedding. He nodded as I spoke and said he knew I would be asking this question. He merely asked the date, verbally noting that it did not conflict with any other events. "Sure, that's fine," he said blandly. I was astounded how quickly he granted me permission.[48] For once, I was pleased with our conversation.

Jenni and I began planning our wedding in earnest. While at Jenni's house, her mom came and sat in the living room with us. She had a notepad and pen and she straightened her back in an effort to become more businesslike. "We need to talk about the flowers."

No one had yet said anything about flowers to me. I felt Jenni's mom was being presumptuous in assuming the role of decorations coordinator. I told her as much, stating that I saw no need to talk about flowers at this moment. She left the room holding back tears.

Jenni reprimanded me, but I fought back. "I didn't tell her to do the flowers, did I?"

"No, but I did," Jenni answered.

"You didn't ask me about it."

"Why? Do you have to know about everything?"

"It is my wedding!"

"It's my wedding, too."

"I'm the man, so I'm in charge. What if something goes wrong? If anything happens, it falls back on me—I could get in trouble for it."

"You're right, you are in charge. But that doesn't mean you can do everything, does it? At your job, your boss is in charge, but she doesn't do everything, does she?"

"I guess I just wished you would have talked to me about it first."

"I didn't think it would be that big of a deal."

"Okay, fine, I'm sorry."

In an effort to get a handle on exactly what was required of a groom-to-be, and to determine what was and was not acceptable at a Witness wedding, I combed through the Society's literature. One *Watchtower* issue featured two articles concerning weddings and receptions.[49] It mentioned that Christians are free to use a Kingdom Hall for their wedding as long as they obtain permission. The elders, the article says, "will not impose their personal tastes as to wedding arrangements." It also said that "only uplifting music, such as found in the songbook of Jehovah's Witnesses" is to be used and that "flowers or similar decorations should be modest and reasonable." I spoke with Rhett on the matter of music, and he agreed to find uplifting music Jenni and I could use. I asked if he would be able to write and record a musical score for us to use, and he said he'd think about it.

The second article concentrated on the matter of receptions. The article left no ambiguity as to who ultimately was held accountable for the reception:

> At a wedding reception the groom is the Scriptural head of the newly formed family (Ephesians 5:22, 23). Hence, while he lovingly ought to consider the wishes of his bride on this special day, and their families' wishes, he primarily needs to accept responsibility for what will go on and for what will not.

I was undoubtedly in charge. Even if people gave us money to use for the wedding, this did not give them the right to insist upon any detail of the wedding nor did it absolve me of my role as head of the gathering. I told Jenni that if anyone offered us money with the caveat that we do something their way, we would categorically refuse the offer.

The article also discussed the matter of invitees. Invitations, the article insisted, were important: Witness couples were under no compulsion to invite everyone in the congregation but instead needed to send them to specific people. We had to arrive at an exact number in attendance and allow only those who were invited to enter the reception.

As it turned out, most invitees were incapable of reading and correctly interpreting wedding invitations. Anything that could happen regarding invitations, did. Some invitees neglected to respond, but still showed up at the reception. Others did respond, but failed to attend. Worse, some replied saying the whole family was attending, when the invitation invited only the parents. Other people responded saying they would be coming with a guest. Such changes made planning very problematic. My grandpa recommended placing ushers at the door of the reception who would allow only invitees who affirmatively replied to enter the building.

After one meeting, when a group of sisters were talking about our upcoming wedding, one of them turned to Jenni's mom and said that she still hadn't received her invitation. This made her uncomfortable, to the point of tears, as she was forced to tell the woman she was not to be invited. While Jenni scolding me for creating circumstances that put her mother in such situations, I argued that it was the woman's cocky comment that had caused the awkward situation: "She was the one pompous enough to feel she deserved to be invited." She was the one acting against the counsel in the *Watchtower*.

Another sister sent back her RSVP claiming that her young son, a boy I had never met, would accompany her. I approached her one day after the meeting and, in accordance with the *Watchtower* article, informed her that my fiancée and I had a limited budget and were unable to make room at our reception for her son. She responded by saying that if her son was not invited, then she would not go without him. I told the sister that I would remove her from the guest list, and I thanked her for making room for others.

Dick Jacobs, meanwhile, made the presumptuous assumption that his children were welcome to attend the reception. So I did what any self-respecting young man would do: I asked my dad to call him.

A week later, Dick and Luther approached me after the meeting and asked if I could sit in the front row with them, where we could have some privacy.

Before saying anything of substance, Luther put his arm around me and shook me, thus showing the maximum amount of physical affection two heterosexual men are allowed to show. "We love you, man," he said, gesturing for emphasis.

"We want you to know that we think you're a valuable member of the congregation," Dick added, drolly. "We appreciate the work you do for us here."

This was a funny comment, as I had assumed the work I did was for Jehovah. Regardless, I accepted the compliment and nodded, thanking them.

"You're certainly a good speaker," Luther said, finally releasing his hand from my shoulder.

"Oh, yes, I've even learned a thing or two from your style of speaking," Dick said.

"Really? Wow. Thank you." I was genuinely impressed.

Then Dick, having finished the formulaic compliments, changed his tone. "Listen, we discussed the matter as a body of elders, and we feel there are some areas where you could use some improvement."

Dick chimed in. He asked if I wanted to know what they wanted me to work on. Since there was no other correct response, I told him I did.

Luther cited a grievance from Howie. Howie disliked how I showed up with my own group of friends every Friday at the meeting for service. "It's like you're trying to prove you have a lot of friends," Dick interjected. "It makes Howie think you don't want to work with the other brothers and sisters." He said it "makes it hard" for Howie to organize people into groups when I show up with "a whole buncha" people.

I was unsure how to respond. I explained that Howie himself showed up with his own group every Friday, notably by bringing in tow his wife and four children. Dick scratched his temple. "That's his family."

"Right," I said, "and I bring my family, too. Jenni is my fiancée, and Sarah is practically my sister-in-law."

"James, that's fine if you bring one or two people with you," Dick replied, "but I guess on a couple occasions you've shown up with a group of people you insisted on sticking with."

I attempted to explain myself. "Once when I was at a pioneer meeting, the Circuit Overseer suggested that we invite people out in service with us, to encourage them. He even said that if we have arrangements with some friends already, it makes it easier for the conductor to organize everyone. I know, speaking from personal experience, that I love it when twenty or thirty people show up for service and I'm conducting and they all already have arrangements. Then I don't have to worry about who to put with whom or who can drive."

Dick looked at Luther, and the two of them emitted tiny laughs. "Brother Zimmerman," Luther said, "Let me just say this: if you show up for the meeting for service ready and willing to work with whomever the conductor puts you with, that makes it easier. That's what we want. Okay?"

I shrugged.

"The one other thing," Dick said, "is more of a personal nature to me. I'd really appreciate it if you could show up on time for bookstudy."

I scratched my head, again not sure how to answer. His request struck me as incredibly pointless, as I had never once shown up for bookstudy late. Before I had the chance to point this out, he added: "I know what you're going to say, that you live far away. And I appreciate that you have to come from a long distance, but it would really help me out if you could show up on time."

"Actually, what I was going to say was that I don't think I've ever been late."

"Technically, yes, you do always get there one or maybe two minutes before we start, but you're my assistant, James. I need to know I can count on you to be there for me. So, when I don't see you until just before it starts, I get a little worried."

I again scratched my head, unable to shake the fact that his words sounded so stupid. *Why did he need to see me any earlier?* If he needed a brother to pray, or to read the paragraphs during bookstudy, it didn't necessarily have to be me. Any baptized man—and there were six in our bookstudy—was qualified. The only real duty an assistant bookstudy conductor possessed was to conduct the meeting in the event the elder could not be present. But in the rare case this should happen, the assistant should be made aware in plenty of time.

All I could do was accept the counsel. I asked Dick: "Is there some sort of ruling regarding the time I should show up, like five or ten minutes before it starts?"

"No, no. There's certainly no hard and fast rules. Just my preference,[50] but if you could be there, say, ten minutes before we begin, I'd appreciate it."

I smiled to signal I was willing to comply. "Okay. Done!" I thought about how easy it would be to fix these problems: I would immediately cease bringing friends out in service. And I would arrive conspicuously early at Dick's house for bookstudy each week.

I left the Kingdom Hall in a haze. Jenni had already gone home, so there was no one for me to talk with about what had just happened. I continually tried spinning the counsel in a positive direction, but I couldn't lose the nagging feeling that the elders' counsel was ultimately discouraging. If they had at least counseled me on something real, like my predilection towards anger, or my arrogance, that would have made sense. Though I wouldn't conscientiously admit it, Dick and Luther were wearing away at my faith. They were discouraging in the extreme. And yet, this wouldn't be the last time the three of us spoke together.

On the walk to my car, a teenager named Kyle ran up to me and asked if I was going out in service the next day. "Can I work with you? My dad keeps saying I need to go out in service more."

I set my book bag down and crossed my arms. I leaned on my car. "Listen, Kyle, I was just talking to Dick and Luther, and I guess they don't like that I bring a bunch of people out in service with me."

Kyle craned his neck, looking around for Dick or Luther as if their appearance would confirm my statement. "They said that?"

"Yeah," I said emphatically.

"Weird. Oh, hey man, no worries. I'll just sleep in tomorrow." And with that, Kyle ran back into the Hall.

Kyle called the next night asking for a ride to bookstudy. His dad had to go to work that morning, so he wouldn't be able to make it to bookstudy unless I could pick him up. I explained to Kyle that Dick insisted I show up for bookstudy earlier.

"Man," Kyle laughed, "they must think you need to work on a lot of stuff."

"I guess."

"I hope they never come tell me all the stuff I need to work on."

I laughed. I told Kyle that I would leave early to pick him up for bookstudy. "You better be ready and waiting when I pull up."

But Kyle wasn't waiting. When I arrived at his front stoop that morning, he was still sleeping. Though his brother managed to wake him up, Kyle said there was no way he'd be ready in time, so I should just go without him.

I got in my car and drove towards Dick's house. While waiting at a red light, the clock on the dashboard rolled over to nine-thirty.

I didn't bother going to bookstudy that morning.

I prayed to Jehovah about these events. I asked Him to help me to understand that the elders had my best interests at heart, and not to dwell on the discouragement they caused.

I talked to my therapist about the matter. She offered that I try to not put such an importance on doing everything I could in the religion. This, of course, was exactly what Satan would have said if he were standing in the room[51] and so I instantly disregarded such a blasphemous suggestion.

She reminded me that the elders were not perfect, and that they, too, were prone to making mistakes. I hated her for saying those things. Worse, I was giving a bad Witness, and for that I felt truly guilty. Nothing good was coming from my sessions with her. I was hindering her from ever accepting the Truth, and she was acting as a minion of the Devil by suggesting I not try so hard.

I never went back again.

Instead, I made a great effort to look for the positive aspects of being a Witness. For a few days, this worked out splendidly. The Xiongs, a family in the congregation, approached Jenni and me one evening after the meeting excited to talk about our wedding. They wanted to hold a wedding shower for us, which we agreed to with much happiness. The children, four of them ranging in age from five to fifteen, asked if there was anything they could do to help with our wedding. "That's so nice of you," Jenni said.

"Jenni, we *have* to give them something to do, that's so considerate," I added. I was enthused that a group of young kids with whom I rarely spoke cared enough to want to help with our wedding. My mind raced through all the matters we had to care for between now and the wedding day, and I hit upon an idea. We asked them if they would like to make a "Just Married" sign to hang from our car as we drove from the wedding to the reception. We were too busy to ever pursue this notion, but now, with these kids offering to do something, we gave them this task. They were delighted, as it both gave them a way to participate in our wedding plans and do something creative. We thanked them profusely and I left the meeting that night feeling good about my brothers and sisters.

But the good feeling was not to last.

Exactly one week later, Jenni was slated to take part in another talk. She was paired with Melvin's wife, Lisa. I arrived at the meeting with a big smile on my face, and kissed Jenni. "Are you all ready for your talk tonight?"

"It's gonna be upstairs." She sounded dejected.

"What do you mean? You're scheduled to be in the second school."

Jenni explained that Lisa had called earlier to say that they would be giving their talk in the main school.

"Why the sudden change?"

"Whoever was supposed to give the talk in the main school cancelled," Jenni said. Canceling at the last minute was a common occurrence in Wheelock, but this was the first time that such a last-minute rearrangement had affected my fiancée.

"I'm sure Luther just forgot that you're Lisa's householder," I said. "I'll go talk to him."

"No, don't. He won't care."

I scowled. Her words hit me like acid on the face. "Come on, Jenni. He *will* care. You know I already talked to him about this once so I'm sure he remembers that you don't give talks in the main school."

"No," she sternly ordered. "I said don't talk to him. Just forget about it. I'll do the stupid talk," her angry words came with a thud of finality.

Things got worse before they got better. Lisa came up and asked Jenni if she wanted to go into the back room and rehearse the talk once more. When Jenni returned, she was white with anxiety. I asked her what was wrong, and she told me that Lisa wanted them to stand up while giving the talk to make it more authentic.

During the first fifteen minutes of the meeting, Jenni kept playing with her hands and biting her lips, fidgeting and agitated and not knowing how to keep her composure. I put my arm around her. "You'll do a good job. Just think: you are making Jehovah very proud of you."

"I'm still nervous, though."

I licked my lips, bracing myself for what I was about to say. "Just say the word and you won't have to give the talk."

"What do you mean?"

"I mean, just say you don't want to give the talk and I'll go tell Luther you are not going to be Lisa's householder."

Jenni looked into my eyes. "Don't do that."

"Why not?"

"Just don't, okay? Luther already doesn't like me."

"So you're gonna give this talk?"

"Yes!" she practically yelled. "But I'm not doing this again."

During her talk, the nervousness in Jenni's voice was indisputable, but she made no mistakes. Lisa tried to give the talk a conversational quality, but Jenni read right from her cue cards. Considering this was only her fourth talk, I felt she was making outstanding progress.

Nevertheless, she had whispered a forceful statement. I committed myself to making her statement come true. After the meeting, I once again walked up to Luther, who was busy packing up his family's books into his enormous briefcase.

"Hey Luther," I began.

"Brother Zimmerman! How you doing, man?"

"Listen, I wanted to talk to you about Jenni's talk she had tonight."

"She sure did a swell job. I was just saying to my wife that a few more talks like that and she'll be an old pro in no time."

I gave a gratuitous laugh, and thanked him on Jenni's behalf. I put my hands in my pockets and stared at the top of his balding head while I waited for him to finished loading his bag. When he looked up at me, he smiled and asked if there was something more.

"I want to request that you take Jenni off the school."

He gave me a look of incredulity. "Come now, brother Zimmerman, you don't really mean that."

"It's not up to me. It's up to Jenni. She doesn't want to give talks in the main school, and you don't seem capable of complying with that request." My eyes locked Luther's and we exchanged no words for two seconds while he assessed my tone.

"She didn't give a talk in the main school tonight; she was just the householder."

"It's the same thing. She's just too nervous to be on the main school right now, and it doesn't matter if she's giving the talk or if she's *just* the house-holder—she's still up on stage."

"Brother Zimmerman, you explain to your girl that I had no choice tonight. I tried to do what she wanted, but the speaker in the main school cancelled on me, you see?"

"I just feel bad because Jenni is trying really hard and I feel like she keeps getting dumped on."

"I see."

"Actually, I feel like her whole family kind of gets ignored. It's kind of sad, you know?"

"Well, Brother Zimmerman, sometimes people have to put themselves in the forefront of the congregation, see?"

No, I didn't see. In fact, I didn't understand his logic in the least. Jesus said he would not extinguish the "flaxen wick"—those who were of a quieter disposition.[52] I wondered what, exactly, was meant by "being in the forefront of the congregation"? Jenni's father was a ministerial servant. Her sister was a regular pioneer, and Jenni was auxiliary pioneering. What more was needed to be considered "in the forefront"? I did not ask. Instead, I said: "I know what you mean, it's just that some people aren't really cut out for public speaking. I give Jenni a lot of credit for trying, but it was really tough for her to give a talk in the main school tonight."

Luther held out his hands as if asking for mercy. "What would you have liked me to do in that situation, Brother Zimmerman?"

"In my old congregation, whenever someone wouldn't show up or would cancel at the last minute, the School Overseer would ask for volunteers. That way, there would still be a complete school and some of the more experienced speakers would have a chance to challenge themselves by preparing a talk on short notice."

Luther stared at me with his mouth agape, and then broke into his trademark laughter. His smile caused a crease to form on each side of his chin, and his mouth took on the appearance of a ventriloquist's dummy. He put his hand on my shoulder. "You know, brother Zimmerman, that is a good idea. I just may start doing that." He patted my arm. "And don't you worry about that girl of yours. She'll come around in due time."

As it was, there were plenty of other things to worry about. Summer arrived at full speed, and soon there were less than one hundred days until our wedding. Jenni and I continued to spar over the plans. We argued over invitations, how to address them, when to send them in the mail. I kept trying to assert my headship in all matters pertaining to the wedding and reception, and kept finding that it was not working as smoothly as I expected.

My parents assisted with some details, but they were distracted by their disintegrating marriage. Their marriage had never fully recovered from years ago. Things had changed. There were no family dinners. My parents acted more like roommates than spouses; they were always doing things apart from one another. One evening, while I sat at the dining room table eating a sandwich my mom fixed for me, she asked if it felt good to be living with the family again. There was no other answer I could give her than *yes*, but in reality, we just didn't seem like one family anymore. It wasn't one family; it was four people.

I worried about my sister. She stayed home from the meetings occasionally, and she wasn't going out in service as often as a good Witness should. She was openly dating Kyle. She frequently joined me at Wheelock's meetings so that she could visit with Kyle, and the two of them stayed up late on the phone every night. I was appalled that my parents showed no concern.

When the Xiong children presented us with the end result of their labors, they were excited and elated. They brought the sign right into the Kingdom Hall and I held it up to take a closer look. It was larger than I'd anticipated. It was made out of wood, painted white, and decorated with flowers in the colors of our wedding. The words were painted in an ornate scroll fashion. It read: "James & Jennifer just got married." There was a hole drilled in the top corners so that we could run rope through and affix it to our car.

We were duly impressed. Jenni thanked them all for doing such a fantastic job. I nodded in agreement. Their mom stood behind them and she beamed with pride as she told us how hard the kids worked at it, and how they were so excited to have done it. "You guys did such a great job," I said, "That was so nice of you." And I meant it, too. Being on the receiving end of such a selfless act of love bolstered my faith and made me feel good about the congregation.

For about a week.

As was our custom, Jenni and I were standing around before the meeting one day when Dick approached. He shook my hand and asked if we had a few minutes to talk after the meeting.

"Luther and I just want to go over a few things about using the Hall for your wedding."

I was relieved the topic would be so benign. "That's fine."

Following the meeting, we watched as people filed out. Sarah asked if we wanted to go out for lunch, but we told her we had to stay and meet with the elders.

She crinkled her nose. "They meet with you a lot, Jimmy."

"I'm beginning to think that, too."

Finally, Dick walked up and asked if we still had a few minutes, as if we had a choice. He directed us into the basement.

Uncomfortable moments ensued. Dick sat across the table and the three of us engaged in nervous banter. He asked how our wedding plans were going. "Fine," I said. I kept looking over at the doorway wishing that Luther would walk in so that we could proceed. When at last he did, he was bumbling and harried, simultaneously complaining and apologizing for his tardiness. He sat down next to Dick and his moustache parted like curtains to reveal a big smile. "How y'all doing?"

We answered quickly, talking over each other.

Dick sat up, straitened his jacket and adopted a pedagogic tone. "James, Jenni," he began, "I'm sure you're both eager to know why we asked you to meet with us here—and we do appreciate you two taking this time to do so."

"Yes, we do," Luther interjected.

"We need to address some things concerning your upcoming wedding. You know, you requested to use this Kingdom Hall for your wedding." My eyes widened, awaiting him to finish his sentence. I wished I could press a button and fast-forward to the end of his sentence. My heart began lashing against my ribs.

". . . and that's okay with us. But we've heard some rumors that we need to clear up here." He looked at Luther before divulging the details. Luther nodded, indicating his approval. Dick arched his back and cleared his throat; he wasn't in any hurry to continue. When the pause began to border on the farcical, he forced himself to continue: "The problem we're having is twofold. First, we've heard rumors that you guys are planning on recording your own music for the wedding ceremony. That's just not appropriate. And second, we heard gossip that you two are planning on having a 'just married' sign hanging from your limousine. Is that true?" He exhaled noisily when he finished speaking, as if the words left him breathless.

I looked at Jenni, then at Dick and Luther. "I thought it was okay if we used whatever music we wanted to, as long as it was uplifting."

Dick squeezed his eyebrows together and looked upwards as if the reply was written on the ceiling tiles. "I guess that's the problem, you know? How can we determine what's uplifting and what's not?"

"I would think that most people would consider classical music to be uplifting," I said. "We're not gonna walk down the aisle to Led Zeppelin." I laughed at my own joke.

Dick didn't laugh. "Maybe most people would be fine with classical music, who knows? Can you be sure that no one will be offended by that music?" Before I could answer, he added: "We think it's just best to stick with music from the Society. That way there's no chance of anyone getting offended. I'm sure you guys wouldn't want that on your hands, would you?"

Jenni shook her head no. I copied her.

Luther jumped in and addressed the second concern: "Now what's this about a 'just married' sign and a limo? Is that true?"

I cleared my throat. "I don't know where that rumor came from, but we're not having a limo."

Dick and Luther looked at each other. "You're not?" Luther asked.

I held up my hand as if giving an oath. "I give you my word: we are not going to have a limo." Then, just to put the matter to rest, I added: "I mean, we thought about getting a limo. Jenni called some limo companies, but they all were too expensive. We thought it would be a waste of money, so we decided not to go with it."

Dick wiped his hand over his face, and brought the death to all reasonableness. "But you *are* planning on having a 'just married' sign, right?"

"It's not going to be on a limo."

Dick raised his eyebrows and cocked his head to the side. "Listen, we don't want to tell you guys what to do, but we want you to consider how that will look to other people."

I folded my arms. I didn't know what to say. I didn't understand what his problem was. Saying nothing, Jenni and I waited for Dick to explain.

He licked his lips. "It just wouldn't be appropriate."

I unfolded my arms and put my hands in my lap. I looked at my hands and I remembered a few days earlier when I'd held the 'just married' sign. I thought about how happy I was—how moved—that someone had shown such a thoughtful gesture. It was such a kind, sincere, Christian gesture. To not use the sign was to slap those children in their faces. I stayed looking down at my hands for many seconds. I was afraid to look at Jenni, lest I cry. I wanted to look at her and tell her that these men were trying to ruin our wedding and that they had no right. I wanted to, at least, yell at the elders for only telling us this now, long after Dick had impetuously agreed to let us use the Kingdom Hall and weeks after we'd mailed out the invitations. But I knew Jenni respected them. They were God's appointed servants—shepherds to watch over His flock.[53] They were balsam in Gilead.

I was afraid to look at them. My state of emotion was balanced between sadness and anger, and a look into their eyes would tip the scale in favor of the latter. I drew in the stale air and let it out slowly, hoping it would slow the sweltering furnace that was my heart. In the second it took me to raise my head upright I dreamed that I was transformed. I became, not a weak, nervous, scrawny boy, but a thing from another world: a thing with wings and talons and fiery eyes and strong muscles. I became an archaeopteryx, a resurrected demon from the Jurassic, who came breaking through the window as if it were tissue, and swept into the room and screeched across the table till at last I grabbed the throats of Dick and Luther—one with each claw—and allowed the momentum of my flight to flail them onto the floor. As they lay there, with blood oozing out from their tracheas and down betwixt my talons, I would speak: *Is this the fruitage wrought from God's own house? Is this love?*

Is this balsam in Gilead?

Instead, I looked them full in the eyes. With an eerie coldness, I said: "I have read all the Society's information concerning weddings and receptions, and there is nothing about 'just married' signs in any of the literature."

Dick snapped his head back like a viper ready to attack. He looked at Luther and cleared his throat. "There's nothing *wrong* with a 'just married' sign, per se, but worldly people driving by might see the sign and it would give a bad witness. At each congregation, the elders have to make decisions between what they feel is acceptable and what's not and here in Wheelock, that's our view on the matter."[54]

Luther jumped in. "We need to make sure we're always giving a good Witness, that we're setting an example. If you go ahead and have that sign hanging from your limo or car, now what do you think people are gonna think when they drive by? We don't want to be making a showy display, do we?"

Luther's comment reeked of ignorance. The vehicle would be waiting for us in the carport, facing the road head-on such that no one would be able to see the sign from the road. While other drivers would see the sign on the highway, this could hardly be considered a showy display and, further, we would no longer be on Kingdom Hall property. Even if someone did see the sign and think to themselves: "Good Lord! That is an abomination against all that is holy!" they would be unaware that we were Witnesses and would be unable to assign their indignation to any religion specifically.

I was disgusted by their counsel, their opinion. I could not respect them. They were wasting my time. I pulled out my pocket knife and began picking the pebbles out of my shoe. After sulking for a few moments, I said: "Last year, I was at a wedding at this very Hall, and that bride and groom had a red carpet rolled out and got into a limo. If a limo was okay last year, why isn't a regular car with a small sign hanging from it okay now?"

The theocratic duo looked at each other and laughed nervously. Dick put his hands on the table. "Whose wedding was that?" Dick's amnesic pretense was insulting. He himself had performed that wedding ceremony with every elder in the congregation present. "He means Jason and Vanessa's wedding," Jenni answered.

"Oh right. James, you're a ministerial servant. As such, you have an added responsibility. As you well know, many of the young kids in this congregation look up to you, and you need to set a good example for them. They see that you're pioneering and that you have all these privileges in the congregation, and they think to themselves that they want to be just like you."

Luther leaned forward. "Those young boys that Dick is talking about, they look at what you older guys are doing and if they see you doing something questionable, they're gonna say: 'Hey, why can't I do that?' So maybe you can ask yourself if you're okay with that, brother Zimmerman."

Dick continued: "We know it's a lot to think about, and we know you guys are already busy with wedding things. We'd just hate for you to do something and later look back on it and regret it, okay?"

"Okay," we both said.

"Again, we're not telling you what to do. We're just throwing out some suggestions, and we'll let you make the final decision. It's your wedding."

I nodded ruefully. I had already made my decision.

Jenni hopped in my car, and we left the Kingdom Hall without a chaperone. I waved to Luther as I drove past, "So long, loser," I said, confident he couldn't hear me through the window. We turned out of the parking lot and sped off down the road.

"That sucked," Jenni said.

"Why, what sucked about it?" I asked, curious to hear her answer.

"The whole thing," she said, acting deplored that I asked. "You were acting like a rebellious teenager the way you were sitting there leaning back like that and cleaning out the bottom of your shoes. I don't think they liked your attitude."

"I didn't like *their* attitude."

Jenni brushed her hand in the air. "Anyways, what are we gonna do now?"

"What do you mean, 'what are we gonna do?'"

"About the music! And the sign! The Xiongs made it for us, and now we can't use it, it makes me feel bad," she sounded crestfallen.

"As far as the music goes, what they said was so stupid. There is not one thing in the *Watchtower* that says we have to use Watchtower music."

"The elders will get mad at us if we use worldly music." She crossed her arms.

"We weren't even gonna go with 'worldly' music. The last time I talked to Rhett, he said he'd already composed some stuff for us."

Jenni furrowed her brow. "Why didn't you tell that to Dick and Luther?"

"They wouldn't listen! They couldn't care less. We'll just walk down to whatever music happens to be in the tape deck at that moment."

"What about the 'just married' sign? I guess we can't use that, either."

I turned to look Jenni in the eyes. "Oh, yes," I said definitively, "*that* we are going to use."

"Huh?" she snapped her head back in surprise. "The elders just told us not to."

"They said they would leave it up to us to decide. I decided that I'm gonna use the sign."

Jenni brushed aside my cocky resolution. "They said that people driving by would see the sign and know that there was a wedding going on."

"Even if we didn't have a sign hanging from a car, they would still drive by and see us out taking pictures. Don't you think they'll see you in a long, flowing gown, and a bunch of girls in fancy dresses and guys in tuxedoes with top hats? I think that might tip them off that there's a wedding going on at the Kingdom Hall. Who even cares if they know there's a wedding? It's not like they're gonna drive by and think, 'Oh no, those crazy Witnesses actually get married!'"

"But you'll get in trouble."

"Maybe," I said, carelessly. "If I get in trouble, then Dick and Luther were lying when they said it was our decision. Besides, they said it was their opinion and I don't give a rat's ass what Dick and Luther's opinion is about anything. Dick's an ass."

"Don't say that!" Jenni shook her head, disturbed by my impiety.

"He *is*, Jenni. I don't care. He's an ass, and if I want to hear from an ass, I'll fart."

"Whatever." Jenni turned away. She crossed her arms and looked out the window. "We can't use the sign."

"Jenni, we are going to use the sign and that's final. I'm the man; I'm the one who makes the final decisions and the final decision is that we use the 'just married' sign. Period. If the elders talk to you about it, just say that it was my decision and you had to obey because I'm your head. Anyways, they won't be able to get mad at us because we're not staying in Wheelock."

"What?"

"You heard me."

"You're just saying that because you're mad."

"I'm serious. We're going to a different congregation."

"Just like that? That's it, we're gonna switch halls right now and start going somewhere else?"

I had suspected Jenni would try to talk me out of changing halls, but I refused to budge. While sitting in the room with those elders, the thought was planted in my brain. Once I considered the prospect of exiting the congregation, I felt a boundless relief. My nerves calmed, and I realized that it was something I needed to do to continue serving Jehovah faithfully. As my dad had said, the important thing is that we just get through this old world. If switching congregations was what I needed to do for the spiritual welfare of myself and my new family, then so be it. I considered Jenni's question: "Let's stay here in Wheelock until we get married. There's too much else going on right now with the wedding, and we don't even know where we're gonna live yet."

"But I thought we were gonna pioneer together here in Wheelock."

"Well, we were, but this place flat-out sucks. I tried to make it work. I wanted it to work. I prayed to Jehovah all the time to help me make it work, but it didn't. So either He doesn't care about me or He doesn't want me here in Wheelock."

"What about pioneering together?"

I tried to sound reasonable. "We can still do that; it doesn't matter what congregation we're in. A different hall would probably be better, actually."

"For you, maybe."

"What's that supposed to mean?"

"This is my congregation," she said sincerely. "This is where I've gone my whole life. This is where I feel comfortable and these are the people I know. This is where my family goes."

I ignored her. "Let me tell you some other things about your wonderful congregation. This is the congregation where elders counsel you because your friend is sitting with a girl he's not dating. This is where Dick tells me that showing up three minutes before bookstudy is not early enough. This is where Johnny goes—you know, the guy who owes me, I mean *us*, hundreds of dollars. This is where debutante Jackie laughed when she first heard you were dating, and where Dick and Gina told Ryan you weren't spiritual. Even Oskar said that about you. I don't know what's so special to you about these people, but I say goodbye!"

"Don't I get a say in it?"

"Fine, what do you say?"

Jenni turned toward the window. She drew a breath. "I guess it's fine. I've never looked at this congregation as an outsider before, 'cause I've been in it my whole life. If you think we should go somewhere else, then we can." She looked at me. "What congregation are we gonna go to?"

"I haven't figured that out yet. This is still new to me, too. We have a few weeks yet to decide."

On the phone that night, I told Jenni that the best option was for us to attend my old congregation. She balked at the decision, complaining: "Didn't the elders hassle you there? That's why you wanted to leave."

"At least when they saw how stupid they were for not letting my cousin come out in service with me, they apologized. I don't see Dick or Luther apologizing for their arbitrary rules."

"Fine, we'll go to your stupid old congregation." She made no effort to conceal the anger in her voice. "I don't think I have a choice, do I?"

I considered her question, not sure how to form a palatable response. "We'll just stay there for like a year or two while we figure out a better place to go, alright?"

"Fine."

I didn't bother attending the meeting that Sunday, even though I was scheduled as chairman. Jenni later scolded me for leaving her in a bad predicament. Luther approached her to ask if I was sick and Jenni had to confess that she didn't know where I was. Luther asked her if I knew that I was scheduled to be the chairman, and Jenni said she wasn't sure. "Why weren't you there?" she asked, "I spent the whole meeting worrying that you got into an accident."

"I just didn't feel like it."

"Is that how you are now? Are you just gonna miss meetings whenever?"

"No," I whined. "Meetings are supposed to be encouraging, right? I just don't think it would have been very encouraging for me to be with those elders."

"Johnny came and talked to me too," Jenni said, ignoring my whining. "He told me he'd heard rumors that he was not going to be the best man in our wedding. I thought you had already told him that," Jenni yelled, "So I didn't know what to tell him."

"What did you say?"

"I told him he should talk to you about it."

"What'd he say?"

"He just felt bad. He thought he was going to be the best man. I think he was planning on using you as his best man, but now I don't know."

This further upset me. From the time we moved out of the duplex, I had written Johnny off as a friend, and the fact that I was using him as a grooms-man at all was, I felt, sufficient.

I planned to speak with Johnny at the next meeting, but Sarah inter-cepted me at the door with gossip to share: Johnny and Tonya had moved the date of their wedding to a point much closer to the present. Instead of December, they opted for their wedding to take place one week after Jenni and I wed. The congregation's attention would be divided between our two weddings. I grieved for Jenni; my shy, quiet girlfriend couldn't even get a moment in the spotlight when it was her own wedding—surely the more popular and extroverted Tonya would overshadow Jenni and win all the attention.

I did not speak with Johnny at that meeting. Or at the next one. Incensed with his flagrant callousness, I couldn't bring myself to even say hello to him for weeks. When finally we were in each other's company at a restaurant one evening, the tension escalated to flashpoint, and I asked him to step out into a nearby causeway to speak in private. For nearly an hour, I berated him on his financial incompetence, reminding him of the money he owed me. I called him selfish and stupid. He answered that I was a tough person to talk to, and that his priorities were different than mine.

I told him how hurt I was that he scheduled his wedding for a week after mine. He claimed that there was no reason to wait to get married. As Tonya already had a child, he wanted to become a father to Riley as quickly as possible. I told him that was respectable, but that there was no reason he couldn't start acting like Riley's father now. Before he could say anything in retort, I launched into another torrent of paroxysms. "You're rushing into it like you do everything else—not counting the cost or stopping for even a moment to think about all the ramifications."

"If you want to think that, Jim, there's nothing I can say to change your mind."

"It's not about changing my mind. It's about the wedding date. Even if we forget about the reasons for getting married—whether it has to do with Riley or being horny or whatever—the point is it still would have been nice if you could have shown some respect to Jenni and me, as your friends, and given us August. Why couldn't you just wait until September or October to get married? Heck, Jenni and I have been engaged longer than you two have even known each other, and we just got engaged five months ago!"

Johnny repeated his earlier statement that we were different people—different men with different needs and different ways of handling life. He put his hands in his pockets. "Maybe we just have entirely different ways of living our lives."

Johnny sat down on a bench and we talked about our relationship since his return from New York. The gradual revelation was that Johnny wasn't my friend anymore. There was no reason to hate him, but at the same time, neither of us cared to be in the other's company. Continuing as his friend was increasingly trialsome, and he said as much about me, too.

When our conversation abated, there was silence. I scrunched my face, perceiving that the words themselves would cause pain. "I don't think you should be a groomsman in my wedding. We're obviously not friends anymore. We can barely even stand each other."

Johnny just shrugged his shoulders. "That's your choice, Jim."

I stared at him for a second. "Okay, then, you're not a groomsman."

"Okay." He got up to leave. "Don't expect to be a groomsman in my wedding, either."

"I won't."

At work the next day, I told Gabe the story of what happened between Johnny and me. I had obtained Gabe a job at the store and in between helping customers and preaching to our co-workers, we gossiped. "I suppose he'll have you as a groomsman, anyways," I said.

"Nope."

I looked at Gabe, unsure if I'd heard him correctly. "Didn't he call you and ask you to be in his wedding?"

Gabe shoved his hands in his pockets. "I turned him down."

"Just like that?"

"Yeah, I think he was surprised I said no. He was like, 'Oh, really, that's too bad.' Then he said something about me being one of his best friends. I laughed at him 'cause I don't know how he can think I'm his best friend when we haven't done anything together in months. He said he was busy spending time with Tonya and planning for their wedding, but I said: 'Yeah, but James and Jenni are busy getting ready for their wedding, and they do stuff with me all the time—they need me as a chaperone!'"

"Great, now Johnny's gonna hate me even more," I said to Gabe.

I asked him how the conversation ended, and he informed me that Johnny simply said he hoped to at least see Gabe at the wedding, but Gabe told him he had to work that day.

"I have to work that day, too." We laughed, and I reminded Gabe that Jeremy was working that day, too.

That evening, Johnny came into the store. I had not expected his visit. I looked at Gabe, who gestured that he didn't know why Johnny was here. Gabe approached Johnny and greeted him cordially. I watched from a distance, trying to ascertain all I could from their body language. Their mannerisms were polite, yet coldly formal. Their friendship had noticeably mellowed. They exchanged few words, and then Johnny came towards me. Gabe stood back and gave me a *he's all yours* signal.

I sat on a stool behind the counter. Johnny closed the gap between us and sat across from me.

"Are you here to buy some glasses?" I asked.

Johnny chuckled good-naturedly. He put his elbows on the table, clasped his hands, and then, in all seriousness, whispered: "Jim, I want you to tell me how much money I owe you. Every cent. I don't care what it's for or how long ago it was, just give me a total."

I knew the exact amount, to the penny. But I did not want to just spew out a number. "I have it all written down at home, but I could probably figure it out."

I rose from the stool and grabbed some scratch paper. I detailed the various debts so that Johnny could see I was not cheating him:

March rent: $208.25
April rent: $208.25
Late fee (for paying April's rent late): $75
Damage deposit: $30
TOTAL: $521.50

I presented the itemization to Johnny. He glanced at the paper and immediately leaned over to retrieve his wallet out of his back pocket. He said nothing. I looked around nervously. Gabe was busy with a customer. I looked back down at the money and watched as Johnny slapped down various denominations until the pile totaled 520 dollars. He dug through the remaining bills in his wallet. "I don't have any ones. Do you have change?"

I pulled out my wallet. It was empty. "Uh, no, no I don't."

"What about the cash register?"

"I can't open it unless I make a sale." We stared at each other. "That's okay, it doesn't matter. This is good. It's fine."

But Johnny spread his billfold open again and thumbed through the bills until he came to a five dollar bill. "Here."

"Okay, I'll get you change next time I see you."

He held up his hand. "Don't worry about it. Consider it interest."

I thanked him, and, in search of something to say, I told him it would be put to good use.

Johnny nodded and stood up. He put his wallet back in his pocket. "If you get home tonight and find I owe you any more, let me know. I want to make sure I don't owe you anything at all. I mean it, Jim, I'm good for it."

"I believe you," I said. And, for the first time, I did.

He said good-bye. He turned and waved to Gabe, still dealing with a customer. Then Jonathan Kamber—my former roommate, pioneer partner, and best friend—walked out of the store. I pulled the cash out of my pocket and thumbed through it. I took out my wallet and placed the money inside. The wallet strained as I folded it.

525 dollars: the price of a friendship.

I began my wedding day as any good Witness should. I woke at six-thirty. I drove around town stopping at laundromats and leaving the latest copies of the *Watchtower*. By nine o'clock, I had been driving around for two hours, which bumped my hours for the service year from 998 to 1,000. For the fourth consecutive year, I had succeeded in achieving the goal, with eight days to spare.

Three hours later, I was with Jenni and her bridesmaids taking refuge in the Kingdom Hall's basement. The guests were arriving upstairs. The feeling of nervousness filled the area. I put my arm around my fiancée. "It's going to be okay."

"I know," she said.

My sister blurted out that she wished there was some wine to pass around. She pegged me as the spoilsport, because, in fact, I was. The idea of consuming liquor prior to a spiritual occasion was against my judgment.

At three o'clock, I kissed Jenni, told her I loved her very much and not to be so nervous. Then I left her in the basement with her father as I walked up the stairs, jostling in between the bridesmaids and groomsmen who populated the staircase.

When at last the bland, generic music commenced, I marched up the aisle. When my feet met up with the tiny 'X' on the floor, I spun in place to watch and wait while seven sets of our friends came up the aisle.

Finally, Jenni demurely walked down the aisle, and in between flash bulbs, I saw how truly gorgeous she was. The dress, borrowed from her grandmother, exuded a stately, classic, elegant allure, and I reveled in the way it curved in and out to make way for her body. I thought about how she had gone through the trouble of looking so radiant, so picturesque on this day, complete with a veil, and pins in her hair, and laces on her shoes, and all manner of clasps securing the gown to her delicate frame. Smiling wide,

I held out my hand. She took it, and we turned to face my grandfather at the lectern.

I was never quite clear on the purpose of the wedding talk. Most people in the audience had heard this same talk at so many weddings that they knew it verbatim. If the idea of the talk was to remind the bride and groom of their responsibilities as marriage mates, well, it was lost on me—I was too nervous to concentrate, though I did hear my grandpa note that this was the second most important day of our lives.

He fully conveyed to us the solemnity of the day. We met with him twice before to share scriptures and assure him our courtship was honorable. He requested a list of our bridesmaids and groomsmen and telephoned their elders to confirm they, too, were upstanding servants of Jehovah. Before leaving his home a few weeks earlier, he drew me close and hugged me tightly, complimenting me on carrying out a clean, Christian engagement. "It demonstrates your love for Jehovah and Momma," he said deeply, looking down into my eyes.

Jenni and I held hands for much of the ceremony, but as the talk went on, we instinctively let go to minimize the sweating in our palms. My neck choked under the tight collar and my fingers swelled from the heat. My feet felt as if they had been smashed with a sledge hammer. I wiggled my toes to make sure they were still functional members of my body.

As the arches in my feet collapsed, I wondered why my grandpa had chosen this day to set a new record in public speaking marathons. I had specifically asked him to keep the ceremony short. When he reminded me that he had to cover all the material in the outline, I requested that he just read the outline word-for-word and then get on with the vows. He disliked this suggestion. Standing there fully immersed in my own wedding, I could not be sure if the talk was proceeding slowly in reality, or if my nerves made me perceive the talk in telescoped time. I had attended Witness weddings where the wedding party sits down so as to not have to stand during the ceremony marathon. Though sitting down during one's wedding looks as stupid as it sounds, at that moment, at my own wedding, I began to understand why wedding parties chose to sit.

"James, repeat after me," my grandpa bellowed, snapping me back to coherence. "'I James Daniel Zimmerman, take you, Jennifer Faye Meissner . . .'"

Jenni and I faced each other and, holding hands, I repeated after my grandpa. Then I recited all fifty-one words of the vow without being prompted. The audience laughed, but considering my upbringing, reciting the vows verbatim was not such an amazing feat. I had sat through many, many weddings.

There was tension in Jenni's voice as she repeated the vows into a microphone. As always, her performance in public speaking was flawless, and her extreme nervousness unwarranted. We looked into each other's eyes, and as she spoke the final word, I thought about how she would never ever again say another word into Wheelock's microphone.

My grandpa next noted that the rings were an outward symbol that I was an owner, and my bride was owned. After the prayer, my grandpa pronounced us husband and wife, averring, "What God has yoked together, let no man put apart." I lifted Jenni's veil and we kissed our first guilt-free kiss. We turned to face our friends and family. I looked at Jenni, and we smiled. We were blinded by camera flashes. The elder-sanctioned, non-Rhett, soulless muzak resumed playback.

We walked down the aisle. As we rounded the corner past the last row of seats, I reached down and scooped Jenni off of her feet. Everyone turned to see us. Some laughed and some clapped. I wasn't sure if such a brazen action was acceptable under the sanctimonious guise of the Wheelock elders, but riding on an overdose of testosterone and adrenaline, I couldn't have cared less. For a vanishing blissful moment in time, I forgot about the present and thought about how amazing it was that I now had a wife. I carried Jenni outside into the sunny late-summer day.

It was then that we saw before us a sight we had not expected to see. Pulling into the carport was not my grandparents' car. I set Jenni down onto her feet and gaped at the shiny white vehicle slowing to a halt. "Oh my goodness."

"We get to ride in a limo!" my new wife exclaimed.

A sparkling, pampered, luxury vehicle—with a tuxedoed chauffer in a top hat—rolled to a stop under the carport. *Crap. I had planned on surreptitiously sneaking the 'just married' sign onto the back of my grandparents' car. But now, here's a limo—and I specifically gave the elders my word that we were not going to have a limo. They are going to assume I lied to them. They are going to be very mad.*

But I said nothing. This was our wedding day, and I didn't want to saddle the bliss with words of worry. So I wore a smile and I kissed my bride, and we lived in our special moment.

The chauffer came around to open the doors. My dad and Sarah, who hadn't been far behind, exited the Hall. Sarah hugged and congratulated us. My dad did likewise, and said: "Are you surprised by the limo, buddy?"

"Ah . . . yeah. I'm . . . quite surprised." And then, nearly forgetting my manners, I added: "Did you get this for us?"

"No. Your grandparents did."

"What about the 'just married' sign?" I asked amid a fluster of activity. Gabe overheard me and ducked back into the Hall. He emerged moments later with the contraband. He handed it to Rhett, who was standing near the limo. Rhett looked at it for a second, unsure what to do with it. My friend Brian, who I'd originally asked to drive Jenni and me to the reception, grabbed it. He asked the chauffer to open the trunk, and he hung the wooden sign in its place of honor.

The chauffer looked displeased. "That's not gonna scratch my car, is it?"

"No, it's fine," I laughed. "*You* don't have anything to worry about."

Jenni and I and several members of the wedding party entered the limo. We popped the champagne and turned on the radio and the air conditioning. I kissed my wife. "How do you feel?" Sarah asked her sister.

"I'm Jennifer Zimmerman now," she said, still overwhelmed by what she had just done. She held out her champagne flute. "I need more to drink."

We soon arrived at the reception hall, where I had the task of ensuring nothing transpired that would cause reproach upon Jehovah or His Organization. To that end, I stationed two ushers at the door, armed with the guest list, to verify the attendees. One family of guests showed up with someone Jennifer and I had never met, and so the ushers came and asked me if it would be alright to let her in. This was a tough decision, because refusing to let her in would mean refusing to let in the family with whom she came—and *they* were invited, and *they* had meals reserved for them. Since so many who said they would come had proven hypocritical in this regard, I allowed the uninvited person to enter. This happened repeatedly throughout the night.

Jennifer's brother Lester came up to us with his girlfriend in tow. He grinned and nudged me on the arm. "I bet I know what's on your mind, James."

I smiled uncomfortably. "Yeah . . . you probably do."

Les leaned into Jennifer's ear, and I hoped to God he wasn't scaring her with thoughts of ravenous, sex-hungry husbands on their wedding night. I waited impatiently to be let in on their clandestine whisperings. Finally, Jennifer said: "Les says we have to take his gift with us tonight."

"I thought we were going to have my dad pack up all the gifts and open them when we got back."

"Yeah," she agreed, "but Les says that we might want to take his gift with us."

I looked at Lester with a bit of disgust. He was sneering like the devil trying to win my soul. He winked. My eyes widened. "What did you get us?"

Les roared with laughter. "Oh, you'll find out. It's stuff you need. Trust me."

I looked back at Jennifer and she sheepishly smiled. *Worldly people are so disgusting.*

While Jennifer talked with her worldly family, Johnny approached me. I had not spoken with Johnny since he paid off his debt. He offered his congratulations. I feared he would yell at me for not using him as a groomsman. Instead, he was gracious, and he joked with me as we had done so often when we were teenagers.

"Isn't it kind of weird?" he asked.

"Isn't what weird?"

"You know—that you can, um, do *it* now."

I laughed. "Well, yes. Yes. I think it's really strange."

"One minute you're, like, forbidden to even touch, and then you just say a few words and sign a sheet of paper and then nothing's off limits."

I thought for a moment and then I agreed, saying: "There's nothing else like that, you know? We can't smoke, but no matter what, we can never smoke regardless of who we are or how old we are. But sex—one day it's the forbidden fruit, and the next day they're like: 'Hey, it's cool with us.'"

Johnny snorted in laughter, and nearly choked on his fruit punch. He looked out among the crowd and saw Tonya standing up from her chair. "Hey man, I wish you the best."

"Thanks," I told him. He sauntered back over to his fiancée. It would be more than four years before I would speak to Johnny again.

Around eleven o'clock, all the good Witnesses, who needed to get home in time to get a decent night's sleep before Sunday's meeting, filed out. Jennifer and I said good-bye to the friends and family who remained to clean up, and then exited the building. I unlocked the doors of my rusted Oldsmobile— *our* rusty Oldsmobile—then ran around to the passenger side to open the door for my new wife.

As we drove down the freeway, Jennifer admitted she was glad it was over. "I'm never doing that again."

"I hope not," I laughed.

We held hands, and I felt a great weight lifted in that we no longer needed to worry about being seen alone in a car. Now, as a married couple, we were *expected* to be alone together. We continued down the road. We had told no one where we were going. We rolled down the windows, and soaked in the cool night breeze. The night air was invigorating. I breathed purposefully and it brought life to my tired soul. The stars were washed out by highway lamps, but the half-moon followed along beside us. The 'just married' sign dangled from our trunk.

After we checked in to the hotel, when the elevator opened on our floor, I picked up my wife and carried her down the hallway. We laughed as I tried holding her in my arms while fumbling to open the door. I left Jennifer in the room while I ran back downstairs to fetch our luggage, including the gift from her brother. When I returned, I wasted no time in secluding myself in the bathroom and striping off the hot, sticky, uncomfortable tuxedo. I reveled in the fun of throwing the suit into a clump on the bathroom floor; for once not having to worry about placing my suit on a proper hanger.

Jennifer lay on the bed, her head propped up on a number of pillows. Her unlaced boots sat in a dilapidated pile in the corner. Her feet were splayed out in front, mercifully recovering from the day's demands. She wiggled her toes.

I jumped onto the bed next to my wife of eight hours. I sidled up next to her and slid one hand onto the small of her back. I laid my other hand on her stomach, softly caressing the fabric of her gown. We zoned out at the television screen for a few relaxing minutes: an amalgam of talk shows, infomercials, and movies from the cinematic dust bin. I felt myself relaxing not just from the busy day, but from a supremely stressful year. I moved my hand back and forth, softly petting her belly. My hand rose and fell in rhythm to her breathing, and I loved the way the gown conformed to her feminine shape. Then I allowed my hand to migrate north.

And we got to *know* each other in the biblical sense of the word.

INTERLUDE

> Has one found a good wife?
> One has found a good thing.
>
> —Proverbs 18:22

W e returned from our honeymoon four days later, and for the first time Jennifer saw the place where she would be living as a married woman. "It's small," she acknowledged, but it was larger than she'd anticipated. We stayed up late into the evening sitting on the floor of our unfurnished living room opening up gift after gift from friends and family.

Jennifer fawned over a set of monogrammed towels. "I'm gonna go hang these up in the bathroom right now." They were burgundy, with stitching of black—a large, scrolling Z flanked by two smaller Js. "But don't use them," she ordered.

"What's the point of towels I can't use?"

"They're just to look nice." She folded the towels and patted them softly so all the fibers pointed the same direction. "They'll make our little apartment look classier."

For a few days, all seemed right with life. The anxieties and pressures of our wedding and Wheelock became irrelevant.

I came to feel remorseful. I knew I had been too inflexible with everyone, most of all Jennifer. I should have allowed her more latitude in planning the wedding. I felt guilty for asserting myself so brashly, so unapologetically. I thought of the petty arguments I instigated, and of how difficult I had made our lives. I wished I could go back in time and do it over. I wanted to tell Jennifer that a small wedding would have been cozier; more romantic. I thought about the beach on our honeymoon, where I had buried her legs in the sand, and I thought about how romantically beautiful it would have been to have said our vows there on the shore. We should have invited only our relatives and closest friends. We should have picnicked in the park, with the cool breeze blowing off the water. We should have had the wedding and reception right there in one place. We wouldn't have had to worry about Dick and the other elders making their arbitrary rules. We could have just

135

been among the people we really cared for, and then left for the night with the 'just married' sign hanging from our car.

I regretted how I treated Johnny. His debts, his wedding, his failure as a pioneer: those were unsatisfactory reasons to reject his friendship. I should have tried calmly reasoning with him, instead of yelling at him and ejecting him from my wedding and my life.

I wondered why the change had come over me. I wondered why, now, I felt so different about how I had carried myself in the months leading up to the wedding—why, now, when it was all in the past, was I finally capable of putting things in perspective? Things that, only days earlier, had seemed so significant, were now wholly unimportant.

Jennifer noticed that I was calmer. She said I had "settled down" and had become easier to converse with. I started to divulge my guilt regarding my outrageous behavior, but I didn't want to embarrass myself. I didn't want the discussion to end up with Jennifer saying: "See, I told you so; I told you that you were unreasonable." Mostly, I didn't want to say as much because I did not want to admit that, in following the Watchtower's guidelines, I had erred.

It was the Watchtower Society that wrote the articles that gave me license to lord it over my fiancée. It was the elders, acting on behalf of the Society, who had caused so much frustration regarding the music and the 'just married' sign. Most notable, it was the Society that dictated dating couples should always have chaperones and that they must not be intimate until after their wedding day.

For months—years—Jennifer and I had had need of chaperones. There was always the hassle of finding a dutiful friend. There was the stress of making sure our chaperone didn't feel left out. There was the pervasive threat that the chaperone would find our hand-holding or kissing offensive, and report back to the elders. On the many occasions when Jennifer and I went off without a chaperone, there was the omnipresent fear that we would be spotted by other Witnesses who might be offended. And there was the overarching worry that we would commit a sin. No kiss, no touch, was ever enough to satisfy my drive, and I became frustrated. This frustration, in turn, was diffused as anger.

Blasphemously, I entertained the notion that if Jennifer and I had been allowed to spend time alone without need of a chaperone or threat of punishment, our time as engaged lovers would have proceeded far more smoothly. I also wished that two people, in love, who had committed themselves to each other, would be allowed to have sex. I was mad at the Organization for forcing lovers to resist their natural urges, while simultaneously expecting them to remain calm when planning the most stressful event of their lives. But I quickly whisked these crazy notions to a dark corner in my brain.

On the sixth day of our marriage, we went to the meeting. I insisted we go, against Jennifer's protests. She wanted to wait another week, contending that we were still on our honeymoon, but I dismissed her argument as lazy and unspiritual. "As head of this new family," I commanded, "I say we go to the meeting."

A few members of the congregation came up and offered congratulations. Sarah and her friend Raven were excited that we were now a married couple; Sarah declared she was tired of being our chaperone and tired of our arguing about the wedding. She gossiped about Johnny and Tonya's upcoming wedding. I looked around for Johnny, but he was not there.

Luther approached me and handed me the assignment sheet for September. "Welcome back, Brother Zimmerman." He gave a hearty smile, "You're a married man, now, eh?" He pointed to the sheet of paper and beamed: "And we got you workin' right away!"

I looked at the paper. I was assigned to give two talks in the next three weeks. I had requested not to have any talks in September, as I wished to get adjusted to my new bride and my new home. The elders had either forgotten, or just didn't care. Luther must have also forgotten about Jennifer; he had her scheduled to give a talk four weeks hence. "I got your wife on there, too," he added, sounding proud. I smiled when I saw Jennifer's name written, for the first time, as "Jennifer Zimmerman." I looked at Luther and said, "Okay, great," and folded the paper into my pocket.

During the meeting, I showed Jennifer the paper. She asked what we were going to do now that we both had talk assignments. "Do you wanna stay another month?"

"No way," I said. "We're outta here."

"They'll be mad at you for leaving without any notice, especially when they gave you talks."

I whispered back: "I told them not to give me any assignments in September. It's their fault for being such idiots."

Afterward, I asked Dick for a minute of his time. My heart raced. I had prepared for this moment for two months, yet it remained an uneasy task. I took a fast breath. "I just want to let you know that Jennifer and I are leaving this congregation."

He cocked his head in surprise and asked where we planned on moving to. I explained that our new apartment was in Apple Valley, and so we would be attending my old congregation. I wanted to tell him that my new residence mattered little in this decision; we would be leaving Wheelock even if we lived across the street, but in my new calmer state, this seemed unnecessarily harsh.

"Do you have a date set?" he asked.

"What do you mean?"

"When's your last meeting? Do you know?"

"Oh, yes." I nodded. "Tonight was our last meeting. In fact, the only reason we came here tonight was so I could tell you this."

"I see." He folded his arms and looked at the floor. "Luther gave you and your wife some talks, though." He looked back into my eyes. "Don't you want to stay to fulfill your duties?"

"First of all," I began, trying not to sound acrimonious, "I told Luther not to give Jennifer any more talks. She specifically asked to not give talks in the main school, and Luther is incapable of complying with that. So I don't know why he assigned her a talk—she's not even in the school anymore. Second, I asked you and Luther not to give me any assignments in August or September because I would be too busy with the wedding stuff. You even gave me a talk in August, and I did it anyways, 'cause I wanted to do the right thing, but I'm not gonna be here in September, so I can*not* do those talks."

Dick diverted his glance around the room, trying to summon a response. "James, the problem is, we can't pick and choose when we're going to be needed by Jehovah. Now, you're a ministerial servant. That means we need you. We need you to help us out, and we tried to do what you asked, but we had to give you a couple talks, because we need the help. Think of it as Jehovah asking you to do something."

I spoke without pausing to check my temerity. "I don't think that's the case at all. In biblical times, the Israelite men had to serve in the military, but when they got married, they were exempted for *one year*."[55] I paused and licked my lips. "I wasn't asking for a whole year off—just two months."

Dick allowed the corner of his mouth to upturn just a little. "Okay. So this is your last meeting then?"

"Yes. It is."

He stuck out his hand as a peace offering and we shook on the matter. "Well, I thank you for all your hard work here in Wheelock."

I thanked him for saying so, and we parted company.

Two days later, our new life began in routine. Jennifer pulled out her camera and took a picture of me leaving for work for the first time as a married man. Meanwhile, fifteen miles north, Johnny and Tonya were wed in an outdoor ceremony officiated by Dick. Sarah visited our apartment the next day, claiming it was "so beautiful." She said the highlight of the evening was when Tonya danced on a table and lip-synced to Aretha Franklin's "Respect." During one part of the act, she reached down her gown, pulled out a wad of cash, and threw it at Johnny's face.

I couldn't help but wonder why it was deemed appropriate for Tonya to get up on a table, sing a worldly song, and extract money from between her breasts. *Didn't Dick worry that the neighbors might peek out their windows and see the blasphemous dancing? Didn't that give a bad Witness?*

But Wheelock was in the past. It was a bad decision, an unfortunate mistake. I tried to pack away the negativity, the discouragement, and the nitpicking. Instead of dwelling on the pessimism and inconsistency that plagued the past year, it was time to face frontward. The new service year was nigh, and I was excited at the prospect of having my wife as my pioneer partner.

Jennifer didn't believe she was ready to pioneer; she was afraid she wasn't outgoing enough or as well-versed in the scriptures as a pioneer should be. I gave Jennifer my word that I would help her; that I would do whatever I could to facilitate her career as a pioneer. She was still hesitant. In what became our first argument as a married couple, I yelled at her for having second thoughts. I reminded her that we had carefully prepared for the day when we would be able to serve Jehovah as fellow pioneers. Now the day had arrived and I was sick to my stomach that she doubted herself.

"Jehovah will help you be a good pioneer," I assured her, half pleading and half yelling.

What was the point of our scrupulous money saving, I asked her, and the way we arranged our affairs so as to live off one part-time income, if not to pioneer?

"What'll we do if we don't? Will we just sit around the apartment all day?" I asked. "And what if Armageddon comes in January or February? What then? What'll we tell Jehovah? Will we say, 'Oh, we had the perfect circumstances to pioneer, but we just decided not to?'"

Jennifer rationalized that there was no reason why I couldn't continue pioneering, and that she had every intention of joining me once she felt comfortable. I countered that our marriage would look ridiculous to the other Witnesses—was I to go out in service all day and then to work all evening, while my wife languished at home and watched television? I asked her why she needed more time to prepare. Two years ago, she was just an average Witness going door-to-door for eight to ten hours a month. Then, we began going out in service together every Friday and she was routinely reporting twenty-five to thirty hours a month. In April and May, she auxiliary pioneered. "If that's not easing your way into pioneering," I said, condescendingly, "I don't know what is."

I promised Jennifer that we would always be together as we went door-to-door. I pledged that I would knock on every door and talk to every householder, if that be her desire.

The pioneer application sat on our kitchen counter for weeks. Jennifer was incessantly apprehensive, and I was continually insistent. "I just don't think I know the Bible well enough to be a pioneer," she argued one morning as I again tried forcing her to sign the application.

I rolled my eyes. "That's not important. Jehovah will help us—he'll help *you*. As long as you have the desire to pioneer, Jehovah will make it possible for you."

"He's not gonna make me magically know everything in the Bible."

"When you go door-to-door, most people aren't even home, right? And if they are home, they'll cut you off before you even say hello. In the rare case that someone does let you get through your presentation, you just leave them the latest *Watchtower*. If they ask any tough questions, just tell them you'll do the research and get back to them. I've had to do that a couple times; there's no shame in that."

Jennifer harrumphed. "I still feel bad that I've never even read the Bible all the way through."

I told her that this was something we would correct. At the next meeting, we walked up to the literature counter and requested large-print editions of the *New World Translation of the Holy Scriptures*. The following evening, we sat together on our futon, and began taking turns reading aloud.

THE DEATH OF ASSEMBLY BOY

> If Noah was a mythical figure and a global flood a fable, the warnings of Peter and Jesus for those living in the last days would be meaningless.
>
> — *The Watchtower*, June 1, 2008, p. 8

We made good pioneer partners. I loved waking up in the morning and driving to the meeting for service with Jennifer next to me. We tried our best to maximize our time; we stopped at laundromats on the way home to drop off *Watchtowers* and when the group broke for lunch, we brought our notebooks into the restaurant and wrote letters.

One day, a sister in our car group asked why we wrote letters during lunch. I told her we had a limited amount of time to get in our thousand hours, and so we wanted to maximize that time. She was unmoved. "Instead of trying to count your time, you should just make sure you make your time count." This rationale was an easy way for a lazy person to excuse themselves from giving all their time to Jehovah. I argued that, as a pioneer, the goal set before me was to attain a thousand hours. "If the goal was to place a thousand *Watchtowers*, or conduct a hundred Bible studies, then that is what I would do." But the Watchtower Society equated giving one's all to Jehovah with the number of hours spent preaching. As such, I was compelled to *count my time* over *making my time count*.

In short order this became challenging. We were exceptionally disciplined in all matters financial, and Jennifer was a skilled budgeter, but I balked at Jennifer's brazen, flagrant disregard for our finances when she came home from a department store one evening having squandered $22.68. I asked her what was so important that she felt it necessary to spend such a sum, and she told me we needed a rack for drying dishes, she wanted a nightlight for the bathroom and a rug for the bathroom, and that we needed a cheese grater. I told her we got along just fine without such indulgences. I was afraid that such carefree spending would soon result in enormous debt and an inability to continue pioneering. She explained that there are some things that are needed—or, at the very least, *wanted*—if our home was to be comfortable and livable. I told her there was no need for comfort now; that sort of luxury could wait until the Paradise. She claimed that she had a good handle on the budget. She knew we could afford the things she purchased, and she felt such spending was acceptable. If we were unable to put any money into our savings account just this once, she claimed there was no cause for worry.

After that, I relaxed my views on spending, but I tried to make sure we continued operating in the thriftiest manner possible. Jennifer suggested we shop at secondhand stores for clothing and kitchen goods. I was apprehensive about this, as many Witnesses were fearful that such merchandise may be demonized from prior owners who dabbled in the occult, but Jennifer reasoned that even new merchandise may have been made at a factory with demonic predilections.

Part of our money-saving plan was for Jennifer to find a part-time job. Such jobs proved scarce. There were part-time options at fast food eateries and local stores, but Jennifer didn't want to deal with the public. Soon, though, a Witness family in our congregation asked if Jennifer would babysit their children. She accepted. The job was once a week, and not much money, but it helped. I also augmented my hours at work; closer to 30 a week, up from 20. I was still employed as an apprentice optician and greatly wished to be promoted to certified optician, as this would have meant higher pay. Unfortunately, being busy as a pioneer meant I lacked the time to invest in the studying and test-taking required for the promotion.

Still, I was proud of our control over our money. Many in the congregation expressed how impressed they were that we were able to provide for ourselves while regular pioneering. Other Witnesses marveled that we got by with neither checking account nor credit card.

A month into our marriage, Jennifer and I spent a quiet evening in our little apartment. Jennifer sat on the bed reading a book, while I was in the living room, sprawled out on the floor organizing my research papers. Our pet parakeets sat on my shoulders, chirping in my ears.

The phone rang. The birds scattered.

"Evening, James," I heard on the other line. "This is Dick Jacobs."

"Hi," I answered, friendly but confused as to why he was calling me. We had, in my estimation, amicably severed ties for the foreseeable future.

Dick demonstrated his consistency in ignoring the usual social niceties and went right on to tell me Luther Lawson was also on the phone, and that he would be listening in on our conversation.

"Hi, Luther," I said, trying to diffuse an increasingly uncomfortable moment.

Luther tried to make small talk by asking how married life was "treating" me, but Dick maneuvered the conversation back to his agenda. He reminded me of the policy wherein when a Witness, or Witness family, moves to a new congregation, the elders from the previous congregation are expected to send a letter to the new congregation's elders. "I am aware of that practice," I said dully.

There are several reasons for sending this letter. The reason that is almost always given, that of introducing the new members, is also the less important reason. I never liked the idea of the letter, because it hampered any chance at a first impression a new person may want to give. Beneath this camouflage, however, the primary reason for the letter is to air any grievances the former congregation may have against the Witnesses.

I felt my soul being stomped on. My legs lost their power, and I reached for a dining room chair. Another aspect of these letters is that they are not shared with the person who is the subject of the letter. The elders from the former congregation send the letter to the new congregation's elders, who then read it and file it in a clandestine cabinet. The only exception is if an elder or ministerial servant leaves a congregation, and the elders judge that that person should not continue as an elder or a ministerial servant. Then the elders read them the letter.

Dick commenced reading the letter, and my heart began to beat rapidly. I was shaking, and I had to keep switching the telephone receiver from one ear to the next because my hands were unbearably sweaty.

The letter began by stating that its purpose was to introduce James and Jennifer Zimmerman. (An innocuous, but bizarre beginning, as the elders who would be receiving the letter already knew me far better than the elders who were sending the letter.)

Dick read the next paragraph, which discussed Jennifer. It said that she would make a fine addition to the congregation *despite her quiet nature* and that, *with some coaching*, she may come out of her shell and be willing to participate more.

Dick, assuredly the letter's author, then read that I had served the congregation well as a pioneer and that I was an encouragement to many of the youths in the congregation. Then came the word *nevertheless*.

In his trademark monotone, Dick condemned me via the letter. It said that I was "presumptuous," that I had my "own agenda" and that I was difficult to get along with. The letter concluded that they could not recommend me for the position of ministerial servant.

When Dick finished reading the letter, he asked if I had anything I wished to say. Lamely, I told them that the only people I did not get along with were the two of them, and their wives. I added that there were quite a few people in Wheelock who were difficult to get along with in their own right. Luther said, while that may be true, their main area of concern was me. If other people in Wheelock were problems, they would handle that separately.

I then asked why they said nothing earlier—if I had so many things to work on, why didn't they bring them to my attention months ago? Why was this the first indication I had that they did not feel I was fit to be a ministerial servant?

"We would have liked to help you out, James," Dick said, "But you left the congregation with no warning. If you had stayed, we would have brought the matter to your attention and helped you out, but you didn't give us a chance."

"Oh," was all I could muster.

"Is there anything else?" he asked. There was much more. But I was too upset to gather my thoughts in any logical way.

I hung up the phone. I was crushed. During my entire life, my single driving desire had been to do as much as possible in Jehovah's service. I wanted to do as much as I could as soon as I could. If I felt I could do more than I was already doing, then I sought out further privileges and responsibilities. I asked the elders if I could do more because I was taught that it was okay to ask to do more. When the elders made requests in the name of God, I tried to obey, even if their requests ran counter to reason.

There was no way the elders in Apple Valley would reappoint me ministerial servant. They would be forced to respect the opinion of the Wheelock elders despite the two-decade history I had with them. There would be no more assembly parts, because there would be nothing outstanding about me. *Maybe I can one day prove myself as worthy of being a ministerial servant—but who knows? Armageddon could be here by then, and what would I tell God? Would he judge me as unworthy to live in Paradise because I had botched my service to him?*

I didn't want my spiritual career to describe an arc; I wanted it to continue reaching new heights. I became consumed with embarrassment at the thought of showing my face at the meetings. *All the elders, including my own uncle, will read the letter and be disappointed. And what will I say to my other relatives and my close friends? What will I say to Rhett? He is my big brother, and now he'll be ashamed of me. And Gabe, who looks to me as a role model, he will be hurt that I'm no longer someone worth emulating.*

Most of all, I was saddened to think that I wanted our marriage to go smoothly. I had dreamed, for two years, that Jennifer and I would be fine examples in the congregation and that, together, we would be doing all that we could for Jehovah. But here, now, only a month into our nascent marriage, that dream was already ripped away.

I was too hurt to speak.

I knew, also, that I would be unable to push this into the back of my mind. It was destined to sit there, like a troll in the window, tapping on my skull and reminding me—forcing me—to think about it. Whether watching TV, or driving in my car, or helping a customer at work, it didn't matter—I would think continually about the bad letter, and about how I was no longer a ministerial servant. I wouldn't be able to focus on anything else.

I began to cry.

I stumbled into the bedroom, onto the bed next to Jennifer. I sobbed, and my emotions became transparent in the dim light. "How could they do that? Don't they know how much it means to me? I tried to do the right thing all the time."

I wanted Jennifer to reach out, to place her hands upon me and absolve me of my trespasses. But she wasn't totally clear what I was talking about, and she asked me to clarify. I relayed the conversation, and she said: "I don't think it's *that* big of a deal."

If I wasn't so sad, this would have greatly enraged me. "How can you say that?" I sobbed, "It *is* a big deal. It's a big deal to me."

"It's not like you got in trouble for anything. They're saying you need to work on some stuff before you're ready to be a Servant again."

"That's embarrassing!" I yelled. "Why did they have to do it that way, anyway? Why couldn't they have told me before that I had stuff to work on? They said they didn't have the opportunity to help me, because we left without giving them any warning."

"I told you we shouldn't just leave like that. I knew they'd be mad."

"That's a load of crap!" I said, wiping my tears, "Where does it say I have to give them any notice, anyways? It's not like a job. Besides, I find it hard to believe they had no time to counsel me on important matters, but they had plenty of time for stupid things like telling us not to use a 'just married' sign and crap like that."

"All that stuff was stressing you out. Maybe you should just take it easy for a while and just focus on being a better Witness."

"This isn't the time to take it easy. We're supposed to give Jehovah our whole mind and soul and strength. And now look! They're not letting me do that."

Jennifer continued to try to calm me, insisting the bad letter was not so bad. She argued that being a ministerial servant was not the end-all of serving Jehovah. She suggested I devote my energies instead to just being a better person. She said I should just make it a goal to be calmer, friendlier, and to try to show more love to the brothers and sisters in the congregation.

This may have been warranted advice, but it was not what I wanted at the moment. There, in our little apartment, as newlyweds, I felt like we were facing our first crisis. I didn't want someone to say it would be alright; I wanted someone to join me in my misery, to sympathize with me.

Later that night, I telephoned Dick again.

Although it was after ten o'clock, I didn't care if I woke him. As it turned out, he was not only awake, he had a house full of guests. After a brief hello, he asked: "What can I do for you?"

I was nervous, but I forced myself to speak. "I want to know specific examples of when I was difficult to get along with."

Dick moaned. "Now, James, I don't want to get into all that. I can't think of any specific day or event."

By stonewalling the conversation before it even began, I could mount no defense, so I said: "There are many people in Wheelock who are difficult to handle, and I think I did my best in dealing with them day in and day out. I just want a chance to defend myself."

"James, that's not the purpose of the letter." Dick cleared his throat. "We met as a body of elders and decided it was best not to recommend you for ministerial servant. It wasn't because of one particular incident here or there. It's not something I'm going to debate."

I sighed. "You just felt like not recommending me, without any specific reasons?"

"No." There was a bit of frustration in his voice. "We had a tough time with you from the start. Like I said, we tried working with you—we wanted to work with you more, to help you out. But you left before we could do that. Even while you were still here in Wheelock, you deliberately went against the elders. We offered you counsel, and you ignored it."

I quickly ran down a mental list of all the counsel the Wheelock elders had given me. In nearly every case, I had obeyed them. There were two ways in which I did not cooperate: First, I defied them by hanging a 'just married' sign from the limo. And, second, I defied them by having a limo at my wedding.

So I asked Dick if he was referring to the wedding.

"That's the majority of it, yes," he said, adding that I did not invite everyone in the congregation to the wedding, including some people's children.

Witnesses are under no compulsion to invite everyone with whom they happen to share a congregation. Dick, therefore, was giving his opinion, a violation of the elder's manual.

I paused to breathe. I closed my eyes and I braced myself to launch into a fiery defense of my actions. I was going to tell Dick that he had explicitly stated that the 'just married' sign was "up to me." He and Luther did not prohibit me from using the sign; they clearly said they were only giving me "something to think about." I obeyed them by thinking about it. I was going to tell Dick that the limo was not my idea—that it was as much a surprise to me as to him. Further, I wanted to tell him that the limo was hired and paid for by my very own grandpa—my *elder* grandpa. I wanted to tell Dick that when I came out of the hall and saw the limo, my first thoughts were of him and how he would react.

Instead, I realized that if Dick does not want me to explain my actions regarding the limo and the 'just married' sign, then he is choosing to remain at odds with me. He would have called, not to condemn me, but to uncover the reasons for recent events. But if he never knew the real reasons about the limo, or why I left Wheelock, then he would forever be wrong about me.

What's more, I reasoned that as long as I withheld that information from him, then I could calm myself about the bad letter by telling myself that he didn't know the whole story. Trying once more to glean specific charges that I could explain or defend, I asked him to give me a particular example of a time when I acted presumptuously. He answered: "James, just by calling me back tonight, you're acting presumptuous."

Dick was correct, but his reply upset me. However poorly I may be acting at the moment surely had no bearing on a letter that was already written. Dick's response set up a catch-22. Like a person accused of talking too much, or a person charged with disagreeing with everything, any defense I mounted would, by definition, only serve to prove Dick's point.

Still, there was one thing I wanted to know. From the time I met Dick, he never seemed to like me. I wanted to know—really, honestly, wanted to know—why he disliked me from our relationship's commencement.

Unsure how to phrase a proper question, I deleted all antipathy from my tone and simply stated: "I think it's too bad that we never really got along."

There was silence for a moment, and then Dick said: "Uh-huh, that is too bad."

"I guess I feel like you never really liked me, even from the start."

"Hmm," he answered, "Now why do you think that is?"

"Maybe it's because you associated me with Jenni's family, and I don't think you ever really liked them, either."

He sighed. "That's probably true."

Our mutual ardor assuaged, he coolly asked if there was anything else I wanted to say. I told him there was not. He wished me goodnight. I never spoke to him again.

I returned to the living room, and commiserated with my wife. Jennifer was disgusted that an elder she had known her whole life would have such a low opinion of her. "Dick and his wife don't like people that aren't just like them." She spoke as if this was an axiom all Witnesses innately knew.

"I believe that," I said, happy to finally have engaged her in conversation. "What's weird, though, is that no one else seems to dislike him that much."

"Maybe people do dislike him; they just don't say anything about it."

Jennifer's words were dead on. Within a year, her family would move out of Wheelock after being loyal members there for a quarter of a century. The elders did not see fit to give them a going-away party, and in a moment of unflinching poetic grace, Jennifer's dad would later refer to Luther as "a self-righteous pompous asshole." Soon after, Kyle left Wheelock and began attending a different congregation. He commented that his new congregation "felt different," and I assured him that this different feeling was Holy Spirit. A year after that, Johnny and Tonya left the congregation, and Johnny confessed that attending Wheelock was trying on his spirituality, and he regretted using Dick to officiate their wedding.

But none of that mattered now; it was all still in the future. For the moment, I still had to deal with my predicament. I couldn't sleep that night. I stared at the ceiling. I wanted the darkness to reach out and embrace me, to give me respite by means of slumber. I wished God would let me die instead of living with such humiliation and embarrassment, as he had once done for Samson.[56] In the morning, I cursed my own existence.

I spent the rest of the year in my own spiritual doldrums. When my grandparents visited me at work one day, I cowered when my grandpa asked if I was looking forward to the upcoming Ministerial Servant School, and I had to honestly tell him I was not invited. When I went to the meetings, and elders came up to greet me, I couldn't help but think that they only saw me as a fallen Witness, a young brother who had performed so well for so long and then squandered his spiritual heritage by flagrantly going against the Wheelock elders.

I prayed to Jehovah more than ever. I wanted Him to know that I still loved Him, wanted to live in Paradise, and had never intentionally acted presumptuously. I apologized for the poor decisions I made, and begged Him for a second chance. I implored Him to show me the way in which I was to walk. I asked Him to guide me as to what to do with my life in the final days before Armageddon.

Awaiting an answer, I felt it best to work in harmony with my multitudinous prayers. I reminded Jennifer of our goal to read the Bible, and we delved back into regular reading, a pattern we had let lapse in the wake of my depression.

I wished that reading the Bible would help me to begin again at the basics; to remind me of what was important in life and in service to Jehovah. It was a sad realization, then, to find that reading the Good Book only served to discourage us further.

Soon the Circuit Overseer made his scheduled visit to the congregation, and I made sure to be in top form. I shaved better than ever, and I polished my shoes. Jennifer and I arrived at the meeting early. I paid rapt attention. Afterwards, I booked an afternoon of service with the Overseer. I felt it was important for him to see that I was a good pioneer. Maybe, I hoped, this would show him that I could also be a good ministerial servant.

I spent the following afternoon with the Circuit Overseer. His easygoing nature, enhanced with a Southern drawl, made him seem very human. I spoke to him about reading the Bible with my new wife, and he raised his eyebrow in admiration. "Reading the Bible through is an admirable goal for a young married couple. As you read God's Word," he added, "You'll notice specific points that the two of you can use to make your marriage succeed."

I wanted to ask if I should get some concubines, show favoritism for one wife over the others, and then have children I can offer to the men of the city. But I didn't.

At the next meeting, I listened closely to the Circuit Overseer's talk, hoping that he would see I was an astute listener. His talk centered on the importance of regular personal study. Reading the Bible daily was of paramount importance, he noted. In doing this, we allow God to shape our thoughts. Also important was preparing for the meetings by reading the articles to be considered and looking up the cited scriptures.

Then the Overseer made some most remarkable comments. "Perhaps there are those among our brothers who are very studious and who are quite adept in keeping up with the spiritual feeding program the Society provides. Maybe you faithfully attend meeting after meeting and study book after book and find that you never learn anything new."

As he said this, my ears perked up. It was as if he knew what I was thinking. He was defining my situation precisely, and I viewed this as God's answer to my prayers. I was eager to hear his next words.

"Let me offer this suggestion," he said. "Pick one subject from the Bible, and make it your goal to learn absolutely everything about that subject.

Become an expert at it." In doing this, he assured us, the Bible would once again come alive, our faith would be strengthened and, as an added benefit, we would become a valuable asset to the congregation whenever that topic arose.

Yes, *this* was the answer to my prayer. This appealed to me like nothing else. Excitedly, I began to contemplate the many biblical topics at which I could become an expert. My mind reeled through all the possible topics. Shall I try to learn everything I can about the prophecies in Revelation, or Mosaic Law? Before I could decide on a topic, however, the Overseer suggested Noah's Flood as one possible topic to explore.

Noah and the Great Flood. I was thrilled with this suggestion, convinced it was a preternatural response to my heartfelt supplications. I thought back to how I had promised myself upon finishing high school I would at last begin my *real* education. Now, more than four years later, I had yet to make good on this promise. In the hustle of everyday life—courting Jennifer, making money, pioneering—I had lost focus of my education. It was time to get back to learning all I could, becoming a better person, enriching my mind! The Circuit Overseer's suggestion was timely and apt. It combined my love of history and animals with God's Word. By studying the Flood, I would learn about history, geology, hydrology, zoology, biology, and meteorology—all subjects I found absolutely fascinating.

Within weeks, I had read everything the Watchtower Society had written in the past thirty years on the subject. I read the entries in their Bible encyclopedia *Insight on the Scriptures* under the headings "Ark," "Deluge," "Noah," and "Animal." I reread the chapters in *My Book of Bible Stories* that detailed the events of Noah's life.

One of the first things I wanted to know was the size of Noah's ark. The *Insight* book said: "Conservatively calculating the cubit as 44.5 cm . . . , the ark measured 133.5 m by 22.3 m by 13.4 m."[57]

Jennifer and I purchased graph paper in an attempt to visualize these dimensions. We defined each square on the paper as equal to one square foot and immediately realized this would require too much graph paper, so we redefined each square as equal to two square feet. We pieced together sixteen pages of graph paper and were awestruck at the size.

Still, a scale model has its limitations. We next went outside, and Jennifer stood in place while I used a tape measure end over end to determine the Ark's length. I carried a roll of yarn, and Jennifer held onto one end while I walked and unrolled it a full 437 feet. There was no doubt about it; the ark had been enormous.

"It would be cool if I could give a talk about Noah's Flood one day," I said. "And while up on stage, I could pull out the yarn and you could walk down the aisle and unravel it so that everyone could see just how big the ark really was."

Jennifer smiled wide. "That would be so neat. I don't think anyone realizes just how big the ark was. I sure didn't know."

"You can read about the dimensions, but until you see it with your own eyes, you never really get it."

"Do you think the Kingdom Hall would be big enough to unwind the yarn?"

I thought for a second. "You'd have to walk all the way into the back, ask someone to hold the yarn, and then come all the way back up front again."

Jennifer's eyes gazed out in amazement. "And that doesn't even take into consideration how wide the ark was—or how tall."

I stopped; arrested in thought by what an awesome task Noah had accomplished. Thinking about Noah and the ark and the Flood made the Bible come alive, and I was grateful to have heeded the Circuit Overseer's advice.

Our next mission was to construct a scale model of the ark and the animals. Jennifer wanted to make tiny sculptures of all the animals, and we concluded that we first needed to obtain a list of all the animals that were on board the ark. So that night, we did some more research.

The Watchtower Society is woefully silent on the subject of which animals boarded the ark. I needed to figure out, for example, if Noah needed to bring two cheetahs, two tigers, two bobcats, two leopards, and so on; or if he just needed to bring two representatives of the cat family. As I thumbed through the Watchtower's publications, I realized I had never before given this matter much thought. I knew that God must have instructed Noah to bring every species of cat. After all, the Watchtower Society teaches that there were two lions in the Garden of Eden with Adam and Eve.[58] So if there were lions at the time of man's creation, then there must have been all manner of cats, as opposed to just some antediluvian proto-cat. Consequently, Noah must have been required to board dozens of cat species.

But there were problems. Foremost among them was size constraint. The ark was big, but it wasn't *that* big. If Noah needed to collect two of every species of land-dwelling animal, he would need room for over a million animals. Assuming they would all survive pent up in cramped quarters for over a year, there was still the matter of food, and many species required specialized diets. And since the only openings in the ark were windows on the top floor, tons of animal dung would need to be shoveled, carried up, and hoisted out the windows several times a day. Noah, even with help from his seven family members, would be unable to even *visit* every animal every day, much less feed them.

Anticipating this dilemma, the *Insight* book provided a tantalizing answer:

> It is true that encyclopedias refer to over a million species of animals. But Noah was instructed to preserve only representatives of every "kind" of land animal and flying creature. Some investigators have said that just 43 "kinds" of mammals, 74 "kinds" of birds, and 10 "kinds" of reptiles could have produced the great variety of species of these creatures that are known today.[59]

I was disconcerted by the word "kind;" it was exasperatingly ambiguous. Was it a species? A genus? An order? Or something in between? The text didn't say. What about all the other animals? Insects, worms, arachnids, millipedes, centipedes, and others were all ignored with nary a word. I decided that this second problem could be dispensed with for the moment, but I needed to know what, exactly, the Watchtower Society (and the Bible) intended with the word "kinds."

I got up from my desk chair, and walked over to Jennifer, who was cleaning the kitchen. "So, do you think that any cat can breed with any other cat?"

She laughed. She set down the towel she was folding and asked: "Why? Are you thinking of breeding cats?"

"No, I'm asking because the *Insight* book says here that Noah only needed to bring only forty-three kinds of mammals into the ark. I know there's, like, thirty different cat species, so if they can't interbreed, that means more than half the mammals Noah brought on the ark were cats."

Jennifer pursed her lips and thought for a second. She tapped her fingers on the counter. "I guess I don't know. But I know that lions and tigers can mate with each other."

"But can a Siamese cat mate with a lion?"

"I don't think they would physically be able to."

"I realize the logistics of sex would probably prohibit any mating, but I wonder if it's possible to take some sperm from a male Siamese cat and an egg from a female lion and see if anything develops."

"I don't think so," Jennifer said, "I don't think they're the same species."

"So then Noah had to bring lots of cats on board, right?"

She tilted her head. "Maybe."

"Maybe he didn't need to bring fifty pairs of cats, but he must have brought more than two; otherwise we wouldn't have the variety that there is today."

"Does the *Insight* book say any more about it?"

I set the book on the countertop and showed her the paragraph. While Jennifer read, I told her that I knew there were over three hundred species of parrots. We knew very well that our pet parakeets couldn't mate with other parrots. "So there are a lot of problems with these low numbers," I told her. "I don't see how Noah could have gotten away with only seventy-four pairs of birds, when he would need more than seventy-four parrots alone. Not to mention owls and starlings and turkeys and penguins and chickens and pheasants and canaries . . ."

"I get it. You don't have to rattle off every bird in the world."

Jennifer suggested we find books about animals and try to determine which animals, exactly, were on the ark. "Maybe there are some biology books out there that say something like 'If you have these forty-three different mammals, you can make all the mammals there are today.'"

The next day, we visited the local library. I approached a librarian, but I didn't want to say that I was doing Bible research, as I knew the majority of worldly people were in league with Satan and would not help me if I told them the religious nature of my quest. "The best way I can explain it is this: Let's say that you plan on leaving earth and colonizing another planet. You want to make sure that this new planet has exactly the same kinds of animals as Earth, but your space is limited, so you're not going to bring, like, every breed of dog; you're just going to bring one pair of dogs. So, I'm wondering, do you also need to bring a pair of wolves, and coyotes, and jackals, too? Or could you just bring one pair of representative canines that could eventually diversify into the variety that Earth has?"

My question sounded ludicrous, but it exemplified what Noah faced when making his passenger list. The librarian listened with undivided attention. "You mean like a Noah's ark kind of thing?"

"Yes, I suppose that would work."

He directed me to the reference section, to one shelf of books. "You'll want to start here." He pointed to *Grzimek's Animal Life Encyclopedia.*

Grzimek's Animal Life Encyclopedia is an imposing publication.[60] Besides its unpronounceable title, the encyclopedia spanned seventeen volumes, each at least three hundred pages long, and every page detailed different animals—animals that were unable to mate with any animal on any other page. Before I even pulled the first book off the shelf, I could sense the sheer enormity—and impossibility—of gathering up all the animals into a single ark. I felt my spirit crush as I realized that birds, reptiles and mammals—the largest of the land animals—accounted for ten of the seventeen volumes.

I left the library without any books.

On the way home, I said to Jennifer: "Where do you think the Society came up with those numbers, anyways?"

"Maybe they just know that there couldn't have been that many animals on the ark," she said, "or else they wouldn't have all fit."

"Right, but why those numbers? Why forty-three mammals and seventy-four birds? They must have gotten the numbers from somewhere. They wouldn't just make it up."

Jennifer looked as though she didn't quite know what I meant. "You think they were able to calculate those numbers somehow?"

"Maybe. It's hard to picture them doing that. They're not scientists, you know. I think what's more likely is that they got that number from some other source."

"Maybe there's a footnote or something that tells you where they got those numbers."

There was no reference. The Watchtower Society used those numbers with no documentation as to where they originated. I was confused. I was sure the Society did not just arbitrarily concoct numbers. Surely, somewhere, there was a reputable encyclopedia on animals, or perhaps some esoteric scientific dissertation that provided detailed proof of animals' relationships to one another and how only a few "kinds" of animals could produce the great variety of today. I wanted to find this source. I *needed* to find this source. It was my goal—my calling—to learn all that I could about Noah's flood, and I owed that much to Jehovah, the Circuit Overseer, and myself to uncover this elusive source.

That evening I wrote to the Watchtower Society.

After Jennifer went to bed, I powered up my computer. It took two hours to craft a letter. I was just about to print it, when the winds of trepidation blew over me. *What if the Society writes back and accuses me of presumptuousness? What if they alert the elders that I was questioning their literature? Then I'll never be appointed ministerial servant. I may even get in trouble, maybe publicly reproved or worse!*

The Watchtower from April 1st, 1986, informs its readers that unity is not "achieved and maintained by each one's independently searching the scriptures, [and] coming to his own conclusions." So, I reasoned, if any negative ramifications came about due to my inquiry, I would simply claim that the Watchtower warns against coming to one's "own conclusions" and, thus, I wanted to learn what the Society had to say on the matter. That same issue says: "If a person just has doubts or is uninformed on a point, qualified ministers will lovingly assist him."[61]

Still, I felt I was teetering on that fine line between sincere inquiry and fault-finding. Not wanting to be accused of the latter, I added a paragraph at the outset praising the Society's fuglemen for the articles they write and I enclosed a money order for ten dollars. Surely, I thought, they would know that a person donating to the preaching work was not, by any means, attempting to undermine it.

On February 5, 1997, I dropped the letter in the mailbox.

"Now all we can do is wait," I said to Jennifer.

Summer closed in, and we felt the pinch of lagging behind on our service time. Jennifer had accumulated more hours than me by going out in service with Sarah on days that I went to work. When we added up our hours, we discovered that Jennifer was over fifty hours ahead of me. On the way home from service each day, we stopped off at a laundromat to leave an issue of the *Watchtower* and, in doing so, accrued fifteen more minutes. In the evenings, we wrote letters while our parakeets and new cockatiel Cosmo sat on our shoulders and nibbled our notepads. One night, I even wrote letters while watching TV, until Jennifer scolded me for counting the most pathetic service time she'd ever seen. Despite all of this, Jennifer pointed out that it didn't look like either of us would achieve the yearly goal.

I made the decision to cut back on my hours at work for a few weeks. I was doubly pleased to limit my employment, as Gabe had just been appointed as a ministerial servant. He was rightfully pleased with his new position, and it prompted him to ask if I had been reappointed. I lied, and after that, made all effort to evade any conversation that could, however circuitously, lead to his inquiring about my ministerial servant status. When Gabe excitedly told me how he attended his first elders/ministerial servants meeting, I nodded courteously, but then ran away as soon as a customer walked in. I was selfishly pleased when Gabe put in his notice to quit the eyeglass store, relieved that I would be spending a lot less time being secretive about my congregational status.

On the seventh of July, I walked out to the mailbox with Cosmo on my shoulder. A single envelope from the Watchtower, Bible and Tract Society gave me cause for both excitement and worry. The envelope was thin. My hopes for a wealth of information vanished, but I knew there was still the possibility that the letter told me where to find the information.

I sprinted into the apartment and announced that a reply had finally arrived. Jennifer jumped up off the futon and met me in the kitchen. Opening the envelope was like uncorking an evil genie. I unfolded the four pages, and quickly scanned the contents. The response letter itself was a single page in length, and the other three pages were photocopies from a back issue of their *Awake!* magazine. They dedicated a mere two sentences to my question regarding animal "kinds":

> With regard to the number of various creature "kinds" that were likely taken along in the ark with Noah, we are enclosing photocopies of pages 14 to 16 of the December 22, 1951, issue of *The Watchtower*, containing the article entitled "Noah's Passenger List." On pages 15 and 16, sources are noted that may help you in your research.

The enclosed article, featuring a cartoon sketching of Noah and the ark, was not an article I had seen before. It was taken from a 1951 issue of the *Awake!* (the Society incorrectly stated the article was from *The Watchtower*), and was thus older than anything I had access to. I sat at the table and read the excerpt word for word.

The article noted, "The Creator makes no effort to itemize the hundreds of thousands of 'species' of the evolutionists. True, a large number of original created types would be found within each main division, but there is nothing to show that such Genesis *kinds* would even approach in number the varieties of them now living."

To which I could only reply: "No kidding."

The article furnished three examples of "kinds" of animals: man, horse, and dog, and stated that just a few "types of each could produce the great variety of each now known." But this avoided the main issue. All dogs, like horses and humans, can interbreed. I was not asking the Society to explain why there are poodles and Pomeranians and Papillons and pugs and Polish lowland sheepdogs. I was asking them for a list of the minimum number of non-interfertile "kinds"—regardless of how "kinds" is defined.

The article contained six references to outside sources, but only one specifically dealt with my inquiry. The final paragraph said:

> *Clarke's Commentary* makes certain interesting observations. Of the six divisions of animal life it assigns, this source eliminates fish, worms and insects as not concerned in the ark calculations. This leaves *mammalia, aves* and *amphibia*.

I threw the paper down on the table. "Hold it," I said to Jennifer, gesturing like a traffic cop, "*Six* animal divisions? What sort of taxonomy breaks animals into six divisions? Certainly none I've ever heard of. And three of those divisions are fish, worms and insects? Does Clarke even know an octopus from an orangutan here? Is he just conveniently ignoring crustaceans, mollusks and arachnids, or is he just hopelessly ignorant?"

Jennifer shook her head in dismay. "I don't know."

The paragraph continued:

> Though the *Commentary* gives the entire naturalist breakdown of each group, it emphasizes that undoubtedly only the basic *genera* or *kinds* would be of concern. With interest we note that they assign only forty-three genera to the mammalia division (excepting the whale kind, certainly of no concern here), seventy-four to the second class, birds (not including web-footed fowls), and ten to the third class, amphibia (reptiles and serpents).

There was all manner of discouragement in these few sentences. First, the Society equated "kinds" with *genera*, and then claimed that whales are a single kind of mammals. Whales are an *order* of mammals, not a genus. This is akin to first claiming that there are fifty states in the United States, and then noting that this includes the state of New England.

Clarke then outdoes himself by declaring that Noah would only need seventy-four kinds of birds, *excluding any with webbed feet*. It was tough to believe that Clarke, and by extension the Watchtower Society, sincerely held that geese, swans, ducks, and loons simply floated for over a year—including forty consecutive days of torrential downpour.

Clarke's Commentary was severely outdated. Still, the Watchtower Society originally quoted from him back in 1951, and here they were continuing to quote from Clarke as if he still knew best.

One thing was clear; I needed to find a copy of *Clarke's Commentary*. The local library did not maintain one in their collection, nor did any library in the state. Except one. The local librarian requested the copy, and Jennifer and I waited again.

On July 24th, we packed our car and made the yearly trek to the District Convention in Rochester. We spent the time in the car trying to plan out the final month of the service year. Jennifer was concerned for our evaporating funds, especially considering the depletion of our savings account to pay for the hotel. These kinds of conversations frustrated me. I trusted that Jehovah would help us continue pioneering, and I implored Jennifer to have faith.

"It's not working," she said, "we're not making our time, and we're going to run out of money."

"We haven't run out of money yet," I countered. "Jehovah will help us keep going. And as far as getting in our time, you need less than a hundred hours, which is a lot better than some pioneers. And I'm doing okay."

"You're not doing okay," she yelled. "We keep doing stupid stuff to cheat, like driving slow and leaving *Watchtowers* in random places, and writing letters."

"What's wrong with writing letters? That happens to be a very good way to preach to people who live in security apartments."

"There's nothing wrong with it, I guess," she admitted. "But it's the way we do it. We write one word every five minutes, or we write letters while we're at the meeting or while watching TV."

"That's more productive than all the times we just sit in a car while we're out in service."

"I don't like doing that either, but that's harder to control," she snapped. It bothered her conscience. She did not feel like she was a good pioneer. She pointed out how the other pioneers did not respect her. She had no return visits, no Bible studies, and she rarely talked at the door. The other pioneers saw this and, with their stares and insidious comments, hinted that Jennifer was merely riding my coattails.

I threw up my hands. "Maybe you're right, but I don't want to think about it right now." I turned back in my seat and wrote one more sentence.

All three days of the convention, I continued writing letters. This was a fairly clandestine procedure, as note-taking was encouraged. During the three days, I managed to rack up nine more hours. This didn't get me ahead, but it made up for not being able to go out in service during those three days.

A week later, while toiling away at work one afternoon, Jennifer called to announce that the library had just phoned: *Clarke's Commentary* had arrived. I was excited. There, sitting on the shelf at the local library, was the answer to my questions. I kept looking at the clock, eager for the day to finish. I sped home via the library and dove into the book.

The first thing that I learned was that Clarke died in 1832. I'd already surmised that the book was old, but I never guessed it was *that* old. Though the book I held in my hand was a reprint, the original work had been completed by Clarke in 1810. My question of Clarke's ignorance was suddenly answered: Clarke was not stupid; he just lived two hundred years ago—prior to the modern discoveries in genetics, heritability, and speciation. Indeed, he lived at a time when humans had not yet discovered all the many known species of mammals, birds and amphibians and, therefore, couldn't possibly have gotten his numbers correct regardless of the research he dedicated to his cause.

Further, Clarke was not a biologist. He was not a scientist of any kind. He was a Methodist theologian. His *Commentary* was not a commentary on fauna, but on the Bible itself. His work was steeped in biblical apologetics; he had created a noble attempt to reconcile the natural world with that of the Holy Scriptures.

Clarke's discussion of the Noachian Deluge included the three numbers that had prompted my letter, but he did not delineate the various animal "kinds." He simply offered the numbers as if this was explanation enough. The Watchtower Society then gleaned this 141-year-old supposition and implanted it into their article.

I contemplated writing back to the Society. I wanted to tell them that they shouldn't use those numbers, because Clarke's book was, quite simply, wrong. Jennifer and I concluded that writing to the Society with such an assertion was treading dangerously. Jennifer pointed out that just because the Society used a flimsy quote didn't mean they were wrong about the Flood. In the Paradise, Jehovah would answer all of our questions, and then we would know which animals (and how many) populated the ark. Noah could answer the question for us.

But the information I'd uncovered pelted my spiritual armor. I had only investigated the topic because the Circuit Overseer recommended it. And now, here I was, more discouraged about the Bible and the Society than when I'd begun my Noah's Ark journey some eight months earlier. There seemed to be no way to reconcile the truthfulness of a global deluge with what I knew about the colossal variety of life on the planet. I played through all sorts of possible explanations: maybe waterfowl *did* float through the flood. Maybe toads and frogs just left their eggs in the water. Maybe Noah corralled only juvenile specimens of the large land mammals onto the ark. Maybe cats *can* mate with bears, and no one's ever thought to try. None of these scenarios felt possible, much less probable. I returned *Clarke's Commentary* to the library at once, and tried to squash its existence out of my mind.

Jennifer continued to do research. I tried to get her to abort the project, but when she asked why, I couldn't find the words. I was worried that there was no answer; no solution to the passenger list of Noah's Ark. Perhaps we were laboring under the false belief that it was possible to tally up all the land animals into a tidy list. Oh, I wished it were true, as that would be a triumph for the credibility of the Ark, and, by extension, the Bible. But with every book we delved into, I drifted further and further from the faith I had in that Bible story. I shuddered to follow that line of thought to its logical conclusion. I wished I could reach out and force her to stop the research to save our faith.

Yet only a few nights later, I stayed up reading the book *Great Disasters*[62] until early in the morning. In reading the chapter titled "Noah's Flood," it was, for the first time, suggested to me that maybe Noah's Flood was not worldwide. This would explicate the animal problem: Noah wouldn't need to board all the animals if the Flood covered, say, only 10 percent of this Earth.

I lay awake that night, considering this idea. There was no way the Flood was global—there was too much evidence against it. At the same time, a localized Flood meant the Society was wrong. As God's mouthpiece, it was unthinkable that they could be wrong. True, from time to time they made refinements in doctrine. But this was simply tacking—adjusting teachings in order to bring God's people into a more perfect understanding of His will.

The following morning, as Jennifer and I walked door-to-door, I asked: "What would you say if I said that the Flood wasn't worldwide?" Jennifer looked down the street and answered: "I would say that makes a lot of sense."

I was surprised. "So you think that's the case . . . that the Flood wasn't global?" We turned to walk to a house.

She shook her head. "That's not what I said. I just meant it would explain a lot."

"But what about—"

Jennifer cut me off: "What about the Society saying it was global?"

"Yeah!"

She hesitated. We approached the house's doorstep and I rang the doorbell. Jennifer whispered: "I don't know. Maybe you should write to them again."

"Should I tell them that there's no way the flood was global and that they've been lying all these years?"

Again, she hesitated. She looked into the house's window, checking for signs of life. "Not unless you wanna get disfellowshipped. Why don't you just ask them if it's *possible* that the Flood wasn't global? Maybe they never thought of that."

I rang the doorbell again. "They never thought of that because that would contradict the Bible." My words fell like a thud.

No one answered the door, so I wrote down the house number and we walked away. She said nothing until we reached the street corner. "Maybe it's not that big of a deal. Maybe we should just let it rest."

"I was only doing the research because the Circuit Over—"

She held up her hand. "What do you want me to say? Maybe that was a dumb thing for him to say." As we approached the next house, she lowered her voice so the householders wouldn't hear us. "Maybe it was dumb for him to suggest Noah's Flood, when there's so much we don't know about it. Maybe you should just leave the Flood alone and research something different."

I shrugged, despairingly.

It was easy to ignore Noah and the Flood for the time being. Our stay in Rochester during the District Convention had caused a dent in our finances from which we were struggling to recover. My two subsequent paychecks had to be cashed; there was nothing to put into savings. I told Jennifer I might need to take off a couple of days from work to get in my service time for the year, but she showed me the budget; we couldn't afford another small check.

Jennifer wanted to go out of town for our anniversary. Looking at our finances, she realized how infeasible it would be. I told her we would just spend a nice day together—no service, no work, no meetings. Our parents sent us cards with money enclosed, and we treated ourselves to a movie and dinner.

While celebrating our anniversary at a restaurant, we talked about pioneering. There was only a week left of the service year, and I told Jennifer I was proud of her for only needing five more hours. She asked how I planned to get in the remaining thirty-five hours I needed and I said: "I'll find a way. I always do." She again brought up the option of discontinuing as pioneers.

I broke off a piece of bread and dipped it in my soup. "I just don't want to quit pioneering."

"I know you don't," Jennifer said compassionately. "I know it's important to you."

Moaning over the inevitable turn of events, I whined: "I wanted us to pioneer as a couple, right up until Armageddon. When I started pioneering, I swore that Armageddon was coming any day. Now, well, who knows when it's coming? I still want to pioneer right up until the End, though, but who knows when that will be?"

"So are you saying we can quit pioneering?"

Her voice carried a whiff of excitement, and I was revolted by her eagerness to quit the Lord's work. I wiped my face with the cloth napkin. "I hate saying it. But I guess so."

Indeed, when I'd considered the year we'd had together, I came to the realization that the only events that cast a shadow over it was the letter from Wheelock and our difficulty pioneering. In the coming year, I couldn't do much about the letter, but I could do something about pioneering. I could end it.

Sunday, August 31st, 1997 was the last day of the service year. My alarm clock bludgeoned me to consciousness at 4:55 in the morning. I gave myself five minutes to find some semblance of alertness, and then I reached over onto my night stand to grab a notepad. I wrote:

Hello neighbor. My name is James Zimmerman and I am . . .

I dropped the pen and rested for five minutes. Then I picked it up again and wrote:

. . . writing to people in your neighborhood today to . . .

This continued for three hours as I intermittently slumbered and counted time. At eight o'clock, Jennifer's alarm sounded. She awoke and rolled over. "Weren't you supposed to get up and write letters this morning?"

"Already doing it," I said, clearing my throat.

"No, you're not!" She propped herself up on her elbow. "You've been sleeping."

I cut her off: ". . . and writing letters."

She plopped her head back onto her pillow. "You're stupid."

"It still counts as time."

"In your opinion," she said, angrily. She sat up. "How much more time do you need?"

I looked at the clock. "Sixteen hours."

"How much time is left of the day?"

"Sixteen hours."

"You'll never make it." She climbed out of the bed.

"Thanks for believing in me, babe."

Jennifer grabbed her clothes and showered. I continued writing letters. When it was my turn to shower, I was careful to keep a dry towel handy so I could dry off my hand and write a few words halfway through my shower.

I wrote letters through breakfast. Jennifer drove to the meeting so I could keep swindling every hour from the day.

After the main meeting, a brief meeting for service was held, as usual, in the far corner of the Hall for people who wanted to go out in service. Jennifer, who needed only three more hours, joined me in the corner. No one else joined us. My dad came over and asked if we wanted to go out to lunch. I told him we both needed to get in our time for the year. The lack of support tinged his conscience and he said he and Diane would go out with us for a bit.

The four of us stopped at a few return visits, and then, after one hour, my dad and sister quit for the day.

Jennifer and I drove home, and she continued writing letters—keeping the time juggernaut rolling for us. At home, we changed out of our dress clothes and sat down to continue writing letters. At three in the afternoon, Jennifer closed her pen and proclaimed her goal was met.

"You did it," I said joyfully. "How does it feel to know you got all one thousand hours?"

"Pretty good."

"That's something to be proud of. You know how many pioneers aren't able to do that?"

"Don't tell me about it again," she said.

I turned back to my notebook, and continued to write. And write. And write. Through dinner, late-night snack, through kissing my wife goodnight. Alone, with only a table lamp illuminating my paper, I achieved my goal for the fifth straight year in a row. At midnight, I closed my notepad, put Cosmo in his cage, and went to bed.

In the week that followed, I oscillated between feelings of remorse and guilt. Jennifer and I spent a lot more time together doing things we wanted to do, but the pleasure I derived made me feel that I was cheating Jehovah. I begged Him for forgiveness for quitting pioneering.

But, I *was* tired. I was tired of rising every morning, donning a suit, and struggling to fill the day knocking on doors. I was tired of driving around the same streets, endeavoring to get along with the people in the car while managing car sickness. I was tired of the claustrophobia that came with squeezing in the back seat between two people; tired of trying to stay warm in the frigid winters and cool in the sweltering summers, all while wearing the same jacket and tie. I was tired of leading car groups and meetings for service just because I was male. I knew so much about pioneering; how to hoodwink the clock and minimize the effort. I knew that a cross on the door inevitably meant an argument. I knew the panic that came with a "No Soliciting" sign, and the slight hesitation that came as I drew close to each doorbell. I could spot a born-again Christian by their staccato speech and unblinking eyes. I could identify the atheist with his condescending, ingratiating posture hidden behind his graying goatee. I knew to offer the magazine about adoption to the white woman holding a black baby, and I knew to offer the magazine about the environment to the college student with the hemp shirt. I knew whether or not someone was home even before stepping onto the porch, I knew how much money they made, how many kids they had, and which god they bowed to. In the rare case I couldn't determine all that, I knew how to ring the doorbell and stand perfectly still, holding my breath, so that the slightest sound from inside the dwelling—a creaking stair, a meowing feline—would betray some information.

It wasn't as if all this would totally stop. Every Witness is expected to join in the door-to-door work on a weekly basis. But the time spent in the Lord's work would now be dramatically reduced. I would now be just a regular Witness, going out once, maybe twice a week for two hours at a time, stopping for long lunch breaks, and reporting only a tenth of the time I used to report.

At the next meeting, I felt no better. Eugene, the Presiding Overseer, announced from the platform: "This is to notify the Apple Valley congregation that James and Jennifer Zimmerman have discontinued their service as regular pioneers." The announcement rivaled my first talk as the most humiliating moment I ever experienced at the Kingdom Hall. The announcement was presented as if we were being reproved or disfellowshipped, and I steeled my nerves against the eyes of my brothers and sisters who turned towards us, anticipating that we were being punished for something. I wished I was invisible.

That night in bed, Jennifer asked: "Are you sad?"

I turned to face her. "Kind of."

She reached out and patted me on the shoulder.

My voice filled with melancholy. "I just wanted to do well, you know?" I reached for her hand. "Thank you for pioneering with me."

"You're welcome," she answered. "Sorry it didn't last."

"We tried."

We said goodnight. I turned to face the wall. The arms of the night reached out and embraced me. In the darkness, I grieved the loss of my identity, and I mourned the death of Assembly Boy.

SCRIPTURAL GROUNDS

The routine of pioneering dissipated, replaced by a gradual realization that I loved life. For the first time in my adult life, I slept in late some mornings. On occasion, I went an entire day without wearing a suit. Even service markedly improved. I no longer fretted over an hourly requirement. When the group stopped for lunch and wasted an hour, it was no worry to me.

In the ensuing weeks, many of my relatives expressed their regrets. This included my mom, who, one Sunday after the meeting, asked if there was anything she could do for Jennifer and me—as if ending our careers as pioneers left us directionless.

My mom had other issues. After twenty-four years of marriage, my dad moved out of the house. Unlike before, this was a calculated, conscientious choice. He called to notify me he would henceforth be living with his parents and attending their congregation. I asked him if he and my mom were trying to work out their problems, but he confessed there were no such plans.

As Witnesses, my parents could not simply divorce. Jehovah "hates a divorcing,"[63] and the Watchtower Society feels no different:

> Christian mates should be able to settle their problems, making allowances for human imperfection. No problem should be so great that it cannot be resolved by praying earnestly, applying Bible principles, and showing the love that is a fruit of God's spirit.[64]

A divorced Witness is not free to remarry unless their estranged mate sleeps with another person. As neither of my parents had cheated on each other, they could not get divorced. Even separating is portrayed as a drastic step to be taken only in extreme cases. According to the Society, the only grounds for scripturally-approved separation are willful nonsupport, absolute endangerment of a believer's spirituality and *extreme* physical abuse.[65] As to a married person's conduct when separated, the same *Watchtower* says:

What if Christian mates do separate? They must "remain unmarried or else make up again." Unless it is a question of divorce obtained on the grounds of "fornication," neither of them is Scripturally free to remarry.

Therein lies the danger: without the constant companionship of each other, the estranged spouses increase their chances of looking outside the marriage union for attention. Even if a Witness couple obtains a legal divorce, they face disciplinary action if they marry another person. *The Watchtower* agrees: "Opting for divorce or separation when a couple has no Scriptural grounds dishonors marriage."[66]

Witnesses who divorce legally are considered fornicators if they marry another person, as they are still married to their first spouse in the eyes of the Watchtower. Should a divorced couple decide to have sex with each other, they are still guilty of fornication.[67] A divorced couple is thus stuck in a sexual no man's land; they cannot marry anyone else, and they cannot sleep with their ex-mate.

Selfishly, though, I was overjoyed they had removed themselves from each other, and my prediction proved accurate as I saw both of them become better people. But I was worried that one of them would sleep with someone else, thereby sinning and risking their prospects for life in Paradise.

My sister, on the other hand, couldn't have cared less if either of them visited a brothel on a nightly basis. She was pleased the arguing had ended. In the year since I moved out, the house had morphed into a staging ground for the full range of emotional battles, and whereas I instinctively withdrew to my room during the parental brawls, my sister chose to stay in their presence and join in the hoopla. Caught in the crossfires, Diane was glad that the house became more peaceful, half joking that she wished they would've split up years ago.

Not everyone agreed. Eugene telephoned my dad within weeks of the break-up and invited him to breakfast. My dad accepted, and Eugene used the jentacular meeting to encourage my dad to return to his wife. He argued that Jehovah wants the two of them to be together, but my dad wasn't so sure. He knew that God wanted us to be happy, and he explained that now he was happier without his wife. Eugene reminded my father that willful, permanent separation from his wife meant he could no longer serve as a ministerial servant, and my dad replied that though he wanted to serve Jehovah, he would willingly step down from his congregational position if it meant ensuring his sanity.

They left the restaurant on poor terms. My dad and Eugene never spoke to one another again. At the next meeting, Eugene performed the solemn duty of announcing that my father was no longer a ministerial servant.

In the meantime, Jennifer and I were riding high on our new life. We deftly maneuvered away from our self-imposed slalom into penury. Jennifer took a job as a housekeeper at a nearby hotel. I began working full-time, and now had time to take a class in preparation for the standardized test to become a certified optician. After passing the test, I was promoted and received a significant raise. Our income more than tripled. Reducing our service to spiritual affairs yielded much financial peace of mind. With a sudden influx of cash, we invited our friends out for entertaining evenings. Primarily, this meant dinner with Jeremy and his wife.

But that lasted a very short time.

In my formative years, I learned that homosexuals were filthy deviants at worst, punch lines at best. Like most Witnesses, I looked forward to the day when God would kill them. It was beyond rational comprehension how any homosexual could trick himself into believing he had God's favor. The Old Testament leaves nothing up for questioning: "When a man lies down with a male the same as one lies down with a woman, both of them have done a detestable thing. They should be put to death without fail."[68] In the Christian era, the Apostle Paul warned: "men who lie with men . . . will not inherit God's kingdom."[69]

The first time I was confronted with gays as anything other than monsters, I was riding the bus to school. My fifth grade class had been assigned to write a five-page essay on an important issue. I, of course, wrote about the impending destruction of Armageddon. The girl sitting in front of me wrote about gay rights. To occupy the time, we swapped essays. In her essay, she argued that homosexuals have no more volition in the matter of sexual preference than heterosexuals; that the proliferation of gays as of late was not due to its sudden vogue, but to greater tolerance, which gave more of them confidence to "come out of the closet"; and that the discrimination of gays was on par with the sexism and racism that scarred the American landscape. The essay concluded by asserting that love between two consenting adults is beautiful, and should not be thought of as a birth defect or abhorrence against morality. I quietly returned the essay to her.

"What'd you think?" she asked.

I made a face betraying the fact that her words were unpalatable. "I disagree," was my tort response.

"Why?" she persisted.

Scurrying for a defense, I said, "It's not natural. I mean, look at animals. There's no homosexuality in the animal kingdom."

"Yes, there is!" She wagged an irate finger in my face. "Actually, 10 percent of the members of some species engage in homosexual behavior."

I looked away, feeling defeated. "I don't believe it."

"Why not?" she pressed.

I threw my hand up. "I don't wanna talk about it."

Ten years later, I was forced to talk about it. When Gabe came over to our apartment for dinner, he asked if I had seen Jeremy at work that day.

"No, why?" I asked.

"Haven't you heard? He split up with Bridgette."

I snapped my head back in amazement. Jennifer's jaw dropped. "They seemed just fine the other day. What happened?"

Gabe leaned forward. "From what I've been told, Jeremy admitted something to Bridgette."

"What?" I asked with wide-eyed interest.

Gabe smirked. "He didn't tell me. But what do you think it was?"

The next day, Jeremy called. He asked if I'd heard about him and Bridgette. I admitted I had, and expressed my sympathies. He asked if I could help him move his things. I desperately wanted to help, if for no other reason than to glean some information about this turn of events, but I told Jeremy I had to work on Saturday. Gabe, however, did spend the day with Jeremy, giving both emotional and physical support while Jeremy moved the remainder of his belongings. Bridgette and her parents waited outside while Jeremy cleared out. As Gabe walked to Jeremy's car with a box of light rock CDs, Bridgette's father Reuben stopped Gabe.

"Why'd you want to help Jeremy move today?"

Gabe shrugged. "He's my friend."

Reuben leaned in and whispered: "If you knew what he told Bridgette, you wouldn't be helping him today."

At work a week later, I looked at the schedule to see Jeremy was working downstairs. I called him. I asked how he was faring, saying I was concerned because I hadn't heard from him in a while. There was a gravity to his voice; a deep, reflective tone that had never been there before. He asked if I was sitting down. He divulged that he had written a letter to the elders. It was a letter of disassociation—written notification that henceforth he no longer wished to be a Witness. The thought of losing Jeremy as a friend confounded me for the moment, but I pushed those thoughts aside, choosing instead to first satisfy my curiosity. I could not fathom why anyone would write such a letter, essentially burning their bridges and severing all contact between them and their friends and family. I asked Jeremy what the letter said. I had to know. He replied: "I have it right here. I'll read it to you."

I turned my back to the customers and, for the next two minutes, I listened to the reading of a document in which one of my best friends removed himself willfully and unambiguously from the Truth. The letter was fascinating, too, in what it did not contain; it was not a hateful, vile desultory bit of spite, but a thoughtful, logical, mature decision set to pen.

I wished I could have said something: some magical incantation or flawless arguments that would spin Jeremy around and make him see the Truth. Instead, I uttered: "Oh, wow. I don't know what to say."

Picking up the lull in the conversation, Jeremy admitted that this might change our relationship. He was aware that Jennifer and I, Gabe, and even his own parents, would shun him. This grieved him, and it made his decision difficult to implement. Nevertheless, he told me that he *was* gay and, therefore, would be forever at odds with the Watchtower Society. He was tired of living a lie in the Truth, and could no longer maintain the façade.

I sat quiet, phone to my ear, for a few seconds more. Jeremy told me he had mailed the letter yesterday; soon an announcement would be made at his congregation. I knew it was over. I would hang up the phone and conclude our friendship. What else could I do? That Jeremy had committed grave sins in his life neither of us doubted. But he took it too far. It was one thing to sin, quite another to quit serving God. This was a test of my faith: Jeremy or Jehovah. I told Jeremy I was sympathetic to his plight and unsure how else he could handle the issue. I lied about customers coming into the store. "I need to get off the phone to help them." Jeremy said we could talk more later. I said "okay," and hung up. There was no "later."

That night, I told Jennifer of my conversation with Jeremy. Cosmo sat on her chest, and she rubbed his head, cleaning his feathers. She asked if I planned to ever speak with Jeremy again, and when I unequivocally said no, she cast her eyes to the ground. "I just think it's sad."

"He made his choice. He didn't have to leave the Truth. He knew it would mean losing all his friends—he even told me that. So what am I supposed to do?"

Jennifer had no answer.

In the days and weeks that followed, we found ourselves persistently conflicted over Jeremy's predicament. I was harsh, writing Jeremy out of my life with a single phone call, but I came to find that I was kinder to Jeremy than many other Witnesses had been.

At an assembly, Jennifer and I bumped into Oskar's wife Charlotte, a woman so fraught with friendliness she could even say kind things about Satan. Our conversation turned to Jeremy. Charlotte asked if I ever saw him at work, and I admitted: "Sometimes." She shook like a small child trying to eat food they detest. "I couldn't even look at him," she said, nearly nauseated at her own words.

On another evening, we paid a visit to my grandparents' house. I told them that one of our friends had recently disassociated himself, and they were sympathetic. Nana used the event as a learning opportunity. "That's one sign of the Last Days. Satan is working overtime to get Jehovah's people to follow him instead. We really need to be on guard."

Aunt Janet concurred. "It's so unbelievable that someone would just give up when we are this close to the End. No one pushes someone to do that."

When they asked what it was that caused Jeremy to leave God's Organization, I told them he was gay.

"Eww, just let him go," Nana said with a dismissive gesture, as if casting off a dirty handkerchief.

While out in service, the others in my group observed that I was unduly quiet. They inquired as to the change from my usual persona. I told them about Jeremy. They had all heard about Jeremy. It was big news. They shook their heads in disgust that a fellow sheep had left the Truth for the temporary enjoyment of sin. One of the sisters in the group, in what was surely one of the most dismal failures in the history of encouragement, said: "It's sad when people decide they don't love Jehovah anymore, isn't it? Especially when they choose to be gay."

Her words called to mind the manner in which Witnesses freely showed their disdain for homosexuals. My grandpa said he didn't mind Oprah Winfrey so much, but he couldn't "stomach" Rosie O'Donnell *because that woman is a lesbian.* Yet Oprah openly admitted to living with a man to whom she was not married and, in that way, is equally culpable on judgment day. Most Witnesses would only say the names of Freddie Mercury, Boy George, or Ellen Degeneres in such a way that it sounded like the very mention of those names made them sick. Ellen, in fact, received a double dose of invective, having her name spoken not only in a sick manner, but also having it routinely changed to Ellen "Degenerate." I feigned illness and left the preaching work early.

Perhaps the Witnesses were not to blame. They only know what they read in the Watchtower's literature, and one thing they read was:

> Isn't heterosexuality superior? Do not the design and natural functions of the bodily parts involved make this obvious? Isn't male with female the obvious norm, and male with male the obvious perversion? Homosexual "love" involves practices the apostle Paul must have had in mind when he spoke of things "not even [to] be mentioned among you" and "shameful even to relate" (Ephesians 5:3, 12). . . . Homosexuality has come storming out of

the closet. With a chip on its shoulder, it parades about as an acceptable life-style.[70]

Jennifer and I tried rationalizing the *Watchtower's* words with our former friend. We reasoned that God must understand Jeremy tried his best. We hoped Jehovah wouldn't judge him harshly. Jeremy, we reasoned, probably desperately wanted to be heterosexual. If only God would give him the chance, surely he would change. Hopefully, God would heal Jeremy in the Paradise and give him another opportunity to choose the straight and narrow road.

Most Witnesses held to the notion that people choose to be gay. I found this a tough stance to accept. *If Jeremy chose to be gay, when did he do so? Surely not as a husband when he had so much to lose. Did he choose to be gay when he was eighteen? Or fifteen? Or six? And if so, why? Why would he choose to be gay?* It made no sense. Jeremy did not *choose* to be gay in the same way I never *chose* to be straight. Nevertheless, he had abandoned Jehovah, and it was incumbent upon Jennifer and me to cast him aside.

We had shunned people before. There was scarcely a time when there wasn't at least one disfellowshipped person in the congregation. At meetings, they'd meekly sit in the corner, ignored. But I never was close to those people. Jeremy was different. Not only had he been one of my best friends, he was still my co-worker. I began contemplating working elsewhere.

In the meantime, my sister became engaged to Kyle. They set a wedding date for mid-July, less than a week after her eighteenth birthday. She asked Jennifer to be the maid of honor and me to officiate the ceremony.

At the meeting the following Thursday, I approached Eugene. "I'm doing the wedding ceremony at my sister's wedding, and I guess I need some kind of letter or something saying that I am a minister so that I can get a license from the state. Can you whip up something like that for me?"

Eugene's eyes wandered. He folded his arms. "Let me talk with the other elders."

I was uncertain why all the elders needed to confer regarding my simple request, but I couldn't fault Eugene for wanting to check with them first. The elders in Wheelock could have learned from him. He said he would let me know next week.

He didn't let me know the following week, or the week after that. I considered reminding him, but I did not wish to seem presumptuous.

Soon, only two months remained until the wedding. As Jennifer and I were leaving after the meeting, Eugene walked up and said: "Say, James? Were you still hoping to give that wedding talk?"

I glanced at Jennifer. "I've got the talk all written out. I'm ready to go; I'm just waiting on you guys."

Eugene cocked his head. The knowledge that I—a non-elder—had secured a copy of the wedding talk outline arrested his thoughts. "A couple of us would like to meet with you after the meeting on Sunday."

Later, Jennifer and I wondered why the elders found it necessary to meet with me about needing a simple note to give to the county clerk. "If I wanted to meet with the elders for permission to sneeze, I would've stayed in Wheelock."

In spite of my misgivings, I smiled when Eugene approached me after the meeting that Sunday. "We're gonna go downstairs for a few minutes, alright?" he said.

I complied, and a minute later I was in the cold basement on the opposite side of a table from Eugene and Uncle Peter.

"James," Eugene began, "we wanted to meet with you in regards your request to perform your sister's wedding ceremony—"

Before he could complete his preamble, my uncle interrupted. "What made you think you qualify to give a wedding talk, James?"[71]

Unprepared for such a question, I turned to my uncle with a startled jolt. "I'm a baptized Witness of Jehovah. That makes me a minister, so I'm qualified. That, and I'm a man."

Uncle Peter was not satisfied. "Where did you come up with the idea of giving a wedding talk?"

"I didn't. My sister did."

"Your *sister*? Why would she ask you to give her wedding talk?"

"Who should she ask?" I said, trying to sound non-confrontational but failing.

"What about one of the elders?"

Lumping my uncle in with all the other elders, I snapped: "She's not close to any of them."

"What about one of her grandfathers?"

"What about them?"

"Why doesn't she ask one of them?"

"I don't know. Because she likes me better. I lived with her for fifteen years and we're not just brother and sister, we're also good friends. I'm friends with Kyle, too."

Peter leaned forward, putting his elbows on his knees and resting his chin on his fist. He exhaled loudly. Then he sat back and clicked his pen nervously. "I gotta be honest with you James, the letter you got from Wheelock wasn't good."

I furrowed my brow. "What does that have to do with anything?"

"Well, it said you were presumptuous—"

"I know."

"—and that was nearly two years ago and you're not a ministerial servant anymore."

"Yeah?"

"So," he stifled a chuckle, "why do you think you're qualified to give a wedding talk now?"

"Like I said, I am a baptized minister. That's enough to qualify me. I don't have to be an elder or a ministerial servant to perform a wedding ceremony."

"Even if you were a ministerial servant, they don't give wedding ceremonies either."

"Actually, my cousin got married last year," I said quickly, "and my Uncle Mitch performed the ceremony. You were there," I said, sounding recalcitrant.

Peter recoiled at the reminder. "That's different. That was his own daughter."

"Yeah, and this is my own sister."

"That was in another congregation. Besides, your uncle used to be an elder."

"I used to be a ministerial servant."

"But you're not anymore."

"Does it matter what my Uncle Mitch or I used to be? Doesn't it just matter what we are now?"

"You're not a ministerial servant. Or an elder."

"But I *am* a minister."

"Why wouldn't your sister want an elder to perform her wedding?"

"Because she doesn't like any of them!" I laughed, realizing the conversation had come full circle. "Like I said, it doesn't matter anyways."

I leaned over to reach into my bag to pull out a *Watchtower* article supporting my position on scriptural grounds, but Eugene held up his hand to stop our pointless squabbling. He said, with uncharacteristic gravitas, "I think the important thing to remember here is not what's done in another congregation or whether or not James is a Servant, but to hear the Society's view on the matter."

Eugene explained that the Society's policy is that only elders officiate wedding ceremonies. Eugene offered no scriptural basis for this policy, and his assertion conflicted with the Society's article nestled in my bag. Wondering whether or not I had read the article correctly, I asked: "Does that apply only to weddings at the Kingdom Hall?"

Eugene said it applied to any wedding, regardless of location. Sensing my confusion, he explained that the Society's policy was spelled out in a recent letter to the elders. It exasperated me to think the Society had changed their policy surreptitiously. When Eugene stopped talking, Peter filled the momentary silence: "Besides all that, the letter from Wheelock wasn't good." He clicked his pen again. "It just wasn't good, James."

I glanced over at my uncle and curled my lip; an outward display of disgust for his immaturity. I never gave Eugene much credit as a communicator, but in this instance, he bested Peter in a surpassing way. I shifted toward Eugene. "I guess I'm more concerned with the Society's feeling on things."

"That's good, James," he nodded. "Now, keep in mind that the Society doesn't explicitly say you *can't* give the talk. So it's really up to you, and ultimately we're leaving it in your hands. If you want us to give you a letter so you can get a marriage license, we will."

Eugene's words conjured up bad memories of Wheelock. In that instance, I chose to go against the elders' opinion, and that decision still haunted me. *In fact, it is haunting me at this very minute, as Uncle Pete seems so fond of reminding me.* So I said: "Let me think about the matter and pray about it, and talk it over with Kyle and Diane and then I'll let you know, Eugene."

Afterward, the more I discussed my conundrum with Jennifer, the angrier I became. "Uncle Pete seemed more concerned about the bad letter then he did about the matter at hand. He's so stinking insecure," I threw myself onto the futon.

Jennifer sat down beside me. "He has never given a wedding talk, so he's probably jealous."

"I was looking forward to it," I said, mournfully. "There are so many aspects of being a Witness that aren't fun, but I was excited to do this. But if I go tell Eugene I'm gonna give the wedding talk, they'll allow it, and the next thing I know they'll take away my privileges and they'll never reappoint me ministerial servant."

"So?"

"So! That's a big deal. How many times do I have to remind you that we're supposed to be serving Jehovah with our whole heart and soul and strength, and if I can't do anything in the congregation, then I'm not really serving Him whole-souled, am I?"

Jennifer leaned forward, pondering my reasoning. "Maybe not."

"You know it's true," I cried, nearly yelling at Jennifer. "The elders told us the 'just married' sign was our decision, and now I get my own uncle throwing it back in my face today like a punchline. It was like he was saying, 'Was it worth it, huh? Huh? Aren't you sorry you defied the elders? Now look, you're not a ministerial servant, and we're not gonna let you do your sister's wedding. But it was all up to you, oh yes, we left it up to you.'"

At the next meeting, ignoring Uncle Peter, I asked Eugene for a moment of his time. Behind closed doors, I capitulated. "I figure if the Society doesn't want me to do it, then I shouldn't do it," I said, as if giving a well-rehearsed speech. Eugene complimented me on my maturity in the matter.

In the weeks leading to the wedding, the conversation with Eugene and my uncle continually churned in my brain. *Why did the elders—including my own uncle—always seem to be punching me down? Weren't they supposed to be providing spiritual food? Weren't they supposed to treat God's sheep with the utmost tenderness and compassion? Weren't they supposed to be balsam in Gilead?*

The more active I was in the congregation, the more stressed and depressed I became. During the years I served as both ministerial servant and pioneer, I was habitually worn down by the elders. Once I was no longer a ministerial servant, the routine discouragement abated somewhat. But even now, as someone who was neither Servant nor pioneer, I was still losing sleep over how I was treated in the congregation. Since Jehovah's Witnesses are "the happiest group of people on Earth" and since there is "joy beyond compare" in serving God, I was forced to ask: *Am I doing something wrong? Why do all my attempts to do all I can for God and the Society keep backfiring? Why are my sincere efforts to help and to bring happiness to others—inviting my cousin out in service, allowing young children in the congregation to make a sign for our wedding, performing my sister's wedding ceremony—incessantly pulverized into a heap of ruins?*

The more I did in the congregation, the more I tried to do, the more frustrated and discouraged I became. Pioneering, serving as a ministerial servant, trying to help in Wheelock, all served to emaciate my faith. This was contrary to all I had been taught. But it was true.

I hated privileges that only served to upset me. I hated being cornered by elders with senseless agendas. I hated pretending to smile when inside I was crying. I resolved to try something new.

I would make it my aim to do only what I wanted to do. In that way, I hoped to be able to stay strong in the final days before Armageddon. If I was not in the forefront (or reaching out to be in the forefront) of the congregation, there would be far less discouragement for the elders to feed me. If I focused only on the basics, and consigned myself to the few congregational activities I unquestionably found satisfying, then in time the elders may ask me to do more. But instead of eagerly accepting whatever they requested, I would consider whether or not I was certain to find satisfaction in the task. If not, I would respectfully decline.

And so, I began a new *me*. A *me* who was not concerned with rank or privilege. A kinder, gentler *me*. It was going to work. It had to work.

ALL ABOUT BIRDS

If you have a means of supporting yourself, do you really need to spend time, money, and effort on further education?

—*The Watchtower*, June 15, 2011, p. 31

I was granted my first opportunity to stretch the new *me* a few days before my sister's wedding. Diane visited me at work to ask a favor: "Kyle and I want to know if you want to say the prayer at our wedding."

Without having to worry about the elders, or any position in the congregation, I was able to decisively answer: "I'd love to."

"Are you sure Uncle Pete won't get mad?"

"Don't care." And then, remembering it was her special day, I amended: "I don't care if you don't care."

Diane shrugged. "I'm tired of his stupid games."

I meditated on the nature of my prayer. I prayed to deliver an articulate prayer in front of the bride and groom and the attendees. Having freed myself of the need to ingratiate the elders, or anyone else, I concentrated solely on giving sincere, eloquent supplication to God in the sight of all the witnesses.

Early afternoon that Saturday, I stood as a groomsman at my sister's wedding. For the first time in my twenty-three years, I was not nervous to be on stage. I stood in a tuxedo; my feet collapsing in the patent leather loafers, listening to Papa conduct the ceremony. When the time came, he called on me to pray. I stepped up to the lectern, grabbed it with both hands, and looked at the crowd as they bowed their heads. I nodded at the bride and groom, bowed my head and prayed.

Feeling confident in the new direction I was taking my life, I began making other changes. I endeavored to become more thoughtful; more reflective. I recognized there was no need to be the leader every time a group of friends got together. I stopped praying before dinner. Jennifer set out the meal, and I'd just begin eating. Jennifer initially balked at my insubordination to tradition, but her resistance withered when I noted the pointlessness of the tradition. From then on, unless we had guests for dinner, we no longer prayed before mealtime. I was glad to dispense with the ritualistic formality. I wanted my worship to mean something—I didn't want it to simply be a motion.

In the same vein, I decided to no longer offer the *Watchtower* and *Awake!* to householders. I had no qualms against the magazines. What I disliked was that we had lost sight of the main thrust of going door-to-door. We were hypothetically supposed to be warning people about God's impending Day of Judgment. When the *Watchtower* and *Awake!* featured cover stories concerning menopause, chronic fatigue syndrome, boredom, and the pagan origins of Christmas,[72] I feared our message would be lost. Householders could not join us if our message was predicated on such mundane topics. So instead, I started offering brochures with titles like *The Government that will bring Paradise* and *Look! I'm Making All Things New!*

The most significant change I made was my employment. I had worked at the same store at the same mall for over four years. I was content there—with one substantial exception. That exception was Jeremy.

Hardly a day went by when I did not see Jeremy. Our co-workers began to push me on my obvious shunning. My paltry attempt to barricade the conversation was woefully transparent. Everyone at the store knew that the only way a person could stay on Jeremy's bad side was by choosing to stay there. Worse, everyone knew that the supposed disagreement was due to Jeremy's sexual orientation. In defending myself, I came across as homophobic and shallow.

I had to escape from Jeremy.

In early October, I transferred to another branch, convincing myself that the 0.75 miles I shaved off my commute was the real reason for the change. I called my previous store several months later needing a customer's eyeglasses prescription, and when I heard Jeremy's voice on the other end, I swiftly hung up. "No answer," I lied to the customer.

Over the ensuing years, Jeremy devolved into a worse and worse person, at least in our minds. When his name came up, it was only to exaggerate a grievance, or minimize an attribute. Meanwhile, the actual Jeremy became an enigma. "Whatever happened to Jeremy? Has anyone seen Jeremy lately?" As if exchanging clues on the whereabouts of a hidden medallion, we swapped stories: "Oh, I saw him at the grocery store the other day; he put on some weight," or "I heard he's working at Southdale Mall now—a friend of a friend of a friend saw him and *he has a goatee!*"

With Jeremy out of my life, my transformation was finally complete. I felt good about myself again, happy to have banished so much stress from my life.

Rhett Sutter walked into my new place of employment one morning complaining of his recent job loss. He'd lost one of his cleaning accounts, and was fretting over his finances. I asked him if it was possible to get another cleaning account, but he told me of his visit to the doctor's office, where he'd been warned that the long hours, hard labor, and harsh chemicals were not doing his body any favors. Nearly crying, Rhett said he had begun pioneering again, but was forced to stop when he had been too sick to attain even half the hourly requirement. "I'm getting old," he joked. I pointed out that he was only twenty-seven.

Then he asked about working in the eyeglass business. "Yeah, that'd be great," I said excitedly. "I'd love to have you working here!"

"Thanks, man," Rhett said.

By month's end, Rhett was working right alongside me. I again had my old friend, brother and mentor back in my life.

Then my daily allotment of Sutters was doubled. As I was walking around socializing one evening before the meeting, the icy winter wind blew Ryan in unexpectedly. In the six years since his marriage, the two of us had been in each other's company only eight times. I promptly walked over to Ryan and told him how good it was to see him. "I've missed you."

"Well, then I got good news for you." He set down his son Sydney and unzipping his coat. "You're gonna be seeing a lot more of me." Ryan, still smarting from divorce, was striking out anew and was moving in with his dad for encouragement and assistance in his inchoate bachelorhood. Jennifer and I quickly included Ryan in our escapades. We watched movies together. We went to concerts together. We made short films together. We philosophized about all manner of life together.

Meanwhile, parallel events transpired in my own family. My mom's encounter with a co-worker gave my dad the cause he needed to leave the marriage for all time. Against Eugene's wishes, he filed for divorce and by the following summer, he was dating a divorcee from a neighboring congregation.

While out in service soon after the divorce was finalized, an elder asked my wife and me: "It's really sad, isn't it?"

I nodded.

"It really shows how unnatural divorce is, and how Jehovah doesn't want anyone to get divorced."

Neither of us knew what to say, so we just nodded in agreement. Looking for more of a response, the elder asked: "How about you, James, how is your parents' divorce affecting you?"

"They were always fighting," I said flatly. "I wish they would've gotten divorced ten years ago."

The elder looked aghast. But I was through with pretenses. My parents didn't belong together. There were no innocent parties, there were no guilty parties. There were just two people who shared a bed at opposite ends of the house. I thought about 1 Corinthians 4:8: "Love never fails." I thought about how their marriage failed, and it made me wonder if ever there was any love between them.

Christmas Eve is just another day for a Jehovah's Witness, and as it fell on a Thursday in 1998, Jennifer and I attended bookstudy as we did every Thursday. When we got home, however, we found Cosmo lying on the floor of his cage. His breathing was loud and laborious, his wings limp. We gingerly wrapped him up and brought him to the only vet open on the holiday.

The next morning, Cosmo was back on his perch, and we spent the day doting over him. One week later, on New Year's Eve, Cosmo again took to the bottom of his cage.

I began including Cosmo in my prayers. I was uncertain if such a thing was appropriate, as God's relationship towards animals was vague. The Society taught that animals would not be granted everlasting life in Paradise. While death is a punishment for humans, it is a way of life for animals.

But I also knew that God cared for his animal creations: "Do not two sparrows sell for a coin of small value? Yet not one of them will fall to the ground without your Father's knowledge."[73] With this scripture in mind, I prayed for Cosmo's well-being.

Time. It's not an absolute, but in this mortality, it is always progressing forward. For all our trying, we can't reverse the arrow. We cannot even budge the arrow. As my last birthday in the 1900s came and went, I began to feel that time was consuming my being. Soon, the only millennium I had ever known would become history. With the Paradise looming in the near future, I knew I would never grow old. Still, the nearness of the year 2000 made me feel old. Where was the promised Paradise? Already eighty-five years had passed since 1914, and though the Society continually chanted that we were closer than ever, there were no more fulfilled prophecies or indications that we were any closer to Paradise than when I was in elementary school.

I might have just pushed this uncomfortable observation into the recesses of my brain, had it not been called to light by the most righteous man I ever met. At work one boring weekday morning, I offhandedly commented that there were only six more months until 2000. Rhett ponderously looked out across the store. "I never thought we'd still be in this world in the year 2000."

I feigned nonchalance. "Maybe we won't. We've still got a little while to go yet."

Rhett smiled. "All we can do is wait, right, man?"

I thought about this for many days. What if the Paradise was still ten years off, or more? Were Jennifer and I willing to continue living in a small, old apartment while working at jobs we hated? I told Jennifer my feelings on the matter, nervous that my thoughts of a far-off Armageddon were blasphemous. But she agreed.

We explored our immediate possibilities: Jennifer worked as a maid at a hotel, and there was no opportunity for advancement. Her job consisted of cleaning peoples' filth from the rooms. "I don't want to spend ten more years emptying ashtrays and picking up used condoms."

My job was marginally better. I hated having to wear a suit to work every day, and the customers grated on my soul. My job offered little advancement, too.

After much deliberation, we came to the decision that I should go to college. I reminded my wife how much I had hated school, but she pointed out that college would be different: I would be in control, not my parents. I argued that we shouldn't be wasting time in this wicked world going to school, but Jennifer pointed out that we both held to the belief that Armageddon was at least two or three years into the future.

We were excruciatingly ignorant of post-secondary education. We visited the library, and Jennifer looked through college catalogues while I browsed the science section. The biggest obstacle was my inability to decide on a profession.

"What do you really want to learn?" she questioned.

It took me days to come up with an answer, but I finally settled on chemistry. Jennifer discovered a community college a half hour away that offered a course in laboratory technology (the closest thing we could find to pure chemistry). I initially balked at the long commute, but when I saw there were no other options, I drove to the college and took a performance test.

Although I could have begun classes that fall, I told Jennifer I wanted to wait until spring semester. I needed time to adjust to the idea of going back to school. Jennifer, for her part, took the six-month interim to look for a better job. She had plenty of incentive: she'd be working full-time while I was in school.

When midsummer arrived, Jennifer and I again headed down to the city of Rochester for the yearly District Convention. Sarah sat by us all three days. Every day, she complained how upset she was that her parents had decided against attending the convention. Sarah shouldn't have been too alarmed at this course of action; after all, they'd been missing many meetings and had been in a downward spiral of discouragement since the bad events at Wheelock. Only recently, their dad had quit being a ministerial servant. The responsibilities that go with that privilege were simply too stressful for him. Though I said nothing, my father-in-law's decision made me feel better about my own decision: being a ministerial servant *was* stressful, and I was glad not to be the only man so affected.

Conversely, I also felt angry with Jennifer's parents for giving up. Behind private doors, Jennifer and I excused their behavior as the symptoms of a mid-life crisis. *We are so close to the End—how can they lose sight of the goal now?* I wanted to ask them what, so late in the stream of time, could make them slack off from attending the meetings and the convention. But I was afraid of the answers I might receive.

One evening that August, Cosmo fell to his cage floor again. I reached in and Cosmo faithfully hopped up on my finger. Petting his feathers, I asked him if he was okay. "I'm a good boy," he said.

His self-diagnosis wasn't very conclusive. The next morning, Jennifer took Cosmo to the vet. The doctor's diagnosis was mostly an exercise in guesswork, and his medical credentials were useless. By the week's end, Cosmo was dead.

His death was so abrupt; so unjust. Jennifer and I had counted on having him as a pet for two decades, not two years. He had been wrested from his nest at too young an age, shoved in a tiny box and shipped across country, where a second-rate pet store gave half-assed information on how to care for him. We, his guardians, had returned his love by squirting him with water and yelling at him. When at last we had educated our ignorant selves, Cosmo's seizures began. For nine months, his major organs failed, until he died.

The next day, we drove to Jennifer's parents' house. Beneath the rose bushes, we buried Cosmo in a tiny plot next to Beaker, our pet parakeet who had died a year earlier.

I tried to put on a happy face for Jennifer's family, but I was depressed. I was sad that Cosmo was gone, but I was also angered. As a Witness, I had grown up knowing that animals will not be resurrected in Paradise; living forever was the exclusive privilege of humans. Dead relatives we would see again. But Cosmo, innocent, naïve, peaceful, friendly, sinless Cosmo? He was dead and would remain so for trillions of eons.

THE LONG LIE

An unbridled, morbid curiosity can lure us into a morass of speculation and human theories wherein genuine faith and godly devotion cannot survive.

—*The Watchtower*, February 1, 1987, p. 29

After Cosmo died, I considered the plight of the animal kingdom: Could God's intentions for the animals be reconciled with his love and justice? If God chose to create life and then destroy it, that was His business. But why create animals with the ability to suffer, and the ability to be conscious of suffering? Humans, of course, had the same consciousness, but they were also promised a reward. At the other extreme, plants were not given any such hope of eternal life, but neither were they aware of any suffering that befell them. How a God of love could create cockatiels, give them the cognition to be aware of suffering, watch them die, and refuse to resurrect them was beyond my ability to grasp. I did not want to think that God was so cruel and calloused. The only alternative then, was that the Society was wrong about animals' resurrection hope. Unfortunately, the Society dismisses such concern over pets as animal worship.

I reread the Society's book *Is There a Creator Who Cares about You?* in an effort to redress my faith. The book's discussion of animals was studded with inaccuracies, and the remainder of the book fared even worse. Too often, the book resorted to straw man arguments to defend belief in God, saying, "The reason many reject the existence of a Creator is that they do not *want* to believe."[74] The book argues that a person should not believe merely what he sees, but should be open to believing in things for which there is related evidence. This same argument had been presented fourteen years earlier, in *Reasoning from the Scriptures*:

> Are there some things that we cannot see with our eyes but that we believe exist because there are sound reasons to do so? What about the *air* we breathe? We may feel it when there is a breeze. We can tell that it fills our lungs, even though we do not see it. . . . And we cannot see *gravity*. But when we drop something we see evidence that gravity is at work. Nor do we see *odors*, but our nose picks them up.[75]

This line of reasoning was wholly unsatisfying. What about blind people—do they believe in nothing? The Society here takes the word "see," in general meaning "to understand," and applies it to literal sight. A better question would be: Are there some things that we cannot perceive with any of our senses but that we believe exist because there are sound reasons to do so?

Most stunning was what the text offered as an example of something we cannot perceive directly. They gave as an example extra-solar planets. Quoting from *Discover* magazine, the book said that scientists had discovered about a dozen planets orbiting distant stars.

When I read this, I threw the book on the floor. For years I held that the strongest evidence for belief in God was that we lived in the only solar system in the universe. But abruptly, I learned there were planets orbiting stars other than our own Sun. Adding insult to my ignorance, I only uncovered this faith-destroying evidence *by reading a piece of literature produced by the Society.*

At the library the next day, I looked up the quoted magazine and, sure enough, there were other planets out there. Lots of them. Astronomers had known about them for over four years. The religious implications are immense; in the year 1600, Giordano Bruno was fastened to a stake and burned alive for his belief in extra-solar planets. The Catholic Church commissioned his death, as well as the burning of all of his writings.

"Of course we were created by God—he didn't make any other planets but the ones in this solar system," I had argued to skeptical nonbelievers at school and work. "If we had evolved, what would be the chances of life forming on the one single, solitary planet in the whole universe that could support life?" Now I felt stupid. My argument was as baseless as those who used to assert we were at the center of the universe. Our place in the universe was not special; neither was our place in the galaxy; nor even our place in the solar system. Now, even planets themselves were no longer unique. As I knew there were more stars in the universe than grains of sand on the world's beaches, it logically followed that there were even more planets than stars; that life would arise on at least one of them seemed practically a given. Indeed, it would almost have been odd if life had not arisen.

The best reconciliation I could arrive at for the conundrum was this: Jehovah created all those other planets with the idea that humans would inhabit them in some future millennium. Jennifer agreed this was a possibility.

Having not seen Gabe in months, we called him to join us for lunch. He agreed, and we met at a restaurant. When Gabe asked if I had any new knowledge to share with him, I decided to talk to him about extra-solar planets.

Gabe laughed in faux-mockery. "We can't live on other planets. Isn't Jupiter like negative five thousand degrees?" He reminded me that the Bible states, "God has given the earth to the sons of men."[76]

I clarified my inquiry, and then asked: "What does that scripture have to do with anything? No kidding that God gave earth to us humans. We're here, on it right now. I'm not saying we'll all leave it. But maybe we'll want to explore other places, or maybe the Earth will start to get crowded. Why is that so hard for you to fathom?"

"James, are you a Witness or aren't you? Don't you know that the heavens belong to Jehovah? We can't go out there. And you think Jehovah will let the earth get too full? He'll shut off our reproductive powers long before then."

I thought for a second. "Okay, first, you don't know when He'll stop us from reproducing. Second, there's a difference between outer space and heaven."

"It just doesn't make sense."

"Gabe, I'll tell you what doesn't make sense: that God would make such an enormous Universe and then only let us occupy 0.000000000001 percent of it. *That* doesn't make sense! Imagine the Universe was just planet Earth and God said, 'Okay, you have to stay in Minneapolis. Don't ever leave. The rest is just stuff I created for you to look at through your telescopes.'"

Gabe was unnerved. "We're not even supposed to be speculating about things like that."

"Don't even get me started on that, Gabriel," I snapped. But Jennifer looked at me, and with her eyes she told me to let the matter rest.

I did let the matter rest, figuring that if I shouldn't speculate on the future, I would bolster my faith by researching the past. According to the Society, Jerusalem was destroyed by Nebuchadnezzar's Babylonian armies in 607 BC. This is the date from which the Watchtower Society calculates that the Last Days began in 1914 AD.[77] I wanted to know not just the year, but the exact date of Jerusalem's fall.

The first Watchtower book I opened simply claimed, "Reliable Bible chronology indicates . . . it took place by early October of 607 BCE."[78] Regrettably, the Society did not list their references for this "reliable Bible chronology." I pulled the *Insight* book off the shelf and turned to the main heading "Babylon," and found only one sentence discussing that eventful year:

> That year, 607 BCE, when Jerusalem was laid desolate, was a significant one in the counting of time until Jehovah, the Universal Sovereign, would set up the world ruler of his choice in Kingdom power.[79]

I browsed the pages covered under "Chronology" and immediately noticed a void of any concrete proof of Jerusalem's fall having been in 607 BCE. Instead, the Society filled the pages with reasons why secular historians and archaeologists should be viewed with suspicion. Meanwhile, the subheading "Bible Chronology and Secular History" commenced with: "Concern is often expressed over the need to try to 'harmonize' or 'reconcile' the biblical account with the chronology found in ancient secular records. . . . Such coordinating would indeed be vital—*if* the ancient secular records could be demonstrated to be unequivocally exact and consistently reliable."

The next paragraph provided one reason why some ancient documents are not reliable: the long life-spans given in the text are obviously mythical. A sad argument this, coming from an organization that taught Methuselah (who died at age 969), was a genuine, historical figure. On the next page, the book said, "The great age of the secular documents is certainly outweighed by the vastly inferior quality of their contents when compared with the Bible." The book slandered secular history further by stating (with nary a hint of irony): "Casual students of ancient history often labor under the misconception that the cuneiform tablets were always written at the same time or shortly after the events recorded on them."[80] I reread that sentence five times. I found it difficult to believe that the Society would call into question Babylonian tablets for their non-contemporary nature when huge chunks of the Bible were written centuries after the fact.[81] The *Insight* book summed up their argument on page 450:

> It is only when the secular chronology harmonizes with the Biblical record that a person may rightly feel a measure of confidence in such ancient secular dating.

I distilled the essence of their arguments to: don't trust any historical record unless it harmonizes with the Society's interpretation of the Bible.

On our next visit to the library, I ran straight to the encyclopedias. Alighting upon the *World Book Encyclopedia*, I grabbed the 'B' volume and scanned the BABYLON entry for coverage of the seventh century CE. Though the entry was silent as to Jerusalem's capture, one sentence began: "During the reign of Nebuchadnezzar II, from 605–562 BC . . ."

I scratched my head. *That's odd.* I knew Nebuchadnezzar was king over Babylonia at the time of Jerusalem's fall, yet this encyclopedia indicated that he did not ascend to the throne until two years *after* that event. Figuring it must have been a typo, I noticed the entry ended with a list of related articles, including "Jews—Foreign Domination." So I grabbed the 'J' volume.

That subheading read, in part: "In 587 or 586 BC, the Babylonians conquered Judah, destroyed the Temple, and took many Jews to Babylonia as prisoners."

This was a singularly staggering find. I read and reread that sentence, slack-jawed at its implications. Refusing to believe the Society could be wrong about so important a date, I moved from encyclopedia to encyclopedia, like a bee searching for the perfect flower. *Collier's Encyclopedia, Compton's Encyclopedia, Grolier's Encyclopedia, the Encyclopedia Americana* and even the mighty *Encyclopædia Britannica* all agreed: Jerusalem capitulated to the Babylonian armies in 587 BC. None of the encyclopedias mentioned 607 as a probable or even a possible date.

I left the library empty-handed.

The Society unapologetically dates events in the stream of time: Isaac died in 1738 BC; Asa became king of Judah in 977 BC; Haggai authored his eponymous scrolls in 520 BC.[82] These dates, though, are mere passing curiosities to Witnesses. Should the Society declare that new evidence proves Haggai was actually written in 540 BC, such a correction would solicit little more than a collective "hmm." Pressed to provide the most important date in the whole of Bible chronology, Witnesses will, without deviation, extol the importance of 607 BC. To alter this date is to eviscerate the Watchtower's most prized doctrine. If 607 BC is wrong, then 1914 is wrong, as the latter is rooted securely upon the former.

Instantaneously, my cognitive powers began constructing apologetics for such findings: The books are wrong. They haven't done the proper research. Satan planted this evidence.

I found it impossible to trick myself into believing so many reputable sources had conspired against the Society. *How could encyclopedias' researchers so carefully scrutinize and document everything else, yet be consistently inaccurate on this one point? If non–Witness encyclopedias were unreliable, why would the Society quote from them? If the Society had the truth about the date of Jerusalem's fall, why did they not hold their sources up for scrutiny to the secular historians?* Such a finding on the part of the Society would give a tremendous witness for Jehovah and give many doubters a change of heart.

There were many opportunities to discuss these accidental findings with fellow Witnesses. One morning before the store opened, I said to Rhett, as offhandedly as possible, "You know, I've been doing some research, and I noticed that no worldly source agrees with the Society that Jerusalem fell in 607."

Rhett cocked his head as if doing so made the comment slide into his brain easier. I could see the change in his expression as the thought registered and he promptly provided a rebuttal. "There's lots of things that worldly people disagree with us about. That's why we should be glad we have Jehovah's Holy Spirit, right, man? We couldn't understand the deeper things if He wasn't directing matters."

"The Society had to get the date from somewhere. If 607 is the right date, then why do all the historical documents refute it?"

Rhett absorbed the argument thoughtfully. "That's why we need to keep checking that what we believe is from the Bible, you know? We don't want to go beyond the things written."

I shoved my hands in my pockets. "That's true."

A while later, an elder from another congregation visited our Hall to deliver a public talk that featured heavily the mathematics involved in calculating 1914 from 607. I joined with other Witnesses in providing lunch for this elder. While eating, I donned a mask of indifference, and asked: "So what, in your opinion, is the strongest evidence that Jerusalem fell in 607?"

The elder paused in mid-chew. He continued masticating until he was able to speak. "Certainly the Bible," he said, with reverential gravitas. "It has a perfect track-record of accurate history and reliable prophecy."

Everyone nodded as if the elder had just confounded them by pointing out that one plus one equals two. A sister at the table shook her head in dismay, lamenting the inexcusability of worldly people who could not perceive such simple truths.

It seemed the only person who fully understood the import of my dilemma was the woman to whom I was married. I told her the Society was wrong about 607, and she began, in full Witness defense, to inquire as to how I could be so sure. I pointed out the lack of substance in the Society's literature, coupled with the near-unanimous accord of secular references.

Conceding my point, she asked, "What difference does it make?"

I elucidated, in an exaggerated tone, that 607 is used to calculate 1914, but Jennifer simply shrugged. "That just means that the Last Days started in a different year, that's all. It doesn't mean they're wrong about everything else."

I reminded her that, ostensibly, one of the most convincing reasons why we have the truth is because *The Watchtower* foretold the End would begin in 1914: "They always point out how much the world has changed since 1914—World War I, the Spanish Flu and stuff like that—and they say that Jesus threw the demons out of heaven in 1918.[83] So, if 1914 is wrong, then none of that holds any weight."

Jennifer dropped her hands between her knees. "Wow," she said, as if she'd just watched a fireworks display, "I didn't think about all that."

Leaning back and resigning myself to fate, I said: "Unfortunately, we can't tell anyone about this, or we risk being disfellowshipped for apostasy."

The apartment filled with a profound, protracted silence.

We paid our regular visit to my grandparents' home some weeks later. Sitting in their living room, with the television blaring, Papa sleeping, Nana rocking in her rocking chair and crocheting, and Aunt Janet sharing the couch with Jennifer and me, we discussed the increasingly apparent point that I had not yet been reappointed ministerial servant. I wanted to tell them of my smarting faith and disagreements with the Society, but I feared they would hate me for such blasphemies. Instead, I told them I wanted to take it easy for a while, and keep some of the stress at bay.

"But James," Nana said, "That's what Satan wants us to do. He wants us to take it easy now, he wants us to slack off, so that we stop doing what's right."

I lamented that she misunderstood: I had no intention of rejecting God, and I still engaged in the key aspects of the religion.

Aunt Janet leaned forward. "If you're doing that stuff for Jehovah already, you should be moved to do more, because you want to please him."

I held up my hands. "You know what? I do want to please Jehovah, and I do want to do all that I can for him"—and it was right at that moment that I wanted to tell them that I couldn't do more if it meant being a hypocrite, but instead, I said, "I just didn't like all the rules."

My aunt was floored by this comment. "What rules?"

"All the rules for being a servant. There's already a bunch of rules for just being a Witness; I don't feel like submitting to more."

"Jehovah gives us those rules for our protection," Nana said. "They're not burdensome, they keep us healthy and make us wise—"

I cut her off. "I don't mean the laws in the Bible, like don't murder, don't steal, and don't commit adultery. I'm fine with those rules. I mean the silly, arbitrary rules that the elders make."

"What rules, James? What rules?" Aunt Janet repeated, "I'm dying to know what these rules are that you're talking about! Name one!"

"You tell me when to stop," I told her, "I can't hang a 'just married' sign from my car at my own wedding. I can't have a limo at my wedding. I can't give my sister's wedding ceremony. I can't watch rated-R movies—"

"I don't know why you'd wanna watch that filth," Aunt Janet interjected.

"—I can't have a beard. I have to wear a tie to the meetings. I don't have to wear a suit coat, but I have to bring it in case I get asked to go on stage—"

Nana raised her voice over my staccato of rules. "James," she said, in a calmer voice, "A lot of those things, too, are for our benefit." She offered the tired adage of providing a good witness by means of our dress and grooming. I countered that guidelines were acceptable, but rules were repugnant, and I asked her how a 'just married' sign at a wedding would negate our attempts to provide a good witness to our neighbors.

"James," Nana said, leaning back in her rocking chair. "What can I say? Sometimes the elders maybe get carried away with what they think is best for the congregation. They're not perfect. And that's a good thing, because if they were perfect, we'd never be able to live up to them, would we?"

I conceded, but argued that I didn't want to be a ministerial servant because those few extra rules hoisted upon them were unbearable.

Aunt Janet flicked her wrist. "Then just do the best you can as an average Witness."

I turned to her. "I will, thank you."

At work the next day, I yearned to broach my floundering faith to Rhett, but Rhett superseded my topic by telling me he was quitting. I was disheartened, but the company we worked for did not pay well. He secured work in the janitorial business once more, surmising that the hard labor, harsh chemicals, and late hours were an acceptable trade-off for higher wages. I congratulated him on the move, joking that it was good he distance himself from the mall's fast food establishments, which, in his short tenure as my co-worker, had caused his belly to spill further and further past his belt line, an observation that was easy to make, as he never indulged on new, roomier shirts. When I told Rhett to make sure he ate better; he laughed. "That's always the goal, man, as long as I can afford it."

And then it was December 31, 1999. As the world celebrated the New Year's Eve of a lifetime, Jennifer and I, like good Witnesses, holed up quietly at home. Two weeks later, my college career commenced. I put in a request to work part-time at my job and, in doing so, lost my medical benefits. Jennifer pulled through with a new job. She worked for a small company that ordered and prepared books for school libraries. It did not pay much better than her job as a hotel housekeeper, but it was a cleaner, easier occupation, and she would be able to work full-time while I was in college. We hoped this would recoup some of the funds we'd be losing from my reduction in hours.

Within a few weeks, I came to look forward to my classes. I took pleasure in writing speeches about things for which I held a passion. I lived in anticipation for the history professor to assign the next chapter in our books. The basic chemistry class, meanwhile, opened my eyes to the fundamentals of molecular and ionic formation—something I had never perfectly grasped in my private studies.

In between each class, I passed my spare time at the college library and took refuge among the tall bookshelves that sprouted like literary plants. One afternoon, I noticed a glass-encased Darwinian shrine: maps showing the progressive spread of humans over the millennia. The base of the display case housed fossils of proto-humans. I found myself utterly disgusted by these icons of evolution; I had no explanation for skulls that looked *kind of* human, but not quite. The best rationale I could erect was that such bones were the remains of deformed children, from an era when disease wracked humanity at a much worse level.

As I walked out of the library and spent the next half hour alone on the drive home, I came to find all manner of turmoil in my head. I hated the mental gymnastics I engaged in whenever I came across anything related to my religion: apologetics when I read Watchtower literature, polemics when I read secular material. I prayed intensely to Jehovah to force me to believe His word and His organization. I faithfully attended all the meetings, and tried to find comfort there.

One such comfort I received at the Kingdom Hall was on a Sunday, when Uncle Peter and his wife, Aunt Nancy approached Jennifer and me to ask if we were planning to attend my cousin Matthew's wedding.

"We were invited," I said. "Are you gonna be there?"

They looked at each other, and then back at me. Uncle Peter placed his hand on my shoulder. "Listen, I'm not gonna tell you guys what to do. You're adults, and you can make your own decisions. But, in our opinion, you shouldn't go."

I furrowed my brow. "Why not? He's my cousin."

My aunt cut in. "He's marrying a worldly girl, Jimmy. He'll be unevenly yoked."[84]

Jennifer spoke up. "But Matthew's not a Witness, so how can he be unevenly yoked?"

"Yeah," I added, "He's never been a Witness."

"Could have fooled me," Peter said. "I've seen him at the meetings here for years."

"He attended meetings because he was a little kid and his mom brought him. But he never got baptized. He's never even been a publisher. I don't think he's been to a single meeting in over a year."

"All the more reason why you guys shouldn't go."

"What do you mean? If I don't go, that will just show him and his bride that I only love them if they're in the Truth. How does that give a good Witness?"

"They'll see," my uncle claimed, "that you are trying to keep yourselves clean, and that if they want a relationship with you, they have to love Jehovah first."

I argued that Matthew would never feel welcome to return to the religion if his family shuns him at his own wedding, and Uncle Peter let out a tiny laugh. "Okay, James. Listen: you make your own decision. Frankly, if you're hoping to be a ministerial servant one day, this is something you should consider carefully." He continued, through no prompting on my part, "If you were a servant, this might not be up to you at all. Because, then I'd be telling you not to go. You'd need to set a good example. I can guarantee no other servants will be there."

"Thanks for your opinion," I said. "We'll give it some thought." Jennifer and I began backing away.

"We're just giving you some things to think about," my aunt said.

"It's up to you guys. We just want you to do what's right," Uncle Peter added.

We ducked out of the Kingdom Hall as fast as we could.

In the evening, we attended Matthew's wedding. Included among those in attendance were six ministerial servants and three elders. At the reception, Aunt Val hugged us and profusely thanked us for attending. "I really appreciate you guys coming." She wiped a tear from her check, exuding an immense gratitude that at least some of her son's relatives did not abandon him. "Now *that's* giving a good Witness," I whispered to Jennifer.

By May less than two weeks of the semester remained. The students turned their thoughts to the impending final exams. I studied for the classes whenever I could, even bringing my notes to the Kingdom Hall to read during the meetings.

During my frequent visits to the library, I noticed two young men from my history class who often studied together. I introduced myself to them one afternoon and asked if I could join their study group. Three days in a row that week, and the following week, I sat with Jay and Martin for over an hour trying to ensure that we knew the material for the final. One day, one of the guys suggested we go out to lunch. I felt uneasy spending time with worldly people outside of school or work, but I figured a quick lunch with them was acceptable.

As we sat in the restaurant waiting for our meals, it occurred to me that this was absolutely the first time I had ever done anything socially with people who did not know I was a Witness. Wondering what their thoughts were on religion, I asked them, point-blank: "So what religion are you guys?"

After both giving me an odd stare, Martin said he had very little to do with religion, though he went to church on occasion to appease his family. Jay said that he did not like to be pigeon-holed to one denomination. "I was raised Catholic, and I respect them, but I don't consider myself Catholic anymore."

"I don't think they have the right religion," I said, trying to steer the conversation.

"I don't think they're the only path to God, either," Jay confessed, "but they do provide a lot for people, you know? They do a lot of good work in underdeveloped nations with healthcare and education."

"Then why don't you do it?" I asked.

"Well, in a way, I do it. I go to mass with my mom on Christmas and I go on Easter."

"You don't mind participating in a religion you know is false?"

Sounding a tad defensive, he answered: "It gives *me* something. I like the community, and the idea that we need to cleanse ourselves of evil. I like the tradition, too. Catholics have these grand traditions and these beautiful churches. You don't see that as much in Protestant religions."

"That doesn't mean it's the right religion, does it? Take Galileo, for example."

He laughed. "I don't buy everything they teach. At least they apologized for Galileo. Besides, I think they have a lot of things right."

I had not expected such a persuasive response to my interrogation. Here was a man who, when pressed, admitted he preferred Catholicism over all other Christian religions. Yet Jay's defense of his faith was not a blanket mantra of "Catholics have the truth." His reply was more nuanced, more thoughtful. He readily conceded the Church's botched handling of Galileo, but rationalized that they had apologized for their error.

I wondered if the Watchtower Society had ever apologized for its mistakes.

Further, the idea that a person could belong to a religion and privately hold—much less publicly proclaim!—that their religion had "a lot of things right" was novel to me. In nearly a quarter of a century, I could not once recall any Witness ever honestly admitting that the religion had "a lot of things right," because implicit in such an assertion is the confession that the religion also has a few things wrong.

Later, as the conversation turned to an upcoming biology final, I asked: "So do you guys believe in evolution?"

Jay shrugged. "Why not? It's the way of the world."

"I don't like the term 'believe,'" Martin said, "because it gives the impression that evolution is a matter of faith. And it's not. Faith is something you believe in even though there's no evidence. There's plenty of evidence for evolution."

In my heart, I knew he was right. In the nearly one hundred books I had read over the past two years, I had searched for something, anything, I could hang on to in an effort to prove Creationism. I would read about how evolution violated entropy, and then a few weeks later I'd read how entropy only applied to closed systems, and life on Earth is not a closed system. I would read about the irreducible complexity of the eye, and then, a month later, learn of light-sensing cells and proto-eyes. I would read that evolution is "just a theory," and then learn that theories are better documented than facts. For every Creationist argument, there was an opposite and superior evolutionist argument. Ernst Mayr once wrote: "There is no longer any need to present an exhaustive list of proofs for evolution. That evolution has taken place is so well established that such a detailed presentation of the evidence is no longer needed. In any case, it would not convince those who do not want to be persuaded."[85] But there I was: not wanting to be persuaded, yet finding myself persuaded regardless. *Why wouldn't God help me?*

I had, in essence, been reduced to accepting methodological naturalism, a kind of "God of the gaps," in an effort to support my faith in the religion. Lately God was filling smaller and smaller crevices.

The next day, I found a comfortable chair in the commons area, opposite a window, and pulled out the latest book I was reading, *Science Matters*.[86] I had been drawn to the book by its inclusive list of all things science right inside the front cover, headed with the words: "What You Need To Know and Where To Find It." Want to know about the Doppler Effect? Turn to page 148. Special relativity? Turn to page 158. Halley's Comet? Neutrinos? Turn to pages 14 and 126, respectively. With chapter titles such as "The Atom," "The World of the Quantum," and "Nuclear Physics," the book practically latched onto me as if the author had named me in the dedication.

Then I came upon chapter 16, "The Code of Life." Underneath the title it read: "All life is based on the same genetic code." The connection between this statement and evolutionary theory was a little too close for comfort. Still, I had read two-thirds of this absorbing book, and I didn't want to quit.

After reading the chapter's last words, my eyes leapt across the page to chapter 17, entitled "Evolution." The sight of this word, as always, caused my heart to beat rapidly. I thumbed through the pages to determine the chapter's length. It was nearly twenty pages long. *Do I really want to read twenty pages about evolution? But if I skip it, then I haven't really read the whole book, have I? But if I don't skip it, it might weaken my faith further!* Turning back to the beginning, I read:

> This chapter will offend some people, but that is nothing new. The
> theory of evolution has been offending people for more than a century.
> Two strongly held views about the origin of our planet and its life are in

severe disagreement. Biblical Creationists accept on faith the literal Old Testament account of creation. . . . If you are a Creationist, the Bible—not nature—dictates what you believe. Creationists subordinate observational evidence to doctrine based on their interpretation of sacred texts.

I resolved to skip the chapter. Chapter 18 was entitled "Ecosystems," a much less problematic topic. I began reading, but my mind was not on the words. *Did I really just skip a chapter? Is it really possible for a single chapter in a single book to unravel all that has been indoctrinated into my mind for a quarter century? How weak is my faith?* I pushed these questions to the back of my mind for a time. That time was forty-five seconds.

As I fumbled for the next page, I froze. I looked up from the text and slowly, cautiously, raised my eyes. In the window, I saw, for the first time that day, my reflection. The usual pandemonium of students talking and walking and rushing to class continued all around, but their lives telescoped into the distance until they were parsecs from my soul. My eyes stared at the reflection, and the reflection stared back. My lips parted, and in the time it took me to breathe my next breath, there came, suddenly, a moment of revelation. My eyes were opened. My subconscious mind had been assembling all the pieces of truth and began beating against the wall to my conscious mind until the light burst through. I felt lifted above the fog. With the cobwebs cleared away, I whispered, to no one but myself, "On the outside, I am a Witness . . . but on the inside . . . I am an atheist." *Atheist.* The word tore at my throat and, even in whispering it, I felt ashamed. What had I done? What bad sin had I committed so that I found myself now, at this moment, an unbeliever? The idea of not believing in the existence of Jehovah was at once too great to bear, and no sooner had I said the word than I bit my lip and turned my head in thought. *No, I'm NOT an atheist—because I've never read anything to disprove God's existence. Instead, I'm . . . an agnostic.* I looked up at the reflection. Was it really so? Yes, it was true. After decades of intense Bible study, I had never, ever had the existence of God proven to me. And now, as I sat there, the thousand little puzzle pieces scattered into the recesses of my brain could be held at bay no more. They forced themselves together, and, for the first time, I looked at the assembled picture. In what was a supreme triumph of Occam's Razor, I knew that I could now explain *everything.*

I could explain why Noah's Flood was so impossible. I could explain why there was no good justification for the ban on birthday parties. I could explain why the Watchtower Society held to 607. I could explain why the *Creation* book offered no good explanation of God's origins. I could explain why the Last Days were dragging on for so long. I could explain why pioneering was not satisfying, why serving as a ministerial servant had not been rewarding, and why my prayers had gone unanswered. But I could explain even more. I could explain a young girl falling at my feet and apologizing for lip-syncing, why some hid their sexual orientation, why the elders reveled in encircling Jennifer and me with a dragnet of interference and—most of all—why I radiated such pride when my dad strode across the lawn and nobly explained our revulsion of birthday celebrations. The explanation was this: *It was not true.*

Did I want it to be true? Oh yes, more than *anything* else in the universe. But that didn't make it true. I walked outside, but the thoughts I tried to shrug off were like an invasive species to the ecosystem of my brain; a Eurasian milfoil in a surrounding sea of theology. Like an archaeopteryx on the horizon, the truth pursued me. His wings wafted the air in great, nuanced flaps and his eyes, like a demon's, bored straight through the back of my skull. I tried to outrun him; to take refuge in my car before he came and carried me off to a land of faithlessness. I could not. His feathers whipped at my neck, and I turned to see him land upon my shoulder. He was no longer an archaeopteryx; he was Cosmo. And the bird, an apparition from beyond the gates of my mind's watchtowers, whispered:

There is no Balsam in Gilead. We are of this Earth, and nothing more.

The bird vanished. His short, suffering life was snuffed out again, and even a God of love did not see fit to bring him back.

Reaching my car, I unlocked the door, threw my bag across the seat, and sat. My eyes stared in the slit of the rearview mirror. Again, I froze.

You know it's not true, James. You have known it for years. . . . Why don't you just admit it and move on with your life? I had to look away from my reflection. Without the religion, there was no life, so how could I move on?

I had been born into the world perfectly suited to be a Witness. I had loved the Truth, and tried to do my best. Still, I had failed. A pervasive, compelling urge to cry consumed me, but I couldn't make myself tear up. Emoting over the new revelation would, I feared, give it fuel to continue. Like a sick patient who receives a diagnosis, I felt that paying any outward heed to my incipient agnosticism would simply confirm it.

I wanted to forget all the doubts and troubles and issues and continue on in the religion as I had always done. Everything was nothing without the Truth, and I did not want to be nothing. I began lying to myself right then and there. "It's not that I think the Society is *totally* false; it's just that I think there's a greater *chance* they're not right." Yes, that was it. I could deal with this sort of self-lie. I convinced myself that my belief system had merely faltered relatively, not absolutely.

That night, I lied. Not to Jennifer, but to myself. When Jennifer asked how the day had been, I could honestly tell her it had been fine. Had I given in to some sort of physical manifestation, I would have had to tell her, "Guess what? I cried today," and then she would ask why and I'd have to divulge the disturbing details. But I had the resolve to not allow the sacrilegious thought to escape into the open. I squeezed and shoved and locked up the thought and so, when asked if I still believed the Truth, I could honestly respond affirmatively. Of course, I didn't know that I didn't believe the Truth because I was so good at self-deception that I was not even conscientiously aware that I was lying to myself. It sounds strange, I know, to hold to such a level of cognitive dissonance. But that's what I did.

After all, it wasn't hurting anyone. Was it?

I WISH I WAS SMARTER; I WISH I WAS DUMBER

> Since our Creator wants us to search for truth, it cannot be wrong to act on the evidence that we find—even if this means changing our religion.
>
> —*Awake!*, July 2009, p. 28

Is it incomprehensible to remain in a religion demanding so much time and energy? To be sure, if it was the only path to God, or if it was fully enjoyable and satisfying, it may be understandable. But the Society was not the "Truth" and continuing to be counted amongst the Jehovah's Witnesses was an act in self-repression and hypocrisy.

So why stay?

1. THE PAST: During my quarter-century of life, I had given over fifty talks, engaged in the door-to-door work for over seven thousand hours, and attended nearly four thousand meetings, assemblies, and conventions. I had served as a pioneer, a ministerial servant, and volunteered at Bethel. The possibility that all had been for naught was unthinkable. I did not want to consider that I had risen early in the morning, donned a suit, and driven around in neighborhoods all day when I could have been going to college. I did not want to think I had submitted to the elders' perpetual harassment, when I could have dismissed them as powerless. I wanted the Witnesses to have the Truth, lest it invalidate decades of hard work.

2. THE PRESENT: Everyone was in the religion. My wife, sister, parents, and grandparents, were all Jehovah's Witnesses. All of my friends were Witnesses. I loved no one else. I knew no one else.

3. THE FUTURE: I deeply desired the Witnesses' conviction of a future in Paradise to be true. No one promised anything better. In essence, I wanted to throw my ante in with Pascal's Wager: If the Watchtower Society is correct about the future, and I remain in their good graces, then I shall gain eternal life. If they are wrong, I will have led a decent life, and, in the end, have lost nothing.

Of course, there was another possibility: Maybe some other religion was correct. It seemed highly improbable, but that was part of being a Witness: every other religion is demonized. The *Watchtower* declared religion to be "a snare and a racket,"[87] and their literature continually pointed out flaws in other religions.

That Witnesses had their foibles and that the Watchtower Society had its inconsistencies, there was no doubt. But the idea that another religion might be the correct path to God? Not a chance.

That summer, I looked into the Watchtower literature in an effort to determine, precisely, to what extent dissenting opinions were allowed. The results were not encouraging.

> Approved association with Jehovah's Witnesses requires *accepting the entire range* of the true teachings of the Bible, including those Scriptural teachings that are unique to Jehovah's Witnesses.[88]

> To turn away from Jehovah and his organization, to spurn the direction of the "faithful and discreet slave," and to rely simply on personal Bible reading and interpretation is to become like a solitary tree in a parched land.[89]

The thought of condemning personal Bible interpretation was frightening enough, but even more so was their condemnation of independent thought:

> Avoid . . . questioning the counsel that is provided by God's visible organization. How is such independent thinking manifested? A common way is by questioning the counsel that is provided by God's visible organization.[90]

Indeed, a good Witness should have no dissenting opinions, because a good Witness would never investigate beyond the pages of *The Watchtower*:

> In Jehovah's organization it is not necessary to spend a lot of time and energy in research, for there are brothers in the organization who are assigned to that very thing.[91]

It was impossible to disagree, even within the confines of one's own brain, with even the most minute of Witness teachings.

I therefore put forth a great effort convincing myself that I was the stupid one; that I had become so wrapped up in doing research I neglected to notice I was going down the wrong path. I told myself that maybe, just maybe, the Society was right and I was too dim-witted to assemble the pieces correctly. My desire, then, was that I could become more knowledgeable on the matters that disturbed me, so as to convince myself of the Society's truth. I prayed to Jehovah about the matter. And this is the prayer that I said:

Jehovah God, my heavenly father,
I am having a tough time right now.
I want to live in the Paradise, and I want to live forever with my wife and
my family and friends,
but you know what has been going on in my head.
I have serious doubts, and I'm not even sure that the Witnesses are the
right religion anymore.
And, Jehovah, you know that this is not what I intended.
You know I wanted to stay strong in your Organization.
You know that I want to become the best Christian I can be.
But so many things lately are not making sense.
I hope this does not sound arrogant, but you know that in my heart I am
not asking this out of arrogance.
I ask that you please make me smarter,
so that I can more fully understand the research I have done;
so that I can know that you are real and the Witnesses are the true religion;
and so that I am not continually nagged by doubts.
I know you are willing to give your servants whatever they ask.
And I know that you once gave Solomon great wisdom so that he could be
a good king.
I am only asking for enough wisdom so I can be a good person.
You know I am asking this just so I can serve you faithfully.
Jehovah, I thank you for all that you do for me.

For a time, I found a tenuous peace by convincing myself that I disagreed with the Society's *interpretation* of the Bible, not the Bible itself. But this rationale, too, soon fell by the wayside when I read a *Watchtower* that arrived in my mailbox just as I was contemplating these issues:

> How inappropriate it would be to challenge or undermine the authority of appointed elders! You should also feel a sense of loyalty to "the faithful and discreet slave" and the agencies that are used to disseminate spiritual "food at the proper time" (Matthew 24:45). Be quick to read and apply the information found in *The Watchtower* and its companion publications.[92]

I hated that I could not speak of my findings to even my closest friends. I kept closed-mouthed on subjects where I disagreed with the Society. This was often problematic, as my friends viewed me as an authority when questions of a scientific nature arose. When pressed, I papered over the topic vaguely and tried to move onto less volatile topics. One day while out in service, a sister asked me point-blank: "You've done a lot of study about Noah's ark, so can you help me out with this one householder who thinks the Flood was just a myth?"

"That was years ago," I said dismissively, "I probably don't remember all that stuff anymore."

It was not my desire to unabashedly lie to my fellow brothers and sisters, but the alternative was far worse. Were I to honestly espouse my findings, I would be labeled an apostate. The elders would evict me from the congregation and I would be shunned by everyone I had ever loved.

Thinking along these lines brought me to the verge of panic numerous times. Witnesses take shunning seriously; they will not speak to a disfellowshipped or disassociated person—even going so far as to avoid eye contact. They go out of their way to dodge being in the sinner's presence, as if a force field prevents them from coming within ten feet of their lost friend. I knew this was true, as I had even transferred jobs just to avoid seeing Jeremy.

The Watchtower admits shunning is a difficult aspect of Christian living, saying, in essence, it would be so much easier if those who leave the religion would simply cease to exist, but in today's world, we are stuck having them around—like walking dead. The Society harbors nostalgia for the days when dissenters were routinely killed by their family:

> We are not living today among theocratic nations where such members
> of our fleshly family relationship could be exterminated for apostasy from
> God and his theocratic organization, as was possible and was ordered in
> the nation of Israel. . . . Being limited by the laws of the worldly nations
> in which we live and also by the laws of God through Jesus Christ, we can
> take action against apostates only to a certain extent, that is, consistent with
> both sets of laws. The law of the land and God's law through Christ forbid
> us to kill apostates, even though they be members of our own flesh-and-
> blood family relationship.[93]

I was troubled by the incongruity of claiming to be Christian whilst ignoring those who had left their faith. It seemed no such trouble existed in the minds of most Witnesses, perhaps because they believed that people only leave the religion because they *desire* to be bad. Others leave because they are mad at an elder or are unable to see eye-to-eye with a fellow brother. Still others leave because they are lazy. It was unthinkable to insinuate that a person left the religion because they discovered it was untrue. *How could the Truth not be the truth?* The very question was nonsensical.

I felt as if I was in a valley—a valley of Witnesses all living their lives under the incorrect belief that they had the Truth. Beyond a great mountain lay a second valley—a valley of honesty, openness, and a bona fide quest for truth. Like a liquid, I could only exist comfortably in one of the two valleys. In between, there was a mountain. And, for the life of me, I could not scale such an obstacle. It was a peak of confrontation, frustration, arguments, disappointments, and heartbreak that I could not surmount. If there was a way to leave Watchtower-dom without adverse repercussions, I knew of no one who ever did it.

My circle of friends received new infusions of life and, unbeknownst to them, this gave me added incentive to continue on in the Truth.

First there was Lester. Jennifer's prodigal brother had long been a peripheral figure in my life, but then he divorced. Lester's wife had never been a Witness. Single and homeless, Les deemed his self-appointed *Rumspringa* concluded. He returned to his parents' home and began gravitating back to the life he had known when last he lived with his mom and dad. Though his parents were all but religiously inactive by this time, the environment in the house was hardly adverse to Witnesses, and Les began attending meetings with the one other person in the house who was still serving God faithfully. Sarah welcomed her brother's return to the religion, especially as she was continually upset with her parents about their lack of religious activity.

I played the same role with my sister. Kyle moved out of their apartment, and they filed for divorce. My sister never spoke against the religion, but neither did she ever go out in service or to the meetings anymore. I simply told her I was there for her if she needed to talk, and when she divulged a waywardness that would cause most Witnesses to shudder with fear (she got a tattoo; she had a worldly roommate), I accepted it with aplomb; knowing that she'd found little fulfillment in the religion.

And then an amazing thing happened.

I walked into our apartment after a late night at work. Jennifer was cleaning the kitchen counters and greeted me as soon as I came in the door. I cast my tie on the floor and bent down to untie my shoes.

She wiped her hands on a monogrammed towel and told me that Johnny called.

I stood there for a second, wondering if we knew anyone named Johnny. Finally, it registered. "Kamber?"

I could imagine what he wanted. He probably wanted to ask if he could borrow money, or just rip open an old wound and fight with me one more time.

"He wanted to know . . ." she paused for dramatic effect, "if we want to go over to their house on Saturday."

"That's it?" I asked in disbelief.

I reluctantly agreed we could use an infusion of friends, but I tried to hold my ground regarding a visit to the Kambers. But when Jennifer said the task of calling Johnny and cancelling the invitation fell on my shoulders, I caved. Five days later, we were standing on the Kambers' porch knocking on their front door. There was no answer. "Let's just leave," I whispered, but Jennifer insisted we try the side door. We knocked on the side door, and saw Johnny and his in-laws relaxing in the backyard. I turned to Jennifer "They'll gang up on us! I don't want to be here—let's go!" I turned to walk down the porch stairs, and I tried leading Jennifer off the stoop.

"Hey guys!" The voice was unmistakable. We turned and saw Johnny— older and fatter, hair cropped short. He had a beer in one hand. He held out his other hand in his trademark manner with his thumb held high and fingers straight out. We shook.

Johnny's in-laws did not plan to stay for dinner; they had stopped by to drop off a borrowed tool. Surely Johnny had orchestrated the whole event: he planned to have his in-laws there when we showed up, as support for him and his wife in case an argument erupted. Seeing we were willing to be amicable, he gave his in-laws the cue to leave so that the four of us could be alone while Johnny roasted me for having been such a jerk years earlier.

But that's not what happened. As soon as his in-laws left, Johnny began showing off the work he had done on the backyard. Tonya was equally proud of her decorating abilities, and proudly played tour guide to the inside of the house. They introduced us to their children. Johnny rocked back on his feet. "Can you believe I have three kids?" he said, filled with delight.

"Wow . . . no," was all I could say. I knelt down to meet my friend's progeny for the first time.

As the evening progressed, I felt more and more comfortable. After sunset, Johnny and Tonya put their kids to bed, and while the ladies spent the next several hours gossiping in the living room, I sat at the dining room table with Johnny.

Financial troubles had never been too far from Johnny. He had temporarily taken on a second job to pay the bills. He and his wife had high credit card debt. They had no savings account.

On the spiritual front, Johnny had similar trouble. With a new wife and son in one day, Johnny found it difficult to keep up with his religious responsibilities. Within a few months of getting married, the elders asked Johnny to step down from being a ministerial servant. Soon after, Johnny had gotten into a row with his mother-in-law. The elders became involved and this culminated in Johnny being privately reproved. He apologized profusely to the elders and tried to explain how remorseful he was for letting his temper get the better of him. Nevertheless, one of the Wheelock elders kept insisting, "I just don't think you're sorry for your actions." This upset and flabbergasted Johnny so that, even now, some three years later, I could still hear the sadness and confusion in his voice. "If you ever have problems with your family, James," he sternly charged me, "*do not* go to the elders. Just handle it yourself." I assured him I would take his advice to heart.

I felt weird around Johnny, as if I should apologize for what I had done but was unable to do so. On the drive home, I told Jennifer that, while I didn't mind the occasional evening with the Kambers, I couldn't fathom becoming best of friends with them again.

But in short order, all of our weekends were taken up with the Kambers. Nearly every Saturday, we made plans to have dinner together, or walk around the mall together, or work on items for Sarah's upcoming wedding. When two weeks elapsed without hearing from Johnny, I whined to Jennifer that I missed him. Jennifer laughed, "That's not what you were saying last year."

"He's a great guy," I said, adding, "as long as there's no money involved."

One evening, when Sarah and her friend Raven were at our apartment planning for her wedding, we took the opportunity to lambaste the Kambers' parenting style: "You know what it reminds me of? It reminds me of Johnny's dad—he always acted like he was some sort of king and the kids should just get down on their knees and be thankful that he even allows them to live there."

Since I said this to Sarah, the news traveled swiftly. When I next saw Johnny, he took me aside. "Listen, man, I heard you had some problems with the way I raise my kids."

I instantly grew nervous, afraid we were heading towards another schism. Stumbling over my words, I reminded Johnny how his father once said, "I'm your father, not your friend," and how much that had affected him. Without irony, bitterness or anger, Johnny said, "I want to be the best father I can be. I don't want to make the same mistakes my dad did. If you ever think there's a way I can improve—you let me know."

I was stunned. From my viewpoint, Johnny had every right to be angry. I spoke out against him and his father in a single sentence. Who was I—a childless man—to toss around opinions on parenting? The Johnny I knew from four years ago would never have humbly heeded his friends' opinions; he was too brash, too cocky. Things had changed, evidently, and on that day my respect for Johnny grew by leaps. There had once existed a pothole on the road to our friendship, and I had widened that whole into a deep, wide chasm. It was Johnny who had reached out first, across the years of time, and offered to shake my hand. For that, I respected him as the better man.

Six months later, Jennifer, Tonya, and Raven stood as bridesmaids in Sarah's wedding. That night, at the reception, Raven's boyfriend Jordan, who I had not yet met, raised his drink in my direction. "I've heard a lot about you."

He named off several people I vaguely recollected. We began swapping stories of mutual acquaintances. Too often, Witness conversations were curtailed due to the religion: *How does one discuss the political landscape when we are supposed to be neutral in world affairs? How does one discuss movies when mass entertainment was just a tool of Satan? How does one debate science when God will answer all our questions in the very near future?* Yet, as I talked with Jordan, I felt none of those limitations of dialogue. Jordan peppered his conversations with oblique references to TV shows and movies. Everything reminded him of an episode of *the Simpsons.* I ended our talk by telling Jordan I would like to hang out with him some time.

But, within a month after her wedding, Sarah stormed into our apartment to criticize how the elders had treated Raven for inappropriate conduct with Jordan. Sarah's major complaint was that Raven was sincerely sorry, but as she was not outwardly emotional, it was difficult for her to convincingly convey her repentance to a group of old men. An elder's wife and close friend of Raven had advised, "Just be honest with the elders. As long as you don't lie, they won't disfellowship you."

And so, Raven, a shy girl in her early twenties, had divulged to the elders every titillating detail of her premarital conjugal visits with Jordan. She was disfellowshipped.

"What happened to Jordan?" I asked, interrupting. "Did he get disfellowshipped?"

Sarah shook her head. "He's not baptized."

This was an incredible bit of gossip. Jordan was raised in the religion from birth. He had two brothers and a sister, and all of them were Witnesses. Raven was also a Witness. I asked Sarah if she knew why he wasn't baptized. She did not know.

I wanted to talk with Jordan to find out what was holding him back. *Did he also know the Society was wrong?* Perhaps he knew the religion was not the truth, yet maintained a façade so as to keep up a relationship with his family. Maybe if I tipped my hand and confided in him, he would be able to confirm my suspicions. But I resisted from ever speaking to him on the matter, because part of me was afraid of what he might say. Besides, with Raven out of our life until she was reinstated, I would not likely be in Jordan's company soon. In fact, apart from seeing Raven at the District Convention (where my wife and I duly shunned her), I did not see her or Jordan again for the remainder of the year.

By then, Jennifer and I moved out of our apartment. When I thought the End was nigh, I felt duty-bound to stay in an inexpensive, simple apartment. But now, fearing this life was all I had, I wanted to improve it to the extent possible. We spent a busy month painting and cleaning our new home. We packed up our birds and gently folded our monogrammed towels, and moved with help from our friends.

It was good, perhaps, that my friends gave me incentive to continue attending meetings, because at every meeting, I kept hoping for proof or evidence of God's existence. I kept praying that, somehow, the Watchtower Society would provide some information explaining their misuse of quotes, their incorrect teachings, and their silly rules.

While lying awake one night in our new townhome, I began to think that maybe I'd gotten everything backward. Maybe it was better to be ignorant. I thought of King Solomon: how Jehovah had made him so smart, and how he wrote "Whoever it is that increases in knowledge increases in pain."[94] Yet Solomon, the wisest man who ever lived, eventually turned his back on God.

I wished I never knew the things I knew. I wished I had never researched Noah's Flood. I cursed myself for uncovering the inaccuracy of 607 BC. Solomon was right; the more I knew, the more painful life became. I daydreamed of being transported back in time, walking up to my younger self and saying, "Whatever you do, don't read another book. You know the Truth is the truth; there's no need to mess with that."

I knew too much. And that was my problem. I prayed to undo my prayer from a year earlier. And this is the prayer that I said:

> Jehovah God, my heavenly father
> I wish I didn't know so many of the things I know.
> I try doing research to increase my faith, but it just ends up upsetting me.
> Jehovah, can you please help me out?
> If it was presumptuous of me to ask for more intelligence, then I humbly apologize.
> Instead, Jehovah, I wish I was dumber;
> I wish I was too dumb to think about those things and too dumb to know of such issues.
> I'm not saying I don't appreciate my brain;
> I'm just saying that maybe it would be best if I was dumber, at least until the Paradise.

For a time my friends helped me regain joy in the religion, but I observed each becoming a worse Witness than any had been only a few years earlier. The Kambers moved into my congregation, which should have been encouraging, but they missed more meetings than they attended. Neither of them enrolled in the Theocratic Ministry School. Tonya never went out in service and Johnny only did so if I invited him to join me.

Ryan was so consumed with the daily affairs of life that he attended meetings sparsely. His new wife Heather attended even less. I would often wonder what was keeping them in the religion; Ryan was an intelligent man who, like me, had an insatiable appetite for the sciences. Heather, meanwhile, did not seem to like anybody, and constantly found fault with members of the congregation.

My sister had not attended a meeting in over a year. She spent time exclusively with worldly people, had a worldly roommate, got another tattoo, and began dating a worldly man. The two of us were growing apart. I did not want to create an uncomfortable situation by asking why she was abandoning the Truth, because I was afraid of the answer. Nana repeatedly told me to encourage Diane. "You're the only one in this family she listens to," she proclaimed. But, as I explained to Jennifer in private, the only reason Diane preferred me was because I did not pester her about the religion.

Even Les, who had displayed the predictable burst of zeal that new Witnesses embody, griped about the religion. He reveled in finding ways to circumvent the *Watchtower's* teachings. Jennifer told me her brother had a history of acting this way. "He gets a high off of being rebellious," she explained dryly.

And then there was Sarah. Though a better Witness than her brother, she was certainly no pillar in the congregation. She freely admitted that she was frequently too lazy to go out in service. She and her husband missed a quarter of the meetings, and when they did attend, they readily left halfway through.

What irked Sarah most about the religion was the elders' treatment of Raven, who continued to attend the meetings. Her mother, who had been slacking in her meeting attendance, supported Raven by accompanying her to the meetings with renewed zeal. After several months, Raven put in a request to be reinstated, but it was denied. Raven was grief-stricken. She had done all she could, including sincere prayers of heartfelt repentance. Her anguish over the matter culminated one night when she contemplated suicide. Sarah drove to Raven's apartment and stayed by her side, consoling her and convincing her to continue her life.

After this incident, Sarah persisted in her relationship with Raven. Jennifer repeatedly told Sarah she was going against the elders by doing so, but Sarah argued that the elders had acted imprudently; the disfellowshipping was unwarranted. She defended her right to have verbal contact with a disfellowshipped friend. She bewailed the elders' continued reluctance to reinstate Raven, feeling that their inaction was, to use Sarah's word, cruel.

I couldn't fathom what was keeping my friends in the religion. A tiny, unacknowledged part of me wished they would all just stop being Witnesses. Then, I reasoned, Jennifer and I could stop, too. We could all be together without the burden of the elders and the endless meetings.

While sitting in our office one day, Diane said, "Did you hear about Norman Penna?"

The tone of her voice gave it away. Norm was neither a ministerial servant nor an elder, but he was incessantly in the company of preteen boys. There was only one reason why Diane would ask such a question.

"He molested Seth," she said, referencing a teenager in our congregation in a devil-may-care manner. She said Norm had been doing this for eight years, and when she began detailing the severity, I had to cut her off.

"Are you sure?" I asked. "How do you know?"

"Mom told me. I guess some kids from Eagan congregation went to the elders and said Norm had sexually abused them when they were younger. They said some other people were involved, so the elders are going around asking all the young guys if Norm ever did anything to them."

"I knew it," Jennifer said, "I knew he was a pedophile. Why else would an unmarried man in his thirties hang out with twelve-year-old boys? I knew there was something weird about him from the day I met him." When Jennifer said those words, she was expressing not anger, but guilt. "We should have said something. All those years he was molesting children in the congregation and we *knew* it!"

"Jennifer," I said calmly, "just because he chose to hang out with little boys doesn't mean he was doing anything sexually to them."

"Oh come on!" Jennifer yelled. "We could have stopped it!"

"Are you telling me I should have gone to the elders and said, 'Norm has a pink feather boa in his bedroom and hangs out with prepubescent boys and, by the way, I think he's raping kids'?"

"We should have asked someone to look into it. Didn't it ever seem weird to you that he was always with kids less than half his age?"

Later I, too, came to feel remorse. I had suspected Norm was a pedophile. I even joked about my suspicion. Instead of joking about it, I should have said something. I reviewed the video footage from our wedding reception and saw Norm—there, cavorting with the young boys—and did nothing. I reminded Jennifer of how, when I asked to take my cousin Matthew out in service, I was denied that opportunity, yet Norm routinely brought Matthew out in service.

"That's the elders for you," I said with extreme sarcasm. "In their wisdom they wouldn't let me take Matthew out in service, oh no—because I wasn't studying the Bible with him. But, Norm, sure that was just fine if Norm wanted to pick Matthew up for the day."

"Why didn't we say anything sooner?" Jennifer cried. "We knew it. We knew it for years! And we didn't say anything!"

I had no answer.

At the next meeting, I asked my mom if she knew more details. She elaborated on the travesty of the whole affair, explaining what she knew in a staccato fashion. She knew a smattering of sordid details, which she divulged punctuated with expressions like "Isn't it terrible?" And "I can't believe it was happening right here in our own congregation!"

What more I did learn came in hushed, piecemeal fashion.

Following a tearful trial and swift jury deliberations, the judge read the sentencing. Norm cowered in his seat, hunched over and grasping a *Watchtower* in his hands. If he hoped to divine some sort of power from the periodical, it worked: the judge sentenced him to a paltry nine months in the work house allowing, of course, leave on Sundays for church services.

The family considered appealing the verdict. Norm assured them he would fight the case, and the end result would only be a further loss of time and money. Norm's father, an elder, offered to help by footing the bill for an expert attorney.

I investigated why the two boys who had initially approached the elders regarding their abuse at Norm's hands never notified the authorities. Looking over her shoulder in worried secrecy, one elder's daughter explained that the two boys were encouraged not to go to the police as that would give a bad Witness. This was unfortunate, as multiple accusations would have resulted in a harsher sentence and the requirement for Norm to be registered as a level-three sex offender. With only one person testifying against him, the court system was unable to give him more than nine months in the work house. As a level-one offender, Norm was not listed on any databases; his crime was hidden from most people—including the majority of Witnesses.

I continually broached the subject with friends and family, hoping that maybe this would awaken any latent misgivings. Many were incensed. The Kambers repeatedly said how happy they were that Norm had never spent time with their sons. Sarah insisted that Norm had never laid a hand (or any other body part) on her husband when he was young. She hated the subject, and abruptly shifted to different topics.

But I observed almost no one questioning the events surrounding our homegrown pedophile. Indeed, I observed that no Witness in my congregation questioned matters even *when they were pointedly asked to supply such questions.*

Service Meeting talks were based out of the monthly leaflet *Our Kingdom Ministry.* The February 2002 issue called for a short talk discussing the video *Noah—He Walked With God.* The *Our Kingdom Ministry* asked ten questions about the video, to be used in audience discussion. Question number one, for example, was: "What was the world like in Noah's day?" Question number six was: "How would you have felt after surviving the Flood?" The most engaging question, however, was number nine: "What questions do you want to ask Noah and his family when you meet them in Paradise?"

Jennifer and I did not watch the video, but I was ready for question nine. When the elder asked, I lifted my hand, confidently punching the sky. I was not alone; about twenty people, mostly children, also raised their hands. As the elder scanned the hall, Jennifer leaned over and whispered: "What are you going to say?"

As the elder called on a young girl in the front row, I whispered: "I want to ask Noah if the flood really did cover the whole earth."

"You can't say that!" she scolded.

"Then I'll ask about the animals."

After the young girl said she wanted to ask Noah if it smelled inside the ark, I raised my hand again, and again the elder called on someone else.

"What are you going to ask about the animals?" Jennifer insisted.

"How was it possible to fit over a million species on the ark, and why did he feel it was necessary to bring mosquitoes, syphilis, and gonorrhea on board, and how was it possible to care for thousands of animals, and how did the animals get to Australia and Hawaii after the Flood."

The elder next called on a ministerial servant sitting in the side row, who said he wanted to ask how Noah maintained his faith while building the ark.

"Put your hand down!" Jennifer said through her teeth.

The elder called on a little boy who wanted to ask Noah if he liked petting the koalas.

"James! I mean it. If you say that stuff, the elders will drag us into the basement and we'll both get disfellowshipped! Is that what you want?"

With my arm still elevated, I slowly turned and looked my wife full in the eyes. The elder called on me, but I withdrew my hand. I looked up at the elder and shook my head. "Change of heart?" he quipped, and then called on someone else.

The Kambers' money troubles led them to move first from their spacious house to a cramped townhome, then to a rental property some miles east in a rural area. Johnny took me up on a hill at the edge of his property, and we surveyed the rolling farmland. He sipped his beer and nodded purposefully. "I feel bad I don't own it, but the landlord says we can paint this place and change the carpet, so it's kind of like we do."

"Tonya was saying they might tear this place down soon," I said.

He looked at me with a dubious expression. "That's years away," he said nonchalantly. "The manager said not to worry about it until 2006 or 2007.

So the whole barrel of Kambers is good 'til then." Spreading his arms to take in the bucolic expanse, he declared: "This is our Armageddon house!"

The toughest financial problems, however, were Rhett's. He restarted pioneering but quit within the year due to financial and health problems. He and his wife now had a son, and the cost of living was rising. At the District Convention, I saw Rhett for the first time in months. He reached out to hug me and, as we embraced, I noticed he was still wearing a cast on his arm. I knocked on the hard cast with my fist and said: "Are you ever gonna get this thing off?" He just laughed and said that the doctor told him his arm hadn't fully healed.

He seemed tired. His eyes drooped; his unkempt hair was thinning. I asked if he had been out partying. His answer surprised me. The convention, as always, was in Rochester, and Rhett and his family were staying in a hotel. The night before, Rhett had to drive over an hour to his janitorial job. He vacuumed and dusted for several hours, then returned to the hotel and collapsed in bed for a scant three hours. After my initial shock at hearing what Rhett had experienced while every other Witness in Minnesota was sleeping in their hotel, I asked why he had another cleaning job: "I thought you said the cleaning accounts were wearing you out?"

"They are," he said, "but they're good money."

Conversely, life was steadily improving for Jennifer and me. I made good on my degree by gaining employment at a chemistry lab east of St. Paul. My employment in customer service belatedly ended, and within minutes I realized I loved my new line of work. I came home on the first day and ecstatically said to Jennifer: "I just got paid for eight hours, and I didn't have to deal with a single customer!"

Another boring Circuit Assembly was held that autumn. Jennifer and I sat in the back, and she elbowed me when I drifted off to sleep. To stay awake, I began counting all the other people who were sleeping, but I lost count at twenty. After yawning, I realized this induced a mild, temporary euphoria, so I started breathing in as deeply as possible, then fully exhaling, repeating the procedure five or six times until I had achieved a natural high.

During the intermission, we walked to a table filled to capacity with my relatives. Nana stood up and hugged us, kissing my cheek as she inquired about my new job. Then she asked "How is Diane *doing?*" emphasizing the last word, a clear indication that the question was asked in reference to her spiritual well-being.

"We had lunch about a month ago," I said, "and we had a nice time together."

"I'm so happy to hear that. I love your sister," she added.

Before the conversation could continue, however, Uncle Peter called my name. "Are you going to your sister's wedding?"

I looked up from my grandparents, surprised. "Of course I'm going to my sister's wedding."

"Why wouldn't we?" Jennifer asked.

Uncle Peter wiped the side of his mouth with a napkin. "That might not be such a good idea."

"Maybe not to you." I looked back to Nana in an attempt to resume our discussion.

Uncle Peter wasn't finished. He opened his mouth and waited until I looked back at him. When I did, he said, "Well, are you a ministerial servant?"

I wrinkled my forehead. "No, I'm not. What does that—"

"You better be glad you're not; otherwise they wouldn't—"

I cut him off: "I *am* glad I'm not a servant!" Everyone gasped at my sacrilegious talk, except for Uncle Peter, who was still lecturing. I held up my hand like a traffic cop. "You know what? I don't want to talk about it anymore. This isn't the time or the place."

There was much commotion at the table. Aunt Janet tried calming her brother down, telling him to just let the matter rest. Nana held her hands out like a referee trying to force apart warring opponents in a boxing ring. "Okay, enough. Enough!"

Papa stood up and turned to Jennifer and me. "Why doesn't he mind his own business?" I asked. I looked over at Uncle Peter, arguing with his sister about the prudence of his vocalizations.

Papa held up his hands and placed one on my shoulder. "It's okay, James. Don't worry about it. There's nothing wrong with going to your sister's wedding if that's what you want to do."

"Why does he think he can barge in to our lives like that?" Jennifer asked.

"He's just trying to do what he thinks is right," Papa answered.

On the eve of Diane's wedding, over dinner, I asked my dad if any of his family planned on attending. With a look of embarrassment over his family's behavior, he confessed that none of them: neither his parents nor his sister, and certainly not his brother Peter, would be there. I told him how sad that was, particularly when Papa had defended our right to attend. "Well," my dad explained, "Papa probably feels it wouldn't be right for him to attend the wedding, but he knows there's no reason you can't go."[95]

The next day, my sister and her fiancé David were married in a civil ceremony presided over by a county judge. Apart from reminding all in attendance that matrimony was a holy union approved by Jehovah himself, there were no religious overtones. While many of the groom's relatives traveled great distances to be at the wedding, the bride's side of the room was appallingly empty, comprising of Jennifer and me, our parents and stepmom, stepsister, and exactly one uncle, aunt, and cousin.

I made it my goal to steer clear of Uncle Peter after that. But when his youngest brother Cal got married for the third time, I was in his company once more. Uncle Cal resided in Florida, as did my dad and stepmom now, so Jennifer and I made a vacation out of the event by flying south and staying at my dad's for a week. All proceeded smoothly for the first ten minutes after Jennifer and I arrived at the Kingdom Hall, but when Uncle Peter made a point of castigating my attire—I was not wearing a tie—my attitude again soured.

The next evening, Uncle Peter stopped by to say good-bye to my dad before flying back to Minnesota. Jennifer and I were in the guest bedroom when he arrived. Jennifer got up to walk out of the room. Seeing that I wasn't budging, she implored, "Let's go say good-bye."

"I'm not moving," I said. "Stay here with me or go suck up to Uncle Pete if you have to."

"Fine." She said angrily. She lowered herself back onto the bed. "I'll stay here."

As soon as he departed, Jennifer and I ventured into the dining room, where Nana said, "You were so rude to your Uncle, James!"

"Maybe it's because he's been rude to me for years and I'm sick of dealing with him."

"How can you say that? Your Uncle loves you very much," Nana said. "He wants to show you love. He does love you, very much, even if you don't think he does."

"Well, we don't need that kind of love," I yelled.

Jennifer agreed, saying that he had often caused us much discouragement. Nana argued that we were looking at this the wrong way. She said we should be happy to have family members in the Truth, who can "look out for us."

"He's been looking out for us all these years?" I asked, sarcastically. "He certainly has a funny way of showing it."

Nana cast a downward glance. She said nothing. I continued: "In fact, he's been nothing but a thorn in our sides for years. He has never once made me feel better. One of the best days of my life was when he moved and switched congregations." I itemized a laundry list of grievances I had against my uncle. "I'm glad I don't see him three times a week anymore."

This brought Nana to tears. She went on to assert that Uncle Peter only wants what is best for me; he wants me to be a ministerial servant again.

"You *do* want to be a Servant again, don't you?" she asked.

I winced and shrugged my shoulders.

"What is wrong with you, James?" she cried. Hitting her fist on the countertop, she interrogated: "How can you not want to serve Jehovah to the best of your ability?"

"Nothing's wrong with me," I said, "I just don't want to be a Servant."

Then Nana turned to Jennifer: "What did you do to him, Jennifer? Why is he like this? He didn't used to be like this."

Jennifer jumped at the unexpected cross-examination. "He's the one who doesn't want to be a servant," she said. "He's the one who has this attitude. I don't know why; I ask him all the time."

Nana turned back to me. "What's your problem? Why have you been so quiet?"

I knew the answer, of course. But I couldn't say it. I couldn't break her heart and tell her how wrong the Witnesses were.

"You've changed, James," Nana said.

My wife diverted the conversation away from my doubts and her supposed evil influence by adding: "One thing that's been bothering him is how you've treated Diane."

I felt my stress ebb with my wife's statement. For a split second, I feared she would divulge our doubts, but I was relieved to hear her pilot the conversation to something less volatile.

"What!" Nana cried, blotting her tears with a tissue. "How do you want me to treat her? I tried my best with her, to bring her back to Jehovah. She doesn't respond to anything. What do you expect me to do?"

"I don't want you to write her mean letters," Jennifer said, referencing a recent card Nana sent Diane wherein she congratulated her on her marriage, but noted that true happiness can only come through Jehovah's Organization. "And I don't want you to reject her by avoiding her wedding."

Nana tearfully claimed, however, that she could not go to Diane's wedding because doing so would have bothered her conscience.

"Are you stricter than Jehovah?" I spat the question out in a fit of indignation. "What's to bother your conscience? The Society doesn't say we can't go to worldly weddings."

"I didn't want to give a bad Witness," Nana said, her voice getting hoarse.

Hopping up to sit on the kitchen counter, I said: "Let me assure you, you did give a bad Witness."

"No I didn't James!"

"Yes you did!" I declared, with full bravado. "How can you not see that? I was embarrassed at the wedding. David had his whole family there, and Diane had barely any relatives. Don't you think David's family asked where Diane's family was? Do you think Diane said, 'Oh, they are in the right and I am in the wrong'?"

"She'll explain the Truth to them," Nana said.

"No, she won't!" I snapped. I was tired of the Witnesses' deluded belief that any who leave the religion continue to defend it enthusiastically. "Diane was upset. Did you expect her to lie for you? She's going to tell them you didn't go to her wedding because of religious differences. Do you think that's gonna make them all think 'Those Witnesses must have the Truth! Let's join them'?"

"But James," Nana said, diverting the question. "Diane and her husband are unevenly yoked."

"How can they be unevenly yoked?" Jennifer shouted. "They're *both* worldly!"

"Oh no, they're not," my dad finally jumped in. "Diane *is* a Witness."

"You may not think so," Nana agreed, "but she is! She's baptized."

"So are lots of ex-Witnesses," I said caustically.

"She hasn't been to a meeting in years—or out in service," Jennifer added.

"But she *knows* it's the truth, Jennifer," Nana pleaded. "She *knows* it."

"So does Satan," I interjected. "Does that make him a Witness?"

A few days later, we were back in our little townhome with our cats. Life resumed, and I spent much of my time alone thinking about the religion. I had asked God to grant me the wisdom to make sense of apparent fallacies. When that failed, I asked him to make me ignorant of the issues I had uncovered. That had not worked, either. I recalled the elder who, speaking at the convention, advised Witnesses to be specific in their prayers. For me, at least, this did not work. Paramount, of course, was the overarching suspicion that the religion was not the Truth, but now I had the equally seditious suspicion that God was not a hearer of prayer. Part of me kept thinking this was because God did not exist. I did not *want* that to be true, so I convinced myself that maybe, just maybe, I had been too demanding. So I prayed again. And this is the prayer that I said:

Jehovah God, my heavenly father
I am sorry for asking to be smarter; that was presumptuous of me.

And I am sorry for asking to be dumber; that was ungrateful of me.
The thing is, I don't care which you do—
I wish I was smarter; I wish I was dumber.
Just do whatever you think is best to ensure my faith and my good graces.

Within the month, I received a phone call from an elder. In sullen tones, the elder told me it was his duty to inform me I no longer was entitled to any privileges in the congregation. I was not in trouble, he assured me, but my monthly average in the door-to-door work was too low. The elder said I could no longer read at the meetings, nor could I assist in the sound department. I took this in stride, responding in a careless monotone: "Oh, okay," and, "That's fine, I understand."

The elder admitted it was with great pain that he delivered this message, and assured me that if my average improved, I would again be rewarded with privileges. But he noticed my attitude was disturbingly nonchalant. After a long pause, he asked: "Are you okay, James?"

"I don't know," I said. "I'm just discouraged. And depressed."

"Well, I hope things turn out okay for you," he answered. "I gotta run." And he hung up.

I walked downstairs and sat on the couch next to my wife and explained the gist of the conversation.

She nodded, in tacit empathy. "Are you sad about it?"

Without turning away from the TV, I answered: "All those privileges just stress me out, you know? Besides, he told me I could have them back if I want. I just have to get out in service more."

"So are you going to?" she asked.

I leaned forward and scratched my chin. "I think it's wrong to go out in service more just so I can look better in the congregation."

"Don't you want to go out in service more?"

I turned and looked at her. "Don't *you* want to go out more?" Jennifer went out in service less frequently than I did, allowing months to elapse without reporting any time. She admitted it was true; neither of us enjoyed service.

After being freed of all congregational privileges, the remainder of the year ensued very smoothly. Raven was reinstated as a member of the congregation, and we could once again be her friend. My postponed camaraderie with Jordan flourished, and there was no end to the things we had in common. Ryan and Heather, meanwhile, continued to be our friends, despite a looming collision in their marriage.

On the religious front, I maintained a workable equilibrium. Jennifer and I missed meetings whenever we felt like staying home. She missed more than me, and would always ask: "Would you be mad if I stayed home to-night?" To which I invariably responded: "Nope."

My sister, divorced again, would often call and ask if we wanted to get together. If this was on a Tuesday or Thursday evening, she'd say: "I suppose you want to go to the meeting." I'd say: "Eh, what are you offering?"

Our door-to-door time slid even lower. In the whole year, I went out in service only seven times.

Thus, I was able to navigate through the boring and inane aspects of the religion. As we lay in bed on the final night of 2003, I recounted to Jennifer how splendid life had been recently. I loved my wife; I loved my cats; I loved my friends, my house, and even my job. I told her how even the religion had been worry-free ever since we came home from Florida nine months earlier. I proclaimed 2003 the best year of my life!

We said goodnight and I rolled over onto my side. It *had* been a good year. There had been few problems in the religion, and I had successfully suppressed any doubts. I wanted to keep that success going in all future years—and I would have, too, had it not been for 2004.

THE LAST DAYS

We are indeed living in "the last days." Just ahead of us is the "great tribulation" also foretold by Jesus Christ. Climaxing in "the war of the great day of God the Almighty" at Har-Magedon, it will bring an end to the present wicked system of things. Then God's promised new world will become a reality.

—*The Watchtower*, July 15, 1991, p. 5

"When are we gonna have a baby?" I asked Jennifer as we lay next to each other in bed.

We had planned to wait for the Paradise, but in seven years of marriage, we spent many evenings trying to verbally rationalize the desire to have a child. It was not enough to simply say we wanted one; we had to deconstruct years of programming that caused us to indefinitely postpone such a natural yearning. It was a major adjustment to even consider having a child in this wicked world.

"What about Armageddon?" she asked.

"I don't know when it's going to come—do you?" I countered, turning towards her. "If we'd had a baby back when we first got married, it would already be six years old."

Jennifer pointed out that it just didn't seem like a good time—our townhome was small; my job provided poor medical benefits. I assured her that I was trying to get a new job with better benefits, and that our townhome had appreciated in value. We could sell it any time and invest in a larger house.

"It just doesn't seem like a good time to have a baby," she said.

I took a deep breath. "Jennifer, it's *never* a good time. There will always be something wrong in our lives; something we want to do; something we need to finish or work on." When she said nothing, I asserted that no matter what we did, or how we lived our lives, we would never be able to sit back, look at the panorama of our existence, and say: "Yes, now our lives are perfect. Everything is in order. Let's have a baby."

We did need more space, though, so I asked Jennifer if she wanted to move. She couldn't say yes fast enough. She reminded me that she had never wanted to be in Apple Valley in the first place; she had only agreed to it when I was being so unyielding. Apple Valley was not intended to be a permanent residence; it was supposed to be a stepping stone on our way to the congregation and house of our liking.

There was another good reason to leave Apple Valley.

The Kambers often invited us over on Friday evenings, along with Jordan, Raven, and Sarah. We usually had a good time in the relaxed atmosphere, and we loved our small circle of friends. Perhaps because they themselves weren't stellar Witnesses, none of them ever asked how we were doing in the religion. Usually, no one asked if we had attended the most recent meeting, or how many hours we had spent in service. Actually, things were a bit too worldly for our liking, and Jennifer and I regularly left the festivities early because everyone else was too drunk to be of any fun. More than once, Jordan, Raven and Sarah spent the night at the Kambers' to avoid driving home while intoxicated.

One evening, before Jordan tapped into his vodka and Johnny began swilling Jägermeister, Sarah asked if we had attended the meeting last Tuesday.

"We stayed home," Jennifer said.

"I wasn't there either. But guess what? Norman Penna got reinstated."

This was such unexpected news I practically choked on my beer. "No way!" Jennifer exclaimed. But Sarah confirmed it was true.

I was appalled. Norm had only been disfellowshipped for a year. To reinstate a disfellowshipped person was to insinuate their sins had been forgiven. I couldn't rationalize such a decision on the part of the elders. *Did they feel justice had been served? Did they feel that Norm was no longer a threat to the congregation?* I asked Sarah if the elders had warned the congregation that, though Norm is no longer disfellowshipped, it still might be prudent to keep him from the children. Sarah said no such warning had been disseminated.

"Johnny, I'm so glad we're in a different congregation now," Tonya said. "Could you imagine being there with our two sons?" Johnny nodded in the affirmative. Apart from this, no one seemed bothered that the religion had created the environment wherein Norm had easy access to children, and was now free to roam among the ignorant sheep in the congregation. I drank heavily that night, allowing my disillusion to ferment in the bottles as they emptied of alcohol.

Norm was at the next meeting. I detested seeing him shake hands with my brothers and sisters. A sister who had only recently moved to our congregation introduced her four-year-old son to Norm. Overhearing two gossipy sisters wondering aloud what sin Norm had committed to cause him to be disfellowshipped, I had to walk away before my sense of justice caused me to inform them of Norm's lecherous actions.

Jennifer and I contemplated switching congregations that weekend. We bided our time until our townhome sold, despite the uncomfortable nature of seeing Norm at all the meetings and even in a bookstudy conducted by Norm's father—the man who had financially assisted Norm in his legal defense.

An invitation to Ryan and Heather's home provided a welcoming respite. Through the winding course of conversation, we alighted upon the subject of animals. Ryan spoke of recent fossil finds and a captivating documentary on ecosystem fragility he had recently viewed. The subject of animals amongst Witnesses was always a cause for trepidation. While I loved animals, discussions of zoology bordered too close to Noah's Flood and evolution for my liking. I instantly was on guard.

Ryan looked across at his wife: "Should we ask them?"

"Yeah," she said, sitting up, "they might know."

Ryan explained that, in viewing the documentary, they began to wonder how it would be possible for the animals to convert to vegetarianism in the Paradise. He spoke in stalling hesitation, as though he didn't want to ask but was being forced to do so.

"All things are possible with God, aren't they?" I asked, ignoring the thrust of the question.

Ryan wasn't so easily distracted. "But if God turns all the animals into vegetarians in the Paradise, that will throw off whole ecosystems." He went on, in typical verboseness, providing specific examples of how entire species were defined and kept in check by predation. As he spoke, I cast my gaze towards my wife. We smiled, recalling too well that we had been troubled by similar issues. Ryan asked if we had ever thought about such matters.

I could have lied. I could have told Ryan that I had never entertained such thoughts. I could have told him to wait on Jehovah, or to pray. Had he been any other man, I would have done just that. But Ryan was the most intelligent man I had ever called a friend. I wished I could lie; I wanted to lie—but such was not the substance of friendships and, further, Ryan's intellect would pierce the façade. So, with lips quavering, I said: "Jennifer and I don't think the animals will be vegetarians in the Paradise."

"What about those scriptures about the lion eating straw with the lamb," Ryan persisted, "and the children playing with serpents?"[96]

I smiled nervously. "We think those scriptures are symbolic."

The words hung in the air uncomfortably. I desperately wanted to know their thoughts but, alas, I was not telepathic. In those protracted seconds, I wondered how Ryan would respond, for never in my life had I ever openly expressed an opinion contrary to the *Watchtower* to anyone but Jennifer. In all my arguments with the elders, I always made sure to hold that my issue was not with the Society, but with the elders' interpretation of *Watchtower* doctrine.

"You think they're *symbolic?*" Ryan asked.

"Yeah," I answered sheepishly, as if I was confessing to a murder.

Ryan was floored. Before he spoke again, I added: "You know, the Society teaches that animals were vegetarians before the Flood, too, and we all know that can't be the case."

A shocked look came over Ryan's face, and, stumbling over his words, he sputtered: "They teach that animals were vegetarians before the Flood?"

"Didn't you know that?" I said, in a manner too casual to comfort him.

"No!" he said with emphasis. "I don't think I ever researched that before. Are you sure?"

"Yeah, I'm sure. Jennifer and I have researched it, trust me," I pointed at Jennifer, who nodded dutifully. "Just look at a tyrannosaurus skull—do you think that thing grazed on weeds?"

Heather laughed. Ryan asked about the animals on the ark. "Were they vegetarians, too?"

Again I glanced at my wife, a silent request for her blessing. "That's another thing. There's no way the Flood was global."

"What?" Ryan asked, aghast equally at my information and at the off-handed nature in which I dispensed it.

"A few years back, Jennifer and I tried making a list of all the animals on the ark." I told them about the numbers provided in the Watchtower publications, the letter we wrote, and the subsequent response. Ryan admitted he had never given it *that* much thought.

"That's not the only evidence against a global Flood," I continued. "Think about this: there's no way all the animals could have gotten to all the different land masses after the Flood."

Ryan's eyes traced a line across the ceiling as if he was scanning the cosmos for an answer. Insistent, I continued: "How would penguins have gotten to Antarctica, or kangaroos to Australia, or Bison to North America?"

"Oh my God!" Heather exclaimed; her face transfigured into one of anguish.

"How did those big, lumbering tortoises make it halfway around the globe to the Galapagos?"

Heather grabbed her hair and wrapped it around her face, literally blinding herself. "Why are you saying those things? I don't want to think about those things," she shrieked.

Ryan ignored his wife's plea long enough to ask: "Do you guys ever wonder about Neanderthal man?"

"We figure they're just deformed humans or something," Jennifer said.

Ryan nodded, indicating he was prepared for this rationale. "Yeah," he said, "but their DNA doesn't match humans."

I tried to maintain a calm exterior. "I've never looked into that. I'd need to do some more research on that subject."

"They're remarkably similar to humans, but they're still a different species."

Heather cried for us to stop, shaking her head back and forth as she said so.

"Maybe we should talk about something else now," Ryan advised.

But the atmosphere was charged with ions of doubt. Though Ryan and I shifted the conversation to movies and music, all in the room could feel the undertow. Driving home, I couldn't stop thinking about Ryan's concerns. His questions indicated he was traveling down a path not unlike the one I had trod years earlier. Back then, I had looked deeply into the Noachian Deluge, and what I had uncovered was nothing short of life-changing. It felt intellectually dishonest to withhold my learnings from my old friend. His wife's distress notwithstanding, he deserved to find answers to his queries.

Sitting at work the next morning, drinking hot tea and trying to come awake for the day, I logged on to the internet. In the search engine, I typed: PROBLEMS NOAH FLOOD. I clicked on the top result, wary that it may be of apostate origin.

It wasn't apostate. It was a well-reasoned essay on the absurdity of a global flood.[97] The essay's author delineated many of the obstacles I had come across in my studies: insufficient space on the ark, the detriment to plant life, water problems, and post-diluvium speciation improbabilities. His essay, unlike my mind, was outlined in a logical, coherent format. I emailed Ryan:

> Hey, we had a good time at your place last night. I would've liked to talk about Noah's ark and the animals more, but I think we were starting to upset Heather. Anyway, I've always had huge concerns with the Flood, too. In fact, here's a link that sums up all of my concerns pretty well. See what you think. You might find it interesting.

That evening, after a grueling commute, I told Jennifer how I hoped to open a dialogue about the Flood with Ryan. "If anyone can clear up our problems, it would be Ryan." I spoke of the link I sent Ryan, and she pounced on my reckless communique.

"You sent him a website against the Flood?" she shouted in fiery denunciation.

"I wouldn't say the site is *anti*-Flood." I tried to stay casual. "It's just a page that lists some of the problems associated with the Flood."

"What's the website for? I mean, is it for or against the Bible in general?"

I hesitated. I wanted to lie, but I knew that would be a bad idea. "It's actually a pro-evolution site. But I didn't send him anything about evolution, just the Flood."

She lunged towards me. "James! You can't send people stuff like that! Ryan will think you're an apostate!"

Her comment made me nervous, but I played it off coolly: "He's looking for answers, I helped him out. That's that. Anyway, he might not even look at my email—he never replied."

"I hope for our sake he didn't. I think you need to call Ryan right now and tell him you don't believe in evolution."

"Jennifer!" I hollered, as if the very thought was revolting. "I'm not gonna do that. Then he'll think we have something to hide."

"You better tell him something. Otherwise he's gonna flip out."

I took a slow breath to calm down. "How about this: tomorrow, at work, I'll email him again and tell him that I hope he didn't get the wrong idea."

Fourteen hours later, I wrote:

> Hey, I was thinking about the email I sent you yesterday and I hope you don't think I don't believe in the Flood. I was just trying to point out there's more involved than most Witnesses think. Jennifer thinks you might have gotten the idea that I believe in evolution, but that's not the case.

Less than an hour later, a message appeared in my inbox:

> No harm done. Thanks for your concern. Don't worry, I don't think you believe in evolution.

Two weeks passed. Late one evening, as I was getting ready for bed, Jennifer called to me as I stepped out of the bathroom. She was in the office, on the computer, visiting Ryan's website. She got up from the chair. "I think you need to read Ryan's latest post." I sat. It read:

> I have gone through something the last month that definitely appears to all my friends and family like a terrible thing. It appears, from without, that I have suddenly rejected Jehovah, rejected my wife, rejected all my friends and family and opted for being some sort of worldly jerk. This is not entirely true and is actually quite misleading.
>
> I have a meeting scheduled with the elders on Wednesday night. I have serious, major issues that I need discussed and, yes, they have left me in a state best described as agnosticism. My faith in the organization and a literal interpretation of the Bible is currently gone, and therefore my

faith in a personal creator and god named Jehovah is as well. Can they be restored? Time will tell. That's why I'm talking to the elders. I admit I'm skeptical that I can go back because "extraordinary claims require extraordinary proof" and I need a lot of convincing. I won't go into any issues here because I don't want to offend or upset anybody. I may have things I don't believe anymore, but I am not at all interested in personally rejecting any of the people I've ever loved or in tearing down or damaging anybody else's faith. I have scientific issues, not a sudden lack of morality or disrespect towards others.

It is true, however, that I initiated a breakup with my wife and that it has pained her greatly. I feel terrible about that, even though she doesn't believe me when I say it. I love her and want her to be happy. . . .

If the elders are able to help me, everybody will know soon enough. If Heather and I are happier and healthier in the long run, it will simply be a matter of time. For now, please, support her. She needs it.[98]

"Do you think it has to do with the stuff we talked about with him, and that link you sent him?" Jennifer asked.

"Absolutely not."

"How can you be so sure?"

"Because that was just one little thing, and I even sent him an explanation the next day. He obviously already had issues before he talked to us."

She looked into my eyes, searching for the source of my confidence. "He said he'd never thought of some of those things before—not until we told him."

She continued looking into my eyes until I turned away. "What do you want me to say?" I yelled. "Do you want me to say 'Yes, Jennifer, we are responsible for causing our friend to leave the Truth'?"

"Why are you getting mad at me? I'm just asking if it's possible that what we said led him down this path."

"And I'm saying, in my opinion, the answer is no. But we'll never know, will we?"

"He's gonna talk to the elders; maybe they'll answer his questions."

"Come on, Jennifer! Do you really think some window washers with high school diplomas are gonna be able to answer Ryan's questions? Heck, I'd be surprised if they even understand his questions."

The new day did not bring a change in conversation. Jennifer and I speculated about Ryan all day, and into the next. We checked Ryan's blog every few hours to see if he posted anything new.

A few days passed, and we were greeted with these thoughts:

On Wednesday I had a 2 1/2 hour meeting with the elders. They were kind, supportive and tried to give me some things to think about. I'm trying to think about them, trying to look at things from a different perspective. They weren't able to provide explanations or answers to my questions or rebuttals to the evidence I have learned about and admitted as much. They did, however, attempt to give me some different ways to think about the issue of whether or not I can honestly continue to be one of Jehovah's Witnesses. They said that the scientific issues I had raised could not really be addressed by the Society and even acknowledged that it was possible the Society was wrong on some points (a surprising thing to hear coming from two elders). They agreed that it was better to be honest about all of this than to be hypocritical and pretending I believed things I did not believe. They suggested, however, that rather than basing my faith on the truth or falsehood of a literal interpretation of Genesis that I consider perhaps judging the organization on the basis of its fruitage. . . . I've never been convinced by that line of reasoning in the past. I always figured that any human group can be good and moral if that is the code they chose to live by. The Amish come to mind, as do lots of other fundamentalist, God-fearing, Bible-based groups. Does it illustrate divine guidance or simply the inherent desire of certain people to live lives that are moral? I've always assumed the latter. It wouldn't be enough to simply say "the morality of the Organization is a good thing and I agree with it so I can be a part of it" because of the witnessing aspect. I could not witness to people things I did not believe. If I believed the Garden of Eden account was a myth, I couldn't tell somebody it was a historical event and the cause for suffering in the world today. I mean, I could, but not without lying.[99]

I was astounded. That the elders were unable to answer Ryan's questions was no grand revelation. But to read Ryan reason on his inability to remain a Witness was the most cerebral, persuasive, lucid opinion I had ever encountered. For years, I had lied to myself about the Organization, and I assumed that as long as it wasn't hurting anybody, I might as well continue. In Ryan's blinding display of light I recognized that I had not been true to myself. Speaking at the meeting and distributing literature to householders was incalculably hypocritical.

It was not my desire to perpetually dwell on Ryan's incipient agnosticism, but Jennifer continually had new information. She persisted in emailing Ryan, like pouring acid on an open sore. I wanted to banish Ryan from my life and purge him from my memories. But for weeks I would come home from work only to have my wife tell me she had emailed Ryan again. The computer screen put out a tractor beam, and within minutes curiosity harnessed me into the office, where I read their most recent correspondence.

In one email, Jennifer asked, "Weren't you happier as a Witness?"

Before he responded, I told Jennifer: "I can tell you what he's gonna say. He's gonna say that yes, he was happier, but he didn't want to be hypocritical." And, indeed, that's what he said.

In another email, Jennifer tried persuading Ryan to return with the impassioned plea. "Don't you want it to be true? Don't you want to live forever, and have your son live forever?"

I promptly castigated my wife. "Why do you keep asking him things like that? Why can't you leave him alone? He's gonna tell you that whether or not he wants it to be true is irrelevant. He'll tell you that the bottom line is that it's *not* true—regardless of his personal preference."

And that's exactly what Ryan said.

Ryan's blog continually reminded me of my feeble faith. One Witness posted that Ryan shouldn't be surprised that everyone he ever knew and loved was shunning him. The anonymous poster explained that faith is a fragile thing, and Ryan had become a baseball bat to everyone's faith.

Then another Witness posted (anonymously) to ask Ryan if he came to the conclusions he had arrived at because of what he had read in science books about radiometric dating. The Watchtower Society devoted entire articles to downgrading this form of archaeological dating, so most Witnesses assumed it was simply a ploy of the devil.[100] But Ryan, in one well-reasoned swoop, pointed out that this was merely one of several converging lines of evidence.

The reality, though I was loathe to admit it, was that any time a Witness put up an argument on behalf of the Truth, Ryan single-handedly defeated it. But Ryan was not some 'baseball bat to faith'; he was sincerely distressed over the things he had learned. It pained him to have to say the things he was compelled to say. He said them because he wanted to be honest with himself and his growing son.

I held out hope that my remaining friends would rid me of thoughts about Ryan, but he incessantly found ways to come up in conversation. Johnny wondered aloud how anyone could leave the Truth this late in human history. "The Paradise is going to be here any day," he said.

Tonya added: "How can anyone believe in evolution? It's just stupid."

The season warmed, and the sun lingered long in the horizon. Jennifer and I took walks in the evening. We found a place—a small lake—that had not yet been poached by suburban sprawl, and we paced the asphalt until we came to the city park each night. The conversation was always about Ryan.

Jennifer pitied Ryan's plight. "I want to invite him over for dinner to show him that we still love him even though he's not a Witness."

This was a tricky request. Ryan was not disfellowshipped, nor had he disassociated himself from the religion. We would not get into trouble with the elders should we decide to share a meal with him. But clearly, Ryan was a danger to our faith. The first few times Jennifer made mention of dining with Ryan, I shrugged the matter aside. Finally, though, I put a stop to her insistence. "We're not having him over, okay? Will you stop asking?"

"He's not disfellowshipped," she pleaded. "Can't we still show him that we're his friends? He's lost practically everyone else!"

"Here's the deal: if we invite him over, I'm gonna ask him what he found out that made him want to leave the religion. Are you sure you wanna hear what he has to say? It might make me want to leave the religion, too."

With fear in her eyes, Jennifer meekly said no. She backed down and never again asked to have Ryan over. She abandoned all talk of that dissident, instead arming herself with Witness apologetics. She asked me how I felt about the religion: what did I like best about the most recent meeting? Was I excited about the coming District Convention? Did I read such-and-such article in the newest *Watchtower*? I tried to summon the zeal to reply like a good Witness, but I just couldn't find it within me.

"What's wrong with you?" she would ask. "Why are you so down on the Truth?"

"Do I have to say? You know the reasons."

"No, I don't. Stop being all secretive and just tell me."

"Jennifer, you know I've been down on the Society ever since we got that letter about the Flood. They're wrong about it. They *must* know. How can they not see that there's no evidence for the Flood being global?"

"Did you ever write back and ask them that?"

"You know I didn't."

"Don't you think you should at least give them a chance to explain things? Maybe you can tell them some of the things you've learned, and they'll agree that the Flood wasn't global."

"They'd never agree to that. The Bible says the Flood covered the whole earth, and they won't go against what the Bible says, regardless of the proof against it."

This gave Jennifer pause. After thinking for some time, her enthusiasm ebbed, and she repeated her proposal that I write to the Watchtower Society again.

So, on my twenty-ninth birthday, I sat at my computer and, with Watchtower publications scattered about, created a second letter to the Watchtower Society.

In a sense, I had been writing this letter for seven years—ever since their reply to my first letter. I knew what I wanted to say; I just had to concoct an urbane, meek manner in which to say it. Two days later, I dropped the letter in the mail and again bided my time as a Witness until a rejoinder arrived.

It arrived less than one month later. Jennifer and I nervously tore open the envelope. I unfolded the enclosed papers and commented on this response being thicker than the previous one. Standing in the dining room, we read together.

The Society frankly admitted that "some persons will accept [the Genesis] account only if the Flood is viewed as merely a *local* one. But that's not what the Bible says." I anticipated their statement to be followed up with a string of supporting scriptures, but this was not the case. In fact, there were no scriptures in the entire paragraph. Instead, they followed up their assertion by reasoning thusly: "If the Flood had been local only, why would not God simply have told Noah to move to another locality?"

I didn't know the answer to this question, but I knew that Jehovah had often asked humans to do more work than is necessary.

During the course of the five-paragraph response, five source references were provided. All references were to other Watchtower publications, and I lamented to Jennifer how stupid it is to use one's own writings to prove a point. "That's like if I say 'Of course the world is cube-shaped. Look, here in this essay I wrote in first grade where I made such a claim.'"

Their response concluded, "We trust the above comments will be helpful," and "We all are eagerly looking forward with you to the momentous events just ahead when God will deliver his people into his new world." I set the letter on the table and looked at my wife.

Jennifer was irate that the Society cited articles from a time when they had taught that the "six days" of Genesis were mere thousands of years long. "They can't quote stuff from when they believed the earth was only six thousand years old. They need to make up their minds—Is the earth six thousand years old, or is it millions of years old? And if it's millions of years old, they can't hand us proof from back when they thought it was six thousand years old, because that's unfair. You need to look up these quotes and write them back."

"I'll have to read the articles they enclosed and look up any references I find in them."

"Do that," Jennifer commanded. "Then write to them."

"I will," I said, definitively, "later."

That night, an elder gave a talk wherein he readily admitted the Last Days had continued longer than most of us had suspected. "It has been ninety years since 1914," he said, confessing that he never thought he would have finished high school. Then he turned to the gist of his complaining: Jehovah must have a reason for allowing the Last Days to go on this long. He asked: "What do you think are some reasons why Jehovah is allowing this wicked world to continue for so long?"

He called on a Dwayne Dunlin, a young brother sitting directly in front of me. Dwayne, scarcely out of his teens, had been raised as one of Jehovah's Witnesses but, upon reaching adulthood, left the religion for a life of sin. He decided to return before it was too late. So, Dwayne, still in his novitiate, commented: "Man, I am so happy the Paradise didn't come sooner. I think Jehovah has let this old world continue so long so I could come back into the Truth."

This was unequivocally the most discouraging comment I ever heard spoken into a microphone at a Kingdom Hall. I'd heard discouraging things before—impudent elders mimicking the Pharisees by passing off asinine rules; Circuit Overseer's making imbalanced comments about the ever-shifting Watchtower paradigm; and average Witnesses gleefully raising their hands and removing any doubts about their stupidity. This was different. This young brother gave an honest, heartfelt response to a valid question.

And that was what was so discouraging. *If I grant that Jehovah has postponed the Paradise these past ten years to win the soul of this one man, then what of the other billion humans born during the decade? Has God allowed them to be born simply to murder them in His impending war? Every day that God delays Armageddon is another day he must kill hundreds of thousands of new babies.* My mind quickly numbed to such large numbers.

To accept that God delayed the coming Paradise so as to gain this one brother was to simultaneously accept that he did so knowing he would lose countless other good people. People I loved. My cognitive powers bristled at the challenge of worshipping a being who was orchestrating the demise of some of my favorite humans.

After that, my meeting attendance dropped precipitously. I would not have attended at all, had it not been for Jennifer. Embodying the Good Witness, she parried my misgivings by redressing the reason we went to the meetings: to one day, very soon, live in Paradise. Over the next three months, she prevailed upon me to attend half a dozen meetings before the end of July, by which time we had purchased a new home over an hour away and were counting down the days remaining in Apple Valley.

Eugene, not having seen us in some weeks, approached and asked when we would be transferring to a new congregation. I told him this was our last meeting, as we were scheduled to move the following weekend. He shook our hands, stating he would miss our presence in the congregation, and invited me to say the prayer at the close of the meeting.

Two hours later, I walked on stage and looked out at the audience as they sang the final line of song. I saw my wife, and my mom. I looked out and saw so many people I had known my entire life. And I saw Norman Penna. I approached the microphone and prayed. And this is the prayer that I said:

Jehovah God
Our heavenly father
We thank you so much for this meeting that we've enjoyed,
And we appreciated the hard work that our brothers and sisters put into it.
And we ask as we go our separate ways tonight
That you watch over us and help us to stay strong in the faith,
And please watch over us as we go to school or work or out in service to-
morrow,
And especially watch over the children
As they are young and inexperienced,
And do not know all the bad things that can happen to them.
And Jehovah please bless this congregation as they try to serve you as best
they can.
And we send you this prayer now
Through Jesus' name
Amen.

Eleven days later, we moved to the small town of Big Lake. We packed up our cats and tossed our monogrammed towels into a box, and moved with help from our friends. But after they left us alone in our new house, so far from all we had known, a deep melancholy came over me. Unlike the last time we moved, I was not happy about the change. I felt indifferent to our new home. We had more room, but the rooms were in need of much repair. In the townhome, we had all of our possessions conscientiously stored or displayed, but here, there was nowhere to put anything. My books languished in boxes, as we had no shelving for them. We didn't bother hanging pictures on the wall, for the walls were in need of painting.

I felt so out of sorts, like my world had totally and irrevocably changed in a single weekend. I wanted to get away from the pedophile, and I wanted to get away from Ryan. But maybe I had gone too far. Our closest friends lived over an hour away, and I feared we would rarely see them.

Two weeks later, embedded amongst unpacked boxes in a house still needing extensive cleaning, Jennifer, sweaty and tired from a day of housework, asked: "Are we gonna go to the meetings anymore?"

"Fine," I said unceremoniously, "I'll look up the address tomorrow and we can go."

"That's not what I meant. I just was asking if you *want* to go."

I tilted my head in thought, as if any answer pained me: "That's what we're supposed to do, right?" I forced a smile. "I'll find out where the Hall is."

I knew I could have seized the opportunity to tell Jennifer I no longer wanted to go, but I was too afraid of how she would react. I wasn't ready to accept the ramifications.

On September 21, 2004, I was sitting in my cubicle at work when the electronic whistle from my computer announced an email had arrived. I raised an eyebrow when I clicked on Jennifer's incoming email to find absolutely no text. There was, however, an icon, which I dutifully double-clicked. It opened up to reveal a small photo proclaiming that, *yes*, she was undoubtedly irrevocably absolutely pregnant. I was directly in the midst of an amalgam of emotions: excited, nervous, apprehensive, privileged.

As if sensing my loss for words, Jennifer helpfully wrote: "You're supposed to wait three minutes, but it turned pink immediately! Then a stripe appeared, and then one appeared in the test side. So it's pretty definite."

Rhett called that evening and asked if anything was new. I smiled, thinking of our big secret. I wanted to yell out: "I'm gonna be a dad!" But it wasn't time for that yet. We talked about other news instead, including Ryan. Rhett asked if I knew his brother Ryan had disassociated himself. Living removed from that world, such news had not yet traveled to my ears. I told Rhett I wasn't surprised; Ryan had been making blasphemous statements on his website for months. Rhett reminded me this meant I should no longer speak with Ryan anymore, and I assured Rhett I had cut off contact with him months ago. "He just seems so full of hate now," I said.

"Ryan has a lot of issues to sort through, and the important thing is to let him know that we are always here for him, and that we still love him," Rhett said.

Ryan, I noticed, had a tendency to come up in conversation at the most unpredictable times. He even weaseled into the dinner Jennifer and I had with my family. I was not paying attention to the conversation, but my curiosity piqued once I heard the name of my old friend.

"Whatever happened to him?" my stepmom asked.

Jennifer swallowed. "He just decided not to believe in the Truth anymore."

"What does he believe in now?" another family member inquired.

"Evolution."

"How can he believe in evolution?" my dad asked incredulously, "How does he explain the fact that humans supposedly came from monkeys, but there's still monkeys around?"

I set down my fork and wiped my face with the cloth napkin. "It's more complicated than that."

My stepmom shook her head in dismay. "I think some people are just too smart to accept the Truth." I nodded politely and remained quiet.

When November arrived, Jennifer and I decided it was time to tell our friends about the pregnancy. We were apprehensive about the reaction we'd receive. For so long, we had viewed childbearing as a wanton test against God. We had talked ourselves out of having children for so many years that no one even suspected we wanted children.

We were delighted, then, when our announcement met with unanimous approval. Johnny and Tonya were elated to learn some of their friends would finally join them in parenthood. Rhett pronounced it groovy, and assured me, "You will love—not like, *love*—being a father." Our families, meanwhile, were refreshingly open to this new development.

At the next meeting, we were approached by Candy, a tall blonde who was exceedingly gregarious—so much so that Jennifer and I had dubbed her "the Congregation Cheerleader." She had been transfixed by the pregnancy since she first heard the news. Jennifer concluded that Candy was vicariously enjoying the event, having earlier confessed to Jennifer that she desperately wanted children, but her husband insisted they wait until the Paradise. "Is anyone planning on giving you a shower?" Candy said. "Because me and some other sisters were talking, and we want to throw you a shower." Then, not getting a response quick enough, she grabbed Jennifer's forearm and added: "That's okay, isn't it?"

"Oh, yeah," Jennifer said.

Another sister walked over, and the two of them started planning the shower, right then and there. We were impressed that these people—who had known us scarcely six months—were willing to host a party for our fetus.

The entire time I was at the shower—including when I was eating the cake with the words "sons are an inheritance from Jehovah"[101] frosted on it—I kept thinking, *These people are so kind. . . . How can I ever leave the religion now?* I knew doing so would disappoint all those good people. When an elder approached me and invited me to join him out in service the following weekend, I was compelled to accept. I went out in service for the first time in seven months.

Jennifer's emotions were more intricate. She began imagining her future as a mother. Though she could picture herself doting on an infant—feeding him, changing him, rocking him to sleep—she realized that the older she pictured her son, the more difficulty she had. The reason was not simply because she was imagining points further and further in time; no, her difficulty stemmed from the religion.

As a lifelong Witness, Jennifer had daily exposure to the adage that the End was "right around the corner." Now, she was nearly a mother: what was to become of her child? Should she tell him that the Paradise would be here any day now—before he was old enough to begin school? Should she impel him to pioneer, like all good Witness parents do? Jennifer regretted that she had not attended college; would her son be sitting around thirty years hence wishing the same thing, cursing his parents for guiding him to a career as a pioneer or a Bethelite? Jennifer couldn't picture herself pushing that life on him; she wanted him to succeed. And yet, somehow, to admit that was to admit that the Society was wrong about their warnings of an impending apocalypse.

Driving home one day, she asked, "Are we going to teach him about Noah and the Flood?"

"He can learn about those things," I said slowly, weighing my words carefully. "But I'm going to tell him that the Flood wasn't worldwide."

"So, basically, you're gonna tell him that the stuff in the *My Book of Bible Stories* book is not correct?"

"Some of it's not correct."

Jennifer persisted. "How will he know the difference between what is true and what's not? Are we going to sit at the meetings, acting like we agree, and then on the way home tell him that the stuff they said about the Flood or about evolution isn't true?"

I was uncomfortable with the conversation. I tried to maintain a dissonance, keeping the heretical thoughts from coalescing into an undeniable conclusion. I could not picture teaching my son what I knew was wrong. I could not imagine encouraging him to forego a quality education in favor of knocking on people's doors. Instead, I could see myself telling him to not make the same mistake I had made: to get a quality education while he was young and make sure he questioned everything, regardless of who it may upset. "We don't have to worry about that stuff right now. He'll be at least five years old before he'll even understand those things."

I laid awake that night, continuously speculating on the prospect of leaving the religion. I wondered if Jennifer would leave the religion with me.

Then Rhett would call. I'd listen to Rhett on the phone—his balanced view of the religion; his good experiences out in service—and wonder how I could possibly leave the Witnesses. Rhett would be so disappointed. I would prefer punching him squarely in the face. That would cause him less pain.

Rhett asked if I'd talked to Ryan lately, and I reminded him that I hadn't seen or heard from him since last summer. "I don't even go to his website," I said, trying to show Rhett I was firm in my resolve against Ryan's godless ravings.

"That's good, man," Rhett said, "he puts a lot of stuff on there about the Witnesses."

"Why would he burn his bridges?" I said. "I'll never get why people leave the religion and then insist on bad-mouthing it. Why can't they just go and leave us in peace?"

Rhett agreed.

The following week was a futile rush to prepare for the imminent arrival of our son. Friday passed quietly. I typed on the computer and Jennifer read the final pages of a baby care book. Before dusk, Jennifer decided to go to bed. I gave her a back massage and she was sleeping by 8:00.

I reclined in front of the computer, taking the quiet evening to document everything that had happened recently. Via email, I was interrupted twice: once by Les, and once by Tonya, who hadn't heard from us in over six hours and were starting to panic. I responded that there was nothing going on and that Jennifer was already asleep.

I shut off the computer and glanced at the clock on the wall. It was after midnight. It was now May 14th, the day my son was due to come into the world. I walked over to the window and, pushing the cheap plastic blinds to the side, peeked at the world. The sky was clear and the air was damp. A chill hung in the atmosphere. A long, cold winter was only now surrendering. I was depressed about the religion. I was anxious about the future. I was nervous to be a father. I felt I had failed at everything. I had disappointed my girlfriend with a frustrating courtship. I had disappointed my fiancé with an exasperating wedding. And now I had disappointed my wife with a crappy house in a God-forsaken location. I couldn't even get the house ready in time for my son. I hoped I would do better in supporting my wife during her labor. I thought about these feelings, and I thought about how I needed to push my own interests aside for the present. This was not a time to pity myself or to become consumed with my own needs. I was now third place in the family hierarchy.

I no longer considered myself a praying man, but I did not want my nagging agnosticism to stand in the way of speaking to God—if, indeed, He was even there. Begging Jehovah to excuse the infrequency of my prayers, I beseeched him to watch over my wife, that she have a good delivery, and my son, that he come into the world in peace and happiness.

Less than three hours later, I was driving a laboring woman to the hospital. The night was black. The boulevards were empty. And we drove into a valley of deep shadow.

THE GREAT TRIBULATION

Woe to the pregnant woman and those suckling a baby in those days! Keep praying that your flight may not occur in wintertime, nor on the sabbath day; for then there will be great tribulation such as has not occurred since the world's beginning until now, no, nor will occur again.

— Matthew 24: 19-21

After parking illegally, I ferried Jennifer into the waiting room and broke up the receptionist's nail-filing festivities. Miffed at the interruption, she pointed to a wheelchair. I helped Jennifer into the chair and left her alone while I sought out a permanent parking space.

Ten minutes later, we were directed into a tiny room with a bed, a counter, and imposing medical devices. This was not the room we had been shown during an earlier tour. Jennifer asked to use the bathroom, but the nurse ordered her first to change into a revealing chintzy gown. Jennifer hesitated, but the nurse repeated her demand.

The morning devolved from bad to worse. Jennifer pleaded to use the bathroom, but the nurse and an older midwife named Agnes strapped belts around Jennifer's ventripotent midsection. Jennifer was lying on her back, a position that was not conducive to comfort during labor. She still had to pee.

The claustrophobic room closed in fast. The room was warm—sweat warm—and I felt feeble. Despite being awake for over two hours, I couldn't shake the just-woken-up feeling. I stood near the edge of the bed and wore a fake smile, hoping it would help.

After an eternity, the nurses acquiesced and removed the belts. Jennifer asked if she would be taken to the midwife unit now, but they told her the midwife unit was full. Jennifer was taken to a regular labor and delivery room—with medical equipment hanging in the open; less-inviting, more imposing, more brightly lit and smaller than the midwife rooms.

The midwife herself was someone Jennifer had never met during any prenatal visits. Jennifer had wanted so greatly to build up a rapport with a midwife; she had wanted so greatly to have a natural birth in a tub. Waves of sadness washed over me. I maintained a supportive approach to the whole pregnancy, determined to let my wife plan and proceed exactly the way she desired. But on the last day, when it mattered most, the hospital refused to cooperate.

I was unsure how to support Jennifer—how to be the coaching husband the birthing class had prepared me for. The events were proceeding too rapidly, and our plans were tossed aside demanding hasty decisions. I didn't have time to dig the iPod out of our bag, much less set it playing with the soothing music we'd selected. Jennifer cried to the nurses to stop their invasive practices, and her mournful tone brought me to tears. The abrupt changes rendered her unable to relax, and she requested Nubain. The nurse, though, had trouble unearthing a vein. She jabbed the needle in several different places, then looked in confusion for assistance. For a moment, in between Jennifer's frenetic contraction screams, they contemplated not administering the drug, but Agnes dismissed this idea, saying "We can't even communicate with her."

Being shunted to this room meant that a natural, less invasive birth was nixed in favor of a policy of poking and prodding. Agnes made two attempts to start an IV, to no avail. She yelled at Jennifer to keep her arm still.

Agnes looked at the nurse: "I can't even control her." If not for the fact that I was endeavoring to be the perfect husband and give a good Witness, I considered punching the midwife. *We did not come here to be controlled.*

Returning to the room after calling our parents, I saw the midwife grab a tiny harpoon to break the water, offering no reason when we asked for one. But they didn't stop there. They continued forcing procedures on Jennifer that didn't seem necessary and for which they offered no rationale nor allowed any questioning. I was confused and frightened. I wanted to help, to champion my wife and my son, but I feared getting in the way of any medically necessary intervention. And so I remained helpless as the time accelerated. Before I could even register that we had come to this point too quickly, Jennifer was actively pushing. With one arm under her thigh, and another in the crook of her knee, I stood like a sentinel holding a weapon. After ten minutes, my arms began shaking. I was tired, hungry, thirsty, and stressed. Our doula, Luna, asked if she could take over, but I said: "That's okay, I got it."

Due to the fast labor, the baby's heart rate was dropping low. To remedy their concern, the midwife gave Jennifer an oxygen mask and told her to change positions. Jennifer tried to get on her knees, but she had trouble moving. When she cried: "I can't," Agnes yelled: "It's not for you—it's for the baby!" I valiantly held a couple wires out of the way while Jennifer turned.

The midwife decreed that Jennifer would tear and ordered an episiotomy. "This isn't the way it's supposed to be," Jennifer wept. But the midwife—who had left her bedside manner in her other smock—curtly told Jennifer that not everything was for her. Despite Jennifer's pleas to the contrary, the midwife performed an episiotomy.

Soon, another contraction came, and Jennifer's eyes widened in pain. Her look was one of terror. It was chilling, unearthly; the kind of face I imagine is on a martyr as they are tortured. I tried to maintain a calm face. The worry in my eyes belied the faux-smile on my mouth.

Eleven minutes after seven, my son Owen slid down the midwife's arms like a water slide and onto the bed. He laid there, curled up tightly in a cocoon of soggy fluids. Jennifer let out a loud moan and shifted her weight. Without thinking, I gasped and my eyes moistened. I wiped the tears with shaky hands. *So this is how it all starts?* I couldn't believe it. *That's my son! A tiny, shapeless bundle of bodily juices? Weird.*

Before I could touch my son, a nurse thrust a pair of scissors in my direction. Under instructions, I reached for the cord and squeezed the scissors together.

The baby was quickly wiped off and, despite my understanding that he would immediately be placed in his mother's arms, a nurse plopped him on a warming bed. I wanted to protest, but I was duped into believing there was something wrong. I fretted he was dying. Remembering my assigned role, I walked over to the baby. I reached out for his hands and held them to his chest. He was covered in blood, water, and cottage cheese. He kicked his legs frantically. His toothless mouth opened wide and with each scream his tiny chin shook. I leaned down and whispered into his little ears, which were aerodynamically plastered to his head. My voice was shaking. "It's okay, little man. Daddy's right here. Shhh." The warm, peaceful, rocking world that was his whole life had given way to a staccato miasma of glaring lights, frenetic sounds and a constant fight against gravity. Alert, he looked around the room. Crying, he exhaled his first breaths as screams.

Early the next morning, a knock at the door jarred us awake. I pretended not to hear it, hoping that ignoring the knock would make the culprit go away. But Jennifer sat up and said: "Come in."

I opened one eye just enough to see Agnes. I pretended to sleep, hoping she would get the hint and go away.

"Good morning Jennifer," she whispered as she crept towards her bed. "I was hoping to have a chance to talk to you about the experience we had yesterday. Is that all right?"

The midwife sat on the edge of Jennifer's bed. She crossed her legs and spoke softly. She explained that she was concerned about what happened. She felt Jennifer acted scary. She didn't think Jennifer's response to labor was *normal*. Agnes claimed she spent all night thinking about the labor and birth. She wondered why Jennifer acted the way she did. She told Jennifer she was out of control, panicky.

Jennifer suggested that the problem may have been that things hadn't gone according to plan. The midwife nodded like a psychiatrist. She offered no reasons why so many aspects of Jennifer's birth plan had been violated, or why so many things were done under the guise of emergency.

The midwife went on to explain that the only other time she had seen women act like that in labor was when she had assisted during the labor of Somali women. In the name of their religion, many of those women underwent a ritualistic mutilation of their genitals as young girls. Labor and birth draws attention and pain to that same region. Having doctors, nurses, and midwifes poking and prodding, the repressed memories reignite. Somali women, she implied, are therefore difficult patients, impossible to reason with.

When Jennifer added that she was not pleased about the episiotomy, the midwife became offended. She defensively stated that she has a very low rate of episiotomies.

Agnes wrapped up the conversation and left. I sat up and smiled at Jennifer. I scooted forward and sat on the end of the pull-out cot.

"That was weird," I said, trying to assess the conversation. Jennifer concurred, but then Owen began squirming for attention.

Owen had trouble calming down that night. A nurse offered to take him out of the room for a short time. Jennifer was adamant that he should remain with us. I was yearning for sleep, so Jennifer eventually consented, with the condition that she be awakened when it came time to feed him. The nurse smiled and nodded. "Of course" she said, as if she wouldn't dream of having it any other way.

The nurse wheeled the bassinette, with Owen in it, back into our room at six in the morning, only after Jennifer had called asking his whereabouts. When she asked how Owen managed to go so long without needing to be fed, the nurse cheerily explained she didn't want to wake us and so she fed him formula.

We arrived home that afternoon. Free of the uncomfortable, policy-happy, stress-inducing hospital, Jennifer successfully fed Owen without incident. He dozed off within minutes of completing his meal.

That evening, the three of us lay down in bed together. I smiled at Jennifer. She smiled back. Quietly reminiscent of the first night we laid in bed together as a married couple, we knew we had just done something big with our lives. A gentle breeze blew in through the window, and the tranquil scent of the lilac bushes lulled me to sleep.

The following evening, Jennifer sat on the futon eating dinner. When I smiled at her, she moved the edges of her mouth up, but all her other facial muscles remain motionless. It was an empty, distant smile. She set her plate down and stared off at some distant point. Expressionless. Her arms were limp at her side. We sat in peace, with Owen sleeping in his cradle.

Finally, she broke the silence. "Did they make you cut the umbilical cord right away?"

This question came out of nowhere. We hadn't talked about the birth all day. "The midwife just held up the cord and told me where to cut and I did."

She didn't answer. She didn't look at me. She pushed her lips together and I could see the tightness in her chin. She straightened out her mouth.

I asked: "Are you mad at me for not videotaping it?"

Jennifer got up and walked out of the room.

"Jennifer?" I called out. I walked into the kitchen, but then she turned and walked back into the living room. I followed her back.

"What's the matter?" I asked her.

First, there was silence. Then she started crying. Her eyes welled up with tears and turned red. I let out a sympathetic "ohhhh," and hugged her. I started crying, too, even though I wasn't sure why. We sat there for some time letting our dinners get cold, trying to loosen our throats so we could talk again.

"I'm sorry I didn't get the cord-cutting on video tape. That was really stupid of me."

She sniffed; then sniffed again. "I'm just upset that things didn't go right."

When she said this, my lungs grew heavy; it became difficult to breathe. Until that moment, I hadn't consciously considered the ramifications, but I was suddenly bowled over with a wave of regret. Wiping my tears, I broke off from our hug. "You mean because you didn't get to be in the tub?"

"That's part of it. I didn't want to take any drugs, either, but I ended up taking them. I didn't want an episiotomy, but they gave me one." She sniffed. "It wasn't the way I had hoped it would be at all."

"Jennifer, you can't get mad at yourself for that. The baby was coming too fast. You weren't prepared for him to come so fast."

Jennifer explained, through her tears, that she had planned it out just right. She had planned for a comforting room—one that didn't smack of medical devices. She had planned for a caring midwife, and a joyous labor. The hospital had ripped those fanciful ideas out from under her.

There was nothing pleasant about the experience. What should have transpired in low lighting, with calming music, warm water washing over her body, and a midwife respectfully waiting at her side, was instead a jarring chiaroscuro of mentally, emotionally, and physically invasive events. I felt sick to my stomach, as if the very thought of what happened was, in itself, an emetic.

"Why was an episiotomy necessary if I was going to tear anyway?" she asked. I tried making up plausible reasons.

When she asked about breaking the water, I repeated that Owen's heart rate was dropping. When Jennifer pressed me as to why breaking the water would help with the baby's heart rate, I was at a loss.

Between sobs, Jennifer cried that she didn't see the cord being cut. Once again, I attributed the cold mentality of the hospital staff to the fact that they were worried about Owen. I didn't know what else to say.

Jennifer toyed with the tissue in her hand.

I glanced out the window. "Jennifer," I said calmly, "Candy is here."

The idea of visitors seemed so incongruous at that moment that Jennifer let out the tiniest laugh. She got up, grabbed Owen and her dinner, and fled for the bedroom.

Candy and her husband had smiles to more than make up for our lack thereof. Candy carried freshly picked flowers, and she danced with glee as she presented them to me. I tried to wax happy, but I was certain they could detect my distraction. They asked about the birth, and I lied. They inquired as to my well-being. "I'm fine, thank you for asking," I said with a courteous nod.

After a quarter of an hour, Jennifer exited the bedroom. Candy practically did a back flip when Jennifer offered to let her hold Owen.

Eventually, Candy's husband pried her away from the baby, afraid that maybe it was contagious. They asked if they could stop by again in the next few days.

Closing the door behind them, I turned to Jennifer. We laughed. "Do you think they could tell I was crying?" she said.

"No, you look fine." Then, sensing that Jennifer knew I wasn't being totally honest, I added: "You look tired."

We resumed our conversation. Jennifer wanted to know the order of events. She said time was messed up while she was in labor. She didn't know how long things had taken. She couldn't remember if one thing happened before or after another thing. I tried filling in the blanks. Each time she posed a question, I paused, trying to figure out the best way to phrase something, hoping to mitigate her grief to the extent possible.

A few times, I left the room, only to come back and see her sitting, staring at nothing. Her eyes were vacant; lost. I didn't know what to do or say. I wondered if Jennifer was sinking into postpartum depression. I didn't know how to handle a wife like that. I was supposed to be the crazy, obsessive, depressed one, not her.

Over the next few weeks, Jennifer incessantly asked me about the birth. It was a conversation that never concluded; just paused for hours at a time. When I was washing the dishes, she walked by and asked: "Why didn't they let me hold Owen right away?" I'd try to answer while still doing the dishes, but eventually I was sucked into another conversation. I couldn't remember exact reasons, or times. I didn't want to say: "Because the hospital staff was in a bad mood and didn't really care about you or Owen!" But that seemed to be the underlying conclusion.

"Why didn't they let me go to the bathroom right when we got there?"

"How long was it from the time they gave me the drugs until Owen was born?"

"How come the midwife said, 'I can't communicate with her?'"

I tried answering as best I could, but I gave accuracy second place, placing priority status to answers that would soothe Jennifer.

She asked if Owen was alert while he was on the warming bed—right after he was born.

"He was." I said. "I stayed right with him," I added quickly, hoping her remorse wouldn't fixate on this detail.

"Why didn't they put him right on my chest?" she retorted. "He was wide awake and alert, and I could have fed him right then. Instead they made me wait for three hours until I was done being stitched up before I got to try breastfeeding. By then he was too tired."

I reluctantly agreed.

"I think that's part of the reason he had so much trouble nursing that first day," she said, crestfallen.

Jennifer grew increasingly distant. She didn't hear what I was saying. I told her I was running outside to get the mail, and she just stared at a spot on the wall.

And so it went on. Jennifer obsessed about the labor and delivery. She cried all the time; a vast change from a woman whom I had scarcely seen cry before. I wanted to tell her to move on, but I didn't want to sound heartless.

My wife was two parts sad and one part mad; my baby, two parts endearing and one part frustrating. Cards and gifts sporadically arrived, and I looked for some excitement, some enthusiasm in Jennifer's face, but it did not appear. People visited, bearing meals and gifts and smiles, but any improvement in Jennifer's demeanor lasted only as long as we were in the company of others. No sunrise or sunset improved Jennifer's state. Quite the opposite, with each passing landmark, she grew more depressed.

I kept asking if I could put away all the paperwork from the hospital, and she insisted we keep the papers scattered about the living room table. When Owen's cord stump fell off, I celebrated this as a milestone, but Jennifer remained glum. She grieved everything that finalized the birth experience. Jennifer kept wishing she could go back in time; to replay and revise Owen's birthday. Every passing hour only served to reinforce that she could never go back.

On the final evening of my paternity leave, I took a break from the housework to sit in the living room with Jennifer. Owen was asleep. I saw deep in Jennifer's eyes, and in her blank expression I could see her despondency. "What's wrong?" I asked. Her lips tightened and her eyes welled up with tears. My eyes heated up and moistened. My throat tightened, like something was jammed behind my Adam's apple. It left me unable to swallow and unable to talk. I swallowed hard and said: "Whenever you cry, it makes me cry, too."

She laughed a tiny laugh.

"Are you sad about the birth again?"

She nodded.

"Oh, Jennifer." I went over and sat by her. I gave her a hug, and we remained in embrace as the day died.

I felt like an automaton going through the motions in a long, repetitive, sad novel. I rose in the morning and drove to work. After sitting in traffic, I sat at a job I didn't like. In the evening, I battled traffic again. I arrived home to a wife conjoined to the couch, staring at nothing or commiserating online with other women who had experienced birth trauma. The house was a mess. The grass was long. The dishes were dirty. The crumpled mound of laundry grew strained and encircled the hamper. All evening, Jennifer wept, singularly focused on her birth experience. She would only finish obsessing over her trauma once dusk settled and Owen screamed unremittingly for three consecutive hours. Then it was time for bed. I awoke languid the next day and the cycle repeated. We did nothing enjoyable all summer. Even my sister's wedding to her non-Witness fiancé Mike taxed our capabilities, and we left the reception early and tired.

I fought with Jennifer about her gloomy, obsessive persona. I was tired of talking about the birth and became angry if I she asked about it. Enough time had gone by, I declared; she needed to get over it. I desperately wanted to revert to our old patterns; I was confused and upset that she wouldn't comply. Empty and aching and torpid, we were broken together.

Nearly every day I saw her cry, and the sight, which had once caused an equal welling up of my own tears, had, after so many weeks, rendered me callous. When she got upset, I sat stiffly with my arms crossed, as if glaring ominously would help her come to grips with her midwife crisis.

After weeks of such overarching gloom, Jennifer contemplated seeking professional help, but I detested the idea of lending credence to her depression by giving it an industry-approved label. I recalled how ineffective my therapist had been, but Jennifer reminded me I hadn't given therapy a fair chance. "Let's just wait a little bit longer, maybe you'll feel better without needing a therapist," I argued. As someone who had spent a lifetime hearing that wives should be in subjection to their husbands, she obeyed.

All other matters outside the house faded into murky insignificance. I felt like an outsider in my own life. I felt like an outsider at the Kingdom Hall. We missed most meetings. At the few we did attend, Owen squirmed and screamed and cried. Jennifer was livid at the lack of facilities for babies. There were no youth programs, no nurseries, no place even to nurse Owen; the bathrooms smelled like feces and the other women sat around by the sinks and gossiped. I encouraged Jennifer to breastfeed in the auditorium, but she feared some would be offended at such an immodest display.

I wished our friends and family would call or stop by simply to brighten the mood. They did, occasionally, and I donned a false mask of happiness. Rhett called. My dad called. Then my grandfather called, concerned that we had attended my sister's marriage to a worldly man, and pointedly asked if I spoke with my disfellowshipped cousin. "Brandi was Diane's maid of honor, right?" he inquired.

"We didn't talk to her," I said. "We know she's disfellowshipped and we were too busy taking care of Owen the whole time to really talk to anyone." Jennifer called me out for lying to my own grandfather, but I growled that I couldn't be bothered with petty matters, like if I had attended a wedding or greeted my disfellowshipped cousin. Such concerns reinforced that we were outsiders.

But never did I feel more like an outsider of my own life than the morning of July fifth. After breakfasting, I checked my email and found a message from Sarah. She wanted to know if Jennifer and I had heard the news: Rhett was dead.

I reread the brief email. Then read it again. Out of courtesy, I responded to Sarah. But then I just sat in the office chair, staring at a spot beyond my computer. *Rhett is dead?* Rhett had broken his leg while helping a fellow Witness install a fence. A blood clot from his broken leg had traveled to his heart. Paramedics restarted his heart but, in the ER hours later, no one could restart it a second time.

Rhett and I had drifted in and out of each other's lives over the years, but I always thought of him as my brother—not the sterile, sanctimonious title of "brother" that Witnesses call each other, but a real, treasured kinship. In effect, I always wished Rhett actually was my brother—an older sibling to guide and care for me. *And now, he's gone?*

I wanted to cry. I wanted to let loose the gigantic sadness within—an accumulation of years of discouragement that now culminated in the demise of my mentor. I knew any sorrow I showed would not be entirely for Rhett. The ersatz emotional outpouring would merely be an excuse; a way to relieve the sadness, guilt, and despondency that had already inhabited my psyche since my son's birth. I could conjure no feeling, sensation, or sentiment for Rhett. It seemed surreal; even unreal. It was one more shovelful of mourning on a mountain of unhappiness.

For the next few days I grieved more over my inability to process Rhett's death than over the death itself. I couldn't do the event justice; I couldn't focus on the loss. In an effort to begin the normal grieving process, I commented to Jennifer over dinner one night: "I feel bad about Rhett dying."

"Yep, it's sad," was her curt, conversation-terminating reply.

"Why does this have to happen on top of everything else?" I said. But Jennifer was too preoccupied with Owen and his birth to focus on Rhett. She couldn't read a book or watch TV, let alone focus on someone else's disaster.

Rhett's friends and relatives planned to meet at his dad's house in Apple Valley to find solace among companions and, in some manner, to feel closer to Rhett. I wanted to go, to be surrounded by Rhett's friends, family and memories. But I couldn't leave my wife for the day; and I knew she lacked the mental stability to join me. I cursed myself for moving so far away.

The memorial service was held a week after Rhett's death. Jennifer and I arrived late, for I had taken us first to the wrong Kingdom Hall. I had been so busy caring for Jennifer that I had neglected to check which Kingdom Hall would host the memorial service.

We were unable to enter the main auditorium, as it was overfilled. We remained in the basement and leaned against a wall, solemnly smiling at other latecomers. I held Owen in my arms, gently bopping him up and down, hoping to allay his crying. But as I looked around, I saw many people crying. Sarah's make-up streaked down her face, and she kept returning to her purse to grab tissues. I gave up trying to calm Owen.

Everyone was crying, except for my wife and me. I kept looking at her surreptitiously, wondering if she would show any emotion. She just stood there and stared at the floor. Her cheeks were red from the heat and humidity, and she slouched under the weight of the diaper bag. I felt I was being disrespectful to Rhett and his family for not crying. But I couldn't make myself do it. Instead, I just looked from my sniffling sister-in-law, to my stoic wife, to so many people I knew from so many years of being in a tight-knit fraternity. I watched them all like someone watching a play.

At the close of the service, everyone sang. I had forgotten to bring our song book, but I knew the words. In between the tears, a thousand cheerless Witnesses sang in heartbroken cadence:

> Can you see, with your mind's eye,
> Peoples dwelling together?
> Sorrow has passed. Peace at last!
> Life without tears and pain.
> Sing out with joy of heart.
> You too can have a part.
> Live for the day when you'll say
> "Life without end—at last!"[102]

I knew it wasn't true. And yet, I couldn't bring myself to admit it. I *wanted* it to be true. I wanted to know that soon—very soon—my wife would no longer feel any pain, my son would grow up in perfect health, and I would be able to reach out and throw my arms around Rhett, not the overweight, sickly, debt-ridden, Rhett of the past, but a strong, revitalized Rhett who would never again have to scrape gum off the floor of some executive's office just to feed his family.

Following the funeral, we followed everyone to a community center. It was uncomfortably warm. The ventilation system couldn't compete with a thousand Witnesses in suits and dresses on a humid July day. Everywhere I looked were Witnesses I hadn't seen in years; all of them crying and wiping their eyes. When I made eye contact, they smiled to show they were happy to see me, then laughed at how incongruous it was to try to smile on this day. The gathering was a grand celebration of Rhett's life; Jennifer noted that it was like being at a convention, without any boring talks and with only cool people invited.

Images and video of Rhett were projected on a large screen. I saw Rhett as a young man, and I heard his music playing in the background; a requiem to my mentor, nearly drowned out by the sounds of mourning. There were posters sitting on easels—each one a poignant photographic montage of a life well-lived: Rhett the son, Rhett the father and husband, Rhett the friend.

I felt a profound loss. My role model was gone. *How could God allow Rhett to die?* I was angry at God. *Why didn't he take me—a man with a surplus of doubt and a storehouse of sin? Why didn't he kill me, so that my sins would be forgiven?* Instead, He allowed an innocent, righteous man to die—a man who did not struggle with doubt, who enjoyed knocking on people's doors, and who was universally loved.

We made our way through the crowd. I held Owen, and Jennifer shadowed behind, trying not to lose me in the mass of bodies. I felt a hand on my back, a deliberate touch that caused me to spin around.

Ryan was balder than the last time I'd seen him, and his eyes bespoke a tiredness. Before I had time to speak, he pulled me closer. I could smell Ryan's sweat, and his face was wet from crying. We stayed in an embrace for several seconds. I did not plan on rekindling a friendship with Ryan, but in that moment—in that fleeting passage of time—I could not toe the Watchtower's line to shun him under the guise of being Christian. I lifted my hand and patted Ryan's back.

As we stood there, two old friends holding on to each other as Rhett slipped away, I observed that his ear was right by my mouth. I opened my mouth to say: *I know that you are right.*

But I didn't speak those words. I wanted Ryan to know that not everyone in attendance hated him. Not everyone would treat him with truculent behavior. I wanted him to know that there was at least one person still trapped in the Watchtower's Ames Room, in full knowledge of the illusion, but powerless to stand up for truth. But it was not the right time. I couldn't dream of going against my wife, who I was certain still believed the religion. More than that, I knew it was wrong to draw attention to myself on a day dedicated to a man far greater than I.

Ryan broke off the hug, and he asked to see Owen. He reached out and took Owen's hand in his fingers, shaking it as he said: "Hi Owen, I'm friends with your dad."

We spoke with Ryan for ten seconds, and then a mutual acquaintance interrupted us. By his body language, I knew he was trying to save us from having to speak any further to the apostate. I submitted to the ploy, and within seconds, Ryan sank back into the shroud of individuals.

When we came upon Rhett's father and stepmother, Jennifer offered her condolences. I didn't know what to say. I bobbed back and forth and smiled. I must have looked like someone who needed comfort, for in his exceeding empathy, Rhett's father opened his arms and said: "Come here, James, give me a hug."

I clasped my arms around his back; and my lungs felt heavy.

"I miss him so much," I said.

He patted me on the back. "We will see him soon. Just a little while longer, okay?" He whispered confidently, "just a little while longer."

His faith was overwhelming. For the life of me, I knew it wasn't true. I *wanted* it to be true. I wanted it to be true *so* bad. I wanted it to be true now more than ever. But wishing didn't make it so.

I gave way to tears. Sobbing into his ear, I eulogized the Rhett that was. "I miss him so much," I sobbed. I drew in for a tighter hug and, unable to stop myself, continued: "He was my best friend. He was my brother. You did such a good job raising him. You should be so proud of the life he lived. He made me want to be a better person."

I could sense that he wanted to say something, but he was too choked up. Regaining his composure, he whispered: "Just a little while longer."

At another time, in another place, Ryan had once said: "If you were going to write a novel, it would be a bad idea to model one of the characters after Rhett, because no one would believe such a person could exist." And now, Rhett didn't.

Our ninth wedding anniversary was decidedly low-key. I spent the day at work. I bought flowers at lunchtime, but by the time I got home, they were dying. We asked a sister from our congregation to baby-sit Owen, but she declined. I forced Jennifer to share some wine with me, but she didn't like the taste of it.

Perhaps I was hoping our anniversary would put us in a better mood. Perhaps I was hoping it would make Jennifer less melancholy. But it didn't. Nothing did. Not the baby shower, not being with our friends, not a visit from the doula. Not even writing an eight page letter to the hospital. I considered it a good night's sleep if I did not lie awake restlessly. I found myself jealous of the cats: mocking me with the carefree manner in which they groomed each other in the sunlight every day. Gray clouds seeped into our house and I wasn't sure if they ever planned on leaving.

I told Jennifer I was tired of coming home to a wife like *this* every day. As she cried, I stood over her and commanded her to snap out of it. She answered: "I am trying! I don't know when I am going to get better! How am I supposed to know that? I don't want to be miserable all day either, you know."

Jennifer again brought up the notion of therapy, noting that her mental state fit the criteria of post-traumatic stress disorder. I continued to fight against her. The idea of weekly visits to a therapist would give her issues the credence—the validity—they needed to become full-blown problems. I asked Jennifer if she really felt it was necessary.

"Of course I do. Otherwise I wouldn't suggest it!"

As summer slipped by, it became increasingly apparent that Jennifer wasn't getting better. I told her to move on; to get on with life, but I knew such a suggestion was as sterile as it was cliché. She cried as I left for work. As I drove down the highway that morning, I tossed off the vestiges of our former selves and accepted the reality of my world. The Watchtower Society, deplete with platitudes for depression, essentially offered an empty toolbox for fixing our crises. And meanwhile, I felt the full brunt of her problems and her needs, and I understood, finally, that I was incapable of mending her by myself.

When Owen was four months old, Jennifer guardedly tread into the world of therapy by visiting Meredith, a psychologist who specialized in adjustment to motherhood. That evening, I asked if she felt any better. I had been nursing the wildly incorrect notion that Jennifer's mood would improve noticeably following the visit. She hadn't even had time to tell Meredith the whole story. In time, Jennifer's depression abated somewhat. Or rather, now that she had a new sounding board for her depression, I was relieved of being her primary mental health caregiver. Every so often, we had stimulating dialogues on non-birth topics; I hoped that these signaled a glimmer of chance that she was getting better.

But over the same span of months, a subtle change took place. More and more, Jennifer began to concern herself with Armageddon. In her hyper-vigilant state, she started dwelling on the doom and destruction that Witnesses long hoped for.

"Do you think Armageddon is coming soon?" she asked one evening as we ate dinner.

"No," I said succinctly.

"How do you know that?"

I set the fork down and looked to the side, hoping to furnish a plausible response. I took a drink to stall. "Because the Society always says it's right around the corner, right? They're always talking like it's gonna happen any day but it never does."

Days later, Jennifer explained that the thought of a worldwide onslaught had always sat uneasy in her mind. Even as a child, she found it tough to accept that her grandparents would soon be killed by a loving God. She sat on the futon, staring off into space.

"Just because someone is not a Witness doesn't mean that they'll be killed at Armageddon," I said, kneeling down on the floor next to her so as to look up into her eyes. "Jehovah reads their hearts, so if they're good people—like your grandma—then Jehovah will let them survive Armageddon anyways."

"You're wrong," she snapped back. "I don't know what religion you belong to, but the one I belong to says that only Witnesses will survive Armageddon."[103]

"No, you just have to be a good person who loves Jehovah. Then He'll remember you."

"Then why do they always say at the meetings that we need to keep doing everything we can? If I only need to be a good person, then why are we always pressured to give talks and go out in service and do tons of studying?"

"Come on, you know the answer to that!" I rose to my feet and stood over her. "If we already know the Truth, then we need to make sure we are doing everything we can."

"Or else . . ." she said with a tone of finality.

"Or else what?"

Flatly, she answered: "Or else Jehovah will kill us."

"Well, I don't know," I blustered, throwing my hands in the air. "I'm not gonna make that judgment."

"That's what the Bible says—remember that scripture that says if you do this and that then you might be saved?"[104]

I cringed in tacit recognition.

"Even if we *are* good people—kind and meek—there's still *only a chance* that we'll survive," she said. Then, to pointedly explain her distress, she added: "The Society strongly suggests that only Witnesses will live through Armageddon.[105] They even say that some Witnesses won't make it into Paradise—remember, in that recent article, where it said some Witnesses who have lost their zeal may not survive? Doesn't that upset you?"

"How do we know that all Witnesses are good people? For all we know, there's an elder feeling up some kid in the back of a Kingdom Hall right now. Heck, we know there are child molesters in the religion. So, no, I'm not upset if some of them won't make it."

She looked up at me. There was confusion in her eyes, as if she could not understand how I arrived at my conclusion. "You're just giving it your own interpretation."

"What do you mean?"

"Whenever they say that some won't survive, they don't say it's because some Witnesses are pedophiles. They say it's because we're not going out in service regularly, or attending all the meetings, or studying for all the meetings. If Jehovah's gonna compare me to other Witnesses, then there's no chance he'll look at me or our friends and think we deserve to be in Paradise."

"Then maybe we need to start doing everything we can," I suggested, pointing to both of us.

Jennifer asked if I thought Jehovah would still love her and let her live in Paradise even though her religiosity had subsided. Before I could answer, she noted how nothing was ever enough. "When you were pioneering, did you feel like you were doing everything you could for Jehovah?" she asked.

"No," I said honestly, "because they're always saying from the platform how we need to be doing more."

"See? If I started commenting once at every meeting, the elders would be on my case to comment twice—it never ends."

In the subsequent months, I hoped and prayed that each meeting we attended would be one that dwelt on the love, or on the Paradise. I recoiled when speakers mentioned the imminent condemnation befalling the bulk of mankind. On the back wall of the Kingdom Hall was a list of upcoming public talks. I inspected this list often, and if the theme of any talk sounded too inflammatory, I made a note of it. When the day of the talk came, I told Jennifer I didn't feel like going to the meeting, and she'd agree to stay home.

It was a harsh trade-off, really. We could stay home from the meeting, staving off the fear for a night; but then Jennifer felt guilty, as if our absence at that one meeting tipped God's scales in favor of killing her at Armageddon. Or, we could attend the meeting, and I would spend several hours afterwards calming her.

"When I wasn't doing that good in the religion before, it didn't matter so much, because I was only dealing with my life." Jennifer said one afternoon. "But now I have to worry about Owen, too."

I looked down at my son playing on the floor. He was trying to master the art of sitting upright. I told Jennifer that she needn't worry—"God reads people's hearts, and I'm sure Owen has a good heart. Why would Jehovah kill Owen?" I asked, almost sarcastically. "Owen has never lied or cheated or stolen anything. He's never had any bad thoughts. If Jehovah can't see that Owen is the purest, most innocent person there is, well, then, He's not a god of love, is He?"

Jennifer nodded, reluctantly assenting. Then she reminded me of the children killed at the Flood and destroyed in Sodom.

"What do you want me to say, Jennifer?" I yelled. "That God is mean and vengeful and that he's gonna kill Owen because his parents haven't been out in service for months?"

Mournfully, she said: "At the meetings they always make it sound like we are responsible for whether or not our children live through Armageddon."

I slouched back in the chair and leaned on my elbow. We looked at Owen. I considered the innocence of childhood, juxtaposed with God's promised to murder millions of children in the near future.

"Maybe it was a mistake to have him," I said.

Jennifer cried. "Don't say that. I'm glad we had him."

"I am, too. But ever since he's been born we've had nothing but trouble. You've been depressed and anxious, and now you keep reminding me that the end of the world is coming any day now, and we're all just gonna die anyways."

She sobbed, wiping her tears with her sleeve. "I didn't have him just for him to die as a baby."

"If I've learned anything in thirty years, it's that things don't go the way you want them to."

"He's so beautiful and so innocent—how can Jehovah kill him?"

"I don't know. Why don't you ask Jehovah? Owen wouldn't be the first infant He's killed. Not by a long shot." I looked out the window, filled with anger.

Jennifer's anxiety did not abate. To the contrary, it grew more pronounced. She was caught in her own private feedback loop: she was worried she would die at Armageddon. In order survive Armageddon, she needed to do more in the religion, yet she harbored grave doubts—doubts that I had planted in her mind over the years—and so she couldn't bring herself to blindly do what the religion required. Thus, she worried about Armageddon.

The majority of the meeting the following week was taken up with whetting our "spiritual appetite" for the upcoming District Convention. Jennifer confided to me that even the theme of the convention—"Deliverance at Hand!"—raised her blood pressure. Just thinking about attending set her on edge. She feared the convention would feature an inordinate amount of discussion of Armageddon and impending destruction.

Her predictions seemed well-founded, as the speaker said the District Convention was especially urgent "In view of the late hour in this time of the end."[106] He also said "one question answered will be 'What can we do now to prepare for "the great and fear-inspiring day of Jehovah"?'"[107] I winced when the elder read that sentence, for I knew Jennifer was right; the convention could bring her fears to a boil. She leaned over and said: "I don't wanna go to the convention." But I whispered into her ear: "Too late, we already booked a hotel room."

As if an approaching convention centered on the wholesale slaughter of billions of humans wasn't sufficient to escalate Jennifer's anxiety, the warming weather also meant Owen's one year birthday was imminent. Reflecting on the assault she had faced at the hospital nearly a year earlier, the days preceding Owen's birthday flooded the emotions back to a strong degree.

Jennifer brought this problem to therapy, and Meredith asked Jennifer what she was planning for Owen's birthday. Jennifer, being the good Witness, said: "Well, in my religion, we don't celebrate birthdays."

Sounding a bit shocked, Meredith said: "So you're not even going to mention birthdays?"

Jennifer squirmed in her chair. "We can acknowledge them; we just don't celebrate them."

"I see," Meredith said reflectively. And she added: "What's the difference?"

Jennifer paused to contemplate the answer. She was at a loss as to how to answer both truthfully and in a way that painted the religion favorably. Somehow, it didn't feel satisfactory to simply say, "John the Baptizer got his head chopped off at a birthday party, so we figure we shouldn't celebrate birthdays." Jennifer couldn't think of any way to answer Meredith logically unless she pointed out that the religion was, at least in some areas, illogical.

"I don't know," Jennifer said dismissively. "You know, with my religion, I have some doubts—and birthdays are one thing I don't really understand or agree with them on."

The confession raised Jennifer's guilt. Witnesses are counseled against being critical of the Society, and to say as much to a non-Witness was tantamount to giving a bad witness.

Silence prevailed for a few moments, until Meredith asked: "What other kinds of doubts do you have?"

Pensively, Jennifer said: "I don't know."

The sun shone brightly in the cloudless sky on May 14th, in vast contrast to the weather exactly one year earlier. Neglecting the circuit assembly, we passed the day at Jennifer's parents' house. We shared dinner with them, and acknowledged—but did not celebrate—Owen's birthday.

As I drove home and squinted at the setting sun, I considered what had happened one year ago. Owen was born, that much was obvious. But so much more: Jennifer and I had become parents. For the first time in years, we were living with a new person. And Jennifer had experienced such great trauma that she was still coping with the ramifications. In my obsessive-compulsive brain—a brain that willfully tracks and records dates and events without any conscientious effort—I couldn't let the day pass with scarcely any memorial. I felt a deep longing, to mark the anniversary of the day. Despite the Watchtower Society, I knew Owen's birthday was a memorable occasion; I couldn't permit the day to elapse without a celebration, however spontaneous and small. I wondered how my parents could have denied similar yearnings to mark the passing years after the births of myself and my sister.

"Let's stop at the grocery store and buy Owen a cake for his birthday."

"Uh . . . okay," Jennifer said unexpectedly.

"Well is that okay? You know, we don't celebrate birthdays," I said uncomfortably.

"Then why do you want to get him a cake?"

"I'm not saying I want to celebrate his birthday, you know? But this is a special day. It's a day that's special to all three of us, not just him. You and I know it's special—because we can read calendars and we know it's the anniversary of his birth. But Owen doesn't know it's a special day. And I want him to know that this is a very important day for him, and for us. Does that make sense?"

"I think it makes perfect sense." Jennifer unzipped her purse to look for money. "I'm glad that you said something." She admitted she had been thinking the same thing, but feared I would get angry if she suggested anything.

So our son, who had been nourished on breast milk, homemade yogurt, organic avocados, and natural cheeses, consumed his very first dessert. Later, we presented Owen with two gifts we had held onto expressly for this day, a book and a toy farm. A warm breeze wafted in through the kitchen windows, and the blooming lilac bushes commemorated the event by offering the same tranquil scent as they had exactly one year ago.

No one got their head chopped off.

As the convention drew nearer, Jennifer switched on to heightened alert, actively looking for signs of Armageddon. She was sure it was coming any minute, and she peeked out the windows several times a day to see if she could detect any signs of it in the clouds or in the demeanor of passersby.

The first two days of the convention were acceptable. Occasionally, a speaker mentioned the "coming great day of Jehovah" or reminded us to "share the good news with everyone you meet before it is too late." Jennifer looked at me nervously. I patted her on her arm, and said: "Don't worry. It's okay."

During one talk, the speaker interviewed a couple of exemplary pioneers. When the speaker asked one of the pioneers why she spent all of her time knocking on doors and preaching to people, she said: "How could I do otherwise? Lives are at stake. The greatest disaster in the history of mankind is about to befall us, and I want to help save as many lives as possible." This was exactly the kind of ominous statement that set Jennifer on edge. Thankfully, she didn't hear the comment. Only a few minutes earlier, Owen had been fussing. He became so noisy and distracting that Jennifer got up out of her seat. Attendants paced the hallways holding signs that read "Please Be Seated," but Jennifer ignored the unsympathetic admonition and paced the hallways with Owen to keep him quiet.

When she returned to the seats, I smiled at her, wondering if she had heard the comment. As she sat down, she leaned into my ear: "Did I miss anything?"

"I wasn't paying attention," I said, lying.

In our hotel room that evening, Jennifer pleaded with me that we should just pack our luggage and leave in the morning. When I resisted, she waved the program in my face. "The last talk tomorrow—do you see what it's called? It's called 'Deliverance by God's Kingdom is at Hand!' Let's just have a nice, calm morning. We can leisurely have breakfast, then take Owen to the pool, and then just check out and leave."

"I honestly don't think it's as bad as you're saying. We always joke that the last talk is the pep rally, right? They talk about good experiences from around the world and they talk about how people in the community have been impressed with our conduct." When I promised we'd leave if Owen was fussy, she acquiesced.

The next morning, I woke early, dressed in my suit, and left the hotel. In the humid July morning, I came upon a convergence of Witnesses, all craning their necks in anticipation. Some people were wearing bathrobes; most had a cup of coffee in hand. One woman leaned down to her little daughter and said: "Stay right by me, okay? 'Cause when they unlock the doors, we have to move fast." The little girl nodded obediently.

Moments later, the doors opened, and Witnesses flooded the building. No one was talking; everyone was too intent on getting the coveted seats. I bounded up the stairs—careful, like everyone else, not to allow my gait to break into a run—and turned the corner into the main auditorium. Gabe moved about on stage, working with a couple other brothers to get the microphones set up. Then I looked up at the top row.

My loafers made a dull thud as they hit each cement step in turn until I was standing at the highest point. I plopped my book bag down on an aisle seat in the top row. I pulled out an assortment of *Watchtowers* and laid them on the chairs; reserving a seat for Jennifer, Sarah, my mom, Jordan, Raven.

I was out of breath from all the walking and stair climbing. So I sat down and observed my fellow Witnesses from misanthropic row. It was comical to watch the filling auditorium from the high vantage; people running to and fro frantically saving seats. Every now and then, I'd spot someone I knew, and I'd watch to see where they planned to sit. There seemed to be such finality to it all. I became nervous, wondering if Jennifer and I had the faith to continue: *would we be at next year's convention?* I couldn't picture it. Yet, I knew it was our tradition, like all Witnesses, to come to the convention every summer. Was this how it felt to know this might be my last day at a convention ever? The thought was unnerving.

I resisted. I didn't want it to be our last convention. I wanted to continue on in the religion for all eternity, with Jennifer by my side. Why, despite my best intentions, was it ending? Where was God at a time like this?

I looked around in a state of panic, as if nearby Witnesses might be able to see my thoughts. No one was paying attention, and I panicked again, wondering if there was no one to help me.

What was there left remaining? What was there left to try? In the entire galaxy, there was, at the end, only one thing to do: Pray. I looked inward and found there was still one more prayer to be offered. I cast my eyes up to the heavens. Seeing only the ceiling, I forced myself to believe that something else was out there. After a lifetime in which I called out to God in prayer over twenty thousand times, I prayed. One more time.

And *this* is the prayer that I wanted to tell you about:

Oh my God.
I don't know what to do anymore.
You know I'm at the end of my rope.
You know I've tried everything.
I keep asking you for faith or peace of mind or whatever,
but I never feel like you answer my prayers.
Am I not praying right?
I guess I don't know.
Aren't you the hearer of prayers?[108]
Don't you answer your humble creations when they call out to you?
I know I have sinned many times, Jehovah,
and I know I have done many things wrong, Jehovah,
but I am telling you now: I am sorry—truly, deeply, sincerely sorry—for all
those things,

and if you want to kill me at Armageddon, then go ahead,
but you also know that I have tried so hard to do what is right.
You know I pioneered—not because I liked it—but because I believed you
wanted me to.
I gave talks and I helped out in so many ways in the congregation.
I'm not materialistic.
I've been faithful to my wife and kind to my son,
and I helped your loyal, loving servant Rhett whenever I could.
If any of that amounts to anything, then I hope you hear me.
Hear me *now*.
I understand if you don't want to answer my prayers for me, but I am ask-
ing you to answer my prayer today for my wife and for my son.
You know that my wife has been depressed and anxious,
and you know that one of the main reasons is because of the doom and
gloom that she hears at the meetings.
You know she didn't want to come to the convention, not because she
doesn't love you, Jehovah, but because she was afraid it would scare her
even more.
So now she's worried about the last talk this afternoon.
She's worried that the speaker will go on and on about Armageddon,
which will make her anxiety reach new heights.
So, please, if it's at all possible, can you please, please make the last talk be
happy
and positive,
and have the speaker dwell on the beauty of Paradise,
and the wonderful aspects of this Organization,
and the wonderful hope in store for Witnesses?
And yet, Jehovah, I know full well that asking You to alter the content of a
talk is probably too much to ask,
so, if you can't do that, then can you at least make sure that Owen is the
most misbehaved child he has ever been?
Make sure he cries and screams and does whatever is necessary to prevent
Jennifer from paying attention to that talk.
I know it's weird to ask that Jennifer not pay attention to a talk that You
provide,
but You know her situation, and You know her problems,
and You must know that not paying attention to the talk will, for her, be
the best thing.

We passed the lunch hour by dining at our seats, then went outside to walk
by the river for a few minutes. Jennifer was fidgety; preoccupied with dread. I
forced a smile for the other Witnesses. Minutes before the afternoon session
commenced, we squeezed back into the auditorium and nearly drowned in
the sea of people. Having clambered above the din and the deluge, Jennifer

serenely seated back into place and held Owen tightly. Later that afternoon, following the morning session and the lunch hour, the chairman introduced the last speaker. He promised that the talk would be a "rousing, encouraging finale to the spiritual banquet we have enjoyed over these three days."

I had been holding Owen for the past hour, even declining to give him to Sarah when she asked to hold him. But as the final talk began, on cue, I handed Owen to Jennifer. I passed him over roughly, hoping to rile him up. I tossed some of his toys in Jennifer's lap, hoping to distract both of them. "I don't want those," she said, looking out of sorts, "put them away."

Within minutes, Owen fell asleep in Jennifer's arms. The speaker, meanwhile, rallied the audience to be alert for Armageddon. A spellbinding raconteur, he provided lines of evidence for the world's impending doom. He spoke of current events lining up with biblical prophecies that evidenced Armageddon was *so* close. Though I didn't know it at the moment, Jennifer began to have a panic attack. She became frozen in her seat and unable to do anything at all, like a rabbit hearing an unfamiliar noise. The speaker ardently railed that we shouldn't expect a mass conversion of humanity into the true religion, and we shouldn't allow Armageddon to take us by surprise. He delineated the futility of seeking higher education, pointing out that, although most Witnesses never attend college, they are the happiest people on Earth. Sarah leaned over and whispered: "That's because ignorance is bliss." We laughed nervously, but it only served to further point out how misguided the speaker's words were.

It was at the summit of Jennifer's anxiety and the speaker's zeal when he invited us to accept a resolution. I hated resolutions. They were pointless in a crowd of people already dedicated and baptized. For example, one declaration on the resolution involved promising to give Jehovah our exclusive devotion. As unnecessary as they were forgettable; they were theocratic Tourette's for the faithful and bored. We were asked to approve a variety of declarations that would keep us in anticipation of Armageddon. The resolution included declaration number seven:

> We will resist with all our strength the spirit of the world manifested in such things as materialism, unwholesome entertainment, overindulgence in food and alcoholic beverages, the plague of pornographic material and *the curiosity or temptation that lure one into association with outsiders through internet chat rooms.*

Speakers at the convention repeatedly cautioned against going online and searching for information about our religion. We wondered what had happened to the standard "be good Christians, be kind and loving to all people, don't do drugs, and don't get involved with worldly people". *Why the sudden change to "don't look online" above all other evils?* When the resolution was presented, all in the audience were asked if they agreed. A booming "yes" filled the auditorium as thousands of Witnesses submitted in unanimous agreement. In her state of overwhelming anxiety and panic, Jennifer stoically sat in silence—angry silence—and Sarah gave a confused side glance. I grew nervous that Sarah noticed Jennifer's noncompliance, but counted myself fortunate that she had not noticed my similar lack of response.

Following the final, tedious prayer, we filed out through the cramped aisle. Jennifer bent down to grab her water bottle. I stood in place, waiting for her to collect our things. Then I cast my eyes to the heavens and, seeing only the ceiling, wondered if there was anything else out there. Jennifer and I did not make eye contact or speak to each other during the march down the bleachers, through the hall, into the skyway, and out to our car. After heaving our bags into the trunk, and buckling Owen into his seat, we slammed our doors shut. I fully anticipated Jennifer to unload her emotions in a torrent of speech, but she said nothing. I wound through the downtown streets, battling traffic and streetlights. At last we were on the highway, heading north.

No longer having to pay full attention to the road, I said: "Well, what'd you think?"

"About what?" Jennifer asked guardedly.

"About the day."

"It was terrible. I don't know why you made me go."

"Okay, we've been over that. What's done is done." I admitted to being baffled by the final talk, reminiscing about past conventions that left us feeling reinvigorated.

Jennifer was too canny to be distracted by my recollections. "The speaker was acting like the governing body is scared of the internet and that most of us are going to die at Armageddon and that it's so close."

I reasoned, as I had before, that Armageddon *was* closer than it had ever been before, but that it could still be far off. Indeed, I spent the entire trek home trying to convince Jennifer that Armageddon lay in the distant future. My words meant nothing. She had the brains to know I was speaking contrary to the Watchtower's teachings. I insisted there was room for personal interpretation, even though I knew very well there was not.

Back home, our routine resumed, but Jennifer struggled. The looming prospect of Armageddon churned in her head. She couldn't figure out how to either find the faith to do more or come to terms with being killed by God very soon.

I rose early each morning and lingered at work later than necessary. I didn't want to go home; I did not want to talk about the religion. I wanted to continue in our habit of attending meetings and papering over our doubts with meaningless phrases.[109] I tried to talk about trivial matters.

Still convalescing from the conventions, Jennifer visited her therapist on Wednesday. Meredith probed into Jennifer's fears, challenging her to confront the religion. Meredith asked how it felt talking about it, and Jennifer candidly answered: "It makes me feel better." She added, "Whenever I allow myself to think it might not be true, I feel better." Meredith asked what she wished could happen, if she was in control, and Jennifer said that she wished she could just believe the Witnesses were the Truth and throw herself into it so she wouldn't feel conflicted. Meredith pointed out that every motivation Jennifer had for remaining a Witness was out of fear. Though my wife had to admit this was correct, the calming effect of the conversation only lasted while she was safely in the therapist's office. Once out in the wicked world again, reality came pressing down on Jennifer once more.

By the next day, Jennifer could neither eat nor sleep, and could barely care for Owen.

We went for a walk, in lieu of attending the meeting. The sun set amidst thick clouds, and the taste of rain hung in the air. I tried to prop up the conversation on secular matters. I talked about a new employee at my job, and a funny website Jordan sent. In between my one-sided diversions were loud, protracted silences.

On Friday, Jennifer awoke to extreme anxiety. She knew there was no chance of healing, or even heading toward relief. There was only the spiraling sensation of exponentially mushrooming anxiety. She distilled her options down to two: death by her own hands, or check into a hospital. Though suicide seemed the preferred option, Owen's presence rendered her unable to carry out the deed.

Freezing in place as she grabbed the phone, Jennifer abruptly became conscious of a third option for redemption.

ARMAGEDDON

I arrived home to a still living, non-committed wife. Bending down to remove my shoes, I asked, "How was your day?"

"Fine," she said, with a note of serenity I hadn't detected in months. I looked up and saw the vaguest flash of a smile, as if she knew something but wasn't letting me in on the secret.

I reached out and picked up Owen. I sat him on my knee and asked him about his day. He babbled. Kissing him on the forehead, I looked at Jennifer. She *was* smiling. She was sitting on the futon with her legs tucked under. She was turned sideways to face me and her arm was on the backrest.

"How are you feeling today?" I asked, probing further.

"Better," she said, clipping off her response.

"Really?" I was pleased to hear good news for once. "Why's that?"

She tightened her lips, and her head swayed around, as if she was searching her brain for the right answer. "Do you want to go for a walk?"

This was not the answer I expected, but I viewed any physical activity, especially one including fresh air, as potentially raising her spirits. Moments later, we stood in silence at the edge of our driveway, with Owen buckled in his stroller, and waited for a car to pass. We crossed to the opposite side and stepped onto the sidewalk. We walked to the end of the block. As we came to the corner and prepared to cross the street, Jennifer said: "How would you feel if I said that the religion wasn't true and there was no Paradise?"

I took a long, deliberate breath, and looked sharply to the left, as if a passing car was taking priority. My brain was doing cartwheels trying to find an appropriate, logical, honest answer. I knew this question was coming. I had known it for years. And yet, I hadn't been prepared for the stagger my heart gave when at last she verbalized it. I pushed my hands into my pockets and said: "I would say that would be very sad."

"How would you feel," she continued, "if I told you that the religion wasn't true, but we don't know if there will be a Paradise or not?"

263

Again my thoughts fired rapidly. I tried to concoct the best answer I could. "I would say that would be better."

"You think so?" she asked. "Why?"

"Well, because . . . I don't like the idea of just dying one day and going off into oblivion. I like the idea of living forever in Paradise. But if there isn't going to be a Paradise, I'd like to think there's something else."

"Like heaven," she said, with a note of happiness.

"Yeah, heaven, or Nirvana, or whatever."

Jennifer nodded, and we walked further, not speaking for a time. Then she admitted to having looked up information about the Watchtower Society on the internet.

"You mean, apostate sites?" I asked, forcing my voice to remain calm.

She hesitated slightly, as if she worried her response might cause me to condemn her as a witch and immediately storm off from our marriage. "Of course," she said bravely, adding that any website about Witnesses, with the exception of the Society's official website, is, by their definition, an apostate site.[110]

She related the things she had read. Unexpectedly, there was little that I did not already know and, for that matter, there was little she did not already know. Seeing it all laid out, in one place, with supporting references, convinced her that the Witnesses were not the Truth.

She reminded me about the Flood. She pointed out the Society's failed prophecies: Armageddon would come in 1914;[111] the last days had begun in the 1800s;[112] the prophets would be resurrected in 1925;[113] Armageddon would come before the twenty-first century arrived.[114]

"A good Witness would say the light keeps getting brighter," I reasoned, "so if the Society was wrong in the past, that's okay, because they're continually refining their understanding."

"How do we know they're correct *now*?" she asked. "Did you know in the book *Children*, they encouraged Witnesses not to have any children because Armageddon was so close? That book came out in the 1940s, when our grandparents were still children!"

Yes, I knew of that book. It sat on my shelf, and I had read large chunks of it.

She reminded me that the Society had suggested Armageddon might come in 1975. I retorted, "A good Witness would say the Society never actually said it would come in 1975; the problem was that many Witnesses just took what they said out of context."

"Did they?" she asked pointedly. "Have you read for yourself what the Society wrote in the '60s and '70s? Because I did, today, and I don't think the Witnesses were taking things out of context."[115]

As if to further the point, she reminded me of how, in 1995, the Society had indefinitely postponed Armageddon and how the increase in the religion's membership had floundered in the years since.[116]

I told her a good Witness would say that such things are in the past, and that it's important we stay current with the Watchtower's teachings.

We turned the corner and headed for a school playground. I unbuckled Owen and he tottered to the sandbox. Jennifer sat on a bench, and said: "Don't you remember what they said at the convention last week—that the best indicator of future events is past ones?"

Feigning ignorance, I asked, "Why do you say that?"

"Look at the history of the religion! They have never predicted anything correctly! You and I both know they are wrong about how long humans have been on earth and about the Flood, so what makes you think they are correct about other things?"

"No one's always right all the time." I sat beside her on the bench.

"Come on, James," she scolded. "You know the difference. You can't go to the meetings and tell people you only agree with half of what they teach. They'll disfellowship you! You know how hard it has been keeping what we know about the Flood secret. We wanted to tell people, we wanted to discuss it, but we couldn't, remember?"

"We talked about it with Ryan and Heather that one time."

"Yeah, and remember how nervous we were? And," she added, to make the point more forceful, "Ryan left the Truth a week later."

I groaned like I was deep in thought. I looked down at the park bench and played with the flecks of peeling paint. "A good Witness would say that you need to talk to the elders, or that you should pray."

"James," she said matter-of-factly, "Of course I prayed. Do you think I didn't think of that?"

I played dumb. "Does it help?"

"Has it ever helped you?"

I didn't need to respond. We both knew the answer.

"As far as talking to the elders," she added, "you're the one who has pointed out to me that the elders won't know the answers to our questions. Whenever I told you to talk to the elders, you reminded me that the elders have always discouraged you, like Dick Jacobs and your Uncle Peter—and the elders have been a discouragement to the Kambers, and Jordan and Raven. Now you're saying you were wrong about all that, and the elders really can help? Were you lying to me all those years? Or are you just saying what you *think* you should be saying?" Her question trailed off, and it hung like a fog over the bench.

I looked away. "I don't know," I said with a touch of anger. "I was just trying to think of *something*." I got up to play with Owen. I carried him to the top of the slide and sat down to go for a ride. I wished that playing with my son would make me forget about what we were saying, but it did no such thing.

As I reached the bottom of the slide, Jennifer walked over to sit by us on a swing. "Did you know that Jerusalem didn't fall in 607 BC?"

"Yeah, I knew that," I said casually.

"You knew and didn't tell me?" she yelled.

"I *did* tell you. You didn't think it was a big deal, so I didn't push the matter."

"Hmm," she said, thinking, "I guess, at the time, I didn't make the connection that 607 was crucial to 1914. When you told me about 607 being wrong, I just thought it was one little fact. I didn't know it was a big deal. But now I know it's a big deal."

"I know! When I found out they were wrong about that, I knew they were wrong about 1914, too."

"Why didn't you say those things to me?" she asked. "For a year now, I've been freaking out that Armageddon was coming and you never told me they were wrong about this or that."

"Jennifer," I said, trying to stay calm, "I thought you knew those things, too. You knew they were wrong about the Flood, and how often did we leave the meetings complaining about stuff? You were worried about Armageddon, and I told you it wasn't coming soon. What more did you want?"

"You could have told me it's not coming at all."

"I didn't know that! I still wanted it to be true."

"So you wanted your wife to go crazy just so you could go on believing that the Witnesses were right?"

I lowered my head into my hands. "It wasn't like that."

"Well, I don't know what you plan on doing, but I'm not going to be a Witness anymore."

In a way, I knew this already. Her statement was the culmination of all we had experienced in nearly ten years of marriage. Still, I was stunned. I thought we had planned to maintain our façade no matter what—regardless of ridiculous doctrines or superfluous rules.

"So what—just like that you're going to stop being a Witness?" I asked, waving my hand in the air.

"Why not?" she said casually. "I looked up information and found it wasn't true. Why would I continue? It's a lot of work! And it made me suicidal!"

"A good Witness would say you're just acting on impulse, though. They'd say you didn't bother to spend the time to do sufficient research," I said, sitting on the swing next to her.

She looked up at the clouds and let herself sway on the swing. "*You* did the research. Your conclusions weren't based on impulse; you took years to come to certain conclusions. I can't tell you what to do. You can keep doing it if you want, and I'll respect that, but I'm not doing it anymore, and I don't want Owen doing it, either."

This caused me great grief, for I realized there was no turning Jennifer around.

"Why are you so against Owen doing it?" I complained. "If I go to the meetings, why can't I bring him with me sometimes? It's not like it's hurting him."

"Because," she answered, as if the reasons were blatantly apparent, "it's *not* true! Don't you get it? It *has* hurt Owen, because it *has* hurt me. I'm his mother, and he's the one who suffers if I am depressed or anxious. It has hurt a lot of people for many years. Do you think your mom is better off because she was raised as a Witness? What about your sister, and Jeremy, and Ryan?"

Weakly, I shrugged my shoulders. "I just don't want to upset anybody."

"If you want to do it, that's your own business, but you and I both know it's not the truth. I want to live my life. I want to do all sorts of things, and I don't want to feel guilty if we have another kid or if I go to college. I want to vote and celebrate the holidays with my family, and I want to celebrate Owen's birthdays, and I know you want to, too."

"That doesn't present any conflicts. Birthdays aren't prohibited by the Bible; that's just another thing Witnesses got wrong. Jehovah couldn't care less about birthday parties. We could remain as Witnesses and still celebrate his birthdays. We just can't tell anyone."

"How can you say that?" Jennifer said, her voice shaking with emotion. "If we continue to celebrate Owen's birthdays, we'll eventually get into trouble."

This rattled me out of my myopic delusions. The thought of disfellowshipping was too much. Imagining myself in the basement before a committee of elders made my fingers numb, and my stomach churned in opposition to the scenarios my brain created. I clenched my teeth as nausea welled in my gut. Jennifer gestured towards our son and continued: "Do you think he can keep a birthday party secret year after year? Eventually, he'll be able to talk, and how confusing will that be when we tell him he has to keep it secret?"

I stood up and paced around the playground. Ignoring the issue of birthdays, I said: "I don't care if I ever vote. What difference does voting make?

I don't care about the stupid holidays. I can celebrate life without needing some greeting card company to tell me it's time to honor this or celebrate that."

"That's what Witnesses are trained to say," she said calmly.

"So? I am a Witness. There's no shame in that."

"But you don't even believe the things they teach. You're just afraid to leave the religion, and you know it. Look at all the things we've talked about here, and you haven't given me one bit of defense against them. You haven't been able to say, 'No Jennifer, you're wrong, being a Witness has benefited our friends and family.'"

"What are you talking about?" I said loudly, getting mad, "All I've done during this whole conversation is respond to your objections about the religion."

"You just keep saying 'a good Witness would say this' or 'a good Witness would say that.' You don't even believe the things you're saying."

I held my hands up to my head, trying to keep the tiny bit of faith that remained from flying away. It was no use. My mind throbbed with the realization that I had been living a lie for thirty years; indeed, I had lived the lie even after I knew it was a lie. I would miss the reciprocal altruism afforded from being in such a tight community, but that didn't change the fact that the Watchtower Society was not the Truth; rather, it was an idealistic perversion of truth. I tried to recall one instance of when the Society made a correct prediction and, apart from vague conjectures, I could not think of one. I became sullen. As Sarah had said at the convention, ignorance really was bliss. I wanted God to give us some sign, some answer, some *thing* to cling to in assurance that He was there for us and would protect us.

But far from my mind being at peace, it felt as if it would detonate. My head hurt, searing in pain from years of trying to contain two conflicting viewpoints. I looked up to the heavens, and in the clouds I imagined I saw an archaeopteryx coming down in a streaking shriek, reaching in with its fiery talons and cleaving my brain in two.

Though I was slow and unwilling to accept her plans, there was nothing I could do to stop Jennifer. What's more, I fully understood and supported her decision.

I looked her eye-to-eye. "What about our friends? What about our family?"

She said that the Kambers and Jordan and Raven were such deplorable Witnesses, it was a wonder they had stayed with the religion as long as they had. "Jordan's not even baptized," Jennifer pointed out. "I don't think he even goes to the meetings or out in service." She opined that some of our friends were simply keeping up appearances. Perhaps they would leave the religion soon, too. Either way, however, Jennifer was resolute.

"You only have one family member in the Truth—Sarah," I said. "Two, if you count Les. I have fifty. How many of them do you think will still want to associate with me?"

Jennifer agreed I had a good point. But as we got up to walk back home, she helped me appreciate that most of my relatives were people I either had little contact with, or were people I would rather not be with anyway. "So what, if your Uncle Pete shuns you?" she said. "I'd view that as a bonus."

"What about my parents?" I whined.

"Look at how they treat your sister," Jennifer said, pushing the stroller, "They still love her and spend time with her, and she's done much more to make them upset than you have. Besides, we have Owen!"

"Ah yes," I said with a note of deviousness, "he's our little ace in the hole."

"I can't believe your parents would shun us when we have their only grandchild."

We arrived home. The long dusky shadows spilled across the dining room and in the twilight, we continued talking.

Eventually, Jennifer prepared for bed. I sat in the living room a while longer, holding Owen and staring out at the darkening sky. When she returned, she asked, "Are you gonna go to the meeting this weekend, or not?"

"I can't make up my mind right now," I said with a tinge of frustration.

I tried to stay up late, to enjoy the quiet time to read. But I couldn't concentrate on the words—they all blurred through my foggy concentration. The last six hours had changed my life.

I tiptoed into the bedroom. My wife was on her side, sleeping soundly. Owen was on his back; his arms up near his head. He had kicked off his blanket and was lying diagonally across my half of the bed. I gently nudged him towards the center and laid my tired body next to his. My heavy head dropped onto the pillow. I looked at my wife. There, lying beside me was, not a Witness, but a worldly person. Jennifer had shed the religion, and honesty behooved me to do the same.

I turned to lie on my back and I cast my eyes up to the heavens. But I saw only the ceiling.

And I knew there was nothing else up there.

I looked down at my chest, and smoke rose up from my heart, the smoldering ashes of a faith that could not survive the crucible.

And I dreamed I was dying.

But in truth, I was not dying. Over thirty-one years after my birth, I had only just lived my first day. My first day in the New World.

THE END OF THIS SYSTEM OF THINGS

I woke with a jolt at three in the morning. My wide eyes darted around the room. All was quiet; Jennifer and Owen slept soundly by my side. I sat up, peeling my sweaty back from the bed, and fumbled to my feet.

I hobbled to the sink and washed my hands. Slowly, I raised my head to see the reflection in the mirror. *Was it good to be alive anymore?* Apart from the tiny Muller's muscles holding my eyelids at half-mast, every muscle on my face was relaxed. I could neither smile nor frown. My mouth drooped to the point of sadness; my tired eyelashes partially obscured my vision. I leaned in closer, through the misty morning haze, and peered into my eyes. In the near darkness, with only the light of a streetlamp illuminating a streak across my face, my pupils were wide. *Had it really happened? Had we really, finally acknowledged that the Watchtower Society was not true?*

I looked into my eyes and saw there was no soul. I was a man of research, facts, documentation, and proof, and I could no longer accept such mythological fantasies as souls, spirits, or God on blind faith. I looked away from my reflection and pondered the thought that *blind faith* was itself a redundant term.

The sun rose like a cancer and blazed across the room early that Saturday morning. I rolled over to see my wife and son. They were both awake.

"How are you feeling?" Jennifer asked, patting Owen's back as he nursed.

"Fine," I said in a monotone voice.

"What do you think?"

271

I rolled back onto my pillow. "About what?" I said dryly.

"Everything."

I brought my hands to my face and rubbed my eyes. "I don't know," I said with a slight whine, "Do we have to keep talking about it? Can't we just have a nice day?"

"I want to have a good day, too. That's why I was checking to see how you were doing."

"I'm fine," I repeated. I got up and went into the kitchen.

As I ate breakfast and Jennifer checked her email, I told her I was nervous.

"About what?" she asked sympathetically.

Sighing, I said, "Our friends, I guess. And my family. I'm afraid of what they will say or do. It's like a tempest is brewing."

"You haven't even told me if you're gonna still go to the meetings or not—"

I cut her off. "I don't know what our friends will do. How will they react, what will they say? Will they still want to be our friends?"

Jennifer raised her eyebrows. "Maybe not, but we need to do what's right, right?"

I squirmed as if her words were binding me in tight ropes. "I just think that if we could sit down with our friends, if we could invite Raven and Jordan over, and if we could calmly speak with them over dinner and say, 'Here's the thing, we're not Witnesses anymore, but we're not bad people. We still want to be your friends, and we won't talk about religion if that's your wish.'"

"I'd like that, too. But don't get your hopes up," she said, closing her laptop. "We can try to calmly tell them that we're not Witnesses, but they'll immediately ask why, and when we say we don't believe it's the truth, they'll assume we were reading apostate information."

"That's just the thing!" I yelled. I stood up and paced the room. "I've never, not even to this day, ever read an apostate book or went to one of their websites. I discovered it was not true because I dug into the things that they told me to dig into." I waved my finger in the air, pointing in the direction of the Kingdom Hall. "They said we should do research! They said we should have 'accurate knowledge' to back up our faith, and that's what I tried doing. Any one of our friends will find out the same stuff if they would only do the studying they're supposed to do in the first place!"

"I know, James, I know," Jennifer said placidly. "But no matter what we say or do, they'll create their own reasons why we left. They won't want to hear our reasons; they'll just invent their own, just like we did with others in the past. It's not like any of them will think, 'James and Jennifer left the

Truth because they found out it wasn't true.'" Jennifer laughed at her own statement. "We gotta stop calling it 'the Truth'."

"Do you think our friends will just say I didn't have enough faith?" I asked.

"Maybe. Some of them might say Satan got to you because you read too many books. Some of them will say I'm just crazy and can't think straight, and then, in turn, they'll accuse you of not keeping our family in the Truth. I mean, the religion," she said, correcting herself.

I hesitated. "Our friends are smart people. Maybe they just stayed in the religion 'cause they wanted to stay friends with us."

Jennifer crossed her arms. "We're smart people, too, but we still shunned some of our friends."

I shrugged off this comment. I walked out of the room and went to shower. As the warm water sprayed over me, I stood there, staring off at the wall, unable to think about something as mundane as showering. I turned off the water, stepped onto the monogrammed towel, and let the droplets of religion splash onto the ground.

Hours later, while Owen fell asleep in Jennifer's arms, I said, "It just doesn't seem like a good time to leave the religion." I reminded Jennifer of upcoming events, primarily our anniversary party. We had arranged for our family and friends to stay at a hotel with us. "They'll all cancel their plans if they find out we're not Witnesses anymore."

I pointed out that my employer had reserved an amusement park two months hence, and that I had already invited Johnny and Tonya, Jordan and Raven, Sarah, and even my sister's ex-husband Kyle to join me that day. "Who will I bring if they all back out?" I cried. "We won't have any friends."

Jennifer raised her hands to calm me. "I'm not saying we have to call everyone up on the phone tonight and say 'Guess what? We're apostates!' We can lay low for now. This is still new to me, too. But I'm not gonna be quiet about it forever. Like I said, I wanna get on with my life."

I leaned back on the futon. "That makes me feel better. If I decide to go along with you in this, I would rather fade than just abruptly stop doing it."

"We've been fading for years."

I mumbled a noncommittal response.

"We can keep this private for now," Jennifer said, sitting forward and laying out our plans. "This is a big adjustment, and we can decide how we're going to handle things before we tell anyone. We'll still have our anniversary party. I'm looking forward to it, actually."

"It might end up being like a good-bye party," I said, making a feeble joke.

"Yeah," Jennifer chuckled.

I stood up and folded my arms, as if I was trying to come to terms with the plans. "So let's not say anything, at least not until after the amusement park. That's about two months from now." I sighed. I looked down at the floor and my face lost all expression. "It's just not a good time right now," I repeated.

Shifting in her seat, Jennifer looked at me. "It's never a good time," she said, smiling. And I caught her smile, and I recalled this as the very same argument I had used when she said it was not a good time to have a baby.

I passed my hand along my chin. Starting slowly, I said: "If I don't do it anymore, then it's all been a big waste, you know? It's all been for nothing."

"It's sad."

I agreed, feeling the gravity of her words.

"If you continue doing it, you're just wasting more of your life. Think about your dad—he's been a Witness for over fifty years. Aren't you glad you haven't wasted that much of your life?"

I scratched my head. "I wish I could've just gone on blindly believing. Or—" I put a lot of stress on the word—"If I'm gonna stop doing it, I wish everyone would stop all at the same time."

"Because then it would be easier?"

"Is that so wrong?" I answered defensively. "I could rest easy knowing my friends and relatives weren't wasting their lives, and we could all lean on each other."

Politely, Jennifer agreed it was a nice wish. But wishing didn't make it so. And this called to mind two questions I had asked myself over twenty years earlier:

The first was this: *Do I want it to be true?* The answer was still yes. Yes, without any doubt, I wanted it to be true. That was my answer then. That is my answer now.

The second question was this: *Is it true?* As much as I hated to admit it, the answer to this question was not dependent upon the answer to the first question. Whether or not I wanted God and the Bible to be true did not affect their inherent trueness in any way. I was just a mortal man. I had no influence over these things.

The answer to this question was . . . No.

I excused myself and went to bed. The air was sticky, and the whirring of the ceiling fan did little to cool my skin. *It isn't true.* The words kept blazing across my mind. *It isn't true.* I had just lived through my first twenty-four hours with a worldly wife. It was hard to believe, but I had survived. If I just took each day on its own terms, perhaps I could survive the ordeal. *It isn't true.* I fell asleep with those words on my tongue.

I was awakened, as I had been every Sunday of my life, to the sound of the alarm clock announcing the meeting hour. I lashed out and slammed my hand on the clock, silencing the noise before it awoke my wife and son. But when I rolled over, I saw the bed was empty.

Jennifer was in the living room, sitting in the rocking chair reading a magazine. Owen was fast asleep, his mouth agape and near her breast. She asked if I was going to the meeting.

I sniffed, and put my hands on my hips. "No." Jennifer let the magazine droop in her hands. She looked into my eyes. She raised her eyebrows and I took that as an indication she wanted more than that. "I'm not gonna do it anymore," I explained, as if this was just a decision regarding the kind of cereal I was choosing for breakfast.

"Do you still believe it?" she asked.

I walked over to the window and pulled apart the curtains. Looking out, I saw cars parking alongside our street—the dutiful attendees of a nearby church. "Nah," I said, "I don't believe it."

"When did you decide this?" Jennifer asked, sounding mildly surprised.

"I don't know," I shrugged, "I guess I haven't believed it for a while now."

"How long?" she asked insistently.

I turned and looked around the room. Casually, I answered: "Oh, like five years. Or maybe six. Yeah, I think six years."

Jennifer sat up. "Six *years?*" she shouted. She looked down at Owen. She shifted him up onto her chest and sat forward. "Six *years!*"

I laughed, unsure why she was so riled about this revelation. "So what?"

"You mean to tell me you haven't believed in the Watchtower, Bible and Tract Society for six *years* and you never told me?"

"I didn't want to—"

She cut me off. "I've been sitting in this living room for months," she yelled, her finger pointing accusatively, "on edge and anxious over Armageddon and thinking about suicide, and you never thought, 'Oh, maybe now would be a good time to tell Jennifer that Armageddon's not real?'"

"I thought you'd get mad at me," I said.

"Oh, you thought I'd get mad at you, huh? Is that more important to you than my sanity? You're right, I probably would've been mad, but I would have gotten over it."

Owen woke up from the sounds of our yelling. Jennifer patted him on the back and wished him good morning. Looking back up at me, she said: "If it was true, I wanted to survive Armageddon. But since it's not true, I wish you would have said something sooner. Thanks a lot."

Owen got down and walked to me. I picked him up and sat on the futon. I kissed his head and told him good morning. Holding him in my arms had a calming effect. Composing myself, I said: "Jennifer, you're right. I'm sorry. The thing is, I wanted it to be true. You know I did. I still do."

Jennifer begrudgingly accepted my apology, but she spent most of the day commenting on how ridiculous it was for me to continue on as a Witness and lie to everyone long after I knew it wasn't true.

"I lied to myself so completely that I hadn't even realized I was doing it," I whined to her that evening. "Even after I stopped doing it." I paused to consider my words. I would never—could never—be a Witness again.

I woke early on the first of October. Jennifer left soon after and spent the day with her parents. Though we said nothing that morning, I could feel the secret was leaving the house that day.

Two hours later, I rendezvoused with my friends at Sarah's house. Johnny offered to drive the seven of us to the amusement park in his minivan. Everyone was in a pleasant mood, excited by the prospect of being together all day at a fun park. The weather was faultless—neither too hot nor too cold. The wind was minimal, and the clouds obscured the sun just often enough to prevent sun burn. As my employer had bought out the park that day, we were able to get on every ride and play every game with almost none of the long wait time that so often plagues such places.

I tried to join in their conversations but felt withdrawn, distant. Even so, I made a concerted effort to be agreeable and amicable. When Johnny tried showing off his manliness by playing a game in the penny arcade, I complimented him. I made a point of telling Kyle to make sure he let his wife know I was sorry she couldn't make it: "But don't make her feel bad," I said, "I know that she has an important job, and it must be hard to get away sometimes."

As we went from ride to ride, I allowed everyone else to decide where to sit. Sometimes, they wanted to sit in the front of the roller coaster, other times, the back. I smiled congenially.

While waiting in line for one roller-coaster, Johnny tilted up his baseball cap and looked at me through his mirrored sunglasses. "When am I gonna install that carpet for you?" he said, nonchalantly referencing the bolt of carpet he'd plopped down in my basement eighteen months earlier. I had a strong sensation that, even as I stood there, my wife was busy telling her parents the tale of our exit from the Witnesses. If my suspicions were correct, then it was only a matter of time before Johnny found out. I had been striving, for weeks, to think of a way to tell Johnny, man-to-man, about my recent decision, but I couldn't formulate a way to get him alone so that we could talk in private. His question all but solved my problem. I asked him to come by in two weeks, just enough time to allow me to prepare the basement. He agreed.

I pretended my friends were too loyal and dear to shun me. I ignored their capacity for hypocrisy and hatred and they, in turn, did not notice the archaeopteryx sitting on my left shoulder. During the car ride back to Sarah's house, I looked around at my friends, pausing at each one in turn. *Is this the end? Are the years of friendship set to vanish today? I can only hold back the secret for so long, and soon they will all know.* Thoughts of losing all my friends raced like wildfire across my brain. Engaged in conversations with each other, none of my friends noticed my breathing quickening. I obsessed about the shrinking time I had left. *This is the last time I'll be on a highway with my friends. . . . This is the last time I'll be at a stoplight with my friends. . . .*

They continued to talk, exchanging gossip and opinions. I wanted so powerfully to just be myself one more time; to forget about the new me and just be a Witness again. In silence, I looked out the window and cursed myself for squandering the few minutes I had remaining with my friends.

Johnny pulled into Sarah's driveway without me even noticing. It was only when the van doors opened that I snapped back to the present. They climbed out of the van. "Thanks for the awesome day," Kyle said. "Yeah, thanks for thinking of us," Johnny said.

Without saying a word, I looked up. I looked at each of them again. My face was expressionless and my heart was asunder. I wanted to pretend they were thanking me for years of friendship, but I knew they were naively thanking me for a measly free day at an amusement park. I opened my mouth to tell them all *you're welcome*, but instead it came out as: "Thank *you* guys for being my friends."

I said it in grave sincerity, with no trace of my usual irony or sarcasm. The moment was thick with silence and my friends exchanged glances. I was never *that* sincere. Finally, Johnny grinned and said, "You're welcome, James." Everyone else followed suit.

I stumbled into my car. Before driving away, I watched them all in the mirror: Sarah fiddled with her keys and went into her house. Johnny and Tonya drove away in their big van. Kyle pulled out of the driveway. Jordan and Raven followed, Jordan flashing a peace sign as he turned away.

Jennifer and Owen were already in their pajamas when I walked in the door. I hugged Owen and laid him on my chest. "I haven't seen you all day, buddy," I said. "I missed you."

Jennifer inquired as to my day, and I gave her the briefest, fastest overview possible. Then I hurriedly asked: "How was *your* day?"

"Well," Jennifer said, bobbing her head back and forth, "I told them we're not Witnesses anymore."

I threw my head back, "Oh man, I can't believe it. There's no turning back now."

Jennifer told me how her parents, especially her mom, were positively elated we had finally exited the religion. Jennifer felt that a barrier between them and us had broken down; for the first time, she was able to inquire as to why they had left the religion, and for the first time, she was able to tell them the many doubts and frustrations and sorrows she had experienced.

In a serious tone, I asked: "Did you tell them to keep it a secret?"

"I told them to not go spreading it around just yet. I told them you were still nervous and that we want to tell our friends in person."

"Okay," I said, relieved, "good."

Squeamishly, I told her I'd invited Johnny to come over two weeks hence to install the carpet. Jennifer was livid that I kept prolonging the inevitable, but I promised her that I would tell Johnny the truth at that time. "When he gets here, I'll take him out for dinner. And while we're eating, I'll tell him that you and I aren't Witnesses anymore."

With a sarcastic bend, Jennifer said: "You think then he's gonna say 'Okay Jim, let's go install the carpet now'?"

I had to confess I didn't know how, precisely, Johnny would react. Jennifer dismantled every recourse I suggested for every possible response my revelation would produce in Johnny. After an hour of this, I shook with anger, not because of Jennifer but because of the double-bind the Watchtower Society had placed us in. I hated that there was no honorable way to explain our position.

Ten days later, Les called Jennifer. I strode into the room with Owen in my arms and sat down to eavesdrop. He knew our secret. He wanted to know why Jennifer had dumped the religion, and she did not hold back from telling him. Les admitted he knew many of the same explanations. When he seemed so agreeable, Jennifer asked why he had resolved to continue being a Witness. Les awkwardly said he felt they might be right about Armageddon and, besides, he liked all the friends he had at the congregation.

When Jennifer hung up the phone, I asked: "How does he know?"

"My mom told him, James," she said matter-of-factly.

"He's such a blabber-mouth," I exclaimed. "He's gonna tell everyone!"

Jennifer assured me she had asked him to keep the information a secret, until we had had time to tell our other friends, but Les was incapable of keeping secrets.

The next day, while I was at work, Jennifer called. "I got an email from Sarah"

"Uh-oh," my heart skipped a beat. Sarah emailed Jennifer nearly every day, but I knew this was different. "What does it say? Read it to me!"

"It says: 'So I had a really good conversation with Les last night. Sounds like they're really serious about going back to meetings.'"

"That's it?" I asked, disgusted at its simplicity. "Are you sure that's all?"

"I have the email open right in front of me," Jennifer scolded.

"She knows," I whispered gravely. Then, my voice rose to frustration: "Oh God, I can't believe it. I knew your stupid brother couldn't keep his big mouth shut. She knows! She knows! And now everyone else is going to know, too."

"You think so?"

"Oh, yes," I said darkly, "there's not a doubt in my mind."

Jennifer's relationship with Sarah—her sister, her oldest and closest friend— devolved rapidly over the next forty-eight hours. Sarah eventually extracted from Jennifer an admission that we were at odds with the Society on major theological issues. She emailed:

> I talked to Les last night and he said that you told him that you and James don't believe it's the truth anymore, which seems to be more how you feel based on your earlier emails. . . . Is that how you feel?

Jennifer responded:

> If I told you that that's how I feel, then you'd have me disfellowshipped for apostasy, right?
>
> Like I said, I'm very anxious, and when I go to meetings that increases my anxiety. We've had some very discouraging experiences over the years. We've had recent emotional troubles.
>
> The advice that elders give for emotional problems is to go to all meetings, pray, [do] personal study, go out in service, and generally do more for Jehovah and keep yourself busy in the work. Since going to meetings increases my emotional problems, that is not going to work. The society even frowns on going to therapists or psychiatrists to receive treatment, and even though they've loosened up on that stance in the last few years, they still say that the best cure for emotional problems is to do more in the truth. They also say that Jehovah's people are the happiest people on the earth. I guess I just don't fit into the mold so well.

A few hours later, Sarah responded:

> Well, that pretty much answers my question. I'm not going to "have you disfellowshipped," I just needed to know.

I was at work, so Jennifer forwarded me the correspondence. Upon reading Sarah's ultimate email, I immediately phoned Jennifer. "What the hell does she mean?" I asked in frustration.

"I thought it was a bit weird, too," Jennifer said. "Why is it so important for her to know if she doesn't plan on going to the elders?"

"Maybe she wanted to know so that she could decide if she was still going to associate with us or not."

"It's strange she wanted to know right away."

"Unless," I said, pausing to gather my thoughts, "she's planning on telling all of our friends."

Jennifer did not respond right away. I could tell she was considering my statement. "I think you're right," she said, "especially knowing Sarah."

"Shit!" I exclaimed hitting my fist on my desk. "She's probably emailing Raven right now, and we'll never get a chance to even say good-bye to her. Oh man," I said, as the idea dawned on me, "She is totally going to call Tonya right now."

"I think you're right," Jennifer said in dismay.

"I guess Johnny's not gonna come over and install the carpet tonight."

"Just see if he says anything. You were going to tell him tonight anyways, so he's only gonna find out a few hours early."

"I wanted to tell him personally," I said dejectedly. "I didn't want him getting the news through Sarah's gossip chain."

I hung up and looked at the clock. In two hours, I would be home awaiting Johnny's arrival. I wondered if Sarah would be able to spread the gossip in so short a time.

I made several feeble attempts to accomplish my duties as work, but my mind was not on my job. I walked down to the cafeteria. When I returned to my desk, there was one message in my inbox:

James,

I will not be able to make it tonight.

I have just caught wind of some things that are disturbing to me. Almost my entire life I have had to limit my association with some of my blood relatives, which has made someone like yourself closer to me than my own family. I truly hope that what I hear is not as bad as it sounds, but only time will tell. I am going to hold off with doing your carpet for at least [a] few weeks.

You have more important things to deal with right now than flooring. Please talk to someone who is qualified to help you. I wish I was, but unfortunately I am not. You do have lots of family who can help you.

Sincerely,

Jonathan

I was stunned. Johnny's email was at once both a bullet between my eyes and a wrecking ball to my gut. My heart thrashed against my ribs, and all the blood left my face. Goosebumps covered me. My hands tingled and grew numb, and I held them up in front of me, astonished that they looked exactly as they did when I gave my first talk: an unearthly white. My lips parted, and my mouth dried up in the heat of the moment. It did not feel good to be alive. I staggered away from my computer, using my desk for support, and headed for the restroom.

I swung the door open with unnecessary force and ran into the stall. *How can he do this? How can he just write me off without even asking for my side of the story? Johnny! You fool! Let me explain, please! It's not my fault. . . . I want it to be true!*

I sat down on the toilet and rested my head in the palms of my hands. My hands were clammy. I rubbed my eyes until I saw spots and flashes of light. When I lifted my eyelids, I peered out at the tiled wall in front of me and I could *see.* "I understand," I whispered. I could see why so many who left the religion became angry—it was not because Satan had entered their heart, but because their family and friends treated them with such contemptuous hatred. I could see the frustration in being castigated by a friend who no longer wishes to be your friend and, further, does not want you to defend yourself.

I began to hate my life. I hated myself for dutifully obeying the elders' whims. I hated myself for not performing my sister's wedding ceremony. I hated myself for not taking Jennifer in my arms and making love to her when first I desired. I hated myself for being stupid, for being weak, for being a sheep.

In the midst of firing synapses, my mind reached back to childhood, when my sister and I had been invited to our neighbor's birthday party. I watched out the window as my father strode across the lawn, *Watchtower* in tow, and explained to our neighbor why birthdays were evil. I suddenly saw that moment, not as one of pride in which we defended Truth, but as one of shame, in which we gullibly followed the dictates of a book publishing company. This toppled each successive event in my life, which shifted in my brain, causing me to see each one in a new light. And it crushed my spirit. I squeezed my knees until my knuckles were white. I emptied myself of my breakfast, and my lunch, and my faith. And I flushed it all away. I hated the Watchtower Society. I hated the Bible. And I hated Jehovah.

Still queasy, I regained a semblance of composure. I returned to my desk and typed:

Johnny—

Wow, looks like you're throwing away a fifteen-year old friendship on the basis of second-hand gossip (oh—wait, it's not second-hand gossip. It must be fourth- or fifth-hand, right? I mean, you're just basing this on something you heard from your wife, who heard it from Sarah who heard it from Les who heard it from Jennifer, right?).

Nice job!

For weeks, Jennifer has been trying to convince me that our friends will shun us the moment they hear we are not Witnesses anymore & she's been trying to convince me the Witnesses are a cult. I didn't agree with her until now, thanks to you! I had entertained the idea of rejoining the religion, but your email helps me remember why I left in the first place. My blood is on your hands.

When your kids leave the religion, I hope you go a little easier on them.

I reached up to click "send," but then I froze. *If I send out an email like this, then I am no better than a stereotypical apostate. If I sound spiteful and hateful, I will feed right into Johnny's preconception of how I should act; I will give him the excuse he needs to shun me.* So I rewrote it.

Johnny—

That's fine, Friday evening is—as I said earlier this week—probably not the best time to trek up to Big Lake anyways.

Of course, I did want you to install the carpet, but mostly I wanted to talk to you about some things in person. I guess gossip travels too quickly these days, though.

Thanks for your advice. I appreciate it.

There, thought I. *He can't possibly find anything incriminating in this email.* In fact, just before sending it, I sanitized it even more; I deleted the word *gossip* and replaced it with *information*. Then I sent the email, shut off my computer, and drove home.

I came home to an empty house; Jennifer and Owen were spending the evening with her parents. The cool autumn air chilled me and I went into the bedroom to don a heavier shirt. I walked downstairs and peaked in on the half-finished office. I gave the bolt of carpet a firm kick.

When Jennifer pulled into the driveway, I ran out to meet her. Owen was sleeping in the back seat, and I lifted him and laid his head upon my shoulder. As Jennifer gathered up the diaper bag and her bottle of water, I said: "They are a cult."

"I told you so," she answered. "Sarah didn't waste any time in telling people, did she?"

"I guess not," I said dryly, "I bet Jordan and Raven know now, too. So we won't get a chance to tell them, either."

Jennifer sighed in agreement. She stayed up late and wrote to her sister, explaining how disappointed she was that Sarah ran ahead and told our very private matters to our friends.

Sarah responded, in part, by saying:

I had a responsibility to let them know the situation (Deut. 13:6–8) no matter how hard it was for me to do it. . . . I'm very sorry that this is the path that you guys have chosen and this has been very hard emotionally for me to come to terms with since you are my sister, and my family. If you are ever open to changing your recent views, please seek help from the elders and know that I care deeply about you and will always be here waiting if you ever change your mind about the truth. Until then, please do not discuss religion with or around me, or argue my position. I am very sad that this is the path you have chosen for yourself and Owen too.

Sarah's rampage did not abate with the informing of our friends. Over the next two months, she continued to visit our website, albeit secretly, and when Witnesses commented, she notified them that we no longer followed the Watchtower Society's rules, even if the commenters were people she'd never met. In time, Sarah wrote to say she would be ceasing all association with us, even to the point of declining to attend family gatherings where we would be present.

Jennifer quickly emailed Raven. This was not the way she wanted to deliver the news to her friend, but as she suspected Sarah had already told Raven, she felt it best to at least make an attempt to tell our side of the story. I held out hope that Raven would answer by admitting that she and Jordan did not believe in the religion, but the next day, Raven wrote:

Are you deciding to not be "active witnesses" (but still hold the beliefs), or are you deciding to not be witnesses anymore (meaning, you're going to hold different beliefs than the WT society)? If you are struggling or deciding to not go to meetings or be active because of some problems you're having (such as anxiety) then I am not one to judge anything, and *of course* it won't affect our friendship. . . .

An elder explained to me recently that it is okay to have doubts as long as I try to get them straightened out because the elders are constantly getting new information that we (the rest of the congregation) aren't even aware of regarding certain issues or apostate beliefs, or whatever. So I'm just wondering if you've asked any elders to help you with the doubts? . . .

I just want you to know that as long as you still believe that the WT society is the truth, I'm here to help and/or support you any way I can.

Jennifer answered Raven by explaining that we did go to the elders—even to the point of writing to the Watchtower's headquarters. We never heard from Raven again.

I then wrote to Jordan, and he replied, in part:

As thinking people I know you and I couldn't maintain a friendship without discussing the reasons why you and Jennifer no longer believe the truth, and I'm just not prepared to do that. Even if we didn't say anything, I can almost feel the uncomfortable silence that would be in the room. It would be like trying to ignore an elephant stampeding around the house, by which I mean impossible. I've just got too much to lose to let anything get in the way of making this work if I can. If our situations were different or if they change in the future I'd be all over this. I hope you understand.

I quickly responded, thoroughly empathizing. I emphatically told him he would always be welcome to contact me. I never heard from Jordan again.

Then I figured it was time to call my dad. There was no more postponing the matter. After talking about selling his motorcycle and giving a detailed breakdown of his newest job, I said, "I wanted to tell you . . . that Jennifer and I are having some problems with the Organization."

It was a clumsy sentence, and a terrible segue into such a meaty topic, but I was at a loss as to how to break my dad's heart gracefully.

There was a pause during which I looked at my phone to make sure he was still on the other line. Finally, he said: "Problems? Like what, buddy?"

Using his question as an opening, I divulged the whole story: my concerns and doubts over the years, Jennifer's depression and anxiety and the lack of answered prayers. My dad listened politely, throwing in an "uh-huh" every so often. When I was done with my speech, I heard him cover the phone and whisper to my stepmom. Prodded by his wife, he asked: "Do you still believe that the Society has the Truth?"

I hated this question, for I had already learned from Sarah and Raven that it was a pointed way to determine how all future contact would proceed. The two possible answers raced through my head: *Do I tell him no and risk never hearing from him again? Or do I lie to my father and hope he never notices?*

"I don't want to get into that," I said with a moan, "that's too complicated of a question, and I don't think it even matters right now." This was a lie. But at least it was a lie by omission instead of commission.

We talked for nearly an hour, my dad calmly offering up every stock Witness solution: *Have you prayed to Jehovah?* Yes, I prayed. *Why don't you talk to the elders?* I did talk to the elders. *But what about the love in the congregation?* What love? Did Uncle Pete love me all those times he furnished me with arbitrary rules? What about the elders in Wheelock? If that was love, I didn't want it. *But look at the growth of the Organization.* You mean the way it's grown to seven million members in a hundred years? The Mormons grew to fourteen million members during the same time; maybe they're God's chosen people.

My dad's final argument was: "Maybe Jehovah is testing you."

This lackluster argument was invoked far too often. Though the maxim never sat right with me, it was not until this moment that I could pinpoint why. I answered: "Dad, I'm so sick of hearing that. You could apply that to anything. If I get a cold, Jehovah's testing me. If I have no money, Jehovah's testing me. How about, for once, he rewards me for my effort? Isn't he supposed to be my best friend?[117] What kind of friend would I be to Jennifer, if I kept testing her? Should I make life difficult for her for years, telling her 'I'm just testing you to see if you love me?' Do you think Jennifer would be okay with that? Or do you think she'd leave me for being such a jerk? You don't test your friends, Dad. You trust them. You do nice things for them. You talk to them."

"I don't know what to say, buddy," my dad conceded. "Sounds like you have a lot to think about. I'm always here for you, and so are all the friends in the truth."

I told my dad that I appreciated his kindness, but that my friends were not there. "As soon as they found out we didn't believe absolutely everything the Society taught, they dropped us like a hot potato," I replied in somber tones.

With some discomfort, my dad explained this in a most novel fashion. He said that those who shun me are weak in the faith. "They want to stay Witnesses, but they're afraid that you'll pull them away from Jehovah."

"Shouldn't they be stronger in their beliefs than that?" I questioned.

"Sure," my dad agreed. "But not everyone is. I'm not worried, you see? That's why I don't mind being with your sister, or you. You guys are my kids and I love you. I know the Society has the Truth and nothing you or anybody says can change that."

"But it's not keeping in line with the official doctrine."[118]

He wouldn't address this directly; instead just assuring he would always be there for us—regardless of what we believed.

I hung up the phone, glad to know that one Witness friend was willing to remain in contact with me. Meanwhile, I returned to work to find a response from Johnny. In part, he wrote:

> You said that information travels too quickly, so I can consider myself informed. You say you want to discuss some things in person. Why in person? I'm not interested in discussing any man's viewpoint on the scriptures.

As before, I had an immediate longing to pick apart Johnny's words. I wanted to tell him that I had only selected *information* because I thought *gossip* sounded too judgmental. I wanted to tell him that *information* isn't necessarily *correct information* and that he was mistaken to assume otherwise. I wanted to ask if he noticed the hypocrisy in knocking on people's doors telling them about his religion while simultaneously squelching any dissenting viewpoints of the Bible. Was he lying to householders all those years when he told them he was stopping by to discuss the Bible? I wanted to ask if his faith was so shaky that he couldn't even have a discussion with someone unless that someone was in total agreement with him. I wanted to ask him how he was able to come to his current beliefs about God and the Bible if he had never been interested in discussing the subject. I nixed this impulse in favor of not giving Johnny any further reason to erase me from his life. If he did not want a discussion, I would not give him one. I merely answered his lone question:

> Johnny—
>
> Why in person?
>> Because it's nice. I think it's kinder, and more personal, to talk about some things in person.
>> Because it's clear. In person, intentions are more clear. Body language, inflection, tone are all lost in email communications.

He replied:

> I do not think that discussing your "intentions" with me is a good idea. Unfortunately I think you are going to try to justify your intentions by having me understand them. Who am I anyways to discuss a situation like this? Have you spoke with your dad or one of your grandpas? Picture you trying to explain your intentions to them. I am not qualified to help you like they are, but my response to the matter is the same as theirs will be. I'm not interested in your intentions. I'm sorry to tell you that. You were probably my best friend, short of Tonya, so I do not mean to sound cold. This is hard for me to have to tell you, but I am not going to discuss your "intentions" with you. I have always had fun debating certain trivial matters, but the subject of the existence of Jehovah and the authenticity of his word is utterly and completely not debatable.

"Does he realize what a lousy Witness he sounds like?" Jennifer exclaimed. "God and the Bible are completely not debatable? What's with that? That's a terrible thing for a Witness to say."

"You're preaching to the choir," I said, laughing at the irony. "How does he plan on *Reasoning from the Scriptures* if he refuses to debate things?"[119] I threw my hands in the air with an air of resignation. "I don't even know how to respond to him. I'm not cut out for this kind of confrontation."

Jennifer wrote a reply for me:

Johnny,

I wanted to talk to you in person so that I could inform you of recent events, not so that I could debate things with you. Spirituality is a private matter, and I am uneasy spreading my personal beliefs to others. I have changed some things in my life, and I am trying to make some hard decisions. It is unfortunate that we all can't just live and let live and be friends even if we have differing views on certain matters. Whether or not I have spoken to my dad, grandfathers, or anyone else about my life is also a private matter (and I have, by the way). Nevertheless, my wife and I are capable of making decisions on our own as two fully informed adults. We of course seek guidance from time to time from others, but I was not seeking you out to provide me with spiritual guidance, therefore there was never any question as to whether you were "qualified" or not. I was simply going to inform you of stuff going on in my life, man to man and friend to friend—things you do "qualify" as. I realize that certain subjects may be too personal to want to debate with others, and this is why through the years Jennifer and I haven't debated them with you or our other friends. Some things are a matter of personal discovery, and choice, and we are fine with whatever others believe, and whatever information others choose to take in, and we respect those choices.

I never heard from Johnny again.

It saddened me to observe my friends acting so delusional. It was clear they couldn't fathom the idea that the Watchtower Society was incorrect, even if only to try to see our point of view. They were intelligent people, yet were unknowingly afflicted with a neurosis. With my newfound freedom of thought, I wrote to the Society yet again regarding Noah's Flood. I collected all of my findings from their last letter and asked why they had taken quotes out of context. I concluded the letter by asking them to answer five questions about Noah's Flood. I wanted, it seemed, just that much more evidence that the Watchtower Society operated under falsehoods.

As the reality of Johnny's loss set it, I grew morose and despondent. Jennifer commiserated with me, suggesting one evening that they were not true friends if they deleted us from their lives so easily. I slumped down onto a dining room chair. "It still depresses me," I said. "We have no friends!"

But we *did* have friends . . . we had just misplaced them.

THE NEW WORLD

It had been years since Diane and I had spoken on matters of belief. I was afraid to speak with her on the subject, having long believed our relationship maintained its amicability by avoiding the topic. When I called, she was on her long daily commute home from her job. She told me a funny story about one of her co-workers. I listened courteously, though my attention was elsewhere. I kept trying to summon the nerve to tell her I no longer believed the Watchtower Society. When at last she asked: "So what's up?" I loquaciously answered: "Um, what . . . what do you mean?"

She laughed. "I mean, what did you call for?"

"Soooo," I started, drawing out the word to stall, "What do you think of the Witnesses?"

There was quiet. Then she said: "Do you mean do I believe it, or do you mean how do I feel about the people, or do I wanna do it—?"

I cut her off. "Yeah," I said, "All that stuff."

"They're good people. Why do you ask?"

"Here's the deal. You're right; most of them are good people. But I don't believe it anymore and neither does Jennifer." I stopped trying to find a reaction in her quietness. "What do you think of that?" I asked.

"It's not surprising," she said casually.

This time I laughed. "Why do you say that?"

"Oh, you know, all those times I used to call and ask what you guys were doing, and you'd say you had a meeting, but then you'd say, 'Why? What are you offering?'"

I laughed again. "I did do that, didn't I?"

I went on to give her an abbreviated history of the past ten years. Diane listened, interjecting words of agreement.

"It's such a relief," she said breathily. "I knew you didn't believe it. I thought you were gonna tell me I needed to get back to the meetings or you wouldn't hang out with me and Mike anymore."

289

Taken aback, I asked, "Why would you think that?"

"The last time I saw our mom, she told me you said you were mad at me for not going to the meetings anymore."

"She said that?" I asked incredulously. "I never would've said something like that! You're living your own life, and that's great."

I confessed to Diane how envious I was: I was jealous that she had been able to fade out of the organization with no trouble from the elders and without having to ever explain herself to our relatives.

She suggested that it was, perhaps, easier for her, because when she had first stopped being an active Witness, it was not due to disbelief; it was because she had been depressed and discouraged. "It was only after I had stopped going to the meetings for a long time that I started making worldly friends and seeing that they weren't any better or worse than the Witnesses," she said, adding, "I haven't thought it was true for years now, but I've never done the homework. So whenever Dad or Nana asks me about it, I just brush it aside. I don't believe in Adam and Eve and all that crap, but I don't know how to prove to them why it's wrong, so I don't bring it up."

In a moment of uncharacteristic confidence, I declared: "If they ever come after you, you refer them to me." Coming back to reality, I confessed how nervous I was about how our family might react. Diane suggested I try to avoid the topic, but I told her it wouldn't be that easy for me.

"Here's a little advice for you," she said frankly, "and don't take this the wrong way—"

"Okay."

"You need to grow a pair." She laughed at herself. "I mean honestly. If Nana or someone asks about the religion, tell them it's none of their business."

Diane was expecting company and couldn't stay on the phone any longer. She promised to get together with us soon, and told me not to worry about the carpeting in the office: "Mike will install it for you guys."

"See?" Jennifer said supportively, "we'll still have some people to hang out with."

"That's good."

But Jennifer wasn't done pointing the way back to forgotten friends.

"I'm going to email Ryan," she announced confidently one evening on our walk to the park.

Stroller in hand, I stopped. The cool breeze sent a chill down my spine. "Ryan *Sutter*?" I asked.

"Yes, Ryan *Sutter*. What other Ryan would I be talking about?"

"I didn't think we were his friends anymore."

"Ugh!" she roared in extreme exasperation. "We weren't his friends because we were stupid Witnesses, and we thought he was evil. Now that we're not Witnesses anymore—"

"I thought we were just gonna fade. If we contact Ryan . . . everyone will know we're not Witnesses anymore."

"Everyone that matters already knows," she yelled. "Despite what you've been deluding yourself to believe, none of them had the decency to stay our friend. Besides, we *are* fading. We haven't done anything that Witnesses would consider bad, and we're not going around looking for trouble. I already told you I intend to get on with my life, and part of that means getting in touch with my old friends. If you don't wanna see Ryan again, that's your own stupid business. But I'm emailing him tomorrow."

Jennifer wrote to Ryan, detailing the long tale of doubts, depression, and deconversion. She apologized for having shunned him and said we would like to get together, no matter where he might be living. While awaiting a response, she forwarded me the link to his website, and I nixed my duties at work in favor of catching up on my old friend by reading two years' worth of blogs. After the initial shock of noticing he now sported a beard, I was enraptured by the story of his life.

Hours later, I arrived home to an empty house. Without bothering to remove my shoes, I ran into the living room to find Jennifer's laptop. Normally, I never touched Jennifer's computer, but my curiosity was overwhelming. I called up her email account: Ryan had answered. In her initial email, Jennifer had asked Ryan if he was surprised to hear from her, and he answered: "Surprised? No. Ecstatic? Yes!"

He said that finding out we wanted to be his friends again was the best news he'd received in a long, long time. He wanted to see us soon, and told us that he would bring his new wife Esther with him. Esther had also been raised in a strict religious household, but was now, like Ryan, atheist. He told Jennifer to not worry about me: "James just sounds like he's nervous right now. I understand; I was nervous, too, when I first left."

Two weeks later, Ryan and his bride came to our home. I was edgy with anticipation as I watched them pull into the driveway, scanning the street to ensure no Witnesses were around to see an outspoken apostate on my property.

I swung the front door wide open. "Hey, James!" Ryan called out in his hopelessly optimistic tone.

"Hey guys," I said quietly.

Ryan walked up the stairs and through the threshold. We embraced. "I missed you, man," he said, and I replied in kind, hoping it would begin to atone for two years of inexcusable behavior.

Esther, a short woman with dark hair and an incessant, impish smile, had brought a dessert, and Jennifer helped her situate it into the refrigerator. Ryan held out a gift. "It's for Owen's birth," he said, admitting it was a tad late.

"Don't worry," I laughed, "It's not your fault."

We gave them a tour of our house, then sat in the living room to reignite our friendship. I told Ryan how I had wished to confide in him at Rhett's funeral but quickly retracted my thought as it was not the right time.

"You were really thinking that at that time?" Ryan asked, bemused.

"I thought it would make you feel better if you knew not all of your old friends wanted to shun you."

"Oh man, I wish you would have said something!"

"I couldn't," I said. "I wasn't ready." I admitted that another thing that stopped me from saying anything was that I knew he considered himself an atheist. "How can you call yourself an atheist, Ryan?" I asked, choking on the word, "Isn't that just as dogmatic as a Witness, except the reverse?"

"Not at all," Ryan answered, setting down his mug of tea. "I'm not *anti-theist*—against god—I'm *a-theist*. 'A-' meaning 'without.'"

As he had done so many times in my past, Ryan's simple, profound words caused my mind to reel. It made sense. I had to know more. "What's the difference between an atheist and an agnostic?"

Ryan shrugged. "In one way, there isn't any. But an agnostic is someone who hasn't looked into the matter, or doesn't think it's possible—"

"How can you look into the matter?" I interjected. "If God is who Witnesses claim he is, then he's outside the realm of space and time. We cannot, by definition, subject him to experiment."

"True," Ryan conceded, "but people make claims about God. People say he answers their prayers, or he healed their sicknesses or helped them win a football game. Those are things that can be tested. It's not like it's a fifty-fifty proposition." He continued, "That's what people think when they hear the term *agnostic*. Do I think there's a possibility of there being a God? Absolutely! But I'm not split fifty-fifty. It's more like one to ninety-nine."

"Good Lord!" I said, purposely creating a pun. "I never thought of it that way." Sitting there with my new old friend, I realized that I had been, not an agnostic, but an atheist for longer than even he had been. All during my youth, I had proposed the hypothesis of God and, in the end, found it failed verification.

Over dinner, Ryan told us his experience when Rhett passed away. As I already knew, he had gone to his father's house for solace the day he learned the news, only to be met at the door by his stepmom, a regular pioneer, who took him into the back yard and austerely told him his presence made everyone uncomfortable. She said she didn't want him preaching his views in front of all the good Witnesses. Ryan, stunned from her harshness, implored her that he had no intention to do such a thing. She answered: "Scientists have discovered that evolution is wrong." Baffled by her non sequitur, Ryan begged to enter her house, but she would not be dissuaded. He stood in the driveway for the next six hours. Then, at the funeral, nearly everyone treated him as if he was invisible. He had prepared a video of Rhett, using Rhett's music as the soundtrack, but when he gave the disk to the Witness manning the projector, he was summarily ignored. When he approached the buffet table, he saw Mary Pallas, Scott's mother, tending to the comestibles. But Mary refused to speak to him, instead asking Esther: "Do you think Ryan would like some salad?" as if Esther were an interpreter for Witness zombies. Ryan admitted that, to this day, his emotions varied from suicidal, blissful, numb, to violent, sometimes even before getting out of bed.

Late that night, long after Owen had fallen asleep in Jennifer's arms, they parted company from us. We hugged again, with a promise that we would stay in touch.

I felt revitalized. It took Jennifer to show me that it was okay to contact people we had been shunning, but once she did so, I ached to heal an even older rift.

Finding Ryan was easy: Jennifer had typed his name in a search engine. This time, I had no such luck. For two days, I wondered how it would be possible—*if* it would be possible—to find the other friend I had shunned. Then, while driving home from work one evening, a long cast-aside memory fortuitously returned.

Several years earlier, Jennifer and I had visited a mall on the other side of town. We rarely patronized the place, but a new computer store was opening, and we wanted to check it out. As we walked through the mall, I turned and looked at an optical shop on the far end of the hall—a habit I had developed from my days in the eyeglass industry. Then I saw *him*. He was older. He looked tired, and he sported a tightly cropped beard. But it was unmistakably Jeremy.

Though I had not noticed the name of the store, the intervening years had not diminished my memory of the store's exact location. I looked it up online and called the next morning, wherein I was promptly told Jeremy now worked for Eyedeals. I telephoned that store. The phone rang once. Twice. In between rings, I heard my breath against the phone, anticipating what might or might not ensue. It rang again.

"Eyedeals. This is Jeremy. How may I be of assistance to you?"

I couldn't believe my ears. After years of shunning, there was nothing between us now but two telephones. I paused, allowing his innocuous greeting to sink in. The voice was unmistakable, even after years of not hearing it.

"Hi," I said, fumbling for words. "Um . . . how are you?"

Jeremy paused, then replied in a voice filled with suspicion: "I'm fine. . . . How are you?"

"Oh, I'm good," I couldn't think of how to introduce myself. Or, rather, how to *re*introduce myself. I feared that I would tell him who I was, and then he would bellow in anger, indicting me as the good-for-nothing friend I had been, dumping him when he most needed support. But then I thought, maybe he already knows who I am. *I recognized his voice; perhaps he recognizes mine.* "Do you know who this is?"

"No," he said coolly, clearly tiring of the game.

"You spent your eighteenth birthday at my graduation party."

There was silence—a ponderous silence, as if I could hear Jeremy thinking. "James Zimmerman?" he asked brightly. "How the hell are you?" He added: "It's great to hear your voice."

"It's good to hear your voice, too."

"What brings this on—why are you calling?"

"Jennifer and I aren't Witnesses anymore," I started, "and so, we thought, why not get in touch with our old friends again?"

Jeremy sounded stunned. "James Zimmerman—Assembly Boy—not a Witness anymore," he said, as if he couldn't believe his words. "How did that happen?"

I hurriedly explained as much as I could, cognizant of the fact that Jeremy had customers waiting.

"Wow," he said, even more stunned than the last time. "You'll have to tell Jennifer I totally understand that whole anxiety thing. I could hardly live with myself for a while there right before I left."

Jeremy told me of his trauma during leaving. He had not seen or talked to either of his parents for a long time. He had no contact with any of his Witness friends. On the brighter side, he was happy and healthy in his current life. And far from being a confirmed bachelor, he was married: "Or, at least as married as this government will allow us to be," he said, with disdain towards the same-sex marriage ban. His contentment reverberated through the phone as he spoke of Charlie, "a wonderful man—very supportive and understanding of what I've been through."

Jeremy took down my phone number and promised to call again that night. He did, and we talked again for over an hour. I was astonished at how willing Jeremy was to let me back in his life. Without asking for forgiveness or even an explanation, he simply picked where we had left off so long before.

Jennifer and I arrived at the restaurant first. We sat on a bench in the entryway and declined the hostess' offer to take us to a table. Each time a car pulled up, I craned my neck to look out the window. *Would I still recognize him? What would he be wearing? What blasphemous facial hair would he be growing?* I had no clue.

"Maybe they're not coming," I said to my wife.

"Chill out. Everyone's not as obsessively punctual as we are."

Looking out into the cool night air, I recognized Jeremy at once; apart from a thin beard, and one or two more pounds, he had not changed: he was decked in cowboy boots and a leather jacket, which, I'd swear, was what he was wearing the last time we'd been in each other's presence. He was still the best-dressed friend I'd ever had.

He held the door open for his husband, and the two of them walked in, bringing a draft of night air with them. Jeremy was smiling, and he approached us swiftly.

"Hello, Zimmermans," he said, laughing.

He hugged Jennifer, telling her it's so good to see her again. And we embraced, and in the space of five seconds, nine years of forced shunning melted away.

"This is Charlie," he said proudly, placing his hand on his companion's back.

"Hi Charlie," Jennifer and I said in unison, and we shook hands. He said he was excited to meet people from Jeremy's past, as he knew of no one else: "Jer's past is such a mystery," he explained. "I want to get all the juicy details."

We were escorted to a table and given menus. As we shifted around to remove our coats and place them on the chairs, Jeremy asked: "So how've you guys been?" he laughed at his own simple question, and we laughed in reply. We told them the tale of the last several years, especially the most recent few months. Jeremy nodded in understanding, and interjected bits of his own experience to compare with ours. Charlie, meanwhile, politely listened and supplemented Jeremy's story with his own viewpoint on the matter. "I just can't believe people can claim to follow God and be so unloving," he said, waving his hand in the air.

Jeremy concurred, and recounted the swift loss of friends and family. "Gabriel was my best friend, and now I haven't seen him in nine years." He asked if I knew how his erstwhile friend was doing. "Fine," I answered, "I mean, he's not as cool as he used to be, and we've drifted apart."

"Is he still shooting to be a rising star in the religion?"

"Oh," I recalled the last time I had seen Gabe. "I would say he's risen."

"Gabe was a good guy," Jeremy said nostalgically, "I miss him sometimes."

He detailed his experience leaving the religion. His friend Wren invited him to lunch shortly after he disassociated himself, and Jeremy accepted, thinking this was out of kindness on her part. But soon after they sat down to eat, he found that she had only rendezvoused with him in an attempt to cure his gayness.

"How did she plan on doing that?" I asked, "Did she flash you her boobs?"

Jeremy laughed, then glowered at me over the top of his pricey eyeglasses. "You remember Wren, right James?"

"Yeah."

"Then you know her boobs would not have sufficed."

Throughout his conversation, I learned that Jeremy, like Ryan, had been treated rougher and crueler than I had imagined. Revealing his sexual orientation in tandem with leaving the religion only compounded the harsh treatment meted out by his friends and family. And yet, he was not bitter. In the aftermath, he had built a new life. "I've never lost my spirituality," he said, "I still consider myself a spiritual person."

The conversation drifted to secular matters. While Jennifer talked to Jeremy about her family, I chatted with Charlie. We had much in common. Charlie also enjoyed making short films; his humor was witty. He was attentive and kind to Jeremy, and he was delighted to laugh with Owen.

As we left the restaurant, Jeremy hugged us again, and said: "We'll have to keep in touch."

And we did.

Learning Ryan's and Jeremy's tales of exiting the Watchtower did not give me faith that Jennifer and I would be able to leave gracefully. Throughout the fall and winter, I maintained an informal vigil at the living room window: keeping a lookout for the approach of Witnesses. They would come. I knew it.

The first visits were innocuous, even pleasant. Two women from our ex-congregation arrived one evening "just checking up." Ten days later, Candy stopped by, inquired as to our overall health, and asked if Owen was talking yet. Then another sister showed up with her teenage son, asking if anyone in the congregation had offended us. I said no, and she pleaded, even to the point of stomping her foot: "What's the problem, then? Why won't you come to the Kingdom Hall?" I wanted to tell her, to reach out and open her mind, but I was afraid any dissent I expressed would be reported to the elders.

Several months after our last meeting, an elder arrived at our door. Jennifer let him in, and I came around the corner a moment later to find Jennifer and Ethan standing around the table. Ethan was a relaxed, amicable man with a round face and thin, yellow hair. Despite being physically imposing (he towered at least eight inches above me and weighed twice as much), he did not intimidate. His mouth hung agape; he'd smack and lick his lips in a frequent attempt to find the right word.

During the past months, Jennifer had tried discussing with me how we would handle a situation like this. "Why don't we just say we're depressed and discouraged?" she'd ask. But I didn't like talking about it, so I never gave her any feedback. Now, however, I had to come up with a plan. And that plan was: stonewall him.

"Hi Ethan," I said, taking slow breaths, trying to masquerade as calm. "How are you doing?"

"Oh," he said, pushing up his glasses with his thick fingers, "I'm doing fine. I came t'see how *you* were doing."

I looked at Jennifer and nodded. "We're fine."

"Is that so?"

"Yeah," I answered confidently.

"Well, then, what's wrong?" he said, allowing a hint of harsh insistence to his voice.

I pretended to think deeply. "Nothing."

Ethan stared, unconvinced. Jennifer, sounding flustered, interjected: "We're just discouraged right now. We don't want to go to the meetings for the time being."

"I mainly wanted to stop by to tell you we haven't seen you at the meetings lately," he said, licking his lips. "We miss y'guys."

Jennifer, trying to be sincere, said, "We miss *you* guys."

Ignoring her, he continued, "We wouldn't want to stay away from the meetings, um, too long, as this system is . . ." He looked at the ceiling, searching for the rest of his sentence.

"Winding down?" I offered helpfully.

"Yes, winding down, exactly," he gestured in my direction. "So see, since you know that, what in particular's been botherin' you guys?"

I tilted my head thoughtfully. "I don't feel like I want to discuss it."

He stared at me, his jaw slack. Rallying, he asked: "Have you guys gotten a hold of some information?"

"I guess I'd rather not discuss it."

The room was silent; filled with tension. Jennifer, who was holding Owen, put his hand up to her mouth as if she was kissing it. She was trying to hide a smirk.

Ethan's eyes darted as he looked for a response. Shepherds are not used to being stonewalled by sheep. "We were hopin' to set up a meeting between you guys and a couple-a elders."

"What would be the purpose of that?" I inquired.

He clasped his hands. "Whenever anyone's been away as long as you guys have, it's standard practice t'begin studying with that person again."

The answer was already on my tongue, but I paused to give the impression I was mulling over his proposition. "I guess I don't see the benefit in that."

Ethan stared at me, stupefied. He tried a different angle: "Are you sure there's nothin' that any of the friends did to upset you?"

"No."

Jennifer lurched forward at my cold reply. She amended, "We like everyone in the congregation; none of them have done anything to offend us."

Ethan turned to look at Jennifer, and then looked out across the room. "So what's goin' on with you guys?" he asked, with a trace of exasperation.

Jennifer explained she had post-traumatic stress disorder, and Ethan nodded. "With kids, I tell you, the meetings can be a real drain. Sometimes it'd be easier to stay home." I folded my arms and nodded, but said nothing. We stared at each other without speaking for many seconds. Ethan broke the silence: "Well, like I said, my main purpose in comin' over was to set up a time when some elders could meet with you guys and maybe help you through some problems. So when would be a good time to do that, James?"

I sucked in air and scratched my forehead. "Like I said, it's something we'd rather not do at this time. Thank you for offering—that's very nice of you—but I don't see what purpose it would serve."

Ethan turned to leave. "I hope you don't mind my trying back in a little while to see if you've changed yer mind."

"I'll let you know if we want to talk with the elders," I said, trying my best to be courteous.

"Okay, James," he said, reaching for the door, "I'll be seein' you guys around."

After he left, I turned to face Jennifer, then reached out for the wall. The wind had been knocked out of me, and I doubled over to regain my composure. When I looked up, I could see Jennifer getting ready to speak, but I held up my hand.

I ran downstairs and grabbed a pen and a notebook and frantically documented the conversation, recruiting Jennifer to ensure I did not forget anything. Then I ran back downstairs to find the video camera and brought it into the front entryway. I set it on a table near the door. Looking at Jennifer, I said: "If any Witness comes to this door again, we are recording the conversation."

"I don't think they would like that."

"Tough. That's not their choice. If they knock on my door or call me on my phone, I'm recording the conversation. If they don't like it, they can stop talking to me."

"I don't see the point of that . . . ?" she said, phrasing it like a question.

"The point? Are you kidding me Jennifer? The point is this: when Johnny told me about how he met with the elders and how they were rude to him, what did we say? Didn't we leave Johnny's house that night saying, 'Well, we don't know what really happened there?' And when my cousin Brandi got disfellowshipped, and I said I disagreed, didn't my dad tell me that I shouldn't think badly about it because I wasn't there? And when the elders told some of the brothers and sisters not to go to Kyle's wedding, what did my grandpa say? Didn't he say that we don't know for sure what that elder said?"

"Yeah."

"I'm gonna make sure people *do* know for sure," I said, waving the pen across the room like a conductor's wand. "If I tell someone—anyone—that an elder said this or that, and they pull that crap saying, 'I wasn't there,' I'll say: 'That's true, but here's a recording. Listen to it and then tell me if I'm lying.'"

The days grew long. While Jennifer sat at her computer, I stared out the window and listened to the sound of water trickling down the gutters. The water streamed down our driveway and pooled in the street, where it eddied into the gutter. The liquid, escaping its frozen prison and running away from the house, made me forlorn about our lost friends, who were noticeable only for the vacancies they left. I sat on the futon next to Jennifer and said: "It's just so frustrating, you know? You can't say anything to them."

She closed her laptop and turning towards me.

"If you send Sarah an email and all it says is 'Hi'," I said, "Sarah will jump on that and say 'Look! She's trying to lure me into her web!' If you try to defend or explain yourself, they say you're trying to destroy their faith. If you say nothing, they say, 'See, she doesn't have anything to say.'"

Jennifer agreed. She mentioned how misguided they were and said we should at least be happy to have freedom of thought now.

"They get it all backwards, don't you think?" I added: "They're their own worst enemy. When they talk about what they do in the congregation, it doesn't make me miss it, it makes me think they're wasting their lives. When they parrot Watchtower answers to us, I don't think 'What good Jehovah's Witnesses they are!' I think, 'Can't they speak for themselves?' And when they shun me, it doesn't shame me, it emboldens me."

"The Society has orchestrated this perfect wall between their members and their ex-members," she said thoughtfully. "Maybe you should talk to a therapist, if you're that frustrated and depressed about it."

I stood up and strode over to the window. I looked out at the dark spring night. "I don't know what I'd say to a therapist."

On Owen's second birthday, we decorated the house with crepe paper and balloons. Jennifer ordered a cake with Curious George decorations. We invited our family: Jennifer's grandma and parents came, as did her sister Roberta and Roberta's daughter. Diane and her husband also came. Everyone brought gifts. Owen was delighted with the event, intently examining his favorite gifts and gesturing for more food. I took the camera from its home near the front door and recorded the event. Jennifer snapped copious pictures. The scent of lilacs wafted in through the kitchen windows. It was the first time a birthday party had been held under my roof. As Owen unwrapped his gifts, Jennifer and I tried to unwrap the practice of this ubiquitous tradition that had, until this moment, eluded our lives.

The experience of celebrating my son's life brought me contentment that lasted days. I deeply and unexpectedly cherished the freedom to rejoice and commemorate the events and the people that had brought Owen to this moment. But this serenity was snatched away by reminders that I was not, after all, free of the past just yet.

The Watchtower Society answered my letter. Or, more precisely, they *recognized* my letter. Of the five questions I asked, only one received any response. The bulk of the letter was devoted to arguing that all humans descended from Noah. This was odd, as I did not take issue with this teaching in my letter, and I was confused as to why they felt the need to defend an issue I never questioned. They concluded by stating:

> It is good to want to be as accurate and precise as we can in such matters, yet we do not want to allow them to become a focal point in our lives. We can be confident that Jehovah's spirit will see to it that any necessary adjustments in understand are made. In the meantime, we suggest that you let the matter rest, and perhaps in time something more will be published to clarify matters.

"What kind of delusions are they operating under?" I asked Jennifer as we read the letter.

"You know the answer to that," she said, with a forced laugh.

I received another letter the very next day. Before even opening it, I knew what was inside. The envelope was not shaped like a greeting card, the kind Nana had so often sent just to say she was thinking about me. It was a business-sized envelope, containing at least three pages, judging from its thickness.

I slid my pocketknife along the envelope's top and began reading the letter right there on the side of the road next to the mailbox.

Nana's six-page letter ran the gauntlet of emotional pleadings urging me to rejoin the Witnesses. After expressing her hurt and disappointment, she provided a litany of assumptions as to why I had left the religion; including feeling the religion was too restrictive, and leaving what is right in an effort to please others. "They want you to join them in their rebellion to make their conscience feel better," she noted.

Nana begged me to think of Owen and how wrong it would be to "rob" him of the chance to know Jehovah. She said I was on "the enemy's side." "Let me tell you," she wrote, "you can stick your head in the sand and make believe that the end of the world isn't going to happen, but *everything* points to this world passing away, and we want it to go." She reminded me, with her characteristic flourish of underlining, that "the Bible has <u>never</u> been wrong, you can depend on it 100 percent. It's the only <u>real</u> truth," and twice pointed out that she *knows* she has the truth. She insisted, three times, that I pray, getting down on my knees to ask Jehovah to clear up my "issues."

I trembled as I read the letter, to the point that I had to lay it on the grass so that it remained still. I was saddened by her words, not because of remorse or guilt, but because I feared I would never speak to her again. She was a caring, loving woman, and to see her condemn her own grandson only served to bolster my conviction that she, like so many others I loved, had been duped by a cult.

In an eight-page response, I made sure, as kindly as possible, that Nana knew I had prayed, thousands of times. I laid out a brief history of the research I had done, providing documented evidence of the Society's misquotes. I assured her that while I envied her conviction, it was one thing to claim she *knows* she has the truth, quite another for her to *prove* it.

I never heard from Nana again.

Throughout June and July, my phone rang with unrecognizable numbers a handful of times. Whether or not these were attempts by the elders to contact me, I will never know; none of the callers ever left a message.

Shortly after she attended the District Convention, my mom called. She said she had heard gossip about me while there. My mom already knew some things about my apostasy; I had even declined to pray over a dinner at her house months earlier.

I asked her who had gossiped about me, and when she hesitated, I stonewalled the conversation until she divulged names. None of the people she mentioned were close friends, so I knew news of my life had spread.

My mom said that finding out we were no longer Witnesses made her very upset, and compared it to finding out her mother had cancer. We spoke on the phone for three hours, my mom discursively bringing up the customary defenses for her faith while I knocked them down, citing references to back up my claims. Each topic we discussed concluded with my mom saying, "I don't know what to say." When I asked her if she had done the research to prove—genuinely prove—the religion to herself, she said, "That's what I took from you—I knew you had done the research, and I trusted that you had proved it to yourself, and that was good enough for people like me who are too dumb to know how to do the research."

"Well, Mom," I said, with a weight to my words, "I did do the research. And I have reached a conclusion about the religion. Are you going to trust that I came to the right conclusion?"

She didn't know what to say.

Near the end of our long talk, she listed off all the things she had endured in the religion over the last half-century, hoping this would ignite within me a desire to return to the religion. But I asked, "Mom, what would you say if someone said all that stuff to you at a door?"

"I don't know what you mean . . . ?" she said, confused.

"I mean this, let's say you're out in service, and you knock on someone's door. The householder says 'I'm a Lutheran,' and then you tell them they should take your magazines and come to the Kingdom Hall. Then they say, 'No way. When I was a kid, my father beat me for the slightest provocation, and even made me wait in the car for hours while he took care of religious duties, and, when I grew up, I forced myself to stay in a loveless marriage because I didn't want to get in trouble by the religion. The elders at my church mistreated my daughter, and my sister, and my niece. Oh, and by the way, children in my congregation were molested by one of the ministers.' What would you say to that, Mom? Would you be impressed with that person's faith? Would you say, 'Oh, you must have the true religion—I want to join that'?"

"No, I guess I wouldn't," she said sheepishly. She was, as I had been, a fideist. Perhaps it was genetic; perhaps religion was in our hemoglobin.

Despite my strong indictment against the religion, or maybe because of it, my mom did not cut off contact with Jennifer and me. When she later came to our house with a gift for Owen and avoided any mention of the Witnesses, we had an enjoyable evening. Her decision to remain on speaking terms, coupled with my dad's similar resolution, caused me even more determinedly to struggle not to get disfellowshipped.

In late July, my dad and stepmom flew to Minnesota for a visit. We spent a day together in which I treated them to a history museum. They were cordial and pleasant, and I observed my dad putting forth an effort to bond with Owen. The topic of religion never arose, though I continually wondered what admonitions my relatives had given to my dad about me. *Did Nana warn him against spending too much time in my presence? Did Papa advise him against entering my home? Did Uncle Pete caution him to not even speak with me?* I did not know. I wanted to know, but I could not ask.

After they departed that evening, Jennifer went out in the front yard to rake leaves. I took Owen in the backyard, and he played in his sandbox, one of his gifts from his birthday party. I stayed nearby in the garden, pulling weeds and watering the tomatoes.

My phone rang, and I pulled it out of my pocket. I did not recognize the number, but it looked vaguely familiar; I assumed it was my co-worker with whom I carpooled to work.

"James, this is Ethan Siskin, from the Kingdom Hall."

My eyes bulged, and my face turned white. I spun in place to face my house. If I was going to talk with an elder, I desperately wanted to record the conversation. But the camera was in the house. "Hey Ethan," I said, staying as calm as possible, "Hold on a second."

I bolted across the yard and vaulted up the steps of the deck. But the backdoor was locked, and I couldn't run around to the front door and leave Owen by himself. Crestfallen that it would not be recorded, I resumed the conversation. "What can I do for you?" I asked, my voice tinged with dejection as I plodded back down the deck.

"James, we need to set up a time to meet with ya," he said, instantly getting to the crux of the matter. "What time works good for you guys?"

I cleared my throat. "I'll have to talk with Jennifer about that first, I hope you understand. She's not here right now." I pointed to the spot directly in front of me. "But I'll tell you what, why don't I talk to her about it and if we'd like you guys to stop by, I'll call you back, okay?"

"That sounds fine, James," he said, adding, "'Cause, y'know, we haven't seen you guys in a long time now."

"I know," I interrupted. "Like I said, we'll call if we would like a visit."

We said good-bye. I pulled Owen to his feet and, brushing the sand off his shorts, ran to the front yard and repeated the conversation to Jennifer.

Having recently changed our phone company, we couldn't figure out how he knew our number. We considered each of our friends in turn, and wondered who was the informant.

Jennifer bit her lip, deep in concentration. There was no strong reason for suspecting one of these people over any other. "Anyway," she said, "It's only a matter of time now. He's gonna call you again, soon."

Thirteen days passed. It was a sweltering summer evening, and the sun was resisting the dusk. Jennifer, Owen, and I were playing in the living room. The phone rattled on the dining room table. Still laughing at Owen's antics, my face lost all expression as I came into the dining room and looked down at the phone.

"Aren't you gonna answer it?" Jennifer shouted from the other room.

"It's him," I said gravely, knowing no further explanation was required.

"Well, then, you better answer."

I carried the phone back to her. "If he doesn't leave a message, then we can just do nothing until he calls again."

"What if he does?"

"Then I'll be able to find out exactly what he wants before I have to call him back."

This is what he wanted:

> This is Ethan Siskin again. I'm just needin' to get in contact with you guys as soon as possible. We got some concerns we need to talk about with you and Jennifer as soon as possible. If you could get back to me soon I'd appreciate it.

"He's fond of the word 'soon'," I said, trying to lighten the mood.

"Call him now," Jennifer urged, "Remember, if he tries to set up a time for a committee meeting, make sure you tell him you have to talk with me about it first and that you *will* get back to him."

My hands were already quavering with nerves. "I need to go somewhere quiet—away from Owen."

I grabbed the handrail and marched downstairs. "And don't confess to anything!" Jennifer said, closing the door behind me.

I entered the library and stood on the carpet Johnny had refused to install. The room was moist from the late summer air. I strode to the window. A feeble breeze entered, refreshing on my hot skin. But I had to close it, for besides a breeze, a window left ajar also let in the noise of crickets and neighbors and rustling leaves. I needed the room to be as quiet as possible.

I sat at my desk and massaged my clammy fingers. I surveyed the landscape: a lifetime of books and magazines, papers, and all manner of office supplies, stacks of books and brochures stuffed with marginalia; lists, photocopies, and print-outs. Fumbling into my pocket, I took out my phone, opened it and, with shaking hand, laid it on the desk. I hunched over and steeled myself against what was about to transpire. Beads of sweat drew together on my forehead and dripped onto the phone. I reached up and wiped my brow with my forearm. With no reason to wait, I pressed the reply button. The phone rang. Soon it would be just me and an elder in the basement—nose to nose and face to face.

There were three rings and then "Hello?" The voice was unmistakably female. I licked my parched lips; my tongue, like sandpaper, scraped against them. Pretending to be ignorant of the voicemail, I said: "I received a phone call from this number a few minutes ago."

"Ethan probably called you," she said.

Ethan came on the phone and got right to the point. "I didn't know whether you and Jennifer could meet with us real soon or not." I could not determine if he was asking a question or merely throwing out an observation.

I reminded him of our previous exchange wherein I told him I would have called him if I desired to meet. Pushing my comments aside, he said: "We've had a sister write us a letter, and some have read your website, and we just need t' get in touch with you guys to see how you're doing. We also heard some rumors that you celebrated Owen's birthday."

His response threw me off. *Who wrote to the elders?*

Avoiding the issue of the birthday for the moment, I said: "I don't have a website. I mean, I used to, but I deleted it a year ago." Even as I spoke, I remembered that Jennifer did have a site—she had surreptitiously set up a new site under a new name with a new address so that she could continue to write about Owen's progress. But I did not divulge this.

All I had to do was tell him I needed to talk to Jennifer and that I'd contact him shortly. The phone call would be over in less than thirty seconds, and then my wife and I would set our plan in motion. I *wanted* to ask who had made the accusations. I *wanted* to ask if he thought it was against Bible principles for these accusers to go directly to the elders instead of coming first to me.

But I was afraid.

I remembered all the times I had been afraid before; all the times I had wanted to say something to the elders, and been too weak to do so.

So, for the first time, I asked what I wanted to ask. "Who's making these accusations?" I said. The question poured out as if I could not stop it.

Ethan repeated that the elders had received a letter from a sister from another congregation.

"These accusations were all made anonymously, then?" I asked.

He hesitated. "For now they are. They're just an accusation right now, that's the reason we need to get with you guys—to see what's goin' on."

Rallying my point, I swiftly added, "If somebody has an issue with me or Jennifer, then they should probably come talk directly to us, according to the scriptures."

To my surprise, he mumbled, "Right."

I continued: "So if someone did make some accusations, I'd like to chat with them. I could probably clear up any issues they have."

He repeated that the sister was from another congregation. I told him this did not matter.

Becoming the champion of the non sequitur, he said, "We just need to meet with you to clear some things up."

I persisted, citing Matthew 5:23 and 24, where it says, without mentioning elder involvement, to make peace with your brothers. Ethan again admitted I was right, and so I repeated my request for the names of my accusers, stating that I would call them tonight to rectify the problem. Ethan simply held fast to his original directive: "We just need to get together, you know, and get this thing straightened out." He said he felt the best way to handle it would be for elders to be involved.

"My understanding," I insisted, "is that the best way is that if someone has an issue with someone else, they should handle it with that person. You even agreed that that was correct."

"Yeah, that is correct," he meekly replied.

"Should we do it the proper way, or would you rather get involved?" I asked.

More silence ensued. And then, "I don't know how to handle it at this point with all these accusations." He said he would have to confer with the other elders, as he was unsure how to proceed. "I'll talk to the elders and see if they wanna give you that information."

"That'd be the right thing to do," I said, "so if they could get that information, I'd appreciate it."

I returned to the living room and deflated onto the closest chair. Jennifer looked up from Owen, and her face told me she could see I was exhausted, but she had to know what transpired. "Well, what did he say?" I grinned wryly. "Why don't you listen to it?" I held up the camera and she reached over and grabbed it from my hands.

She held the camera's tiny speaker to her ear and listened to the conversation. After earnestly complimenting my performance, and noting the shakiness of my voice, we contemplated who tattled about the birthday party.

"Oh come on, Jennifer," I said. "It was Sarah."

"I don't know. I think it was your family. Probably Nana."

I didn't want to entertain that idea. "No way," I said flatly. "Your sister's the one who's been rude to us—she even talked Les into shunning us."

"If my brother and sister were going to do something," she said, "they would have done it months ago, when they first found out. Your family just found out recently. And you told them a lot more than I told Sarah. You probably really scared them with all the points you brought up. Anyway, they're super-righteous Witnesses; they're the ones who probably think you need to be disciplined. They probably want you disfellowshipped so that they can turn to your dad and tell him he needs to shun you."

I mournfully agreed. Jennifer reasoned further: "They probably hoped to have us disfellowshipped before your dad came to visit, but they hadn't counted on you stalling for time."

I clapped my hands and rubbed them together diabolically. "A-ha!" I laughed, "I bamboozled them!"

My time to gloat did not last. As I was in the midst of complimenting myself, the phone rang. Jennifer and I stared at each other with apprehensive smirks as each ring came and went. *Ring! Ring! Ring!* Then quiet. An electronic PING alerted us that a message awaited. I listened to the message with bated breath:

> This is Ethan again. I did some more checking and I guess they got twenty-eight pictures of the birthday party. And it's just more than you can handle. We just need to meet.

"Dammit!" I shouted. I stood up and kicked one of Owen's toys across the room. "They know! They know! They have proof!"

"Proof of what?" Jennifer said, sounding lost, "What are you talking about?"

"What do you think, Jennifer? The birthday party. Ethan said there are twenty-eight pictures online."

Jennifer held her hand to her mouth, stifling a giggle.

"What's so funny?"

"Twenty-eight pictures?" she laughed. "He sat and counted the photos?"

I brushed aside her flippant attitude. We were counting on the elders not having any evidence—just accusations. "I wish you wouldn't have put those pictures online."

"Don't yell at me," she said, defensively, "I asked you if you minded, and you said it was fine."

"I know," I whined, "I'm not mad at you; I just wished we hadn't done it. Now look what it's caused."

She folded her arms. "If it wasn't this it would've been something else."

"What the hell am I supposed to do now? If I tell him I don't want to meet with him, he'll just say, 'We know you're guilty. We'll just disfellowship you without meeting with you.'"

"You just have to tell him you'll get back to him," she said. "It will work—trust me."

"I guess there's no putting it off," I said, dejectedly. I turned to leave the room.

"Don't forget," Jennifer said, as I walked downstairs again, "Whatever you do, don't decline a meeting with them—"

"—But don't accept one, either," I finished her warning. "I'll remember."

I reentered the office. The sun had nearly set, and the room was a hazy darkness. I sat, pressed the record button on the camera, and called Ethan's number. I looked up at the Watchtower literature on the desk, and in the dusk the silhouetted stacks looked like headstones. A haphazard cemetery of a euthanized faith.

Ethan explained that he had called another elder, who had shown him the birthday party photos. "This is beyond you being able to handle it on your own," he said in deep seriousness. "We're gonna need to meet with you." Ethan said he just wanted to make a shepherding call on us, adding, "We haven't been in contact with you guys for a long time."

When I did not respond, Ethan asked: "Do you know what's involved with this?"

I was fairly certain I *did* know, but I told him I would play ignorant while he enlightened me. He said: "It's pretty serious because, you know," he paused dramatically, "we don't celebrate birthday parties. And if you invited somebody else, it could turn into apostasy."

This was a bold accusation, but he was correct: if a Witness invites other Witness to engage in sinful behavior, such deeds are viewed as apostasy.[120] He was wrong to believe that I was still a Witness and, further, his assumption that the people at Owen's party were Witnesses was likewise in error.

I told Ethan that the meeting he wished to set up sounded more like a judicial meeting rather than a shepherding call, and he admitted it could turn into a judicial hearing. As soon as he verified my suspicion—that the meeting could devolve into a disciplinary tribunal—I did not need to play games any more.

"Since you said it's kind of a serious thing, I hope you don't expect me to make a decision right this minute, especially when my wife is already in bed," I said. "I'll tell you what, let me talk to my wife about it and we'll contact you in a few days." I asked him to respect my wishes by giving us a week to think on the matter.

"We will," he said, speaking for the elders collectively, "'Cause, you know, our first thought is to gain you guys; we don't wanna lose you guys." I found his comment highly suspect, as the elders had not bothered to contact Jennifer or me in over seven months, but I let him continue: "We know that sometimes mistakes are made, and things can be turned around and be fine, y'know?"

I wasn't sure exactly what he meant, but I agreed and thanked him for his politeness. After assuring him that I would contact him within a week, we said good-bye.

The sun rose early the next morning and split the bedroom into crepuscular slats. The humidity mounted to an uncomfortable degree before I even lifted my head from the pillow. Shortly after rising, Jennifer printed out our letter, delineating twenty-five rights we wished to secure before meeting with the elders. In it, we did not refuse to meet with them, but stipulated we be told of the exact charges and times of the meetings in writing. We requested to know the names of our accusers and to be allowed to record the meetings. Knowing that they would be in contact with the Watchtower Society's lawyers, we requested that we likewise be allowed to invite legal representation to the meetings. Further, we made it clear that the information shared thus far was ecclesiastically privileged—they were legally and morally bound to share it with no one. We stated that, should we be disfellowshipped, then from that moment forward we would no longer be members of their congregation. "From then on," we said,

> we will consider any attempt to convince by speeches, talks or teaching; to coerce by implied or actual threat of similar judicial action; or to encourage by private counsel or suggestion any of Jehovah's Witnesses to treat us differently from any other persons that are not Jehovah's Witnesses, to be a serious violation of our civil rights. We may then initiate any legal action, civil or criminal, that we deem appropriate. This includes any attempt to convince by speeches, talks or teaching; to coerce by implied or actual threat of similar judicial action; or to encourage by private counsel or suggestion any present Jehovah's Witnesses to shun or avoid us, cease or otherwise modify their doing business with us.

We unequivocally stated that we would not be disassociating ourselves, as such a move bore no scriptural precedence and was merely a matter of convenience for the Watchtower's legal department, and, at any rate, we had no desire to cut off association with the majority of Witnesses we knew. We concluded by saying we would respectfully await their written response. Perhaps, we surmised, they would find a loophole and officially eject us from the congregation at some point in the future, but in the interim, this letter would make them squirm, and it would buy us time to adjust to our new lives.

On Thursday we walked to the post office. I opened the hinged metal flap of the mailbox. I brandished the letter, signed and sealed, turning it over and examining it one last time.

"Are you having second thoughts?" Jennifer asked.

"Nope," I said. And with a flick of my wrist, I cast the letter into the belly of the blue box.

Jennifer let out the slightest squeal. "What have we done?" she said, her hands covering her impish smile.

"What we have done is what we were pushed to do," I said with an air of finality. "There is no going back."

"It's such a relief!" Jennifer exclaimed.

"It's so nice to not be in limbo any longer." I took hold of Owen's stroller and we walked toward the setting sun. "Now I'm gonna move on with the rest of my life."

"Isn't that the *truth*!" she said, wrapping her arm around mine.

By late August, there was still no response. Supposing we were in the clear, I printed out a fourth letter to the Society—bolder and more indicting than the others—and sent it on its way.

Autumn came and the bulky trees in the yard shed their leaves. Jennifer snapped photographs of the vibrant fall colors; the crimson and green mix created a vibrant pastiche with the gold and russet. I raked piles of crisp leaves four feet tall and twice as wide. I lifted Owen by his hands and tossed him in. He giggled with innocent abandon, as only a child can do, and gestured the sign for 'more.' We had not heard from the elders or the Watchtower Society in over two months. It *was* good to be alive.

Postlude

Life moved on, and soon our first calendar year as non-Witnesses drew to a close. I moved through the new world, and I saw noble and treacherous people. There are those I prefer to never speak with, and those with whom I trust my life, just as in the Watchtower. When I observed my co-workers, Jennifer's doula, and Owen's speech therapist, I came to know that they were not wicked; their actions, attitudes, and words belied such a label. I could find no deficit in worldly people that justified the chasm Witnesses placed between themselves and all others. If members of the Watchtower Society are good, then so are people of the world.

I often wondered how life would have been different if I had left sooner. Such a hypothetical scenario is farcical; there is no way to picture my years past without having been a Witness. The subsequent unfolding of life is impossible to calculate; it is academic and ultimately meaningless. I had moved on from being a Witness to being an ex-Witness. Would I ever become an ex-ex-Witness? Such a prospect seemed highly doubtful. After all, I was continually reminded of the life that was each time I heard news of my old friends and was unable to join in the procession of their lives. They merely appeared as blips on my radar, and then vanished. I am forced to wait for them.

In the dank black of a summer midnight, a boisterous storm visited. Globs of rain bombarded the house. The thunder cracks jerked Jennifer and me to consciousness. "God must be angry," I joked, in a lethargic, half-sleeping tone. The wind whipped through the neighborhood, and I heard branches breaking off trees and landing on the roof—an act of God.

The next morning, I ventured outside, and the air tasted like the salvation after a tempest. I began collecting sticks and tossing them into the fire pit. As I did, I came across a fallen nest. It was exquisitely designed; leaves and grasses intertwined with twigs. But it had not had the ability to weather the storm. I picked it up and examined its intricate detail. As I walked over to

311

toss it into the fire pit, I happened upon a baby bird. Or, rather, what had been a baby bird. It was in a death pose, back curved and tiny wings, only partially fledged, splayed out. Its large head was cocked to the side, as if its last action was to try to comprehend what was happening.

I dug a hole in the ground near the side of the garage and picked up the fatally wounded baby with a spade. Gently, I lowered it into the ground. I shoveled the soil back into place. I looked at the small mound and leaned on the handle of my shovel. I could not do much for the baby bird, but I did more than God did. I thought about this dead bird, and I thought about all the birds I ever knew. And I thought about the scriptures that say God feeds the birds[121] and that none of them fall to the ground without His knowing of it.[122] And I thought about how beautiful that was.

And I thought about what a bunch of bullshit it was.

Theologians dedicate a whole branch of thought to the reconciliation of evil in a world created by a God of love. It's called Theodicy. But I wondered why theologians, and so many biblical apologists, felt the need to reconcile this supposed contradiction. God himself says: "I form the light and create darkness, I bring prosperity and create disaster; I, the Lord, do all these things."[123] "Is it not from the mouth of the Most High that both calamities and good things come?"[124] "When disaster comes to a city, has the Lord not caused it?"[125] Those who are distressed as to how God can allow evil are asking the wrong question: God doesn't *allow* evil; he *causes* it.

Were you to ask a Witness why God permits suffering, they would say that He does so for the greater good. But in my mind's recently unfettered state, I perceived that justice delayed is justice denied. *Aren't we God's children? Who denies their children life's necessities?* A good Witness would argue that God is only allowing suffering temporarily, such as when a parent allows a son to undergo a painful operation for his own benefit. But this suggests humans were designed purposely flawed, and God now needs to fix them. It ignores what Witnesses claim to be the theme of the entire Bible: God allows innocent humans to suffer not to make them better, but to prove a point: His point. Is such suffering justified by the end?

Witnesses say that God is good. But humans yearn to live peaceful happy lives with a measure of health, and denying humans these basic desires is obscene; God is not merely less than "good"; he is evil. *Who denies his child's wants and needs for six thousand years?* When once I asked my dad this question, he reminded me that to God a thousand years go by in but a day. What kind of parent denies their child his needs for six days? Only the very evil and the very insane. Neither deserves respect, much less worship.

I thought about these things during the months after dropping the letters in the mailbox. Safe in the knowledge that God's self-appointed minions could no longer restrict my thoughts, I had the audacity to wonder if God's creation is inherently bad. *Why, when left to our own devices, did we devolve so quickly? If God took his leave of us after man's fall, this may explain murders, rapes, accidents; but why congenital defects? Why earthquakes? Is God's handiwork only 'good' if he continually tweaks it? Were we so special as to have a Universe designed for us to inhabit, and then deemed so unworthy that we were thusly forgotten?*

An elder once halted a sardonic discussion about the purpose of appendixes by declaring: "We can't question God—his ways are higher than our ways."[126] Sitting alone in my living room, I stared dead-on out the window. Looking out at the mailbox that autumn evening, I recalled the teaching that I was made in God's image. If this is true, then what is powerful to me should be powerful to God; what is just to me should be just to God. "We can't question God?" *Why can't I question him? I thought He wasn't far off*[127] He had fourteen hundred pages to explain himself. Who possibly could commission a book to be written about himself, only to have it fail to explain the very questions people find most perplexing? Is God, then, both evil and incompetent? This is a most unfortunate combination. We are fortunate, indeed, that the God of the Bible is fictitious.

In this way, I exorcised the demons and angels from my thoughts. Freed from the fiction of theocracy and the farce of theodicy, logic no longer needed to struggle for possession of my mind. Jennifer and I moved on to unpack and unravel our wasted lives, to acknowledge the death of every day, and the future.

I came to know that I am not wicked, or demonized, or hateful. I am not full of rage. I am not uninterested in my son's future or my family's happiness. I am only a mortal who has clambered above the din and the deluge, stood at the edge of doubt and, looking into the canyon, witnessed a tiny speck of truth. With dogma and tradition and hypocrisy rushing down, I jumped into the canyon. I have been free-falling in the world – the Earth – ever since. And, to quote my late mentor, are we "of this Earth" and nothing more? Is there no respite from expectation; no relief from suffering? Is there no reward; no solution; no goal; no solace?

Is there no Balsam in Gilead?
Is there no Deliverance at Hand?

Notes

1. *The Watchtower* (Feb 1, 1961): 80. All citations below are published by the Watch Tower Bible and Tract Society unless otherwise noted.

2. Isaiah 25:6 (brackets theirs).

3. *Sing Praises to Jehovah* (1984).

4. Jeremiah 8:21, 22.

5. Isaiah 65:17.

6. Psalm 90:10.

7. *The Watchtower* (Nov 1, 1986): 25.

8. *My Book of Bible Stories* (1978), story #10, "The Great Flood."

9. "Noah and his sons obeyed Jehovah and started building. But the other people just laughed. They kept on being bad. Nobody believed Noah when he told them what God was going to do." *My Book of Bible Stories*, story #9, "Noah Builds an Ark."

10. Some Witness families set aside non-birthday celebrations for their children, often on the day of the parents' wedding anniversary. The Watchtower Society did not condone this practice. My parents refused to engage in such a practice, claiming that it implied there was something missing in a Witness child's life and that such celebrations were a way to circumvent the birthday ban.

11. "Parents are truly wise when they teach their children to pay attention rather than provide coloring books or other things that hinder children from listening and learning." *Our Kingdom Ministry* (July 1979): 4.

12. "When did God create the dinosaurs, and when did they become extinct? . . . At the very latest it seems likely that they must have disappeared off the earth at the time of the flood of Noah's day." *The Watchtower* (July 15, 1973): 447.

13. For a discussion of the caution needed regarding "Thriller" and its accompanying music video, see *Awake!* (May 22, 1984): 19 and 20.

14. Exodus 34:6–7.

15. Exodus 4:10.

16. *The Watchtower* (April 1, 2006): 22 (box).

17. "A university degree may or may not improve your employment prospects. But one fact is indisputable: 'The time left is reduced!' For all its presumed benefits, would four years or more in a university be the best use of that remaining time?" *Questions Young People Ask—Answers that Work*, 177. Statements to this effect in Watchtower literature are many.

18. *Life—How Did it Get Here?, By Evolution or by Creation?*, 20, 79.

19. *Life—How Did it Get Here?*, 55 (italics mine).

20. *The Watchtower* (Jan 15, 1989): 12 (italics theirs). This wording appeared only in the original print edition of the magazine. Subsequent electronic versions altered the final words of the sentence to read: "in our day."

21. Matthew 24:36.

22. "To reduce expenses, some Pioneers share an apartment with other Christians. In assisting their children to Pioneer, parents sometimes provide lodging free or at a minimal cost. Others help Pioneers with food and transporta-

tion costs. But Pioneers would not want to be a burden to others, for they have a Scriptural duty to support themselves." *The Watchtower* (Sept 15, 1993): 28, 29.

23. "Bad association spoils useful habits" (1 Corinthians 15:33).

24. Matthew 6:33.

25. "Like the locust horde of Joel's prophecy, the mighty army of Jehovah's Witnesses, now 5,413,769 strong, continues to fill the earth with its witnessing." *1997 Yearbook of Jehovah's Witnesses*, 253, 254.

26. Romans 6:9 and 10 (italics mine).

27. 1 Corinthians 7:8.

28. The term "make the Truth your own" was popularized among Witnesses due to the song (#191) of the same name from *Sing Praises to Jehovah*.

29. "Understanding the Miracles of the Bible," *The Watchtower* (May 15, 1971).

30. For examples, see John 14:14 and Matthew 7:7.

31. Malachi 2:16.

32. "Be Upbuilding and Helpful to Others" (unit 14a), *Shining as Illuminators in the World*, 155.

33. Hebrews 11:1

34. "Dating one of the opposite sex is not mere recreation but should have marriage in view. If a person does not have marriage in view or is too young to take on marriage responsibilities, then he ought to examine his motives as to why he wishes to have dates with one of the opposite sex. In what direction is he proceeding, or, stated another way, for what is he beginning to live?" *The Watchtower* (Feb 1, 1973): 74.

35. "Surely it would be unclean to allow one's hands to stray under someone's clothing, to remove someone's clothing, or to caress another's intimate areas, such as the breasts. Why, in the Bible the caressing of the breasts is associated with the pleasures reserved for married couples." *Awake!* (Oct 22, 1993): 22 (italics theirs).

36. Only permanent volunteers received a stipend; as a temporary volunteer, I did not receive any money.

37. Matthew 19:26.

38. This included *Awake!* (Aug 22, 1967): 27, 28:

The facts show that the headship of a man is both somatically and psychologically sound and in the best interests of all concerned, even as we shall see. Thus a leading authority on the human body (soma), Gray's Anatomy (1966 Edition), tells the interesting fact that as regards the human skull there is no difference between the male and the female until the time of puberty; but then as adulthood is reached the difference becomes more and more apparent. The female skull is lighter and its cranial capacity is about 10 percent smaller than that of a male, even as is the rest of the anatomy. . . .

True, mere brain size in itself is not as important as brain quality, but where the quality is the same the larger brain size has an advantage. . . .

That it is in the best interests of both sexes for the man to take the lead is also supported by psychological evidence.

39. *Questions Young People Ask*, 259.

40. Sal's opinion violated the Elders' manual, *Pay Attention to Yourselves and to All the Flock*, 23, 24: "Take note of ways that you *and others* can assist and encourage young ones in the congregation, and continually assure them of your interest" (italics mine). The text goes on to delineate nine ways Elders and others can encourage youths, including: "Work with them in the field service."

41. "The form of worship that is clean and undefiled from the standpoint of our God and Father is this: to look after orphans and widows in their tribulation, and to keep oneself without spot from the world." James 1:27.

42. See Matthew 22: 41–23:24.

43. She photocopied this form from Bob Bowersox's "The Form for Reacquaintance," *48 Hours to a Stronger Marriage* (St. Martin's Griffin, 2002).

44. By gossiping, Dick violated the counsel: "So we should guard against gossip, even if it does not seem harmful." *The Watchtower* (Oct 15, 1989): 11.

45. For larger congregations, the Watchtower Society recommends a second school. This consists of a small portion of the congregation retiring to a different room where an auxiliary school is held. Students deliver talks just as the other students give talks in the main school. The appeal of the second school was the smaller crowd, and no microphones. See *Our Kingdom Ministry* (Nov 2002): 4.

46. *Pay Attention*, 46.

47. Though not baptized, the boys were publishers and, as such, were approved participants in the door-to-door activity.

48. In granting my request immediately, Dick violated the instruction in *Pay Attention*, 86: "Individual Elders should not take it upon themselves to handle matters that ought to be judged by an assigned judicial committee or decided by the body of Elders."

49. "Christian Weddings that Bring Joy" and "Find Balanced Enjoyment at the Wedding Feast," *The Watchtower* (April 15, 1984).

50. In pressuring me to abide by his opinion, Dick violated *Pay Attention*, 65: "Avoid imposing personal viewpoints, opinions or arbitrary rules on the congregation or the body of Elders."

51. See Matthew 16:23.

52. Matthew 12:20. See *The Watchtower* (Nov 15, 1995): 21–24.

53. "Thus, when Elders meet, and they pray for Jehovah's guidance to shepherd the flock of God." *The Watchtower* (Dec 1, 1994): 30.

54. Dick's admission that the counsel he was giving was based solely on his opinion violated the direction in *Pay Attention* regarding giving counsel to other members of the congregations, 91: "Always give them direction from God's Word; avoid giving your own opinions."

55. "In case a man takes a new wife, he should not go out into the army, nor should anything else be imposed onto him. He should continue exempt at his house for one year, and he must make his wife whom he has taken rejoice" (Deuteronomy 24:5).

56. See Judges 16:25–30.

57. *Insight on the Scriptures*, vol. 1, 164.

58. *My Book of Bible Stories*, story #3, "The First Man and Woman."

59. *Insight on the Scriptures*, vol. 1, 327.

60. Bernhard Grzimek, ed., *Grzimek's Animal Life Encyclopedia* (Van Nostrand Reinhold Company, 1975 [1968]).

61. *The Watchtower* (April 1, 1986): 31.

62. Kaari Ward, ed., *Great Disasters* (The Reader's Digest Association, 1989).

63. Malachi 2:16.

64. *The Watchtower* (Nov 1, 1988): 21

65. One is willful nonsupport. When getting married, a husband assumes the responsibility of providing for his wife and children. The man who willfully fails

to provide the material necessities of life "has disowned the faith and is worse than a person without faith" (1 Timothy 5:8). This suggests separation is possible. Another is extreme physical abuse. If a mate physically abuses his wife, the victim may separate (Galatians 5:19–21; Titus 1:7). "Anyone loving violence [God's] soul certainly hates" (Psalm 11:5). Another ground for separation is the absolute endangerment of a believer's spirituality—one's relationship with God: "When a mate's opposition, perhaps including physical restraint, has made it impossible to pursue true worship and has imperiled the believer's spirituality, then some believers have found it necessary to separate." *Awake!* (Feb 8, 2002): 10.

66. *The Watchtower* (May 8, 2004): 21.

67. "A *divorced couple* (even if only legally divorced) who has sex relations with each other commits fornication." *Pay Attention*, 135 (italics theirs).

68. Leviticus 20:13.

69. 1 Corinthians 6:9 and 10.

70. *Awake!* (March 22, 1986): 14.

71. For what made me think I qualified, see *Our Kingdom Ministry* (Nov, 1973): 8: Weddings and funerals may be conducted by any dedicated, baptized brother as permitted by law. . . . When it comes to the selection of someone to conduct a wedding or a funeral, this is a personal matter for the individuals or the family involved to determine. Since weddings and funerals are not viewed as public talks, appointment as an Elder or Ministerial Servant is not a requirement for one to perform such services.

72. The cover article of *Awake!* (Feb 22, 1995) was "A Better Understanding of Menopause." Another *Awake!* (Aug 22, 1992) cover article was "Chronic Fatigue Syndrome—How to Deal with It." Another *Awake!* (Jan 22, 1995) cover article was "Is Your Life Boring? You Can Change It!" Each year from 1990–2006, the Dec 15 issue of *The Watchtower* featured a series of article relating to Christmas, from its popularity in Japan (1991) to materialism (1995) to the historicity of Jesus (2001).

73. Matthew 10:29.

74. *Is There a Creator Who Cares about You?*, 9.

75. *Reasoning from the Scriptures*, 151 (italics theirs).

76. "As regards the heavens, to Jehovah the heavens belong, But the earth he has given to the sons of men" (Psalm 115:16).

77. *The Watchtower* (April 1, 1984): 6–7; *The Watchtower* (Feb 1, 2004): 19–20.

78. *Reasoning from the Scriptures*, 96.

79. *Insight on the Scriptures*, vol. 1, 238.

80. *Insight on the Scriptures*, vol. 1, 453.

81. For a listing of the Watchtower Society's teaching on when each Bible book was written, see *All Scripture is Inspired of God and Beneficial*, 12.

82. *Insight on the Scriptures*, vol. 1, 183, 1019, 1218.

83. "'The End of the World' Is at Hand!" *You Can Live Forever in Paradise on Earth*.

84. "Unevenly yoked" is a reference to 2 Corinthians 6:14, where Paul warned of pairing a mule with an ox—the parallel being that good, strong Witnesses (oxen) should take care not to marry spiritually weak people (mules).

85. Ernst Mayr, *What Evolution Is* (Basic Books, 2001), xv.

86. Robert M. Hazen with James S. Trefil, *Science Matters: Achieving Scientific Literacy* (Knopf Publishing Group, 1990).

87. *The Watchtower* (April 1, 1988): 16.

88. "Questions from Readers," *The Watchtower* (April 1, 1986; italics mine).

89. *The Watchtower* (June 1, 1985): 20.

90. "Avoid Independent Thinking," *The Watchtower* (Jan 15, 1983): 22.

91. *The Watchtower* (June 1, 1967): 338.

92. *The Watchtower* (Aug 15, 2000): 28.

93. *The Watchtower* (Nov 15, 1952): 793.

94. Ecclesiastes 1:18.

95. "Questions from Readers," *The Watchtower* (May 15, 2002): 28.

96. "And the cow and the bear themselves will feed; together their young ones will lie down. And even the lion will eat straw just like the bull. And the sucking child will certainly play upon the hole of the cobra; and upon the light aperture of a poisonous snake will a weaned child actually put his own hand" (Isaiah 11:7, 8).

97. Mark Isaak, "Problems with a Global Flood," 2nd ed., The Talk Origins Archive, accessed 1 Nov 2012, http://www.talkorigins.org /faqs/faq-noahs-ark. html.

98. Ryan Sutter website, accessed Dec 29, 2009 (private records).

99. Ryan Sutter website, accessed July 11, 2009 (private records).

100. See "The Radiocarbon Clock," *Awake!* (Sept 22, 1986): 21–26; "How Old Are the Fossils?" *Awake!* (Nov 22, 1981): 13–15; and "Science or Bible Chronology—Which Merits Your Faith?" *Awake!* (April 8, 1972): 16–20. In the final article above, note particularly the subheading "Carbon-14 Dates a Rickety Structure."

101. Psalm 127:3.

102. *Sing Praises to Jehovah*, #15, "Life Without End—At Last!"

103. "But Jehovah's servants already belong to the only organization that will survive the end of this wicked system of things." *The Watchtower* (Dec 15, 2007): 14.

104. "Before there comes upon you people the burning anger of Jehovah, before there comes upon you the day of Jehovah's anger, seek Jehovah, all you meek ones of the Earth, who have practiced His own judicial decision. Seek righteousness, seek meekness. Probably you may be concealed in the day of Jehovah's anger" (Zephaniah 2:2,3).

105. "Only Jehovah's Witnesses, those of the anointed remnant and the 'great crowd,' as a united organization under the protection of the Supreme Organizer, have any Scriptural hope of surviving the impending end of this doomed system dominated by Satan the Devil." *The Watchtower* (Sept 1, 1989): 19. "Similarly, Jehovah is using only one organization today to accomplish his will. To receive everlasting life in the earthly Paradise we must identify that organization and serve God as part of it." *The Watchtower* (Feb 15, 1983): 12.

106. *Our Kingdom Ministry* (April, 2006): 6.

107. Joel 2:31, 32.

108. Psalm 65:2.

109. In discussing astronomers' reactions to discoveries that "confirmed what was written in the Bible," the Watchtower Society states: "It turns out that the scientist behaves the way the rest of us do when our beliefs are in conflict with the evidence. We become irritated, we pretend the conflict does not exist, or we paper it over with meaningless phrases." *Life—How Did It Get Here?* 202.

110. "Noticeably, there have been a number of individuals who have created Web sites ostensibly to preach the good news. Many of these sites are sponsored

by indiscreet brothers. Other sites may be sponsored by apostates who wish to lure unsuspecting ones (2 John 9–11). Commenting on whether there is a need for our brothers to create such Web sites, *Our Kingdom Ministry* (Nov 1997), page 3, stated: "There is no need for any individual to prepare Internet pages about Jehovah's Witnesses, our activities, or our beliefs. Our official site [www. watchtower.org] presents accurate information for any who want it.'" *Our Kingdom Ministry* (Nov, 1999): 5.

111. "The 'battle of the great day of God Almighty' (Rev. 16:14) which will end in A.D. 1914 with the complete overthrow of earth's present rulership, is already commenced. The gathering of the armies is plainly visible from the standpoint of God's word." *Studies in the Scriptures*, 1889 ed., vol. 2, 101. The 1915 edition of this text was altered to read "A.D. 1915."

112. "The indisputable facts, therefore, show that the 'time of the end' began in 1799; that the Lord's second presence began in 1874." *The Watchtower* (March 1, 1922): 68. "The [Napoleonic] campaign is briefly, yet graphically described in the prophecy, verses 40–44; and its being completed in 1799 marks, according to the prophet's own words, the beginning of 'the time of the end.'" *Creation*, 293.

113. "There will be no slip-up. . . . Abraham should enter upon the actual possession of his promised inheritance in the year 1925." *The Watchtower* (Oct 15, 1917): 6157. "Therefore we may confidently expect that 1925 will mark the return of Abraham, Isaac, Jacob and the faithful prophets of old." *Millions Now Living Will Never Die* (1920), 89, 90.

114. "The Apostle Paul was spearheading the Christian missionary activity. He was also laying a foundation for a work that would be completed in our 20th century." *The Watchtower* (Jan 1, 1989): 12. This was changed in subsequent reprinting and on the Watchtower's CD-ROM, the last few words now read: "be completed in our day."

"Some of that 'generation (of 1914)' could survive until the end of the century. But there are many indications that 'the end' is much closer than that!" *The Watchtower* (March 1, 1984): 18, 19. "Jehovah's Witnesses, in their eagerness for Jesus' second coming, have suggested dates that turned out to be incorrect." *Awake!* (March 22, 1993): 4 [footnote].

115. "Within a few years at most the final parts of Bible prophecy relative to these 'last days' will undergo fulfillment." *The Watchtower* (May 1, 1968): 272. "Behind this passion for convert-winning is the firm conviction of the Witnesses that the end of human history is imminent. They expect it to come at any hour, and almost certainly within the next 10 years." *The Watchtower* (Aug 1, 1968): 466 (quoting news editor Louis Cassels). "Only a few years, at most, remain before the corrupt system of things dominating the earth is destroyed by God." *Awake!* (Oct 8, 1968): 13. "What about all this talk concerning the year 1975? Lively discussions, some based on speculation, have burst into flame during recent months among serious students of the Bible. Their interest has been kindled by the belief that 1975 will mark the end of 6,000 years of human history since Adam's creation. The nearness of such an important date indeed fires the imagination and presents unlimited possibilities for discussion." "Why Are You Looking Forward to 1975?," *The Watchtower* (Aug 15, 1968): 494.

116. Between 1980 and 1995, the number of Jehovah's Witnesses increased an average of 5.54 percent per annum. Between 1996 and 2008, the number of Jehovah's Witnesses increased an average of 2.39 percent per annum.

117. "[Jehovah] is the best Friend we could ever have." *2002 Yearbook of Jehovah's Witnesses*, 5.

118. "Disfellowshipped and disassociated ones are shunned by those who wish to have a good relationship with Jehovah." *Pay Attention*, 103.

119. *Reasoning from the Scriptures* is the title of a Watchtower publication.

120. "If an individual is trying to influence others to take an unscriptural course or is trying to deceive others, all should avoid him." *Pay Attention*, 103.

121. "Observe intently the birds of heaven, because they do not sow seed or reap or gather into storehouses; still YOUR heavenly Father feeds them" (Matthew 6:26).

122. "Do not two sparrows sell for a coin of small value? Yet not one of them will fall to the ground without YOUR Father's [knowledge]" (Matthew 10:29).

123. Isaiah 45:7.

124. Lamentations 3:38.

125. Amos 3:6.

126. Isaiah 55:8, 9.

127. Acts 17:26, 27.

Acknowledgements

I first owe a debt of gratitude to the following individuals for offering feedback and encouragement as I created the first draft of this book: Stan Meissner, Debbie Meissner, Roberta Meissner, Ryan Sutter, Jeremy Davis, Diane Korinek, and Mike Korinek.

For assisting in various ways throughout the revising and editing process, I thank: Grant Steves, Farmer Rachel, Nick Votrobeck, Patricia Larsen, Carrie Lloyd, Ryan Benson, Mike Gallagher, Professor Mark Olson, Chris Edwards, Jeff Ritter, Tom Flynn, Mike Haubrich, Eric Jayne, and Mindy Rhiger.

Thanks, too, to everyone at Freethought House who guided this book to its finished product: Bill Lehto, Cassandra Farrin, David Orr, and Robaire Ream.

Finally, I thank my wife Jennifer for offering immeasurable assistance every step of the way, and my children, Owen and Isla, who provided encouragement as only children can.

Resources

More about the Author's Story

Recordings of the author's 1993 district convention interview, phone
  conversations, and more: youtube.com/user/CircuitOverseer

The author's correspondence with the Watchtower Society:
  watchtowerletters.com

To contact James Zimmerman, email authors@freethoughthouse.com

Support Groups

Jehovah's Witness Recovery: jehovahswitnessrecovery.com

Jehovah's Witness Discussion Forum: jehovahs-witness.net

Solace for Mothers: solaceformothers.org

Further Reading

Captives of a Concept (Anatomy of an Illusion). Don Cameron. Lulu, 2007.

Crisis of Conscience, 4th edition. Raymond Franz. Commentary Press, 2002.

Doc Bob's Blog: Information for and about Jehovah's Witnesses: docbob.org

The Gentile Times Reconsidered: Chronology and Christ's Return, 3rd edition.
  Carl O. Jonsson. Commentary Press, 1998.

Facts about Jehovah's Witnesses: jwfacts.com

Official website of Jehovah's Witnesses: jw.org

Discussion Questions

- The book's subtitle is *The Redemption of a Devout Jehovah's Witness.* What meanings does the word "redemption" have in the narrative?
- Give examples of the Witnesses' use of a unique vocabulary. What purpose does this serve, and how does it influence their thinking and reasoning?
- How are Jehovah's Witnesses portrayed by the author?
- What level of control do the elders exercise on the local congregations? How do the elders compare and contrast with leaders in other religions with which you are familiar?
- How does the author come to understand the use of evidence by Watchtower publications?
- Jehovah's Witnesses are stratified by gender, especially in congregational duties and privileges. What are the different obligations and expectations for men and women? Which gender role would you find most challenging, and why?
- Jehovah's Witnesses often quote Isaiah 1:18, "Come now, let us reason together" (KJV). What does this mean to Jehovah's Witnesses? Why do the majority of Witnesses in the book seem unwilling to question their faith or even deviate from the established doctrine even when pointedly asked to do so? How does this differ from other religions with which you are familiar?
- How is shunning defined in the text? What purposes does it serves? Is it effective, in your opinion?
- Dr. Caroline Schroeder once wrote, "Some people change their ways when they see the light, others when they feel the heat." In what ways might this observation accurately describe the experiences of the author and his wife?
- Jennifer and, later, James come to the conclusion that they had been members of a cult. How would you define a cult? Do you agree that Jehovah's Witnesses belong to a cult? Is it important to draw a distinction between religions that are cults and those that are not?
- Which of the author's friends and relatives seem most likely to leave the religion? Give reasons and examples from the story to support your response.
- In a moment of self-searching, the author labels himself as an atheist, and then quickly revokes the description. He later discusses the term

with Ryan and hesitantly accepts that he is an atheist. Why does he avoid the term? Are descriptive terms such as "atheist" applicable whether or not we want them to be? Does the difference matter substantively or rhetorically?

- The few people in the book that leave the religion appear to do so in one of two ways. Some exit the religion immediately, such as in the wake of trauma. Others do so gradually. How do James and Jennifer fit into these methods? Are there other means of leaving?

- How does the author understand the concept of evil? Cite from the text to support your response. Is his resolution the only logical conclusion for those who believe in the god of the bible?

- What role does emotional attachment play in the process of questioning one's religion? How might emotional attachments overcome reason and evidence? How do reason and evidence overcome emotional attachments? How does emotion influence your decisions? How do reason and evidence influence you?

About the Author

James Zimmerman was a contributing editor to *Atheist Voices of Minnesota: an Anthology of Personal Stories* (Freethought House, 2012), in which his essay "Losing My Head" appears. His writings have also appeared in *The 2013 St. Paul Almanac* and *Breathing In: Stories from the Century College Community, Volume II*, and several periodicals including *The Humanist*, *American Atheist*, and *Free Inquiry*. He is a frequent host of *Atheists Talk* television show and is a former editor for *The Minnesota Atheist*. A lifelong Minnesota resident, James currently lives in St. Paul with his wife, Jennifer, and their son, daughter, and cat. James is also a licensed minister who has performed several weddings in the Twin Cities area.

CPSIA information can be obtained at www.ICGtesting.com
Printed in the USA
BVOW01s0734300913

332411BV00007B/16/P